T0265580

THE PEOPLE VS. GOD

VS. GOD

The Lucifer Lawsuit

Re: The Problem of Pain, Evil and Suffering

R. A. VARGHESE

BlackBox
228 Park Ave S, #19611
New York, NY 10003-1502

ISBN 979-8-35093-492-2
eBook ISBN 979-8-35093-493-9

ABOUT THE AUTHOR

R. A. Varghese is the author and/or editor of numerous books on the interface of science, philosophy, and religion. His *Cosmos, Bios, Theos*, included contributions from 24 Nobel Prize-winning scientists. *Time* magazine called *Cosmos* "the year's most intriguing book about God." *Cosmic Beginnings and Human Ends*, a subsequent work, won a Templeton Book Prize for "*Outstanding Books in Science and Natural Theology.*" Varghese's *The Wonder of the World* was endorsed by leading thinkers and was the subject of an Associated Press story. He co-authored *There is a God— How the World's Most Notorious Atheist Changed His Mind* with Antony Flew. He subsequently edited *The Missing Link*, a study of consciousness, thought and the human self that includes contributions from three Nobel Prize winners and scientists from Oxford, Cambridge, Harvard, and Yale. He also authored *Metaverse of Mind – the Cosmic Social Network*.

Comments from scientists and others on Varghese's book
The Wonder of the World –

"Varghese explores the basic and critical questions we face concerning this remarkable and wonderful universe. Why are we here? Where are we going? This is no doctrinaire treatise, but a sensitive, profound and clear discussion of the important issues of our universe and our existence, including questions, answers, and uncertainties. It is written with a deep understanding of philosophy, spirituality, and the complex science involved, yet expressed in a way which is interesting and very understandable to the non-specialist."
– *Charles H. Townes*, Nobel Prize winner and inventor of the laser

"Though I found myself arguing with both protagonists, the issues raised and Guru's lucid outline of modern science's framework of understanding, helped me to challenge and refine my own answers to the ultimate questions that each one of us must ask." – *Arno Penzias*, Nobel Prize winner who discovered the Cosmic Microwave Background Radiation that established the Big Bang theory

"Congratulations on a fascinating book! I found *The Wonder of the World* to be a highly illuminating and thought-provoking discussion of all the important issues on the borderline between science and religion." – *Robert Jastrow*, Founder of NASA's Goddard Institute of Space Studies and Director of the Mount Wilson Observatory

"You have in your book deployed abundant evidence indicating that it is likely to be a very long time before such naturalistic [atheistic] explanations [for the origin of life and reproduction] are developed, if indeed there ever could be. . . I was hugely impressed and substantially challenged by it." – *Antony Flew*, at the time the best-known philosophical atheist in the English-speaking world

I am deeply grateful to Wayne L. Fisher, Esq., one of today's foremost plaintiff attorneys and past President of the International Academy of Trial Lawyers, for his invaluable guidance on all matters relating to legal format and procedure. Wayne also kindly provided the "Introductory statement by the Court" section. He bears no responsibility, however, for any errors of omission and commission.

TRIAL STRUCTURE

The People vs. God is a lawsuit. "The People" ("the Plaintiff"), ostensibly all human beings, are suing God ("the Defendant") for the pain, evil and suffering that are a part of human existence.

The Plaintiff is represented by Lucius HellMan, Esq. The Defendant is represented by Misha-El Angelini, Esq.

The court proceedings follow the structure common to jury trials. After the Judge issues instructions to the jury, the Plaintiff's counsel makes an opening statement. This is followed by an opening statement from the Defendant's counsel.

The Plaintiff's counsel then brings his expert witnesses who present evidence in support of the Plaintiff's Complaint. These experts are then examined by the Plaintiff's counsel and cross-examined by the Defendant's counsel. Next, the Defendant's counsel introduces his expert witnesses who present evidence in support of the Defendant's position. These experts, in turn, are examined by the Defendant's counsel and cross-examined by the Plaintiff's counsel.

Once the expert testimonies are completed, the Plaintiff's counsel makes a Closing Statement following which the Defendant's counsel makes his Closing Statement.

After the Closing Statements, the Judge instructs the jury to enter into deliberation until it reaches a verdict.

The expert witnesses testifying on behalf of the Plaintiff or the Defendant include cosmologists, physicists, biologists, logicians, philosophers, psychologists and theologians. The domains under discussion include modern cosmology, physics and biochemistry, evolutionary biology, genetics, Artificial Intelligence, linguistics, mathematics, philosophy, psychology, sociology, comparative religion, theology and history – to the extent that these domains pertain to the Complaint. The expert witnesses were required by the Court to use language intelligible to the lay public with minimal technical jargon.

Given the identity of the Defendant and the nature of the Complaint, the media dubbed the case "the Lucifer Lawsuit" under headlines like "Satan Sues God."

CONTENTS

www.ThePeoplevsGod.com

DRAMATIS PERSONAE

Judge, The Honorable Solomon King

Plaintiff's Attorney, Lucius HellMan, Esq.

Defendant's Attorney, Misha-El Angelini, Esq.

Witnesses for the Plaintiff

Percy Maersk, *Cosmologist, "New Atheist" blogger,* author of *When Nothing Became Something*

Eminent cosmologist and a prominent member of many national academies of science. His book *When Nothing Became Something* was an international best-seller, praised by both academics and the popular press. Critics of the book have mainly been theologians and religious believers. They are even more incensed with his widely popular blog, *Cosmic Darwinism,* which regularly takes on not just the religious right but its left and center as well. You might say he wears his New Atheism on his sleeve.

Joyce MacIntosh, *Analytic Philosopher,* author of *Evil-Doer – The God of Religion*

MacIntosh's book is widely considered by atheists to be the final word on the problem of evil. In this book, Professor MacIntosh examined various ideas of a divine being and tried to show that the concept of an omnipotent, all-good being cannot be reconciled with the existence of evil.

Robert Atkinson, *Evolutionary Biologist,* author of *The Self-Made Gene*

One of today's most celebrated molecular biologists. His book *The Self-Made Gene* has changed the whole perception of evolution with the elimination of all traces of a designer deity.

Richard Peterson, *Professor of Comparative Religion,* author of *A Dangerous Book*

His work, *A Dangerous Book,* exposes what he considers the darkness of the Old Testament deity.

Bartholomew Endicott, *Ex-Christian Theologian,* author of *Diabolic Delusion – the Invention of Hell*

A former Christian, Professor Endicott is now a trenchant critic of Christianity and, in particular, of the doctrine of Hell.

Witnesses for the Defendant

Raquel Prendergast, *Symbolic Logician,* author of *The "Enlightenment" and Its Reign of Error*

Known as a logician and not a diplomat, Professor Prendergast is best known for her critiques of modes of thought associated with the Enlightenment.

Stanley Genereux, *Theoretical Physicist,* author of *Mindverse – An Unbrief History of the World*

In addition to a lifetime of research in theoretical physics, Professor Genereux has explored the nexus of science, philosophy and religion and has critically scrutinized and occasionally demolished scientific ideas that are primarily based on speculation.

Gabriel Kantor Chesterfield, *Theologian,* author of *The Jesus Cloud – What You Don't Know About Christianity Can Hurt You*

A prolific writer on theological topics, Mr. Chesterfield's *The Jesus Cloud* presents Christianity in an entirely new light.

Mary Lucas, *Cognitive Psychologist,* author of *Not thy will But MINE Be Done*

Specialist in cognitive-behavioral therapy who has published peer-reviewed papers on diverse motifs ranging from the psychology of atheism and the claims of evolutionary psychology to the question of meaning in life and the metrics of personal success.

Jose Mendoza, *Exorcist*

Rev. Mendoza is an exorcist who has been called upon to expel spirits from Hell – also called demons – that oppress or possess people on Earth.

Harold Montefiore, *NDE Survivor*

Mr. Montefiore is a survivor of a Near Death Experience (NDE) who was shown Hell. Fortunately for him, it was a round-trip visit!

ANTECEDENTS

Accuser

"The LORD said to the *satan*, 'Have you noticed my servant Job? There is no one on earth like him, blameless and upright, fearing God and avoiding evil. He still holds fast to his innocence *although you incited me against him to ruin him for nothing*.'" *Job* 2:3

"Then he showed me Joshua the high priest standing before the angel of the LORD, while the *adversary* stood at his right side to *accuse* him." *Zechariah* 3:1

"Then I heard a loud voice in heaven say: "Now have salvation and power come, and the kingdom of our God and the authority of his Anointed. For the *accuser* of our brothers is cast out, who *accuses* them before our God day and night." *Revelation* 12:10

Tempter

"Now the *snake* was the most *cunning* of all the wild animals that the LORD God had made. He asked the woman, 'Did God really say, 'You shall not eat from any of the trees in the garden'?' The woman answered the *snake*: 'We may eat of the fruit of the trees in the garden; it is only about the fruit of the tree in the middle of the garden that God said, 'You shall not eat it or even touch it, or else you will die." But the *snake* said to the woman: 'You certainly will not die! God knows well that when you eat of it your eyes will be opened and you will be like gods, who know good and evil.'" *Genesis* 3:1-5

"Then Jesus was led by the Spirit into the desert to be tempted by the *devil*. He fasted for forty days and forty nights, and afterwards he was hungry. The *tempter* approached and said to him, 'If you are the Son of God, command that these stones become loaves of bread.'" *Matthew* 4:1-3

"He remained in the desert for forty days, *tempted* by *Satan.*" *Mark* 1:13

"For this reason, when I too could bear it no longer, I sent to learn about your faith, for fear that somehow the *tempter* had put you to the test and our toil might come to nothing." 1 *Thessalonians* 3:5

Liar

"The huge dragon, the ancient *serpent*, who is called the *Devil and Satan*, who *deceived* the whole world, was thrown down to earth." *Revelation* 12:9

"You belong to your father the *devil* and you willingly carry out your father's desires. He was a murderer from the beginning and does not stand in truth, because *there is no truth in him.* When he tells a lie, he speaks in character, because *he is a liar and the father of lies.*" *John* 8:44

"But Saul, also known as Paul, filled with the holy Spirit, looked intently at him and said, "You son of the *devil*, you enemy of all that is right, full of every sort of deceit and fraud. Will you not stop twisting the straight paths of [the] Lord?" *Acts* 13:9-10

"And then the lawless one will be revealed ... the one whose coming springs from the power of *Satan* in every mighty deed and in signs and wonders that *lie* ... a *deceiving power* so that they may believe the *lie.*" 2 *Thessalonians* 2:8-9, 11

Killer

"Be sober and vigilant. Your opponent the *devil* is prowling around like a roaring lion looking for [someone] to *devour.*" 1 *Peter* 5:8

"He was a *murderer* from the beginning." *John* 8:44

Denouement

"How you have fallen from the heavens, O Morning Star, son of the dawn! How you have been cut down to the earth, you who conquered nations! In your heart you said: 'I will scale the heavens; Above the stars of God I will set up my throne; I will take my seat on the Mount of Assembly, on the heights of Zaphon. I will ascend above the tops of the clouds; I will be like the Most High!' No! Down to Sheol you will be brought to the depths of the pit!" *Isaiah 14:12-15*

"Jesus said, 'I have observed Satan fall like lightning from the sky.'" *Luke 10:18*

"The Devil who had led them astray was thrown into the pool of fire and sulfur ... forever and ever." *Revelation 20:10*

SEQUENCE

Opening Statement –
Plaintiff's Attorney, Lucius HellMan

"God Does Not Exist. Jesus Did Not Exist. Christianity Should Not Exist"

How Can There Be Evil in a World Created by an Infinitely Good and Powerful being?

The Belly of the Beast – the Revelation of the Christian "god"

A House of Horrors – the Story of Christianity

Emancipation

Copernican Revolution

Reparation

Opening Statement –
Defendant's Attorney, Misha-El Angelini

"God Does Not 'Exist' – God is EXISTENCE. Jesus 'Did' Not Exist – Jesus IS. Here. Now. Christianity=Human Rights, Freedom, Science, Hospitals, Universities, et al."

GOD Does Not "Exist," GOD is Not "Morally Good," "Evil" is Not a "Thing"

MindField

The Jesus Cloud

Evil, Interrupted

GodSpace

7

Witnesses for the Plaintiff with Cross Examination by Defendant's Attorney

"'Thou Shalt Have No god Before Me' Saith the Universe"

Witness – Percy Maersk, *Cosmologist, "New Atheist" blogger,* author of *When Nothing Became Something*

    Examination and Testimony

    Cross-Examination

"Cruel and Unusual"

Witness – Joyce MacIntosh, *Analytic Philosopher,* author of *Evil-Doer – The God of Religion*

    Examination and Testimony

    Cross-Examination

"Red in Tooth and Claw"

Witness – Robert Atkinson, *Evolutionary Biologist,* author of *The Self-Made Gene*

    Examination and Testimony

    Cross-Examination

"Moral Monster"

Witness – Richard Peterson, *Comparative Religion,* author of *A Dangerous Book*

    Examination and Testimony

    Cross-Examination

"Hell No!"

Witness – Bartholomew Endicott, *Ex-Christian Theologian*, author of *Diabolic Delusion – the Invention of Hell*

Examination and Testimony

Cross-Examination

Witnesses for the Defendant with Cross Examination by Plaintiff's Attorney

"From Error to Terror"

Witness – Raquel Prendergast, *Symbolic Logician*, author of *The "Enlightenment" and Its Reign of Error*

Examination and Testimony

Cross-Examination

"The Universe is a Social Media Platform"

Witness – Stanley Genereux, *Theoretical Physicist*, author of *Mindverse – An Unbrief History of the World*

Examination and Testimony

Cross-Examination

"The Jesus Cloud"

Witness – Gabriel Kantor Chesterfield, *Theologian*, author of *The Jesus Cloud – What You Don't Know About Christianity Can Hurt You*

Examination and Testimony

Cross-Examination

"Homo Sapiens 2.0"

Witness – Mary Lucas, *Cognitive Psychologist,* author of *Not thy will But MINE Be Done*

    Examination and Testimony

    Cross-Examination

"The Hellfire Brief"

Witness – Jose Mendoza, *Exorcist*

    Examination and Testimony

    Cross-Examination

Witness – Harold Montefiore, *NDE Survivor*

    Examination and Testimony

    Cross-Examination

Closing Statement – Plaintiff's Attorney

Closing Statement – Defendant's Attorney

Statement by the Court

INTRODUCTORY STATEMENT BY THE COURT

LADIES AND GENTLEMEN:

You have been selected to serve as a juror in this case. By the oath you take as a juror you become an official of this Court and an active participant in the public administration of justice.

For more than six hundred years, since the Magna Carta in 1215, there has been the right to a trial by jury not only for criminal cases but also for civil disputes.

You will be the sole judges of the credibility of the witnesses and the weight to be given their testimony but in matter of law you must be governed by the Court's instructions.

The trial of this case will involve issues of monumental importance. Lucius HellMan represents "The People" (Plaintiff) in this epic attempt to "try" the Creator for the pain, evil and suffering in the world.

The Defense is led by Misha-El Angelini who argues that the Plaintiff has created a fake god who bears no resemblance to the infinite–eternal God revealed in Jesus of Nazareth.

Among the issues raised by the Plaintiff:

If the Creator is all good and all powerful, why doesn't he, or she, prevent or eliminate the evil and suffering in the world?

Why are innocent people subjected to pain, disease and deprivation?

Why do animals have to suffer?

Doesn't the Old Testament show a violent, merciless God?

How can a God who condemns his creatures to eternal suffering in Hell be called loving?

Hasn't science already shown religion to be false?

You will undoubtedly have questions or concerns about how the evidence has been developed in this case. It may be helpful to explain several aspects or rules of evidence that help determine what is admissible evidence in a trial.

A number of very prominent experts will be called as witnesses. They include Theologians, Scholars, Scientists, Biologists, Historians, Physicists and Mathematicians.

Federal Rule of Evidence 702 deals with testimony by Experts. It provides: "If scientific, technical, or other specialized knowledge will assist the trier of fact to understand the evidence or to determine a fact in issue, a witness qualified as an expert by knowledge, skill, experience, training or education may testify thereto in the form of an opinion or otherwise, if:

> the testimony is based upon sufficient fads or data,
>
> the testimony is the product of reliable principles and methods, and
>
> the witness has applied the principles and methods reliably to the facts of the case."

The Court, in pre-trial procedures and/or based upon agreements between Counsel for the parties, has ruled that each of the attorneys representing the parties and each witness to be called is qualified as an "Expert" to testify or express opinions.

You have undoubtedly heard that "Hearsay" cannot ordinarily be considered as evidence. But there are exceptions to that rule. Hearsay is defined as a statement, other than one made by the declarant (a person who makes a statement) while testifying at the trial offered to prove the truth of the matter asserted. The exception to the Hearsay Rule that will be most applicable to this trial is the one dealing with "Learned Treatises". The many books and articles you will hear referenced by witnesses that are published treaties or periodicals on the subject of history, medicine or other science or art established as a reliable authority have been ruled admissible and are not precluded as "Hearsay."

Now, on to the trial.

OPENING STATEMENT –
PLAINTIFF'S ATTORNEY

Plaintiff's Attorney – **Lucius HellMan (LH)**

"God Does Not Exist. Jesus Did Not Exist. Christianity Should Not Exist"

How Can There Be Evil In a World Created By An Infinitely Good And Powerful Being?

The Belly of the Beast – the Revelation of the Christian "god"

A House of Horrors – the Story of Christianity

Emancipation

Copernican Revolution

Reparation

Your Honor, Ladies and Gentlemen of the Jury:

God truly is on trial today. The Christian God.

"He" is on trial for crimes against humanity of which he is author, accomplice and accessory.

But I have to start off by sharing our three foundational assumptions. These, I think, are accepted by most reasonably intelligent people in the 21st century:

God does not exist. Jesus did not exist. Christianity should not exist.

And yet the non-existent Christian God is on trial because belief in the existence of this moral monster has brought untold suffering over two millennia.

The god of the Old and New Testaments is vicious and vengeful. From the first preposterous pages of *Genesis* to the unhappily ever after ending of *Revelation* we see a domineering deity who imposes diabolic rules, indentures all who fearfully follow him, inflicts cruel and unusual punishment on friends and foes and invents imaginary enemies (the "Devil"). Most revolting of all is his threat of eternal punishment. Those who dare to dissent from his demand of mindless submission are condemned to roast forever in the fires of hell – a foolish fantasy but one that has unleashed untold suffering on millions of impressionable minds.

This sordid saga of tyranny has, in turn, created a race of brainwashed, brain-dead slaves. Christians say that man is created in the image of God. This claim is right in one respect: they have been recreated in the image of their loathsome "creator." The last two thousand years is a horrendously tragic history of oppression, persecution, exploitation, torture, war, all carried out in the name of the Prince of Peace. The Crusades, the Inquisition, the witch-hunts, slave-trading, the burnings at the stake of scientists and thinkers, the wars fueled by religious intolerance, the destruction of indigenous peoples and cultures across the world, the pogroms, the Holocaust, the prohibition of any form of enjoyment in the short span between womb and tomb with a virulent and obsessive focus on eliminating sexual freedoms and reproductive rights – this is the legacy of the Christian god. The Christians themselves have single-handedly created a problem of evil that convicts their creator of crimes against humanity!

This trial is about holding this bloodthirsty Tyrant and his followers accountable for their gruesome reign of terror and stopping them from wreaking any further damage while also securing reparations for the irreparable harm they have caused. Since the Tyrant exists only in the minds of his followers, it is his followers that we must indict for their weapons of mass hatred.

I'm not going to waste the Court's time right now trying to show that the Christian God does not exist for the same reason that I do not have to spend time showing that Zeus or Baal or Pan do not exist. If someone wants to say that fairies exist, the burden of proof is on them to make a case for fairy existence – not on those who do not believe in fairy tales! Of course, some of our finest philosophers and scientists have already done this job for us as our witnesses will show.

The great philosopher Bertrand Russell, the intellectual godfather of the New Atheist movement whose writings led modern philosophers like Simon Blackburn and Colin McGinn to atheism, annihilated all the so-called arguments for God's existence. The most popular of these is the argument that you need a creator to explain how the universe got here. About this, Russell said, "If everything must have a cause, then God must have a cause. If there can be anything without a cause, it may just as well be the world as God, so that there cannot be any validity in that argument. ... There is no reason why the world could not have come into being without a cause; nor, on the other hand, is there any reason why it should not have always existed."[1] As you will see from the testimony of our cosmologist witness, modern science has indeed shown that the universe could come into existence without a cause.

The distinguished scientist Richard Dawkins said, "An atheist ... is someone who believes that there is nothing beyond the natural, physical world, no supernatural creative intelligence lurking behind the observable universe, no soul that outlasts the body and no miracles – except in the sense of natural phenomena that we don't yet understand."[2]

Russell also said that "modern science gives us no indication whatever of the existence of the soul"[3] and "today no serious neuroscientist will entertain the idea of a soul."[4]

Then there is the question directly relevant to this trial. If there is a god who is infinitely good and powerful, how is it that we have all this pain and suffering and evil? According to Christians, God is the cause of everything and so he must be the cause of all the evils as well. It is part of the whole package.

When asked, *What is the strongest argument against God's existence?* Simon Blackburn said: "Undoubtedly the fact of appalling human and animal suffering makes it hard to believe that the world is the product of an all good, all powerful, and all knowing intelligent designer."[5]

As for Jesus, like the God question, I do not have to spend time at this point to show that he did not exist. The self-styled New Testament scholars have already performed that task over the last 200 years with their systematic

---

1 Bertrand Russell, *Why I Am Not a Christian* (Watts & Co., for the Rationalist Press Association Limited, 1927), https://users.drew.edu/~jlenz/whynot.html

2 Richard Dawkins, *The God Delusion* (London: Bantam, 2006), 14.

3 http://www.personal.kent.edu/~rmuhamma/Philosophy/RBwritings/whatIsSoul.htm

4 Bertrand Russell, *Let the People Think* (London: Watts & Co, 1941), 113.

5 https://philosophynow.org/issues/99/Simon_Blackburn

demolition of the historicity of the book they supposedly study. After denying the actuality of almost every one of the events in the Gospel, "de-mythologizing" is what they call it, they leave us with a work of fiction. This raises the question of why these "scholars" should be employed at all. But, no doubt in the interest of their continued professional relevance, even the most radical of them have insisted that the central character existed – while also admitting we know nothing about him and all the stories surrounding him are false. But other more honest scholars have taken the scholarship to its logical conclusion – namely that there is nothing historically factual in the Gospels including its prime protagonist. In short, Jesus never existed.

Our focus is not on the existence of god or Jesus but on what is concrete and indisputable. Accordingly we will be showing that the god of the Christians is a morally despicable being. We propose to show this in a systematic sequence by

> first pointing out the kind of world in which we find ourselves with all its pain and cruelty and the absence of benevolence of any kind;

> then highlighting the kind of terrifying deity that we find on display in Old and New Testaments;

> and finally exposing the barbaric behavior of those who are morally depraved enough to believe in such a deity, a depravity they have balefully manifested in their every interaction with the rest of humanity.

These three considerations will be a final nail in the coffin of this moral monster – "god" – that has been the single greatest enemy of civilization, rationality, innovation, tolerance, progress, peace and human happiness.

Now it will not all be doom and gloom in our presentation. There is a silver lining to these menacing clouds hanging over the human enterprise. The dark night of faith has been dispelled by the heroes of humankind ranging from Galileo to David Hume to Jean-Jacques Rousseau, Voltaire to Charles

Darwin to Lord Russell, who have deployed science and reason to over-throw the idols of religion. They have spurred on the human spirit damp-ened by superstition to regain confidence in our own powers of exploration and discovery. Instead of attributing lightning to the wrath of the gods, we come to see its electrical origins. The rebirth of the human spirit inaugu-rated by the Enlightenment has borne fruit in the new world of science and technology and humane behavior in which we live today. In his breath-tak-ing book *Enlightenment Now*, Steve Pinker first says, "The Enlightenment principle that we can apply reason and sympathy to enhance human flour-ishing may seem obvious, trite, old-fashioned." He then goes to show that because of the Enlightenment "The world has made spectacular progress in every single measure of human well-being."[6]

Of course, the biggest obstacle to all of this is religion. Russell had already warned us of this in the preface to *Why I Am Not a Christian*, "I am as firmly convinced that religions do harm as I am that they are untrue"[7]

I turn now to some of the main themes that will be addressed by our witnesses.

How Can There Be Evil In A World Created By An Infinitely Good And Powerful Being?

The first and most obvious refutation of the superstition that there is a kindly old man in the sky tending to the affairs of his minions on Earth is the pandemonium we actually find here below – most of it caused by reli-gious fanatics. The Christians have the audacity to claim that their deity is a perfect being that is both infinitely good and infinitely powerful. Well, if that is the case, why is there so much pain and wanton suffering, destruc-tion and death, cruelty and waste in his world? (I say "he" because this is

6   Steve Pinker, *Enlightenment –The Case for Reason, Science, Humanism, and Progress.* (New York: Viking, 2018), 4, 52.

7   *Why I Am Not a Christian and Other Essays on Religion and Related Subjects* (New York: Simon And Schuster, 1957), xi.

the pronoun Christians use when referring to their deity. In any event, no woman would be so odious.)

Why do babies suffer horrible deaths with inoperable tumors? Why do plagues and pandemics arise throughout history bringing with them slow and painful death? Why is there humanly caused destruction and suffering in every era? Why are there famines and floods, earthquakes and tornadoes, parasites and viruses? If the deity is all-powerful, he could easily prevent all this mayhem.

But since he does not stop any of it, this means that either he is not omnipotent or he is not all-good as his followers claim. You cannot have it both ways. Maybe he is not all-powerful in which case he is not perfect and doesn't deserve worship. Maybe he's not all-good in which we should spurn him not praise him. Or, maybe, as all the evidence indicates, he doesn't exist except in the minds of the gullible and the perverse.

All this is obvious. Asked to defend the indefensible, the few Christians who claim to have thought about it evade, ignore or explain away the facts before us. Recently, after much squirming, they concocted a scam they call the freewill defense. Allegedly, their god is almighty and all-good but wanted his creatures to freely choose to be his slaves by following arbitrary hare-brained rules. But because they were created as imbeciles, they messed up and ended up offending him. As a resulted they created hell on earth to be followed shortly by hell hereafter.

This preposterous freewill gimmick only creates new problems without solving any of the initial issues. If the creatures are such numbskulls, should not their creator be responsible for making them that way? And if the deity is all-powerful, why could he not create a world in which these helpless beings do not make mistakes or where their mistakes would not have such dire consequences? Why should the baby in a cancer ward or the family blown to bits by religious terrorists suffer for the mistakes of their ancestors?

Neurobiologist and primatologist Robert Sapolsky has demolished what is left of the freewill runaround with his encyclopedic masterpieces, *Behave – the Biology of Humans at Our Best and Worst* and *Determined – A Science of Life Without Freewill.* In *Determined,* he points out that "we are nothing more or less than the sum of that which we could not control—our biology, our environments, their interactions. ... These are not all separate – ology fields producing behavior. They all merge into one—evolution produces genes marked by the epigenetics of early environment, which produce proteins that, facilitated by hormones in a particular context, work in the brain to produce you. A seamless continuum leaving no cracks between the disciplines into which to slip some free will."[8]

He adds that what the science in his book "ultimately teaches is that there is no meaning. There's no answer to 'Why?' beyond 'This happened because of what came just before, which happened because of what came just before that.' There is nothing but an empty, indifferent universe in which, occasionally, atoms come together temporarily to form things we each call Me."

Sapolsky has permanently ended the illusion of freewill:

"We have no free will at all."

"We are not captains of our ships; our ships never had captains."

"When people claim that there are causeless causes of your behavior that they call 'free will,' they have (a) failed to recognize or not learned about the determinism lurking beneath the surface and/or (b) erroneously concluded that the rarefied aspects of the universe that do work indeterministically can explain your character, morals, and behavior."[9]

---

8   Robert M. Sapolsky, *Determined: A Science of Life without Free Will* (New York: Penguin Press, 2023), 240.

9   Ibid., 386, 6. 386, 8.

Sapolsky's work is, in some ways, as important for human self-understanding as the works of Darwin and Freud. He has liberated us from yet another of the harmful superstitions foisted on us by religious fanatics. We have to now radically change our ideas of crime and punishment, praise and blame.

Going back to the "creation" of the "infinitely good and powerful" deity, when you look at the world revealed by evolution, you see nature "red in tooth and claw." It is kill or be killed all across the animal planet. There is no trace of providence in the snarling lion or the spitting cobra. Charles Darwin, perceptive as always, put his finger on the problem: "I cannot persuade myself that a beneficent and omnipotent God would have designedly created the Ichneumonidae with the express intention of their feeding within the living bodies of caterpillars."[10] And remember, Earth itself is nothing but a gigantic graveyard.

When you look at human history, you see savagery in every society. Human sacrifice to please deities, cannibalism, rape and plunder, slavery, torture, holocausts. And always we see wars mostly caused by religion and religious intolerance – war after war with unthinkable savagery. If this is how the "image of god" behaves, we shudder to think what that god is like. In fact, the only societies that have been civilized are those that expelled god from their midst.

If their god is morally perfect or good as the Christians claim, there is no evidence of that in the world in which we live. Quite the opposite. Rather, what we see is a nightmare domain of such unthinkable evil that if it had a creator, then that creator would have to be what previous eras called the Devil. Some Christians say, "trust us, our god will bring about what is best in the end." To this we say how downright delusional and callous can you be? What good could possibly come out of such monstrous cataclysms as the Holocaust and the killing fields of Cambodia?

---

10   Charles Darwin, Letter to Asa Gray, May 22 1860

If anyone chooses to ignore all that is palpably self-evident and still professes belief in a god that is all-knowing, all-good and all-powerful, they are showing their criminal indifference and outright contempt for the suffering endured both by their fellows and all living beings. Such a belief is not simply obscene but evil. Psychotics who profess such beliefs are simply immoral. And irrational. As A.C. Grayling put it, "to believe in the existence of (say) a benevolent and omnipotent deity in the face of childhood cancers and mass deaths in tsunamis and earthquakes [is an example of] serious irrationality."[11]

Let's say you are a compassionate person. If you saw a stranger suffering from some ailment for which you had a cure and you had the opportunity to treat them without incurring any cost or effort, would you assist them or not? Simply by virtue of being compassionate, you would help out – even if it meant great cost, which in this example it does not. Now if there is a being that is both infinitely compassionate and infinitely powerful and that sees his creatures writhing in pain, at the very least by virtue of his compassion and using his power, we would expect him to relieve them of their suffering. Otherwise, it is meaningless to call him compassionate or loving. But the creatures continue to suffer in the most terrible ways. So, snap out of it! There is no infinitely compassionate and powerful being. And if there is an infinitely powerful being, he certainly isn't compassionate.

Since this "god" is clearly immoral, we hold him guilty of the suffering bedeviling the human race and demand reparations for the suffering he has inflicted on his creatures. Since he does not exist, he cannot pay up. But his followers who inflict most of this suffering on their fellows saying that they are just "following orders" have no such escape clause. They need to be held responsible. They have to put their money where their mouth is. Put up and then shut up.

---

11   A.C. Grayling, *Against All Gods* (Oberon Books, 2007) p. 37.

The Belly of the Beast –
the Revelation of the Christian "god"

So far we have stayed with the evidence of our eyes. Now let us peer into the depths of the darkness that makes up the Christian religion.

Somehow or other, Christians have conned the world into believing that theirs is a religion of love. A simple reading of their scriptures will cure you of any temptation to believe this pipedream.

Here is what you see in their so-called holy books, what they grandly call the Old and New Testaments:

- A god who banishes his first creatures from a mythical paradise and condemns them to suffer death and destruction for daring to think and act on their own.

- A god who tells his followers to slaughter their enemies to the last man, woman and child.

- A god who orders the immediate execution of any of his followers who transgress his arbitrary commands.

- A god who arranges for their enemies to slaughter his followers because they didn't keep his laws.

- A god whose wisest follower had 700 wives and 300 concubines.

This is just the tip of an extraordinarily bloody iceberg. The Old Testament is full of these kinds of ghastly, grotesque events and individuals all following a script directed from on high. But the Old was simply a preview for the coming horrors of the New Testament.

In the New Testament, we meet Jesus, a man we now know never existed but who is acclaimed to be god by his followers. At the foundation of this New Testament are five terrifying teachings that have terrorized vulnerable populations for centuries:

Unless you claim that the mythical Jesus is god and take him as your "lord and savior" you are not going to find salvation.

We are all born totally depraved and incapable of any good action but are nevertheless guilty of being this way.

We are all under attack by a spiritual underworld that is presided over by someone called Satan who is also known as the Devil: the serpent in the garden of paradise has been repurposed to play this new infernal role.

To surrender to Jesus means you must repress all normal sexual urges and say goodbye to all earthly pleasures – or else!

Worst of all, if for some reason you fail to follow the teachings of Jesus or follow the various commandments he laid down (especially the sexual ones), you will suffer everlasting torture in the flames of Hell.

Many of us do not realize the true savagery of the last of these teachings, the terrible doctrine of Hell. What the New Testament tells us is that most human beings will live forever in unthinkable suffering because they broke a few arbitrary rules and despite the fact that they had no control over their actions.

To add insult to injury, the Christian theologian John Calvin, the godfather of many evangelicals, gleefully said: "All men are not created for the same end, but some are foreordained to eternal life, others to eternal damnation."[12] He added, "The wicked themselves have been created for this very end – that they may perish."[13]

In other words, God created most people simply and solely to damn them! No wonder enlightened atheists have said that the god of Christianity is a

---

12   John Calvin, *Institutes of the Christian Religion* (Philadelphia: Presbyterian Board of Christian Education), Book 3, Chapter 21, 1.

13   Citation in John Murray, *Calvin on Scripture and Divine Sovereignty* (Michigan: Baker Book House, 1960), 61.

megalomaniacal, cosmic sadist. A monster. I ask you, what kind of savage could believe in such a savage god?

The Christian god has evolved from the genocidal tyrant of the Old Testament who rained terrestrial fire and brimstone on the earthly enemies of his "chosen people" to the hellfire and brimstone tyrant of the New Testament who promises, through the so-called "son of god," eternal suffering to those who don't "get it." This is the deity we indict.

Some may ask why we are not arraigning the Islamic god or the multiple gods of the Eastern religions. The Islamic god is a later gnostic evolution from the Christian god but the root of all evil is the Christian deity because it introduces demented beliefs about this deity being a "trinity" along with nauseating beliefs about human destiny such as hell. The Eastern religions are superstitions and oppressive in their own right but none are intolerant and doctrinally savage in the same way as Christianity. In taking on the Christian deity, I charge him not only for the cruelty and the enslavement we find in both Testaments but also all the resident evil that we find in offshoot religions like Islam.

A House of Horrors – the Story of Christianity

The horrifying narratives of tyranny, savagery and degradation that we find in the "Holy Bible" are matched by the sadomasochism, malevolence and depravity of the Christian Church. One thing that the Jesus of these texts got right was his aphorism, "by their fruits you shall know them." This was certainly true of his followers who massacred and mutilated their fellows by the millions. We see popes delighting in their debauchery, priests sodomizing boys, knights of the "true faith" butchering innocents and robbing their earthly possessions, stern clerics torturing the supposedly heterodox in the name of truth, merchants selling opium while purporting to distribute Bibles, Christian colonists killing indigenous peoples so as to grab their lands and goods, slave traders and slave holders who claim to follow biblically sanctioned practices, televangelists raking in cash from little old ladies by promising financial blessings, and on and on.

To sum up, the Christian religion has been the most oppressive, poisonous and murderous force in history. It destroys human dignity, manufactures irrational guilt, forbids all natural human pleasures, demands intolerance, burns heretics at the stake, launches murderous crusades and pogroms against dissenters, and terrorizes its followers with the fear of divine wrath and the burning flames of hell. Its goal is to produce puppets who dance to the tune of its puppet master. It creates a slave mentality with its demand for subservience and the enforcement of superstition. In all this, the religion mirrors the deity it worships and propagates. Christianity is the summit of all the wickedness of the religions that came before it and the source of the evil of all subsequent religions.

It is a force for evil because it demands total unthinking allegiance to a bloodthirsty, genocidal tyrant. As is to be expected, you become like the being you worship: intolerant, judgmental, murderous. You not only become incapable of independent thought but are brainwashed into barbarism. Righteous indignation gives you the right to inflict any kind of suffering on pagans and heretics. To believe in Hell is to be Hellish.

Let me lay out a partial laundry list of "war crimes" that were conceived and executed by Christianity:

- Suppression of thought that resulted in ignorance on all matters of human welfare.

- Suppression of science by death threats or actual death, Galileo simply being the best-known case.

- Torture as a means of control as exemplified not just by the Inquisition but the standard practice of hanging as well as drawing and quartering in all the so-called Christian kingdoms of Europe. Think also of the countless women who have been burned as witches simply for being women!

- Terrorism in the name of God that has led to the massacre of millions.

- Fanatics slitting throats while shrieking "God is great."

- The Church has always sought political power and has used every possible means – bribes, spiritual threats, pleas – to be part of the ruling establishment. This pattern of avarice and power grabs began with the Israelites using divine authority to steal the land of the Canaanites and Amalekites purportedly because they were ordered by their god to plunder their neighbors' possessions.

- Slavery, in which human beings are treated as property, was given sacred sanction both in the Bible and by the Church. The Christians simply practiced what they were taught.

- Racism always prevalent in Christian churches.

- Apartheid created by the Dutch Reformed church.

- Oppression of the female sex with the establishment of a patriarchal society where women have no rights.

- Sexual repression and exploitation that has caused more misery than virtually anything else.

- Persecution of various sexual orientations that has led many to depression and suicide.

- Denial of abortion and other reproductive rights which has led to the increase of poverty.

- Specific biblical injunctions to do evil that Christians practice with gusto.

- Celibacy, another practice that demonizes natural sexual urges.

- Child abuse, a specialty of religionists of every stripe.

- Church leaders including Popes and Orthodox bishops who have been tools of intelligence agencies, dictators and kings.

- Adolf Hitler, the mass murderer whose main followers were Lutherans and Catholics. And, as historian William Carroll demonstrated, Christian antisemitism was responsible for the Holocaust.

- The Fundamentalists, Evangelicals and Pentecostals who have been all about making money whether by propagating capitalism or the prosperity gospel.

- Self-appointed social justice Christians who themselves live in the lap of luxury. Among Christian leaders, economics and power take precedence over doctrine.

- Sexual double lives of the leaders of all the different churches.

Christianity, as you can tell from this short checklist is a house of horrors, a plague that continues to defile the human race. Some of its apologists argue that despite its shortcomings it has been the source of many benefits. In reply the courageous and prescient Lord Russell said that he could think of only two benefits that religion has given humanity – one is the construction of calendars and the other the chronicling and prediction of eclipses. Both of these predated Christianity. Christianity itself, he said, has only bequeathed fear and misery.

Now some might say that there are liberal forms of Christianity that have discarded many of the primitive notions of the early Christians – such as benighted views of sexuality – while embracing science and rejecting superstitions like the doctrine of hell. Unfortunately, this is an all or nothing situation. You are in or you are out. You cannot pick and choose when dealing with an ideology that is corrupt from root to shoot. To call yourself "Christian" is to aid and abet the religion's savagery.

In another twist, some Christian leaders today think they will be accepted by the freethinking world by piously paying homage to our rationalist principles: fighting climate change by eliminating fossil fuels, empowering women, denouncing consumerism, ending global poverty through social spending. They downplay their reactionary views on sexuality and some-times even disown them (when no one's listening). They strip away all references to the supernatural.

Of course, we welcome all who want to join us in the fight for a scientifically run society. But when it comes to these Christian Lite pretenders we demand that they first denounce their own institutions and reject their superstitions. Then, they should give up their opulent properties and work for a living. Otherwise, they are simply self-serving hypocrites trying to save their skin by selling out. To them we say, we do not need you and we do not want you!

One reason that Christianity is so intolerant is because its existence depends on all other religions being untrue. But this is its Achilles Heel. Since the world has thousands of religions, there is no reason to prefer one over the other claiming it to be true or a divine revelation. What about all the other religions out there? This is deadly for Christianity's claim to be true. This is why Christians are so intolerant. Other religions represent a mortal threat to its claim to be the one true religion. So the solution is to stamp them all out as works of the devil.

To rub salt in the wound, the Christians add, for good measure, that anyone who believes in a rival religion will go to hell. So, all those millions of people who have never heard of the mythic founder of the Christian religion or were born and brought up in another religion are summarily sentenced to eternal torment. What kind of monstrous deity would do this and what kind of sociopath would believe such a vile doctrine?

Because of these and other unholy beliefs, Christianity has spawned wars, persecution and intolerance, inflicting incalculable evils on the human race. To believe in its god is to be servile, depraved, ignorant and intolerant.

The Age of Faith is also known – and, more accurately I might say – as the Dark Ages and our liberation from this nightmare was rightly called the Enlightenment.

Emancipation

The Enlightenment was the Emancipation Proclamation of the human race. The Enlightenment Era, a glorious period between 1685 and 1815, is also called the Age of Reason. It was the Enlightenment, through the great thinkers of this period, that gave birth to modern science as well as freedom and reason. Science has liberated us from the superstitions of religion, improved our quality of life and made us civilized people.

The Old and New Testament writers, of course, were aware that the human spirit would always seek freedom and discover reason. Both these capabilities represent the greatest threat to organized religion. This is why the writers of these books created myths about an evil figure who would tempt humans to think for themselves. But these myths themselves show that the priests who wrote the stories feared the potential for progress represented by freedom and reason. In the *Genesis* myth of the Garden of Eden, a talking serpent, whom Christians identified with their primary bogeyman, the "devil", tells them "God knows well that when you eat of it [the forbidden fruit] your eyes will be opened and you will be like gods, who know good and evil." (*Genesis* 3:5) When they end up eating of the fruit, the god of *Genesis* is fearful of their new power and banishes them from the Garden. He punishes the serpent for liberating the couple.

Later in the Bible, the so-called devil is called Lucifer or light-bearer. This actually happens to be an appropriate name because it describes a being who is opposed to the dark obedience demanded by the biblical deity and brings light to those trapped in darkness. You might say that the Lucifer figure in the Bible represents the true hope of humanity because this is the kind of figure we can be if we exercise freedom and reason and break the fetters of religious superstition and fear. I am glad to say there is a greater interest today in Lucifer than ever before, across the board – from the entertainment industry to academia to the popular realm.

We will be showing all this in more detail but it is clear that the greatest fruit of the Enlightenment is science and science is the one hope that humans have to be liberated from the straitjackets imposed by the Christian religion. Science has delivered! When it comes right down to it, the fate of humanity depends on the success of science. We are free at last but the price of freedom is eternal vigilance! The only obstacle standing in the way of the continued success of science is Christianity.

Copernican Revolution

Among the freedoms won by the Enlightenment was liberation from the Christian penitentiary of moral bondage. This was indeed a Copernican Revolution.

Christians claimed that the moral code created by their corrupt clergy lies at the center of the universe of human action. But the Enlightenment freed us from this sick fantasy. We came to see that the human universe is awash with various moral planets which are narratives created by different societies at different times. What is wrong in one narrative is right in another. Christian morality is only one of many moral narratives. All were formed by evolutionary advantages, cultural conventions and patriarchal power structures and nothing more. They have no deity behind them – or over them.

And yet what the Enlightenment took away with one hand it returned with another. It struck down the golden calf of religion-based morality. But it gave us a New Morality built on something acceptable to all civilized people and provably beneficial – science! As Steven Pinker has said, the Enlightenment thinkers gave us "a secular foundation for morality."

The precepts of the New Morality are easy to recognize and practice:

> All ethical rules are human creations and should be changed depending on circumstances and goals. They have no supernatural source. We create them depending on our needs and interests.

At all times, these rules should maximize human pleasure. To adapt Freud, this is the Pleasure Principle and it should rule all our actions. This means no restriction on all the ways in which we enjoy ourselves especially in spaces like sex which primitive societies have repressed and persecuted. Sexual orientation and expression of every kind should be cherished not criminalized.

There is one exception to the Pleasure Principle. In seeking our pleasures, we should not harm others. This is in our self-interest. If we are permitted to cause harm to another in the pursuit of pleasure, then others can do the same to us in the same pursuit. This is not a question of right or wrong but of pragmatism.

Religionists should have no say in any ethical matter and especially when it comes to science. It is science that has brought us greater prosperity and pleasure than was ever dreamed possible. Religion has been its chief obstacle at every step of the way. Now that science has won the day, these obscurantists have changed their tactics. They piously proclaim that their moral mumbo-jumbo should guide the applications of science. What chutzpah! It reminds me of the man who killed his parents and then pleaded for the court's clemency because he was an orphan. After failing to kill science in the cradle, they want to now become its legally appointed guardian! The answer is no.

Social constructs created by religion such as marriage should be de-constructed. They are oppressive structures and often instruments of torture. Everyone should have the freedom to enter into and leave relationships as they see fit.

I am happy to say that the Copernican Revolution has reached its zenith with the discovery and celebration of gender fluidity. "Gender" is one more of those oppressive structures bequeathed by Christianity. Generations of children and adults have been forced to adopt the gender roles they were assigned no matter how disfiguring it was for their psyches. Gender dysphoria has driven millions into depression and even to suicide.

But no more! No mas!

Science has made it possible for us to adopt the gender of our choice! We have entered the trans-gender age! Non-binary, binary, agender, gender fluidity – anything we want gender-wise is now possible.

This transformational breakthrough shows us how science can and will shape the ethics of the future. It will demolish every element of religious morality and replace all the "do nots" with "do"s.

It is a Copernican Revolution for human happiness.

But we have to go further – much further!

Progressives have celebrated the legalization of same-sex marriage. But here is the problem. By agitating and achieving for this sort of thing, they implicitly accept the legitimacy of such institutions. To fully embrace the freedom offered by science, we have to abolish these retrograde ideas – marriage, family, even pregnancy. The end of gender is just the first step.

We now have artificial wombs in which embryos can gestate. We will soon be able to create human eggs from skin cells. So, here is how it all comes together. We create embryos using frozen eggs and sperm donors. The eggs themselves may come from skin cells so there is no limit to the number of embryos we can create. Someday we might even have synthetic embryos. We then use gene editing to remove genetic defects in the embryo. We can even magnify desirable attributes. These embryos are then finally "hatched" in the artificial wombs – ectogenesis. We edit film footage to create movies and verbiage to create books. Why shouldn't we do gene editing to create healthy, happy humans?

The bottom line is this. If science makes something possible and this something augments social efficiency, drives down costs and contributes to human happiness, we have a rational obligation to go for it. Science has made it possible to end pregnancy as we know it with its human and financial costs and to prevent genetic defects with its waste of resources.

Since we have separated pregnancy and birth from its current messiness, all of us are now free to live our lives to maximize the Pleasure Principle. Anything that comes in the way of this Principle has to be eliminated. Commitments are a crutch that holds back our growth. So, goodbye marriage and family, two of the many ways in which the Church sought to control its subjects.

Religions and their moralities have only produced misery. Science has set us free.

Reparation

All this shows us why the present proceeding is of the greatest urgency for the well-being of humanity. Amusing as the absurd teachings of Christianity might be to the modern mind, they have been a regressive force acting against science, reason, progress and civilization. They have been responsible for the annihilation of entire nations, the Inquisition, the Crusades, slavery, racism, sexual and every other kind of oppression.

And they continue to fight a rearguard action against the advancing forces of reason and science.

But enough is enough. As our presentations will show, there is nothing more important for humankind today than to be liberated from the most dangerous force in the world. It is the ideology of a moral monster who prohibits science, reason and freedom and commands his followers to silence all those who proclaim tolerance, pluralism, inquiry, progress and civilization. It is an ideology that seeks total dominion and will never compromise with its perceived enemies.

For the very survival of our civilization, of a decent morality, we have to end this threat. Just as we cannot allow a Nazi party or a KKK group to enter into public discourse or impose its beliefs, we cannot allow this religion of a moral monster to continue operating in the public square.

It has to be banned. And its followers must pay for their crimes.

Our demands are very simple: we want the Court to ban any further propagation or practice of this evil and odious ideology, and we want all Christian churches, starting with the Roman church and moving to include every group or individual that touts itself as Christian, to pay restitution and reparations for these abominations. We want both compensatory and punitive damages commensurate with the magnitude of the destruction of life and liberty entailed by this savage religion. These reparations will not heal the wounds but they will confer a small measure of justice. Most important, they will remove today's greatest threat to human well-being and development.

Thank you, Ladies and Gentlemen of the Jury. Thank you, Your Honor.

OPENING STATEMENT –
DEFENDANT'S ATTORNEY

Defendant's Attorney – **Misha-El Angelini (MA)**

"God does not 'exist' – God is EXISTENCE. Jesus 'did' not exist – Jesus IS. Here. Now. Christianity = Human Personhood, Rights, Freedom, Science, Hospitals, Universities, et al."

How We KNOW There is a God – A One-Minute Exercise

How We Know Jesus IS

The Matrix of Modernity

GOD Does Not "Exist," GOD is not "morally good," "Evil" is Not a "Thing"

God Does Not "Exist" Just as Life is not "Alive "

God is Not "Morally Good" Just as the Moral Law is Not Morally Good or Bad

Evil is Not a "Thing" But a Lack of Something

MindField

The Achilles Heel of Atheism

The Supra-Physical – Non-Physical Realities

Seeing is Believing

Fish Don't Know They're in Water

The Supra-Physical Should be the Starting Point of Evolutionary Theory

What the Pioneers of Modern Physics said about the Supra-Physical

The Jesus Cloud

GodSpace

Ladies and gentlemen of the jury, as we notified the Court at the outset, my Client does not accept the legitimacy of these proceedings. Neither the Plaintiff nor the Court has any standing as far as my Client is concerned and, of course, no jurisdiction whatsoever.

In fact, if anyone should be on trial, it should be "The People!" What has been obvious throughout history is humanity's inhumanity to itself. It takes a lot of nerve to blame human savagery on anyone other than human-kind itself.

We have, however, chosen to participate in this "mock" trial because we want to protect the freedoms of those who have remained faithful to the truths revealed to humanity by its greatest Benefactor. Our participation is also an opportunity to correct common misconceptions about my Client as graphically illustrated by my opponent's opening statement.

The outcome of the proceedings depends on the way in which you, the jury, exercise your freedom and your reason. We hold that freedom and reason are the two greatest gifts we have been given after the gift of existence. My opponent's comments to the contrary, these gifts are celebrated by followers of my Client and denied by the children of the misnamed Enlightenment as we shall show. At any rate, the outcome of this trial, whatever it might be, will have no effect on my Client – only on "The People."

To begin with, I will show that my opponent was obviously and undeniably wrong in his first three claims: namely his claims that neither God nor Jesus existed and that Christianity has been an irredeemable blight on humanity.

How We KNOW There is a God – A One-Minute Exercise

Let's start with his first claim, the non-existence of God. Your brain is made up of 80+ billion neurons. Each neuron is made up of some 100,000 mole-cules and is mostly water. As neuroscientist Mario Beauregard notes, these molecules change about 10,000 times over the course of your life. And yet you remain the same at two months old, two years old, 20 years old and all the way to now. Of course, you grow and learn and change but it is the same "you" that undergoes these changes. So what is it that stays the same?

It is clearly not something physical because the physical – for instance, your neurons – is in a constant state of flux. You could not even complete a sentence if you were entirely physical. Indubitably, then, there is something about you that is non-physical.

Where did this non-physical dimension come from? It could not have emerged from the physical for two reasons. All the cells in your body, and not just your neurons, are constantly dying and being replenished, so they cannot serve as the basis of a continuing identity. Secondly, the laws of physics have no room for the creation of the non-physical from the physical. Ergo, the non-physical "you" must come from something that is itself non-physical. And where did this non-physical reality come from? It must always have existed without limitation. This is the Ultimate Reality we know as God.

How We Know Jesus IS

The second claim made by my opponent concerns the existence of Jesus. The life and indeed the death and resurrection of Jesus are evident facts of history. The most compelling feature of the Christian story is the transformation of the followers of Jesus and the genesis of the Christian movement. As we shall see, no serious historian whether atheist or Christian denies that Jesus existed and was crucified. The greatest of the Jewish and Roman historians, who wrote in the first century, testified to his existence. But there is a bigger question.

What transformed 11 fearful peasants and fisher-folk into superheroes who preached the Good News across the world despite trials and tribulations and eventually horrendous deaths? What galvanized them to take on the most powerful empire of the day? They claimed that Jesus rose from the dead and appeared to them.

Critics say this was a hallucination or a hoax. But the hallucination hypothesis is not remotely plausible for those who know the causes and characteristics of such illusions. Hallucinations are individual experiences caused by drugs, mental illness or an expectation of seeing that which is allegedly witnessed. None of these applied to the hardy peasants who never expected Jesus to rise from the dead.

The idea of a hoax is wildly implausible given the improbability that anyone would deliberately seek out a grisly fate in order to perpetrate a fiction. Ten out of the 11 died horrific deaths in faraway lands: skinned alive, crucified, stoned, speared. The notion that a myth about a non-existent Jesus was the impetus behind the conversion and martyrdom of a ragtag band of one-time cowards and whiners is self-condemned simply in its utterance. These kinds of counter-explanations remind us of what George Orwell once said: "One has to belong to the intelligentsia to believe things like that. No ordinary man could be such a fool."[14] It seems undeniable that the extraordinary transformation of the 11 could only be explained by an extraordinary event and, in this respect, the Resurrection makes perfect sense.

The Matrix of Modernity

Finally, there is the Plaintiff's third claim about the harm caused by the Christian religion. This is, again, obviously mistaken. It is the cultural and intellectual matrix of Christianity that produced all the essential elements of modern life. These include modern science, the modern university, hospitals and the very idea of us being persons which is essential to freedom and human rights. Despite all the evils perpetrated by individual Christians, the revelation of Jesus transformed human history and built modern civilization.

---

14   George Orwell, "Notes on Nationalism", May 1945. http://www.resort.com/~prime8/Orwell/nationalism.html

If the Plaintiff can be so wrong on these issues that are fundamental to his case, it should be clear that the rest of what he has to say is likewise flawed.

Let me illustrate.

GOD Does Not "Exist," GOD is not "morally good," "Evil" is Not a "Thing"

First, let us let get a better understanding of what we mean by God and evil.

The Plaintiff's counsel and those who filed amicus briefs – the angry atheists and assorted malcontents – have one thing in common: they know virtually nothing about their target. So I have to start with elementary lessons on what is meant by "God."

Some of what I say may sound surprising. But only for the poorly schooled.

First, God does not "exist."

Second, God is not "morally good."

Third, there is no "thing" called evil.

In case you are wondering, no, I am not trying to make the Plaintiff's case for him. Rather, I am trying to show why the Plaintiff has no case!

So before my opponent celebrates victory, let me explain why these truths and a host of others are fatal to his whole "cause of action."

God Does Not "Exist" Just as Life is not "Alive"

First, God does not "exist" because God is EXISTENCE itself in all its fullness. To say that God exists is like saying "Existence exists" or "Life is alive."

Mr. HellMan, like atheists in general and some theists, makes the erroneous assumption that, in addition to all the things in our universe such as galaxies and giraffes, there is also a super-item we call "God."

At the start, we should exorcise the idea that God is a being, even a "Supreme Being." God is not one of the beings in the Universe. God is not a "being" because a being is something that belongs to a class or category whereas God cannot thus belong to a class. God cannot be placed "alongside" finite beings.

In talking of God, we are talking of that which brought all that exists into being from absolute nothingness. That which continues to keep them in being like the sun keeps sunlight in being.

What we call "universe" or "multiverse" is not a thing in itself.

It is just a way of talking about the entire aggregate of things and beings that "exist" – from virtual particles, vacuums and stars to unicellular and multi-cellular life-forms. Not one of the members of this aggregate existed always in its current form: gases begat fundamental particles which begat stars which begat galaxies and so on.

Neither this aggregate of things nor any individual thing has the power of "creating" itself. Nor does it have any inherent logic of always existing. But nothing can come to be from nothingness. So how did it get here? It had to come from Something that did not come "to be." Something that has the inherent Power of always existing. Something that exists by its very nature.

If anything at all exists, then there must be Something that cannot not-exist, Something that must BE by its very nature, Something that is self-existent. Nothing would exist if there was not Something that always existed and is the Source of existence for everything else.

We do not UNDERSTAND how there could be Something that exists by its very nature. But we do KNOW that It has to BE because we are here!

God is this Something that does not depend on anything else for BE-ING. The Something that is the Source of the initial and continued existence of all things. Our ability to be, our be-ing, is "powered" entirely by God much as *an electric current can "be" only with a power source.*

All this is relevant here because the Plaintiff talks of evil as a "problem" *caused* by a *being* acting in the Universe that we call God. But God is not a "cause" in this sense. God is the Source of all the "causes" in the universe not one of these causes. Neither is God a "being" acting in the universe but rather That which keeps the universe in being.

This last point about God keeping the Universe in being becomes clear when we recognize what it means to exist.

Any "thing" that exists – whether it be a sub-atomic particle or a bird – is essentially a collection of "powers." When we say it exists, we are saying that these powers exist and are exercisable. That which can exercise the powers is the "thing" itself which is the unifying agent that "operates" the powers.

Once we understand that a thing is a unified collection of powers, we ask how these powers continue to function on a regular basis and how they stay unified by an activator.

The powers we are talking about are myriad. Think of energy, the laws of Nature, our consciousness, our thoughts, the colors of the rose (with the underlying framework of light emission, photoreceptors and neurons), the melodies of a song (with its interplay of vibrations in the air, fluctuations of pressure, electrical impulses and like). All of these powers have to be supported in being on a continuous basis by the Something that "invented" them out of nothingness.

The activators that individually exercise these powers have to likewise be supported in being. The activators are of different kinds from photons and stars to microbes and mammals.

The powers and the activators are as dependent on the eternally existing Something as a sunray on the sun.

This becomes clearer with an analogy. To fly in a plane means to leave the ground and move through the sky. All kinds of things are required for this to happen: a vehicle with an engine that can move at such a high speed that the air pressure above its wings is lower than the pressure below thus lifting the whole plane skyward; sufficient fuel for the flight; various electronic and other mechanisms, a pilot who knows how to manage take off, flight and landing.

The passengers on the plane may be unaware of all these background activities and can simply sit back and enjoy the flight. But every instant of their staying suspended in the air is dependent on the support provided by each one of these activities. If just one of the crucial activities go wrong (say, if the engine fails or the pilot passes out), the flight could come to an abrupt end with fatal consequences.

We are in the same position with respect to our continued existence – and are just as blissfully unaware of our dependency as passengers in flight.

God is Not "Morally Good" Just as the Moral Law is Not Morally Good or Bad

Once we understand that God does not "exist" but is Existence, other related insights will become apparent. We will come to see that it is absurd to talk of God as a morally good being or agent with obligations to fulfill.

God is not morally good. God is Goodness. To say that God is morally good is like saying "Goodness is good." To have the fullness of existence is to have the fullness of all the perfections of existence: goodness, power, knowledge, love. God does not "have" these perfections: God IS each of these perfections.

Returning to "goodness," we say something is good in relation to their nature or structure. You are a good runner because you are capable of running and you exercise this capability very well. It makes no sense to say that you are "bad" at flying with your hands because self-propelled flight is not a human capability.

This is what we mean by "goodness" with respect to our human nature and the same can be said of other beings with their own nature. Some mice are better at locating cheese than others because, to begin with, mice have the capability of sniffing out food items. Hence it makes sense to say a mouse is good at this activity.

But in human beings, we also talk of "goodness" on a moral level. Normally, this refers to certain traits that we call virtues and to certain choices made with respect to what we call the moral law. Thus, a person can be courageous or honest to the extent that they conform to the virtues of courage or honesty. And a person can choose to follow the moral law as manifested in conscience, the collective moral codes of humanity and, above all, divine revelation.

The Source of the natures of different beings, of virtues and of the moral law is God. The natures of different beings manifest the infinite creativity and wisdom of God. The virtues are pathways to align ourselves with the infinite goodness, holiness and love of God. And the moral law is an insight into the plenitude of perfection that is God and to which we unite ourselves through our choices and actions.

To say that God has to follow the moral law is like saying that Nature has to follow the laws of Nature. By laws of Nature we simply refer to what we understand about Nature and not something "outside" Nature herself. Likewise, what we mean by "goodness" and "moral law" is what we understand about God at a finite level.

God has no moral "obligations" or duties against which we measure divine activity just as Nature has no "obligations" to the laws of Nature.

But while we do not speak of Goodness (i.e., God) being morally good, we can speak of God being "just." By this we mean simply that God's actions remain true to God's nature. This includes actions taken with respect to the finite creatures that God brings into being with their specific natures and destiny.

God does not have any obligation to bring finite creatures into being or to bestow them with gifts conducive to their happiness. But he does both out of his infinite generosity. And he does this by creating a dynamic realm of diverse creatures enjoying varying levels of autonomy. To say God is just is to say that. once he creates this ecosystem, he will sustain it in being in order that we can make the choices that form us and thereby map our future.

Evil is Not a "Thing" But a Lack of Something

But if we are creations of That which is infinitely good and infinitely powerful, how is it that evil exists? Since God is the Source of all that exists, is God the Creator of evil as well?

These questions are the products of verbal confusion. We have been misled by words. "Evil" is not a thing like a quark or a plant. Nor is it a positive attribute like courage or purity. Evil is a lack of something good just as a hole is the lack of a physical mass. Cowardice is the lack of courage just as a hole is not a "something" but the absence of something.

All that God is created is good. And it is God that sustains all causes and actions and laws in being. But in sustaining these, God also grants autonomy in different degrees. Subatomic particles have one kind of autonomy, plants another and animals yet another.

Human beings have the highest level of autonomy in the physical world because they have the power to freely say "No" to the infinite Good that is God. All the power we have comes from God including this one capability of turning away from the will of God. It is a "negative" power in the sense that it is a matter of rejecting the Good. Evil is *our* exercise of this negative power.

Our sense of moral obligation and our moral outrage over injustice or evil are inexplicable in terms of genes and molecules. They point to another order of reality that transcends the physical. All the finite goods in the world are oriented toward the Absolute Good that is God. All these goods derive from God: they are not our creation.

But it is possible for us to misuse these goods. It is possible to choose a finite good over the infinite Good or to use one of these goods in a way that is detrimental to our being (gluttony, for instance). The laws of Nature describe the kinds of behavior built into the fabric of the physical world. The moral law concerns our interaction with the goods that fulfill our being as human persons. It is not just an impersonal set of laws but a participation in the infinite Good that is God. We are drawn to this Good and our moral choices are in that respect our response to the Voice of God beckoning us towards participation in his Being.

Evil, as we have seen, is not a "thing" but our exercise of our negative power to refuse the good. It is an absence, a corruption, misuse or perversion of the good for which we alone are responsible. It resides in our intentions and choices. It resides in us.

Thus understood, evil is not an illusion. It is real but real as an "absence" and not a "presence": an absence of goodness: just as blindness is the lack of sight. It describes our alienation from what our being, our human nature, needs – God the Absolute Good. It is a descent into the darkness of the divine absence. It is OUR descent for which we alone are responsible.

MindField

From just these three misconceptions unwittingly illustrated by the Plaintiff, we can see that the god portrayed by the atheists is a figment of their imaginations. We have no desire to defend the existence of the atheists' god or justify its actions. It has about as much of a resemblance to the infinite-eternal God as the lightning bug has to lightning. We are talking about two different things – one a fiction and the other a Fact. God is BE-ing not a being.

The Achilles Heel of Atheism

Atheism today is heavily dependent on evolutionary theory. In fact, Richard Dawkins said once that Darwinian evolution enables atheists to be intellectually fulfilled. This is because evolution provides a mechanism for the variations in living beings without pointing to a Creator. Yet evolution is entirely and unavoidably silent on fundamental hard facts that demonstrate the divine. And that is especially clear today.

The origin of variation in living beings is, of course, an important issue to be investigated by the life sciences. This is where evolutionary theory with its tale of genetic variations and population pressures has a place. But evolution as such is an irrelevant distraction when it comes to a consideration of the existence and ceaseless activity of God.

Evolution talks about how things change *once they exist*. Evolution does not talk about how things as a whole *came to exist*. It talks about the origin of changes not about the origin of the thing that changes. For instance, evolution does not address the origin of energy. Most important, evolution concerns changes to the physical but can say nothing about non-physical mental realities.

As even atheists now admit, evolution cannot address the existence or origin of consciousness or conceptual thought.

This last point is of central importance. Everywhere around us we see conscious beings – beings that are capable of being aware of their environment through the senses. When we come to fellow humans, we recognize our ability to communicate using a world of symbols with non-physical ideas such as justice – or the concept of evolution! And, as pointed out earlier, we ourselves maintain our self-identity despite the constant change in our neuronal make-up.

But where did these non-physical mental realities come from – consciousness, symbolic thought and the continuing self? Evolutionary theory is entirely centered on changes to the physical structures of living beings. It has zero, zip and zilch to say about the non-physical capabilities of these very same beings. This is because science is solely concerned with the measurement of physical quantities. Hence the phrase "the physical sciences."

Of course, you have to have a physical nervous system to feel or think. But this is a transmission vehicle for the non-physical not the non-physical itself, as will be illustrated.

The Supra-Physical – Non-Physical Realities

For clarity, we will use the phrase "supra-physical" to talk about the non-physical dimensions relevant here. *"Supra-physical" refers to non-physical mental realities that are obvious in our experience and that have no physical attributes or properties and thus cannot be "measured" and that cannot be explained by physical laws or constants.* The supra-physical is nevertheless integrated with the physical (e.g., the brain does not think in symbols but we cannot think in symbols without a brain). And though they are not physically "measurable" they can "organize" and unify the physical while also, at times, entirely transcending it.

Perceptions, feelings, emotions, images, memories, concepts, reasoning, intentions, choices, selfhood are the primary instances of the supra-physical. Supra-physical phenomena are characteristic not simply of the human animal but of various other species which have different degrees of intelligence and various kinds of mental powers. Nevertheless, there are specific dimensions of the supra-physical, those which totally transcend the physical, that are peculiarly human. These include the capacity for language and symbolic and conceptual thought and the continuous self/person.

The supra-physical is immediately evident in our experience. For instance, in seeing, hearing, smelling, tasting and touching, a mechanical stimulus is transformed into a nerve signal that is sent to the brain and then converted into a conscious state. Decades of scientific study have helped us understand the network of proteins, ions, signals and cellular structures involved. But, despite all these advances, the bridge between these two worlds, the external stimulus and the corresponding sense-perception, remains as much a mystery today as ever.

On the one hand, we have an efficient chain of precise physical processes that monitor, transmit and respond to an immense variety of sensory inputs. On the other, we have a mysterious and radical conversion: the merely physical becomes something of which we are conscious, something in which we "participate".

Consciousness, by which we mean awareness of our environment, is a fundamental reality that cannot be described or explained in physical terms. It is supra-physical.

Some of the knee-jerk atheists will say that everything we say about the supra-physical depends on the physical equipment and so the non-physical is irrelevant. This only means they've missed the point. The question isn't whether the physical plays a central role. Rather they should ask first how anything non-physical exists. Then they should consider how it is so seamlessly integrated with the physical. And, finally, they should ponder how the physical + non-physical system exists at all.

As mysterious as the very existence of the supra-physical is the question of how the supra-physical is integrated with the physical. How can two such entirely different realities work together?

Seeing is Believing

Take the phenomenon of seeing. How do we explain it? This is not a question of the origin of the eye.

> Here is the central mystery in the phenomenon of physical vision: the fact that you and I can become directly and immediately aware of the world around us. Why is it the case that one piece of matter attains the capacity to become aware of another in so intimate and complete a fashion? Can anything in physical reality explain or

even describe this ability to *be aware*? Viewed as a mode of awareness, the phenomenon of seeing is irreducible to anything physical or material.

Second, how and why did the most primitive light-sensitive cells come into being? Why is reality structured so that there can be a symbiosis between light and the eye, between photons and neurons, that results in sight? Light waves, incidentally, are the only kind of electromagnetic radiation with the energy level required for biological systems to detect them and the wavelength of light is just the right size for the high-resolution camera-type vertebrate eye.

Third, what lies at the basis of the amazing transformational interfaces between eye, brain and mind that convert electromagnetic waves into electrical signals and then into subjective visual images – activities that take place so effortlessly that we take them for granted?

Fish Don't Know They're in Water

Fish swimming in water are not aware they are in water because they take the water for granted and never ask how it came to be. Likewise, everything we do – seeing, hearing, thinking, feeling, having a first-person perspective – is totally embedded in the supra-physical and hence we never think of focusing on it or asking how it came to be.

Speaking about the fish-water analogy, David Foster Wallace observed that "the most obvious, ubiquitous, important realities are often the ones that are the hardest to see."[15]

We are conscious, we think with concepts and ideas that have no physical correlation, we continue to be the same person despite the constant change in our physical being – this is the water, "the most obvious, ubiquitous, important realities," which for us is "the hardest to see."

---

15 https://www.theguardian.com/books/2008/sep/20/fiction

The physical-supra-physical integration issue is evident in the history of life. There is a finely tuned synchronization in the history of life between particular kinds of supra-physical powers and the specific physical platforms required to sustain them.

Biological history points to the invention of four different but integrated worlds. Life, consciousness, conceptual thought and the self appeared in a systematic sequence. That they are different from matter is self-evident. But to be functional they required a precise physical base. Yet as Paul Davies noted, "No known scientific principle suggests an inbuilt drive from matter to life. No known law of physics or chemistry favors the emergence of the living state over other states. Physics and chemistry are, as far as we can tell, 'life blind.'"[16] This is even truer of consciousness, thought and the self.

The Supra-Physical Should be the Starting Point of Evolutionary Theory

Millions of words have been written about evolutionary theory by thousands of specialists. *But no one has even asked the question of how there could be a perfect match between the physical platforms that arose at different stages of the history of life and the supra-physical realities that mysteriously appeared and operated them just-in-time.*

The physical platform, as, for instance, the eye, and the corresponding supra-physical reality, namely, visual consciousness, belong to two different orders of reality. Science cannot tell us how the latter (the supra-physical) exists. Still less can it tell us how consciousness became operational just when the eye was ready for use – including the different kinds of visual consciousness in various types of eyes (all of which have the same universal master control pax 6 gene).

Of course, most evolutionary biologists say nothing about the more fundamental question of how such supra-physical realities as consciousness

---

16   Paul Davies, "What is Life?", https://iai.tv/articles/what-is-life-auid-1249

and the processing of meaning through conceptual thought exist. This is because such realities are entirely inexplicable by evolutionary theory. Evolution cannot "produce" anything non-physical and yet evidence for its existence is everywhere. *The nature and origin of the supra-physical should be the true starting-point of evolutionary theory. And yet, to date, it has yet to be addressed or even admitted.*

It is in this context that Freeman Dyson of the Institute for Advanced Studies at Princeton made this comment: "[Is mind] primary or an accidental consequence of something else? ...Mind was a primary part of nature from the beginning and we are simply manifestations of it at the present stage of history. It's not so much that mind has a life of its own but that mind is inherent in the way the universe is built."[17]

Most compelling of all was the revelation that dawned on the Nobel Prize-winning biologist George Wald who started off as a physicalist but ended up recognizing the supra-physical as foundational.

Wald noted that:

> "Mind, rather than emerging as a late outgrowth in the evolution of life, has existed always as the matrix, the source and condition of physical reality – that the stuff of which physical reality is constructed is mind-stuff. It is mind that has composed a physical universe that breeds life, and so eventually evolves creatures that know and create: science-, art-, and technology-making creatures."[18]

Wald also observed that:

---

17 Interview with Freeman Dyson, *U.S.News and World Report*, April 18, 1988, 72.

18 George Wald, "Life and Mind in the Universe," in Henry Margenau and Roy Abraham Varghese ed. *Cosmos, Bios, Theos* (La Salle: Open Court, 1992), 218.

"This universe is life-breeding because the pervasive presence of Mind had guided it to be so."[19]

What the Pioneers of Modern Physics said about the Supra-Physical

The founders of modern physics had already highlighted the undeniability of the supra-physical For instance, Max Planck, the father of quantum physics, said, "All matter originates and exists only by virtue of a force which brings the particle of an atom to vibration and holds this most minute solar system of the atom together. We must assume behind this force the existence of a conscious and intelligent mind. This mind is the matrix of all matter."[20]

Niels Bohr, one of the great patriarchs of quantum physics, said, "We can admittedly find nothing in physics or chemistry that has even a remote bearing on consciousness.... [Q]uite apart from the laws of physics and chemistry, as laid down in quantum theory, we must also consider laws of quite a different kind."[21]

Erwin Schroedinger, yet another of the quantum pioneers, observed, "Consciousness cannot be accounted for in physical terms. For consciousness is absolutely fundamental. It cannot be accounted for in terms of anything else."[22]

---

19   George Wald, 1986 address to the First World Congress for the *Synthesis of Science and Religion.*

20   Max Planck, *Das Wesen der Materie* [The Nature of Matter], speech at Florence, Italy (1944) (from Archiv zur Geschichte der Max-Planck-Gesellschaft, Abt. Va, Rep. 11 Planck, Nr. 1797).

21   Bohr N., quoted in Heisenberg W., *Physics and Beyond* (A.J. Pomerans, trans.) (New York: Harper and Row, 1971), 88-91.

22   Erwin Schroedinger, "General Scientific and Popular Papers," in *Collected Papers*, Vol. 4. (Vienna: Austrian Academy of Sciences. Friedr. Vieweg & Sohn, Braunschweig/Wiesbaden,. 1984), 334.

My main point here is that my opponent's brand of Victorian atheism may have seemed impressive two centuries ago when Darwin first got going. But it is dead on arrival today as scientists wrestle with, what they call, the "hard problem of consciousness" and puzzle over the origin of semantics, syntax, concepts and language as a whole.

So where did the supra-physical come from? Evolutionary theory has no answer beyond the truism that consciousness provides evolutionary advantages – which does not answer the question of how it arose in a physical universe.

The only plausible answer is that mind arises from infinite Mind and consciousness from infinite Consciousness. Before exploring this further, we should review the universality of the supra-physical.

Why Physicalism/Materialism is Obviously Untrue

Physicalism is the philosophy that only the physical exists. It is the denial of the supra-physical. It is the fish denying the existence of water.

But the falsity of physicalism can easily be shown.

Here are the hard facts that sound the death knell for physicalism:

- We are *conscious* and conscious that we are conscious. We are aware of things around us. None of the laws of matter describe or explain how it is possible to be conscious.

- We have *thoughts* and *intentions*. These are what drive our neurons and not the other way around. So where did this capability of thinking and intending come about?

- When we use language, we are encoding and decoding signals and processing *meaning*. Matter and its laws know nothing of meaning or reasons or purposes.

- *I* see, not my eyes. I think, not my brain. The "I" that does the seeing and thinking remains the same throughout our lifetimes.

Our brain is a flux of chemical reactions, electrical impulses and constant molecular change. We could not even complete a sentence or remember what happened a minute ago if there was no "I" that is stable, enduring and non-physical.

I am alive, I am conscious, I think, I intend, I communicate meaningfully and there is an "I" that does all of this. *All these non-physical powers must have a non-physical Source. And it is this Source that "grounds" them all and allows them to continue operating.*

The demonstrable reality of the supra-physical also happens to be the fatal flaw of the neo-Darwinians and the new atheists because their ideologies are built on a foundation of physicalism, the idea that matter is the only reality.

Born Free

Once we recognize the supra-physical, we can eliminate physicalist errors such as determinism, the idea that we have no freewill. My opponent cited the neurobiologist Robert Sapolsky in rejecting the reality of our obvious experience of freewill.

But Sapolsky is simply selling an 18th century idea wrapped in 21st century clothes. Consider, for instance, what the determinist Baron Paul d'Holbach said in 1770:

> Man's life is a line that nature commands him to describe upon the surface of the earth, without his ever being able to swerve from it, even for an instant. ... his organization does in nowise depend upon himself; his ideas come to him involuntarily; his habits are in the power of those who cause him to contract them; he is unceasingly modified by causes, whether visible or concealed, over which he has

no control, which necessarily regulate his mode of existence, give the hue to his way of thinking, and determine his manner of acting.[23]

d'Holbach's view is not essentially different from Sapolsky's unoriginal thesis that "We are nothing more or less than the cumulative biological and environment luck, over which we had no control, that has brought us to any moment ... Why did that behavior occur? Because of biological and environmental interactions, all the way down." He admits that when we focus only on a single field, such as genetics, "you can't disprove free will with a scientific result from genetics." But, "put all the scientific results together, from all the relevant disciplines, and there's no room for free will."[24]

Ironically, all the "free-thinkers" in history (going back to the ancient Greeks) were adamant in rejecting the fact that they are free!

In Sapolsky, as so often with other determinists, we witness the spectacle of an eloquent, learned scholar claiming that he is nothing but a temporary random configuration of law-driven atoms and that this configuration is entirely a product of its genetics and environment. The collection of atoms named Sapolsky then freely proclaims that it has no freedom and uses rational arguments to make its case that there is no rationality.

Citing data from innumerable sources and studies – neuroscience, endocrinology, anthropology, evolutionary psychology, genetics, zoology, game theory, complexity science, quantum physics – he reiterates the idea that every thought and emotion, every choice and act, is determined by factors entirely beyond our control. We have no say in what we do or think although we suffer from the illusion that we do. No one is to be blamed or praised for anything. There is no truth or falsehood, good or evil, no love. In Sapolsky's view, "all human behavior is as far beyond our conscious

23 Baron Paul d'Holbach, *System of Nature* (1770), https://rintintin.colorado.edu/~vanc-ecd/phil1020/Holbach.pdf

24 Robert M. Sapolsky, *Determined: A Science of Life without Free Will* (New York: Penguin Press, 2023), 4,8.

control as the convulsions of a seizure, the division of cells or the beating of our hearts."[25]

But here is the fundamental problem with this line of thought. It is self-contradictory through and through. If everything is "determined," so is the writing of Sapolsky's book *Determined*. If it is "biological and environmental interactions, all the way down," there is no place for rational thought or accurate acts of judgment – and therefore no reason to believe anything in *Determined*.

Sapolsky says he is motivated by a need to promote compassion and greater equity. But if everything is truly determined by impersonal factors entirely outside our control, how can WE make a difference – and WHY should we?

It is not just the self-contradiction that is calamitous. More detrimental is the unarguable fact that all human beings have an inborn awareness of acting freely. We make choices constantly. Many of our actions are driven by purposes and reasons not just external causes. What unarguable grounds do the determinists have for insisting that this is all an illusion?

Finally, the determinist ship runs aground on the actuality of moral advancement in individuals and societies. Barbaric practices like slavery were outlawed over the years as people became aware of human rights and dignity. Countless self-improvement methods have been devised to overcome bad habits. None of this makes sense if we are helpless marionettes entirely manipulated by particles and forces, upbringings and cultural structures.

Here is Sapolsky's challenge to those who claim to have free-will: "Show me a neuron (or brain) whose generation of a behavior is independent of the sum of its biological past, and for

---

25   https://www.latimes.com/science/story/2023-10-17/stanford-scientist-robert-sapolskys-decades-of-study-led-him-to-conclude-we-dont-have-free-will-determined-book

the purposes of this book, you've demonstrated free will."[26] It is precisely at this point that he shows why his physicalism dooms any attempt to plausibly eliminate freewill.

Sapolsky's challenge assumes that neuronal activity is all there is to thinking. But then is his challenge simply a result of neuron action potentials and firings? Or did HE assemble various reasons expressed in THOUGHT *as a result of which* his neurons are activated? If it's just a matter of neurons and ions and action potentials, his challenge is as irrelevant to the issue of freewill as an asteroid collision. But if his challenge is based on reasons and a rational process of thought, it is worthy of consideration – which also means that his physicalism and his determinism are false.

Sapolsky is aware that his physicalism is not without its problems. When asked, "Do you think the concept of "the hard problem of consciousness" presents a real challenge, and why or why not?," he replies in all honesty, "It sure presents a challenge for me. Consciousness is beyond me to understand — every few years I read a review from the people trying to understand it on a neurobiological level, and I cannot understand a word of what they are saying. For me, consciousness arises as a "complex emergent property" — which explains everything and nothing."[27]

If "consciousness" is a hard problem, conceptual thought and self-identity are immeasurably "harder." As we shall see, the acceptance of the supra-physical is the only possible explanation of human experience.

Other fundamental problems await Sapolsky's kind of dogmatic determinism: why do humans have the awareness of being free and responsible in making choices? Simply piling up libraries of studies on the "influences" acting on human behavior in no way proves that these "influences" are the whole story.

---

26   Robert M. Sapolsky, op cit., 15.

27   https://medspire.net/en/from-stanford-to-medspire-an-exclusive-interview-with-robert-sapolsky/

From the chaos of subatomic clouds, gene expressions, biological pro-cesses, psycho-dramas and socio-cultural pressures, there emerges a world of rational agents who act autonomously in order to achieve their pur-poses. How did this happen? How do we know that the phenomena of agency and autonomy are "illusions?" This is especially a problem if a par-ticular autonomous agent claims it is all an illusion since they can only make their case if they are both autonomous and an agent – in which case they have no case.

Without question, most of our choices and acts are products of our genet-ics and environment. If we are born and brought up in a slum or a refugee camp, we will act differently than someone brought up in suburban luxury or a jungle village. Our childhood, our schooling (or lack thereof), our nutrition, our addictions, our traumas and the like will affect the way we think and make decisions.

But to say that we are mostly the product of our influences does not log-ically lead to the conclusion that we are ENTIRELY the product of such influences. There are commonalities shared by all human beings of which our supra-physical being is fundamental.

Sapolsky himself observes that "unless there is some serious neurodevelop-mental disorder, we all have brains that are very similar but not identical."[28]

He points out that if a DA asks, "Would every single person with the same head trauma have committed this murder? Could it have been pre-dicted beforehand?" … the answer has to be no, we can't predict that."[29] Sapolsky abandoned belief in God and freewill at the age of 14. Was his decision the result of a process of thought or simply environmental factors?

On the positive side, in his book, Sapolsky performs a signal ser-vice by exposing the vacuity of two contemporary approaches to the

---

28   Ibid.

29   https://lareviewofbooks.org/article/everything-is-embedded-in-what-came-before-a-conversation-with-robert-m-sapolsky/

freewill-determinism debate. In the first, many scientists and philosophers claim to believe in both determinism and freewill and call themselves compatibilists. As Sapolsky says, this eat-your-cake-and-have-it-too view is incoherent. Likewise, he arraigns those who claim that freewill emerges from quantum indeterminacy – this freewill-of-the-gaps is little but a form of quantum quackery.

Here is what we know: we are agents who make choices constantly and many of these choices are constrained by our environment. But clearly not all people and not all our decisions are entirely the product of environment. We sometimes (if rarely) advance morally or make difficult choices. We have remorse and regret. We repent.

Why did Abraham Lincoln or Martin Luther King make the choices they did? How do thousands of people wean themselves off biochemical addictions in organizations like Alcoholics Anonymous? How is it that people sometimes have conversions? Why do some become more selfless or devote their lives to serving others? It is simply absurd to dogmatically proclaim that these choices and acts were "determined" at every level.

Which leads us to another dimension. In all our acts, our goal as individuals and societies is and must be to enhance our supra-physical capabilities. A good example is the growth we seek in our capabilities of reasoning. Likewise, we seek to advance in the worthwhile exercise of our freedoms and progress in our moral character.

Sapolsky's deterministic ideology sadly undermines all such efforts. As one of his critics, Paul Tse, rightly said, "Those who push the idea that we are nothing but deterministic biochemical puppets are responsible for enhancing psychological suffering and hopelessness in this world."[30]

---

30   https://www.latimes.com/science/story/2023-10-17/stanford-scientist-robert-sapolskys-decades-of-study-led-him-to-conclude-we-dont-have-free-will-determined-book

And it retards efforts at growth in all the values treasured by humanity – from selflessness to heroism.

All this goes to show that physicalism and its offshoots are disastrous for human progress.

Mind-ish Universe

But physicalism is primarily a disease of the academics. The existence of the non-physical is taken for granted by even the non-religious population. The perennial popularity of TV shows like *Paranormal* and *Supernatural* and the horror and exorcist movie genres testify to the public's instinctive belief in the non-physical.

The mind-ishness of the Universe comes to a climax in the supra-physical dimension of the human person. But this mind-ishness is all-pervasive.

The Universe is mind-ish in its blueprint and behavior. In other words, it is a template of embedded and embodied intelligence. This is the great discovery of modern science:

- from mathematically precise cosmic laws to the enigma of energy fields,

- from the Big Bang to the Cambrian Explosion,

- from the fine-tuning of the Anthropic Principle to the virtually instantaneous emergence of life, consciousness and language,

- and from the epigenome that manages the activity of our genes to the universal genetic tool-kit that governs the body plans of diverse species,

- the Universe is a manifestation of Mind.

It is teeming with mind-bots and mind-fields and mind-forms. In its mind-fullness, it testifies to an underlying Mind-Grid, an infinite Mind.

The founders of the greatest physical theories of modern science – of the very small and the very large – made the connection. We have heard what pioneers of quantum physics like Planck and Schroedinger stated. Albert Einstein, the discoverer of Relativity, famously said, "My religion consists of a humble admiration of the illimitable superior spirit who reveals himself in the slight details we are able to perceive with our frail and feeble minds. That deeply emotional conviction of the presence of a superior reasoning power, which is revealed in the incomprehensible universe, forms my idea of God."[31]

Consider a few examples of the mind-ishness of the Universe:

There is a recurrent pattern of diversity and multiplicity springing from a simple, single starting-point:

- A physical universe of trillions of galaxies springing into being from an infinitesimally small quantum state of being (billions of times smaller than a hydrogen atom).

- All biological life-forms taking a unicellular organism as their launchpad.

- All humans of all races rising from a universal common ancestor.

- Einstein pointed to the unity of the physical world, Darwin to the unity of living beings and Aristotle to the unity of the physical and the supra-physical in the human person and to the unifying matrix underlying vegetative and animal life.

Then there is the undeniable fact that the entire cosmos cooperated in the creation of our physical being with countless just-right physical ratios and values such as:

---

31   *The Quotable Einstein*, ed. Alice Calaprice (Princeton, NJ: Princeton University Press, 2005), 238.

- *The expansion rate of the universe*: If the rate of expansion had any higher, there would be no time for galaxies to form. If it was lower, with the force of gravity being higher, matter would have fallen back on itself and formed one giant lump.

- *The age of the universe*: The universe has to be at least 13 billion years old for human life to form. If it was any earlier, there would have been no time for the stellar furnaces with its 20 life-essential elements (e.g., iron) to form. If it was any older, the stars would have gone dim and life would not have been possible.

- *The mass of the universe*: If the universe would have been any larger than it is, its expansion would have been slower; no light elements would have formed. If it was smaller, the expansion would have been faster; no heavy elements would have formed. In either case, there would have been no life.

- *Nature's fundamental constants*: If there was any change in the numerical value of myriad constants such as the strength of the electromagnetic force or the constants that govern the masses of elementary particles and their interactions, life could not have formed.

Some atheists have said that the coincidence of these constants is no surprise if you make the assumption that there is an infinite number of universes – a multiverse. But their escape route argument does not explain the existence of their own speculative multiverse. Nor does it tell us why reality is structured such that there are any constants at all in any universe. Most important, the multiverse route applies only to laws of matter and cannot explain mind. The multiverse deals with the physical world and not with supra-physical realities like consciousness.

Five Leaps

Moving on, we should consider, too, the sudden leaps of embedded intelligence that cannot be explained in terms of what came before. This is most obvious in the emergence of five utterly new kinds of reality – five distinct realities – in a progressive sequence, that we will explore in more detail:

- energy, what we call the physical, which is manifested at the most fundamental level as quantum fields and follows precise laws at both the micro and macro levels

- autonomous actors or agents (i.e., living beings), starting with unicellular organisms like bacteria,

- consciousness (awareness of the environment),

- conceptual thought (the world of meanings as expressed in language) and

- the human self (I, you).

These sudden "leaps" are found both in the physical and the supra-physical realms:

- In his paper *The Biological Big Bang model for the major transitions in evolution*, E.V. Koonin pointed out that: "Major transitions in biological evolution show the same pattern of sudden emergence of diverse forms at a new level of complexity. The relationships between major groups within an emergent new class of biological entities are hard to decipher and do not seem to fit the tree pattern that, following Darwin's original proposal, remains the dominant description of biological evolution. The cases in point include the origin of complex RNA molecules and protein folds; major groups of viruses; archaea and bacteria, and the principal lineages within each of these prokaryotic domains; eukaryotic supergroups; and animal phyla. In each of these pivotal nexuses in life's history, the principal 'types' seem to appear rapidly and fully equipped with the signature features of the respective new level of biological organization. No intermediate 'grades' or intermediate forms between different types are detectable."[32]

- Evolutionary biologist Marc Hauser noted in *Scientific American* that "Charles Darwin argued in his 1871 book *The Descent of Man* that the difference between human and nonhuman minds is 'one of degree and not of kind.' ... Mounting evidence indicates that, in contrast to Darwin's theory of a continuity of mind between humans and other species, a profound gap separates our intellect from the animal kind. ...Our mind is very different from that of even our closest primate relatives and ... we do not know much about how that difference came to be."[33]

Mind-ish Life

The pioneers of modern physics always saw the "big picture" of Mind-at-work. But the 20th century neo-Darwinians were entranced by a picture of mindlessness – random variations, random mutations, randomness of every kind. Innate purposiveness and embedded intelligence were forbidden topics.

There is a reason why their minds reject any evidence of mind. Evolutionary biology is an exercise in history rather than an investigation into the laws of Nature. We use fossils and genes to try to reconstruct the past. Such reconstructions can be persuasive when studying the relation between genotype (the set of genes carried by an organism) and phenotype (the external expression of these genes in characteristics), for instance. But they are less

32 https://www.ncbi.nlm.nih.gov/pubmed/17708768/

33 "The Origin of the Mind," *Scientific American*, September 2009, https://www.scientificamerican.com/article/origin-of-the-mind/

convincing when they dogmatically dismiss the possibility of underlying laws in the history of life. Fortunately, in recent years, new findings and methodologies have made it impossible to maintain that randomness is the fundamental source of diversity.

The neo-Darwinians have traditionally explained purposive and intelligent behavior and systems as results of natural selection acting on random variation. But neo-Darwinians themselves have to assume capabilities of self-reproduction at the earliest stages of life. Yet reproduction is an irreducibly purpose-driven act and it is also one that cannot simply spring from matter. How is it that the first living beings had the powers of replication? How is it that life came with this fundamentally purposive capability pre-installed?

John Maddox, a former editor of *Nature*, admits that we do not how sexual reproduction itself evolved despite decades of speculation.[34] Replication is the engine that runs evolutionary theory. *It is the horse of reproduction that draws the cart of natural selection.* If you put the cart before the horse, you cannot get started. But who came up with the idea of replication? And who then imprinted material structures with a vast variety of replicational capabilities?

Also, what triggered off the Cambrian Explosion? Alison Gopnik has noted that "A number of biologists and philosophers have argued that consciousness was born from a specific event in our evolutionary history: the Cambrian explosion. ... Quite suddenly by geological standards, most of [the first multi-cellular organisms] disappeared. Between 530 and 520 million years ago, they were replaced by a remarkable proliferation of animals who lived quite differently. These animals started to move, to have brains and eyes, to seek out prey and avoid predators. (...) These creatures

---

34   John Maddox, *What Remains to be Discovered* (New York: Touchstone, 1998), 369-370.

developed the first simple brains, as well as new sensors like eyes and new tools like limbs and claws."[35]

All the body plans of all living animals were formed during this period of five to ten million years, a relatively short time in the multi-billion year history of life. If it was a question of certain genes being switched on, why did it happen at that particular time, why all of a sudden and why never again?

Although the Victorian atheists of today (aka the New Atheists) hang on their neo-Darwinian dogmas, modern biology has moved on:

- Oxford biologist Denis Noble points out that "The 'Modern Synthesis' (Neo-Darwinism) is a mid-20th century gene-centric view of evolution, based on random mutations accumulating to produce gradual change through natural selection. Any role of physiological function in influencing genetic inheritance was excluded. The organism became a mere carrier of the real objects of selection, its genes. We now know that genetic change is far from random and often not gradual. Molecular genetics and genome sequencing have deconstructed this unnecessarily restrictive view of evolution in a way that reintroduces physiological function and interactions with the environment as factors influencing the speed and nature of inherited change. Acquired characteristics can be inherited, and in a few but growing number of cases that inheritance has now been shown to be robust for many generations. The 21st century can look forward to a new synthesis that will reintegrate physiology with evolutionary biology."[36]

- James Shapiro, in *Evolution: A View from the 21st Century*, asks: "Do the sequences of contemporary genomes fit the predictions

---

35 "The Explosive Evolution of Consciousness," https://www.wsj.com/articles/the-explosive-evolution-of-consciousness-11559746175

36 https://physoc.onlinelibrary.wiley.com/doi/pdf/10.1113/expphysiol.2012.071134

of change by 'numerous, successive, slight variations,' as Darwin stated, or do they contain evidence of other, more abrupt processes, as numerous other thinkers have asserted? The data are overwhelmingly in favor of the saltationist school that postulated major genomic changes at key moments in evolution. ... Little evidence fits unequivocally with the theory that evolution occurs through the gradual accumulation of 'numerous, successive, slight' modifications."[37]

Shapiro moves from the Darwinian natural selection-random variation dogma cage to an information- and systems-based approach. He highlights, for instance, the intrinsic intelligence of all organisms shown in their capability for "natural genetic engineering."

- In *How Life Works – A User's Guide to the New Biology*, former *Nature* editor Philip Ball contends that "Biology is undergoing a quiet but profound transformation. Several aspects of the standard picture of how life works – he idea of the genome as a blueprint, of genes as instructions for building an organism, of proteins as precisely tailored molecular machines, of cells as entities with fixed identities, and more – have been exposed as incomplete, misleading, or wrong." Instead, says Ball, we now know that "life is a system of many levels – genes, proteins, cells, tissues, and body modules such as the immune system and the nervous system – each with its own rules and principles." The new understanding is irreversible: "The new story that is emerging is, it's true, sometimes more complicated than the old half-truths. But I think this story is coherent, cogent and consistently supported by many independent strands of research in genetics and molecular biology, cell biology and biotechnology,

---

37   James Shapiro, *Evolution: A View from the 21st Century* (Upper Saddle River, NJ: FT Press, 2011), 89, 128.

THE PEOPLE VS. GOD

evolutionary theory, and medicine. Many of the details remain unclear and contentious, but the broad outline seems now unassailable."[38]

Among other things, says Ball, the new story spells the end of both mechanistic views of life and genetic determinism. "The rules that govern life are, then, not *prescriptive* but *generative*."[39]

- According to developmental biologist Alfonso Martinez Arias, author of *The Master Builder: How the New Science of the Cell Is Rewriting the Story of Life*, modern biology shows that cells control genes and not the other way round, thus spelling the end of genetic determinism. "It would be foolish to argue that genes have nothing to do with who and what we are," writes Arias. "They do. But they are not the masters of our being and fate that they have been made out to be. The well-settled cultural importance of the gene can probably be traced to Richard Dawkins and his Selfish Gene idea that claimed the gene as the essence of biology. That idea suggested that in the grand scheme of things, genes rule and, as he put it, organisms are survival machines created by genes for their spread into eternity. For Dawkins, cells do not exist. … Surprisingly, it is when we try to describe a genome that we realize that something is missing between the gene and the organism. … The genome is also often referred to as a "toolbox." This is a better analogy but one that begs the question of who or what uses the tools in the box. Could it be the genes themselves? It must be a strange toolbox then, in which its contents are the users. When you think about it, in the context of an organism, the only possible user is, of course, the cell.

38 Philip Ball, *How Life Works – A User's Guide to the New Biology* (Chicago: University of Chicago Press, 2023), frontispiece, 16.
39 Ibid., 294.

"It is the cell as a sensing, deciding, calculating entity that reads the environment, its neighbors, and its state. A cell chooses which genes to activate and use to fulfill its needs or those of the community it belongs to. The genome contains information for tools and materials that cells use to build other cells, to repair themselves, to create societies; ensembles that we call organs and tissues weave them into an organism. Far from being an instruction manual for an organism, a genome is a collection of tools and materials at the service of life's true expert builders: cells. ... It is cells that control genes and not genes that determine cells. ... I sense a shift in our views about how we are made and who we are in which genes are integrated within the activity of cells. Such a cell-based understanding of biological systems promises to help us tackle diseases, improve our lives, and also see ourselves in a richer and less deterministic view than that provided by our current gene-centric view of biology."[40]

- Simon Conway Morris, Chairman of Evolutionary Palaeobiology at Cambridge University who is renowned for his work on the Cambrian Explosion, has shown conclusively that the "chance" or random model of the history of life must be replaced with that of convergence and inherency. There are fundamental organizational principles underlying life that inevitably lead to certain key outcomes even if there are entirely independent pathways. There is a "map of life" that governs the way in which living beings develop. The development of proteins, eyes, limbs, tool-making, etc. are inevitable once life appears. Instead of the old randomness model, we have a rigid set of rules that govern all aspects of the development of life. In *The Runes of Evolution*, he writes: "It

---

40   Alfonso Martinez Arias, https://nextbigideaclub.com/magazine/master-builder-new-science-cell-rewriting-story-life-bookbite/44654/

is high time that just as Einstein transmogrified the Newtonian world, so we need to move beyond evolution."[41]

- Evo-devo (evolutionary developmental biology), which is sometimes hailed as the third revolution in biology, holds that the same fundamental "tool-kit" genes that lay out an animal's basic body plan and oversee its development are found across all animals and, in fact, perform the same functions in various kinds of animals (as mentioned previously, the same pax 6 gene switches on the development of eyes in both humans and fruitflies). Despite the fact that the genes are the same, there is diversity in design because of differences in their expression. This means new forms evolve not because of a series of "random" mutations or the appearance of new genes but through modifications of existing genes and body plans: the recycling and repurposing of one set of ancient genes. In *Some Assembly Required*, Neil Shupe notes "The genetic architecture that builds the bodies of flies, mice, and people reveals that we are all variations on a theme. From a common toolkit come the many branches of the tree of life."[42]

Beginnings

Science, as it is practiced, comes down to observation and measurement. In both dimensions, mathematics plays a fundamental role. The workings of physical nature can be represented in mathematical symbols and equations (as, for instance, the laws of physics). Scientific theories themselves are constructed with mathematical models. Thus, Nature's interactions can be described in the language of mathematics. But whether these

---

41   Simon Conway Morris, *The Runes of Evolution* (West Conshohocken, PA: Templeton Press, 2015), 299.

42   Neil Shupe, *Some Assembly Required – Decoding Four Billion Years of Life, from Ancient Fossils to DNA* (New York: Pantheon, 2020), 118.

descriptions are accurate can be determined only through observation and measurement.

It should also be remembered that the mathematics as applied is simply a representation of what is already there, what exists. It does not create the reality that is studied or bring it about. While the interactions of the foundational quantum fields can be represented in mathematical terms, these terms cannot explain the existence of the fields. The existence of the entities studied by science precedes the mathematics used to represent their interactions. Their existence is the cart that draws the horse of observation and measurement.

Further, the mathematical models only work in modeling one of the five fundamental realities we experience, namely physical energy. They cannot describe autonomous agency (life), consciousness, thought or self-hood. And they cannot explain the origin of any one of the five realities.

Of course, both atheists and theists have been mesmerized by questions about the beginning of the universe and the possibility of life on Earth. Hence, they have been fixated by cosmological speculations about the Big Bang and what happened "before" it or the Anthropic Principle or the hypothetical multiverse.

But this is a fundamental mistake. We are looking backward in cosmic history when we should be looking at what is right in front of us.

When we turn to the here and now, we see the manifestation of these five realms: energy, agency (life), consciousness, thought and self-ness (you and I). Five realities each of which has its own unique attributes that are qualitatively different from the others. *The fundamental question is not whether there was a Big Bang or how the Big Bang came about – important as these issues might be – but how these five independent hard facts exist here and now.*

To be sure, agency/life needs matter (condensed energy) to operate; consciousness needs life; thought needs consciousness; and the self needs consciousness and thought. But none of them are inter-changeable with the others. For example, there are living beings that are not conscious and conscious beings that are not capable of conceptual thought.

They are five totally different realities! And we cannot explain the origin of any one of them – even energy. If we say that the universe originated in the energy event that is the Big Bang or that the Big Bang was part of an infinite number of energy events involving fluctuations of the vacuum, we still have not explained the origin of energy.

Nobel Prize winning physicist Richard Feynman even said that in physics "we have no knowledge what *energy* is."[43]

Science has to pre-suppose the existence of energy. To ask how energy or consciousness came to be is to ask a question about be-ing and nothing-ness, about the Source of all be-ing. As Wald put it, we are asking about the matrix of Mind.

Mind-ishness Explained

The mind-ishness of the universe comes to a climax in the human person.

We humans are born into a mystery. What we encounter is a world of matter, trees, flowers, birds, insects, squirrels, tigers, and, at the center of it all, selfs: self-conscious beings with a first person perspective.

We have no idea how any of these – let alone the last, the self – exists. How did reality come to be and come to be the way it is? How did we gain the capability of looking back at cosmic history? At the center of all our inquiry is the embodied self that inquires. There is no explanation at all of the existence of a continuing self with all these powers of assembling data, inferring, speculating.

Neither the Big Bang with its initial quark-gluon plasma soup nor the Cambrian Explosion can explain the "I" and the "you" or the first-person

---

43   https://www.feynmanlectures.caltech.edu/I_04.html

perspective. Quantum fields do not generate selfs. They just constitute our physical being.

The evolutionary biologist Julian Huxley (grandson of Darwin's colleague Thomas Huxley) observed, "The clear light of science, we are often told, has abolished mystery, leaving only logic and reason. This is quite untrue. … Why is the world-stuff what it is? Why does it have mental or subjective aspects as well as material or objective ones? We do not know. … But we must learn to accept it, and to accept its and our existence as the one basic mystery."[44]

Remember, we are simply "born into" this mystery beyond belief. It was here long before any of us existed. We did not contribute anything to its reality. This includes Einstein, Darwin and all the scientists and philosophers who ever lived. We and they were just born into it and had nothing to do with its origin. How it all came to be, and continues to be, we do not know if we stay on the level of the physical. It is only when we grasp the reality of the supra-physical that we know that it has a Source, one which is infinite and eternal and all-perfect. God.

Any discussion of God necessarily requires figures of speech like metaphors. But this is hardly unusual. Almost everything we say, any use of language for that matter, involves metaphors, similes, analogies and symbols.

Serious thought, profound insights, breakthrough discoveries, effective communication all depend on metaphors. The natural sciences depend on metaphor in theory and inquiry: Big Bang, DNA bar coding, Book of Life (genome). So do the social sciences: unseen hand, class struggle, the Unconscious. Likewise, symbols convey complex messages simply and immediately. Think of the swastika or the hammer and sickle – or the Cross!

---

44 *Science, Faith and Man*, edited by W. Warren Wagar (London: Macmillan and Co, 1968), 91.

For these reasons, theists in general have no choice but to use metaphors when talking about the Infinite-Eternal Spirit. Beyond this, any discussion of God invariably uses analogy, and often this centers on the negative, on the absence of some limitation. When we talk about God we normally talk about what he is not. "Infinite" means "not finite," not limited in where he can be present, in his power, in his goodness. "Immortal" means "not mortal." "Immutable" means "not mutable."

Truths about God necessarily have to be expressed in metaphors and analogies because we are dealing with a Reality that transcends the resources of human thought and language. And this is true about God's relation with the world – not just Incarnation but Creation and Redemption. We say God is present in the world but this does not mean that he is present in the way a stone is present or the wind is present. He is present because he holds all things in being. He is "present" where his power is exercised.

Analogy and metaphor are again inevitable and inescapable when we talk about truths specific to our next topic, the Incarnation, the Infinite acting in and through the finite. "Incarnation truths" necessarily have to speak a language that preserves the incarnational meaning and mystery just as "Creation truths" do when we speak of the mystery of creation: *creatio ex nihilo* – creation from nothing. *To profess the Incarnation is to say that the infinite being of God is manifested in finite terms in Jesus.*

Before turning to that, as a footnote, I must say I was amused to hear my opponent treat Bertrand Russell as the ultimate authority on the existence of God, et al. Russell, the author of some flippant forgettable attacks on religion, has become the patron saint of today's budding atheists – the one to whom they turn when they want to justify belief in their unbelief.

But Mr. HellMan seems unaware that Russell beat a hasty retreat from serious philosophy for the last half century of his life. This is after, quite early on, Ludwig Wittgenstein, the most influential philosopher of the 20th century, rigorously criticized Russell's academic work in philosophy.

Russell was so shaken by this critique that he said in 1916, "His criticism ... was an event of first-rate importance in my life and affected everything I have done since. I saw he was right, and I saw that *I could not hope ever again to do fundamental work in philosophy* (emphasis added). My impulse was shattered, like a wave dashed to pieces against a breakwater." He was so affected he even said, "Only yesterday I felt ready for suicide."[45]

Wittgenstein's comments on religion, in contrast, were so profound that they sealed the fate of logical positivism, a philosophy that sought to brandish science as a weapon against religion. We might call it scientism. Wittgenstein's critique of scientism was fatal for this infantile ideology.

The Jesus Cloud

From the inescapable reality of GOD, we turn to the undeniable existence of evil, pain and suffering. In our response, we are not concerned with "defending" my Client from the ludicrous and rather recent idea that the Creator of autonomous agents (any being that acts on its own) and free rational creatures is somehow responsible for their actions.

What and who caused and causes moral evil? Why are there physical evils? We will address these questions but even more important we will try to show how we can overcome the reign of evil and its associated suffering.

Our starting-point is my Client's revelation of reality: a revelation progressively unveiled to all peoples at all times: a revelation that came to a climax in the Jesus Cloud.

The Jesus Cloud is a manifestation in human terms of the innermost reality of the Godhead. It is also a disclosure of the eternal destiny of the human person. On the level of action, the Jesus Cloud liberates humankind from its self-chosen bondage to evil and offers the gift of divine Life.

---

45   Bertrand Russell's letters to Ottoline Morrell, 4 March 1916 and 19 June 1913, https://blog.oup.com/2015/06/bertrand-russell-suicide/

The fulcrum of the Jesus Cloud is Jesus of Nazareth whom his followers called the Christ, the Anointed One, the Messiah.

Jesus is the human embodiment, the Incarnation, of the Infinity Field we call God. He was given the name Jesus because his primary mission was to "save his people from their sins" (*Matthew* 1:21) through his sacrificial death. This mission meant also having "to destroy the works of the devil" (1 *John* 3:8), the Adversary of the human race who was also its ruler. With the coming of Jesus, "the ruler of this world will be driven out" (*John* 12:31).

These are affirmations, of course, and must be supported by evidence which we will provide throughout these proceedings. Here it should be said that these affirmations are rooted in the universal experience of humanity and not simply in an abstract argument.

In one of his many faux pas, my opponent said that Jesus did not exist. In making this confident assertion, he relied on the outermost scam-ridden fringes of the Dark Web. Of course, Bertrand Russell, Richard Dawkins, Michal Onfray and other evangelists of atheism had flirted with this insane idea so I will spend a few moments to put it to bed permanently.

Did Jesus Exist? Check Your Calendar

The 18th century Jesus-did-not-exist school suffered a mortal wound when its best known modern advocate, G.A. Wells, admitted to Jesus' existence in 1999. Michael Grant, the noted historian of the classical world, pointed out that "no serious scholar has ventured to postulate the non-historicity of Jesus."[46]

In any case, quite apart from the Gospels, it is startling to find that not only do we find mention of Jesus in extrabiblical Jewish and Roman writings, but these references come principally from two individuals who were, respectively, the greatest of the Roman and Jewish historians,

---

46   Michael Grant, *Jesus – An Historian's Review of the Gospels* (New York: Charles Scribner's Sons, 1977), 200.

Cornelius Tacitus (ca. ad 56–120) and Flavius Josephus (ca. ad 37–100). Referring to Tacitus, *The Oxford History of the Biblical World* observes that "it is significant that Tacitus – making one of the earliest direct references to Jesus' followers outside the New Testament – uses the popular name *Christiani* to describe them. The name *Christian* is not used in the earliest New Testament literature, the letters of Paul, and the Gospels."[47] About Josephus' references to Christ, historian James Charlesworth writes, "We can now be as certain as historical research will presently allow that Josephus did refer to Jesus"[48]

We know that Jesus existed from a variety of sources including:

- the Gospel accounts, which are treated as historical (the acts narrated in the Gospels were commemorated in Christian communities across the Roman Empire even before the Gospels were written);

- the transformation of the apostles of Jesus after his proclaimed resurrection from the dead;

- the personal experience of Jesus in the lives of his followers;

- the extrabiblical evidence available from near-contemporary historians and

- the undeniable fact that Christianity spread rapidly across the Roman Empire at a very early date.

Jesus' existence is not just a historical datum but a phenomenon. In him we find a Person manifested in proclamation, discovery and encounter, word

---

47   *The Oxford History of the Biblical World*, ed. by Michael Coogan (New York: Oxford University Press, 1998), 536-7.

48   James Charlesworth, *Jesus Within Judaism* (New York: Doubleday, 1988), 96.

and act. A work of "history" usually involves a writer transmitting records of memories of persons and events to a reader. But in Jesus' instance, we have a Person transmitting his writers to us, the readers; the senders themselves are sent to us. They come as his proclaimers not as mere recorders of memories. Consequently, what we have here is not the recording of a phenomenon but a proclamation that is itself an integral part of the phenomenon. It is not as if we read the writings to discover the phenomenon. It is truer to say that the phenomenon, the reality of Jesus, discovers us through these writings.

The vehicles manifesting the phenomenon are not simply the books that constitute the New Testament. The phenomenon reveals itself through a plethora of platforms: the religious history of humanity, the unique experience of the people of Israel, the witness of the community centered on Jesus, the startling claim that he rose from the dead, the worldwide missionary journeys of his apostles and missionaries, the ancient liturgies that testified to the faith of his followers, the Councils that defined an organic body of doctrine centered on his identity, the martyrs and the mystics, the claims of miracles that always accompanied the expanding universe of faith.

Further, we can be certain about the existence of Jesus as an actual, historical person in a way that we cannot about any other historical person. We know about every other person in history, whether they be from the distant past such as Alexander or Abraham Lincoln or the recent past such as Hitler and Stalin and even Chavez of Venezuela and Mao of China – from such sources as contemporary reports, monuments, videotapes, the writings of these individuals and the like. We believe they existed even if we have not personally seen them ourselves.

Jesus is the only person about whom his followers say that they know him from personal encounter in the present – whenever that "present" may be. Nothing similar is even claimed about any transformational figure in world history. In contrast, right from the start, Jesus was believed to have been present to his followers and this has continued over the centuries and in the lived experience of hundreds of millions of people.

Take, for instance, the revivalist who claims to personally experience the presence of the Savior or the missionary of charity who sees Jesus in the poor or the believer who hears Jesus speak to her directly through the Gospels or the evangelist in a remote jungle who feels the hand of the Lord in the face of travails and turmoil. For those who have come to see that Jesus is a real Person who lived at a specific place and time on planet Earth, it is not just the texts that are relevant but their own personal encounters with him.

A singular element of the phenomenon of Jesus is the understanding of who he is:

- He is worshipped as God incarnate.

- He is experienced as personally present.

- He is seen as Redeemer. His very name means Savior.

- His whole identity is tied to the historical facticity of his resurrection from the dead ("The Lord is risen").

- His life and acts altered the future of humanity and history had a new start that began with his coming. His "second" coming will signal the end of history.

- He brings about the presence of God, the Holy Spirit, in the very being of his followers.

- He demands the total allegiance reserved for God by most religious believers and his teachings are to be preserved to the end of time.

- He identifies himself with his church as shown most remarkably in a statement he made that was reported by the Apostle Paul on his way to Damascus: "Saul, Saul, why do you persecute me?" (*Acts of the Apostles* 9:4)

- His whole mission is focused on the purpose and meaning of life – specifically on the eternal destiny of each human being: It is for this that he came; it is for this that he died.

- He embodies unconditional and self-sacrificing love and asks the same of those who follow him.

- He has irrevocably changed the human understanding of God by presenting a window into the inner nature of God – God as Spirit and God as Trinity.

This is the Jesus that speaks to us from the Gospels, the Jesus who was proclaimed by his followers from the beginning, the Jesus who was worshipped in the earliest liturgies, and the Jesus who has transformed the lives of millions of people around the world from the first century to the present.

Revolutionizing Reality

Jesus presented a new, unprecedented, and, indeed, revolutionary *vision* of reality:

- God is Spirit.
- God is Trinity (Three "centers" united in One spiritual reality) .
- God (specifically the Second Person of the Trinity) is incarnate in him: He is the human locus of the divine who manifests through his life the tri-personal Being of God.
- He, Jesus, atones for the sins of humanity.
- He is the path to eternal life.
- He enables our souls to be sanctified.
- He lays out an ecosystem of self-giving love.

Jesus also represented a rendezvous of the religions that came before him.

The great religious movements, ideas and rituals that preceded the birth of Jesus – from India to Persia, China to Israel, Greece to Babylon, Africa to Meso-America – pointed to sacrifice and expiation, incarnation and salvation. These themes came to a climax in the life and teaching, the death and resurrection of Jesus. If Jesus was part of a divine plan of revelation and incarnation and salvation, then it would seem that the minds and hearts of the human race would be prepared for his coming. Multiple historical vignettes indicate that the psyche and intellect of humanity in the first century A.D. was indeed thus "prepared." Let us consider two examples.

The *Rig Veda* of India (circa. 2000 B.C.), the most ancient and authoritative of the *Vedas*, has a prophecy of the sacrifice of the mysterious *Prajapathi* ("Savior of man"), a being who is both divine and human. As laid out in the Vedic texts, the sacrifice of the God-man *Prajapathi* was performed by the kings and the priests. It is a sacrifice that is required for the redemption of humanity and only those who accept *Prajapathi* will be redeemed.

Then there is China which had an ancient tradition of a covenant with God as well as the annual sacrifice of an unblemished victim performed by the emperor. Interestingly, Chinese court records describe an eclipse that took place at the time of the actual death of Jesus (becaise the Chinese capital was five hours to the east of Jerusalem, it was experienced as a solar and a lunar eclipse). The most extraordinary of all the interpretations of that two-thousand year-old event was this commentary in the Record of the Latter Han Dynasty, "Eclipse on the day of Gui Hai, Man from heaven died."[49]

The Inner Being of the Godhead

This same universality of theme is found in the greatest revelation of Jesus – the inner being of the Godhead. As described in the Gospel narratives, Jesus' identity is inextricably "related" to two other Persons, the Father and

---

49   Chan Kei Thong, *Faith of Our Fathers – God in Ancient China* (Shanghai: Orient Publishing Center, 2006), 319.

the Holy Spirit. At the center of the Jesus Cloud we find him embedded in a matrix of Three that was yet One. There is the Father who "sent me" (*John* 20:21) and the Holy Spirit that "I will send" (*John* 16:7). Everything in the being of Jesus involved the action of the Three Persons. He was the Logos/Son made flesh. He was filled with the Holy Spirit. He was sent by the Father and to see him was to see the Father. Jesus is the human locus of the divine. And the divine is seen to be tri-une, Three-in-One: Father, Son and Holy Spirit.

The revelation that the Godhead is "tri-personal" is continuous with the understanding of the Godhead in the religious traditions of India, China and Israel which represent the three main human approaches to God: cyclic-mystical (India); unity-in-multiplicity/harmony (China); historical-linear (Israel).

In the Hindu holy books of India, God is seen as Saccidananda: Being, Knowledge, Bliss. In China we have the ancient Taoist belief in God as the "Three Pure Ones;" "The Universally Honored One of Origin" or "The Celestial Worthy of the Primordial Beginning;" "The Celestial Worthy of the Numinous Treasure" who reveals the scriptures; "The Celestial Worthy of the Way and its Power" or "The Universally Honored One of Virtues." In the Tanakh, the Hebrew Bible, God is described as Father, Word/Wisdom and Spirit/Shekinah. God is called *Elohim*, a plural noun used in a singular sense to honor the divine majesty. *Elohim* appears 2,570 times in the Hebrew Bible, the Old Testament, starting with *Genesis*.

Jesus' revelation also confirmed what reason suggests about God's inner being: God is infinitely perfect. This means the infinite Spirit is perfect love just as it is perfect goodness, knowledge and power. But love implies distinction, otherness. Love is necessarily personal and in fact necessarily inter-personal: it is a relationship between at least Two. Furthermore, love, as we know it, involves not just two but a third who is the fruit of the love between two. Love is fulfilled and manifested in its fruit. For the love of an I and a You to be complete, it must culminate in a third who likewise loves and is loved by both. Lover, beloved, co-beloved. I, Thou, Ours. Father, Son, Holy Spirit.

Again: since God is infinite love, there has to be love *within* God. Since God is infinite, this loving, its object and its fruit must likewise be infinite: Three inseparable "centers" that ARE the One. And in what would such love consist? In a giving, receiving and sharing in full of the divine nature, of all that it means to be God. A child receives its human nature with all its powers from its parents as a manifestation and fruit of their love. Likewise, the love within God is a giving, receiving, and sharing in full of the divine nature with all its infinite power and glory. It is a love without beginning or end, a LOVE that IS. "Trinity" is not God's proper name. It is simply a way of saying that God is infinite love. To say that God is Trinity is simply to say that God is LOVE.

If God is Love, how is this relevant to humanity? One of the most moving passages in the New Testament tells us that the rationale for the coming of Jesus was love: "For God so loved the world that he gave his only Son, so that everyone who believes in him might not perish but might have eternal life. For God did not send his Son into the world to condemn the world, but that the world might be saved through him." (*John* 3:16-17)

Evil, Interrupted

You might be wondering why I took this excursion into the Jesus Cloud. The reason is that it lies at the center of any authentic discussion of evil. The rejection of love is the essence of moral evil. By its very structure love is something that must be freely accepted and reciprocated – or not. Since the fundamental fabric of reality is infinite Love, finite beings that are free and rational face a choice. They must choose whether or not to participate in this Love that "moves the sun and the other stars."[50]

---

50   Dante, *The Divine Comedy, Paradiso*, Canto 33.

Therein lies a story – a saga of two realms, the City of God and the Empire of Evil.

The Plaintiff points to all the evil in the world. No one denies that moral evil is pervasive across the human enterprise: Evil individuals and systems seem to always triumph and reign; evil choices and actions continually cause horrendous pain and suffering; evil behaviors are the norm in most societies.

There is, of course, pain and suffering in the animal world and there are natural disasters that afflict all living organisms. These are inevitable in a world with autonomous beings, as we shall see. But animal violence is driven by instinct and not by moral choice. It has been rightly said that the only real "wild animals" are human beings.

But how did evil originate, and how is it even possible in a universe created by Infinite Love?

As with the Plaintiff's case as a whole, this question betrays ignorance of the nature of the Godhead and therefore of the kind of world God brought into being.

In brief, the Jesus Cloud shows us that infinite-eternal "self-giving" is what the Godhead is all about. Love means giving of oneself – freely, unconditionally, totally. The paradigm instance of love is the infinite-eternal Self-giving that is the Godhead: the beginning-less, endless Love of Three infinite Persons: each of the Three Persons giving entirely of all that they are to Another.

This Love that is the Godhead manifested Itself most fully to the human race in the Person of Jesus who gave of himself freely, totally and unconditionally for the liberation and eternal victory of humanity because "God so loved the world."

Love as self-giving is the destiny to which all free finite beings are called and this includes both human persons and the pure spirits who are called angels.

Fundamentally, angels and humans are characterized by the capability to know and to love. To love is a free act of the will. And to love means to give of one-self.

The self-giving that is love is a free act. It is also an act that affects others.

Yes, angels and humans were created to participate and enjoy eternal bliss in the infinite-eternal Love of the Godhead. But this participation had to be freely chosen. And the invitation to participate in this Love comes as a still, small voice.

> "Go out and stand on the mountain before the LORD; the LORD will pass by. ... the LORD was not in the earthquake; after the earthquake, fire—but the LORD was not in the fire; after the fire, a light silent sound. ... A voice said to him, Why are you here, Elijah?" (1 *Kings* 19:11,13)

> "This is the word of the LORD to Zerubbabel: Not by might, and not by power, but by my spirit, says the LORD of hosts." (*Zechariah* 4:6)

The voice is still and small because, unbelievably, such is the nature of the divine Love – tender, sensitive, poignant, humble. This is why Jesus said, "Whatever you did for one of these least brothers of mine, you did for me." (*Matthew* 25:40)

The Love that is God, then, is not coercive or overpowering. It does not compel or demand. It invites in the most subtle and vulnerable way possible. For us to accept this invitation and to love means to surrender our selves, to give our being to the Source of our being. And giving our selves to God means giving our selves to our fellow beings: "whoever does not love a brother whom he has seen cannot love God whom he has not seen." (1 *John* 4:20)

The choice is simple but it is a choice. And there is the rub. We have the option of serving ourselves instead of God. We do not have to give of ourselves. We can be lords of our selves rather than submitting our selves to our Lord. Which brings us to the implosion of the angels and the Fall of the human race.

God had no need or obligation to bring us into being. But Infinite Love knows no bounds and sets no conditions. We the beloved – angels (pure spirits) and humans (ensembles of spirit and matter) – were freely brought into being from nothingness solely for our own benefit. The divine Lover seeks only what is best for its beloved. What was best for the beloved was to love the Lord their God "with all their hearts." For it is in loving the Source of our being that our hearts are fulfilled – i.e., joy-filled.

But this was not to be. The greatest of the pure spirits, Lucifer, said "No" to Love. Instantly and forever he became the ugliest and unhappiest of beings: the Satan or Adversary. Multitudes of the spirits made the same choice and shared the same fate – eternal separation from the Source of all joy and entrance into the state of endless misery known as Hell. Angels do not "change" their minds or develop their characters over a period of time: their superior intellects allow them to see immediately the eternal consequences of their actions and their superior wills enable them to instantly make decisions that they know will bind them eternally.

Contrary to what the Plaintiff's counsel said, Lucifer is not a role model for humanity. Rather, he serves as a dread warning that pride goes before a fall.

But not all the spirits said "No" – and the greater part of them (the "good" angels) chose the path of love.

Breaking and Entering –
Paradise Lost, Paradise Regained

The human choice was different in nature and outcome than that of the angels. In the first parents, "Adam" (man) and "Eve" (mother of the living), all of humanity was given a primordial choice – freely to do the will of God or not. They chose "not." The consequence was catastrophe: suffering, death, impending damnation for the human race. And, for all time, the effect of the "Original Sin" taints human life, action and thought.

Evil clogs our arteries. The human will has become a will to evil, driven by an innate seemingly irresistible inclination towards wickedness. Always at war with God and itself. The serpent of sin lurks in the holiest of hearts, ready to strike any time and all the time.

Infinite-eternal Love, however, would not abandon us to our self-chosen destiny of death and damnation. Instead, divinity bore the consequence of humanity's insanity and malice to set it free. The Heart that is God became Man: as Jesus of Nazareth: "You are to name him Jesus, because he will save his people from their sins" (*Matthew* 1:21)

The Old Testament narratives show the unfolding of the divine plan to rescue the human race and should be understood in this context. We will respond to our opponent's caricatures of the God revealed in the Old Testament in due course. Here, we note that this plan was consummated in the coming of Jesus.

From the very start, there was no doubt as to the meaning of the mission of Jesus. "Just as through one transgression condemnation came upon all, so through one righteous act acquittal and life came to all." (*Romans* 5:18) The suffering for the sins of humanity that Jesus took on himself was for sins past, present, and future – "Through his suffering, my servant shall justify many, and their guilt he shall bear.... He shall take away the sins of many, and win pardon for their offenses." (*Isaiah* 53:11–12)

Here we see the logic of the laws of Love. The slightest offense against Infinite Goodness and Holiness is infinite in its impact: Thus humanity's "Fall" created an unbridgeable gulf between Creator and creatures. Only an atoning sacrifice of infinite value could re-open the path to God. And it would have to be a sacrifice performed by the offending party – a human being. But only an infinite Person could perform a sacrifice of infinite value. In Jesus, an infinite Person took on a human nature. Since he was divine and human, his death was the reparation required for redemption from Original Sin: His divine nature sufficed to make the infinite reparation; his human nature made it a truly human act.

But the redemptive death of Jesus does not "assure" salvation for every human. It simply makes salvation possible for anyone and everyone. We still must accept God's invitation of union with him. We are not puppets predestined for salvation or damnation but "free agents" capable of self-giving who are invited to give ourselves to our God.

Our whole life is a string of choices – free acts in which we either give of ourselves or not. We are our choices. What we become through our choices is our destiny. Unlike all other earthly creatures, human beings freely determine their own destiny. But human destiny was never about just the here-and-now. As all human societies across space and time recognized, the endgame is eternity. All nations and peoples – India, China, Persia, Greece, Egypt, Israel, Mesomerica, the hunter-gatherers – recognized too that our ultimate self-chosen destiny is either Heaven or Hell.

The destiny to which we are called is Heaven – the everlasting vision of the Godhead, our union with That which we need and desire above all. But those who blind themselves will not see; those whose hearts have hardened will die. The eternal self-deprivation of the sight of God, the loss of all that we need and desire, is Hell.

Heaven is not reward. Hell is not punishment. Heaven or Hell is what we become. The state of our being at the moment of death is its state forever.

Yes, there is pain and suffering in this world. Yes, there could be endless horror in the next. But no, God is not responsible for either state of affairs. Above all, God is a Savior who seeks everyone to be joyful and united with him, always and forever. Suffering is simply the other side of the coin of love. You have been created with the capability to freely give of yourself in love. If you were not free you could not love because love means being able to say Yes or No to the Other. But not even omnipotence can "make" someone love God.

Yes, God could create a robot or a machine that has been programmed to show the signs of love but this would not be love. It would be like your car or your bed "loving" you. The divine objective in creation was not to create robots but beings who could give of themselves in love. This means loving freely. This means the ability to say "No" even to omnipotence and even forever.

Infinite Love creates an ecosystem of self-giving love with all its potential catastrophic consequences for three reasons:

a. Love is not possible without free self-giving.

b. God will intervene to assuage the suffering of those who choose to love by bringing them to eternal joy.

c. God's Providence will bring about a greater good despite the prevalence of freely-chosen evil in this world.

The still, small voice that is the Infinite Lover speaks to every human heart at every instant. It also appears on the horizon of human history speaking through individuals and communities. It draws all to sorrow for the evil choices of the past and inspires all to remain true to their first love, the Triune God. The voice is often drowned out by the competing alternatives of hate and evil but its echoes never die out. And the voice was often amplified and broadcast to their fellow humans by those exceptional persons of every era who made the choice to love the infinite Lover.

In the fullness of time, the Voice came to us as a Person. "There was in him no stately bearing to make us look at him, nor appearance that would attract us to him. He was spurned and avoided by men, a man of suffering, accustomed to infirmity, One of those from whom men hide their faces, spurned, and we held him in no esteem. Yet it was our infirmities that he bore, our sufferings that he endured, While we thought of him as stricken, as one smitten by God and afflicted. But he was pierced for our offenses, crushed for our sins, Upon him was the chastisement that makes us whole, by his stripes we were healed. We had all gone astray like sheep, each following his own way; But the LORD laid upon him the guilt of us all."

This was the divine response to the calamity of human suffering. It was a response, above all, of love. No reductionist, no skeptic can explain the mystery of the message of love that lies at the center of this vision. We are told that the infinite Creator of trillions of galaxies is an infinite Lover, that he can be known most fully in the poor and the lowly, that he asks nothing of you but your love. Who could have thought up such an idea? Who but the Lover that is Love Itself?

The "man of suffering" was to be named Jesus precisely because he came to "save his people from their sins." And his "saving" was a story of love – total, unconditional Love: Love that he offered to each and every person and asked that they show to "the least" among them. No one else ever came with a message of such overwhelming, overpowering, all-embracing, all-pervasive love: asking total surrender, total trust and offering total love. Of those who drove nails into him, he said, "Forgive them for they know not what they do." Never before in human history was there such an unimaginably poignant utterance.

Exceptionally holy men had spoken of detachment from the world, of showing compassion to all living beings and of leading a pure life. But none had spoken of actively loving your enemies, of selflessly serving your fellow beings and thereby serving God, of giving up your very life to save your neighbor. The very idea of loving and forgiving your murderers *while* they are driving nails into your flesh is so unthinkable, so unnatural, that it could not have been invented. This is Love itself. This is GOD.

Because Jesus is God incarnate, his life on Earth is the divine response to the human predicament. But if the Godhead is changeless and perfect, how is it possible to speak of God suffering? How can God become man, suffer and die and yet be without change? Can God suffer if he is infinite perfection? Can he feel our pain if there is no change in him?

The answer is this: From all eternity, God is self-giving love: unconditional, infinite, perfect love: that is who he is: he is Trinity. If God becomes man, then he will necessarily be seen as unconditional and perfect love. If he becomes man in a sinful world, then he will be encountered as unconditional love suffering at the hands of sin: he is seen as perfect love and perfect sacrifice: because his eternal reality is sacrifice. Thus, he can only be sacrificial and suffering love in a world of sin.

There is no change in God. God's unchanging love is seen in this world and by this world as a sacrifice, as suffering, as self-giving. This is a photograph in human terms of the Trinitarian God. This is what he is. There is no change in him. The change is in us. This is how the unchanging Lover is perceived and experienced in a world without love.

You Will Know That They Are Christians By Their Love – At times ...

The Jesus Cloud has come to be known as Christianity. The Plaintiff's account of Christianity in history is about as accurate and plausible as a narrative about the Jewish people written by Adolf Hitler.

The idea of personhood emerged from Jesus' revelation of Three Persons within one God. Historically, there was no idea, no concept of human persons before Christianity. Embedded in the idea of the person are the insights into the irreplaceable value, dignity, and inalienable rights of each human being that serve as the foundations of modern civilization. These insights preceded the Enlightenment by centuries and have, in fact, been systematically erased by the progeny of the Enlightenment.

It was also the Christian cultural matrix that gave birth to modern science. The Christian revelation showed that the universe is the creation of an infinitely intelligent Mind, and therefore followed laws embedded in it by its Source. "There is a certain Eternal Law, to wit, Reason, existing in the mind of God and governing the entire universe," wrote Thomas Aquinas. As to the nature of this governance, Aquinas said, "God imprints on the whole of nature the principles of its proper actions. And so, in this way, God is said to command the whole of nature, according to Ps. 148:6: 'He hath made a decree, and it shall not pass away.' And thus all actions and movements of the whole of nature are subject to the eternal law."[51] This conception of a divinely implanted order of being gave rise to the whole quest for the laws of Nature that gave birth to the science of today.

It is a striking fact of history that Copernicus, Galileo and Kepler, Newton, Faraday and Maxwell, Einstein, Planck and Heisenberg, all believed in a divine "mind" behind the world. They saw Rationality at the foundation of reality. Further, the doctrine of the Incarnation showed that the universe is not a "part" of God and should therefore be studied without fear.

It was the Christian theological matrix that produced two institutions that are fundamental to modern society – the modern university (beginning with the University of Bologna in 1088), which cares for the mind, and the hospital, which cares for the body. (There were, of course, centers of learning in the ancient world from Nalanda in India to Plato's Academy in Greece.)

Anything good that emerged from the Enlightenment era came from the Christian vision underlying the societies of that time. But the Enlightenment was also a rebellion against the Christian restraints on

---

51   "Question 93: The Eternal Law," *Summa Theologiae*, https://aquinas101.thomisticin-stitute.org/st-iaiiae-q-93

human evil and, consequently. as we shall see, it produced the greatest kill-ing machines in human history starting with the Reign of Terror known as the French Revolution.

My opponent has detailed the wicked acts of individual Christians and Christian institutions. While his account includes fabrications and exag-gerations, it is a matter of record that Christians have been guilty of great evil over the centuries – for instance, intra-Christian warfare or mercenary assaults against non-Christians. But let us remember that the first three centuries of Christianity were marked by a display of superhuman love in the face of wholesale slaughter never seen before. The first Christians marched to their deaths forgiving their murderers and praying for their transformation. It is by their love that the Christians conquered the forces of hate arrayed against them. For some religions, martyrs are killers, those who die while killing their enemies. For Christianity, on the other hand, martyrs are those who meekly offer up their own lives to their enemies who kill them for spreading the Gospel of Love.

Some of the Plaintiff's charges are simply silly.

For example, Adolf Hitler was as much an enemy of Christ and Christianity as he was of the Jews. Hitler said:

> The heaviest blow that ever struck humanity was the coming of Christianity. Bolshevism is Christianity's illegitimate child. Both are inventions of the Jew. The deliberate lie in the matter of religion was introduced into the world by Christianity.[52]

> Leave the hair-splitting to others. Whether it's the Old Testament or the New, or simply the sayings of Jesus, it's all the same old Jewish swindle. It will not make us free. A German church, a German

---

52   Hermann Rauschning, *Hitler Speaks: A Series of Political Conversations With Adolf Hitler on His Real Aims*, 1st edition, 1939.

Christianity is a distortion. One is either a German or a Christian. You cannot be both.[53]

Christians have often and inexcusably been guilty of antisemitism as have many other groups before and after the coming of Jesus. But the Holocaust was a product of the Nazis and not Christianity.

Jewish historian and rabbi Yosef Yerushalmi said that "between this [Christian antisemitism] and Nazi Germany lies not merely a 'transformation' but a leap into a different dimension. The slaughter of Jews by the state was not part of the medieval Christian world order. It became possible with the breakdown of that order."[54]

Hitler was not simply anti-Christian but an occultist. His elite fighting force, the SS, was driven by is own satanic cult. The Israeli newspaper *Haaretz* reports that mainstream scholarship is finally recognizing the occult undercurrents in Nazism. "Literature dealing with esoteric dogma, satanic cults and mysticism created a broad space for discussion on worship of the kind found among the Nazi leadership. ...Now many researchers have come to recognize the fact that we don't have enough tools to explain everything that happened between 1933 and 1945, as Tel Aviv University historian Shulamit Volkov wrote a number of years ago. One example of this is the popularity of satanic cults among SS officers."[55]

But the Christian revelation, as we have seen, warns us that there is an evil streak in every human person. This includes those who themselves profess the Christian faith. To be a Christian is to fall in love with God but love is a relationship of constant commitment albeit with the assistance of the divine Lover. Sadly, as the Apostle Paul said, the spirit is willing but

53 *Hitler's Table Talk 1941-1944: His Private Conversations*, translated by Norman Cameron and R.H. Stevens.

54 "A Response to Rosemary Reuther," *Auschwitz: Beginning of an Era?* (New York: Ktav, 1977), 104.

55 https://www.haaretz.com/opinion/2014-02-11/ty-article/.premium/a-mystic-glimpse-of-evil/0000017f-df0d-d3ff-a7ff-ffad004e0000

the flesh is weak. Power and money tend to corrupt and, when Christians attained both, they often walked away from the Love of their lives. And that is when all Hell breaks loose!

Despite this, Christianity has often served as a restraint on the baser urges of individuals, institutions and societies. And even where institutional Christianity lost its moorings, individual Christians have continued to live lives of self-sacrifice and quiet heroism working among the poorest of the poor and ministering to the sick and the disabled. This is how orphanages, homes for the poor, hospitals and universities were born. And for every one member of the clergy that has sexually abused the vulnerable, there have been twenty others who have given of themselves in thankless lives of service and commitment to their fellows.

These are the kinds of enduring fruits by which we should evaluate the faith rather than the failings of those who betrayed their birthright.

Would-be gods

In contrast to the Christian vision, we have the "new morality" outlined by the Plaintiff that is increasingly the norm in modern consumerist societies.

- The highest value of all is unlimited personal freedom with no constraints other than the use of violence against another.

- Consequently, all laws and societal conventions pertaining to human behavior must conform to this non-negotiable, non-debatable, and unquestionable provision. The only rule is that there are no rules.

- Religious institutions and systems are retrograde structures that will soon wither away and can only be tolerated if they uphold the canon of unrestricted freedom. Modernity is a deity-free zone.

- Moral laws and codes are nothing but instruments of torture instituted by oppressors. The fact that they vary from society to society means that there is nothing absolute about them.

- Virtues are replaced by virtue-signaling because the new morality has its own taboos that are rigorously enforced by its disciples.

The Plaintiff calls all this a Copernican Revolution in morality. But it is more accurate to call it a regression than a revolution. It is a repackaged version of the plunge into darkness recounted in the Book of *Genesis* that, amazingly but accurately enough, the Plaintiff cites. "When you eat of it your eyes will be opened and you will be like gods, who know good and evil." This is actually the enticement that comes before entrapment.

Given its underlying assumption of no boundaries or barriers, the demolition path taken by the "New Morality" can be easily predicted and was, in fact, partially laid out by the Plaintiff:

> All pleasures are permitted – this is the pleasure principle. First in line is the "sexual revolution" since this involves the most powerful of human desires. Every form of sexual indulgence and experimentation is to be encouraged. Hetero and homo, of course, but why stop there? Not just sexual "formats" but the very idea of sexual gender is up for grabs. Hence, we now have binary and non-binary and the freedom to identify ourselves as whatever we wish to be. Nothing must come in the way of the all-consuming passion that is sex.

> Institutions like marriage and family – let alone monogamy – have no relevance in this new era. Neither do biological conditions like pregnancy. While "the use of violence against another" is taboo, this does not apply to human embryos – or, for that matter, those individuals whose age make them cost-prohibitive to "maintain." When needed, you just "take out the trash."

Of course, sex is not the only item on the new agenda. Children are now products created in labs and since we want only the "best" product, we can easily discard those that do not meet our marketing specs. Ends dictate the means in all matters in the New Morality. Cloned human embryos to create replacement "parts", gene editing for favorable traits, aerosol injections into the Earth's atmosphere to fight climate change – everything is on the table since there are no rules.

The vision of society laid out by the Plaintiff is a formula for hell on Earth. It is survival of the fittest on steroids. No commitment, no love, no human-ness. Self-indulgence – shop till you drop, party like there's no tomorrow. The Plaintiff's New Morality has been adopted not only by consumerist societies but by authoritarian and totalitarian regimes around the world. The only difference is that the autocrats-in-charge set their own rules for their societies driven by governing agendas and power plays.

But those who aspire to "be like gods" soon discover they are not really gods. If we try to violate the laws of Nature – say, by rejecting the idea of laws of motion and standing in front of a speeding truck – we soon realize that there is a price to be paid. Likewise, those who dispensed with the moral codes of humanity found out that these dispensations came with a cost. The dissolution of marriage and family has torpedoed succeeding generations with outbreaks of violence, abuse, addiction, gangs, depression and suicides. Societies that mandate one child families face demographic collapse. The sick and the elderly in societies with legalized euthanasia risk being "terminated" during hospital visits. God is replaced with gods.

Especially dangerous – for the entire race – is the pursuit of scientific research without moral fenceposts. We are one technology away from annihilation. This is all deadly serious stuff.

Let us remember here that the traditional moral codes were rooted in an understanding of the weakness of human nature and were meant to ensure our protection and well-being.

If we look at the principle of entropy – the progressive descent into disorder of a closed system – we might say that there is a law of moral entropy at work in human affairs. Once we reject the rule of moral law, the law of the jungle will become the law of the land.

The Plaintiff has said that all moral laws are relative to particular societies and cultures, so there are no moral absolutes. All moral codes, he said, simply embody a particular narrative that is dominant in a society.

Now it is true that there are culturally conditioned differences in the moral codes governing different societies. But there is a fundamental commonality that transcends such differences. The members of different human societies are, after all, members of the same species, homo sapiens.

There are universal values (moderation in consumption, social stability, etc.) that are undeniably beneficial for the optimal development of human persons no matter when or where they live. All humans have similar desires and drives and all come to recognize, in different degrees, a hierarchy of values. They also recognize the prevalence of evil and the need to wall it off with proscriptions against certain behaviors (addictions, for instance). These values and proscriptions are embodied in the traditional moral codes recognized by all of humanity.

Even more important, almost all the codes across history recognized that there is a transcendent Source of the moral order. As such, these moral laws are the rules of reality just as the laws of Nature are the rules of the physical world. We come from the Divine and are "built" to be united to the Divine. Anything that is not beneficial for our optimal growth as human beings is an obstacle to this union; anything that is beneficial facilitates our union. We have a common human nature. Our nature has a divine Source and it is made for ultimate communion with this Source. All morality is built around these two truths – the commonality of our human nature and its built-in orientation to communion with its Source. This is the universal "narrative" of human morality.

When he talks of "moral narratives", the Plaintiff draws attention to the problems with his own approach. Those who reject moral absolutes create their own impoverished narratives of the human enterprise. For the atheistic evolutionary biologists, morality (old or "New") is simply a reflection of the "survival of the fittest" dynamic. For the Marxist, it is simply part of endless material cycles. For the hard-core physicalists, all human activity is just a perturbation of quantum fields. All these narratives ignore the structure of human nature because they do not recognize its reality. As such, what they offer is not "liberation" from oppressive structures but personal tragedy and societal implosion.

The Plaintiff's idea that science will provide guidance on moral matters was rejected by one of the greatest of all scientists, Albert Einstein, who said science can only tell us "what is, but not what should be."[56]

The witnesses I call will delve into more detail in these areas.

Now, I will say something on the question of gender since it is apparently a key part of the Plaintiff's self-proclaimed revolution.

For all the talk of "transgender" and people identifying themselves with various genders, it is a biological fact that there are only two sexes, male and female.

Richard Dawkins, an authority often cited by the other side, made this very clear in his analysis of the gender debates: "As a biologist, there are two sexes and that's all there is to it."[57]

---

56 Albert Einstein, "Science and Religion", 1939, https://www.panarchy.org/einstein/science.religion.1939.html

57 https://talk.tv/news/6378/richard-dawkins-there-are-two-sexes-and-thats-all-there-is-to-it-piers-morgan

In fact, there are 6,500 genetic differences between males and females. Geneticists Shmuel Pietrokovski and Moran Gershoni of the Weizmann Institute identified "6,500 Genes That Are Expressed Differently in Men and Women." This is practically very relevant to our everyday life because "the differences between men and women in the genes that cause disease or respond to treatments."[58]

Then there is the matter of the chromosomal differences between the sexes. A National Institutes of Health publication observes that "The biological differences between the sexes have long been recognized at the biochemical and cellular levels. Rapid advances in molecular biology have revealed the genetic and molecular bases of a number of sex-based differences in health and human disease, some of which are attributed to sexual genotype—XX in the female and XY in the male. ... The male genome differs from the female genome in the number of X chromosomes that it contains, as well as by the presence of a Y chromosome."[59]

As this paper put it, "Every Cell Has a Sex." Removal of genitalia or various kinds of behavioral and hormonal and surgical treatments cannot modify the DNA that is imprinted in every one of our cells. In short, so-called sex-change treatments (which began in the 1950's) cannot change anyone's biological sex. As *Genesis* has it, "in the image of God he created them; male and female he created them."

N.T. Wright notes that "in Genesis 1 it is of course male plus female that is created to bear God's image. The male-plus-female factor is not of course specific to humanity; the principle of 'male plus female' runs through a great deal of creation. But humans were created to bear God's image, and

---

58   https://wis-wander.weizmann.ac.il/life-sciences/researchers-identify-6500-genes-are-expressed-differently-men-and-women

59   https://www.ncbi.nlm.nih.gov/books/NBK222291/#:~:text=The%20male%20genome%20differs%20from,of%20the%20male%20gonadal%20phenotype

given a task, to be fruitful and multiply, to tend the garden and name the animals."[60]

Which brings us to the larger point. No one knows better about what is best for us than the One who created us. The moral law dismissed by the Plaintiff is, in fact, a health-and-wellness plan that enables each of us to fulfill our potential as human persons. The glory of God is the human person fully alive, said Irenaeus, one of the early Church Fathers.

Many of those who today turn away from the law of God that was built for their betterment have been previously traumatized in one way or another or shunned or despised by their fellows. Adopting behaviors that infringe on the divine law, however, will not bring them happiness. Quite the opposite. Our hearts go out to them in their state of distress and loneliness. We ask them to turn to their Heavenly Father who loves them unconditionally and seeks to bring them home to the fullness of joy.

Best Possible World?

Is this the best possible world that God could have created? Was it not possible for him to improve on it? Since he can "foresee" everything why did he create people he knew would go to Hell?

These questions in themselves show complete ignorance of both God and the world we live in. It is ignorance that thinks of God in human terms (anthropomorphically) without realizing he is infinite and eternal. He does not "foresee." He knows all things from all eternity. There is no "best possible world" when you are dealing with a world of autonomous agents. Autonomous agents are beings that are able to cause their own actions from "within" themselves for their own sake. The kind of world we live in is co-created by the agents who make it up. Thus, God "makes his sun rise

---

60 https://ntwrightpage.com/2016/07/12/communion-and-koinonia-pauline-reflections-on-tolerance-and-boundaries/

on the bad and the good, and causes rain to fall on the just and the unjust." (*Matthew* 5:45)

It is easy to see that there are only certain kinds of beings that are possible – purely spiritual beings (angels) where spirit is understood as something that does not occupy space; purely material beings (the physical universe); beings that are combinations of matter and mind which range from beings that are alive but have no mental properties (bugs, plants) to beings that are alive with certain mental properties (birds, dogs, chimpanzees, etc.); and beings that are combinations of matter, mind and spirit where spirit is the reality that does not occupy space but, in this case, is nevertheless integrated with matter (human beings who have the attributes of intellect, will and self, all of which are "spiritual").

Any world involving such beings will be co-created by them. It is senseless to talk of God creating a best possible world if you have autonomous agents who partially determine their own destiny. Of course, God can create a robotic universe entirely controlled by him but this would not be a best possible world. It would be pointless.

In his infinite-eternal love and generosity, God created spiritual beings (angels and humans) capable of loving him and, consequently, enjoying eternal bliss. But this meant that they had to be free to love him or not. Whatever world we have would be one that we and all other autonomous agents co-create. This is the only possible world.

It is a world governed by natural processes. This includes the unity of the human race inasmuch as we all ultimately share the same parentage and DNA. Since our autonomy is real, this means that all those in our blood-line choose their own destinies. By the very nature of the case, God cannot and will not "intervene" to prevent the existence of anyone in the human race since its genetic unity is intrinsic to its autonomy.

The world we have is the only one that is possible given a world of autonomous agents directed toward ultimate union with the Godhead. Also, as explained by the logician James Ross,

"There is no point … in imagining that God picks among worlds and individuals, or among icons for them, like a child picking among pictures for toys to make. Possibility is consequent upon being not prior to it or explanatory of it. … God's knowing extends as far as his causation … God does not make what will never be, so there is nothing to know beyond what is. … The actual – and the potential in it – exhausts the possible."[61]

Once we recognize what is obvious – the reality of God – we should look back at our lives in its light. In all the pain and suffering, chaos and confusion, choices good and bad, we will inevitably come to see God bringing good out of evil and turning around impossible situations. In this snapshot, we can see something of the big picture as it applies to our own lives.

As Holocaust survivor Victor Frankl said, "Those who have a 'why' to live, can bear with almost any 'how'". (…) Suffering ceases to be suffering at the moment it finds a meaning, such as the meaning of a sacrifice."[62]

When it comes to world history, God does the same thing – bringing about the triumph of love in the midst of evil and disorder. But this triumph can be seen only if we have the big picture – of which we only have a few jigsaw pieces.

And yet, there is one paradigm jigsaw image that makes it all clear: the life, suffering, death, and resurrection of God incarnate *who met us where we are to take us where he is.*

---

61   https://www.sas.upenn.edu/~jross/realfreedom.htm

62   https://medium.com/mind-cafe/7-viktor-frankl-quotes-to-motivate-you-to-find-your-purpose-2ece0c64f1d8

GodSpace

Jesus' concern was not simply with the life to come but life here and now. His prescription for earthly life was transformational for all who put his teachings into practice.

At the center was his revelation that God is "our" Father, that the purpose of life is to become children of the Father – through his Son and his Holy Spirit – and that we are called to live from this moment forward in the Kingdom of the Father, GodSpace.

Jesus tells us that "true" worship must be directed to the Father.

The Father that Jesus revealed was prodigal – i.e., extravagant, in his love and generosity.

Even more astonishingly, Jesus calls God *Abba*, the intimate and affection-ate Aramaic term for one's own father – a first in religious history. He tells us we are all called to become children of this *Abba* and thus live with him forever.

Jesus further tells us that God is "Our" Father, who insists on meeting our every need and who urges us to turn our lives over to him. As his chil-dren, in this world we are all invited to live in the Kingdom of the Father, GodSpace, Heaven here-and-now.

Thus the Father unveiled to us is the Prodigal Father, *Abba* Father, *Our* Father.

This revelation was transformational simply because it changes the entire understanding of our origin and destiny. It transfigures our thoughts and feelings, our plans and perspectives, our choices and actions. For the first time, we see that we are dealing not with a hostile universe nor a distant deity but with an infinitely loving, constantly present, ever-providing Lover – the Father. And we live as his children in his Kingdom on Earth as it is in Heaven.

We learn, too, that Jesus is the incarnation or human embodiment of the Father's eternal Son whom the Father sends to us because he "so" loves us. And that the Father through the Son sends us the divine Fruit of their infinite Love, their Holy Spirit.

There is a reason for the Father's sending of his Son and his Spirit. Through the incarnation, death and resurrection of his Son on our behalf, the Father offers us redemption from our sins. Through the sending of his Holy Spirit into our "hearts," the Father makes us his children who are invited to live with him forever. We can only become his children if we live with his own Life – his Spirit – and when filled with his Spirit we are thereby able to call him "Abba."

This revelation was a revolution at the level of knowledge. But, just as important, it was a revolution in terms of our relationship with God, and the way in which we lead our lives. To discover the Father is also to discover our identity as his children who live in GodSpace.

God, from our standpoint, will never be the same again. He is no longer an impersonal abstraction, a remote sovereign or an extra-cosmic Force. He is God 2.0 – our prodigal Father, present with us here and now, fulfilling our deepest desires and leading us to eternal ecstasy.

In Closing

Your Honor, Ladies and gentlemen of the jury, I have sought to give an outline of all the salient issues relating to the Plaintiff's accusations.

It is our contention that the Plaintiff has no standing to bring any action against my Client. In addition, it should be obvious that he has no case for a case given his claim that my Client does not exist! Irrespective of these issues, we are confident that the testimony of our witnesses will show beyond any reasonable doubt that the source of moral evil is to be found in the intentions and choices of free agents. My Client seeks only to overcome evil and mitigate pain on behalf of humanity and the response has been this egregious lawsuit. I guess it is true that no good deed goes unpunished!

I hope the Plaintiff's witnesses have something more substantial to offer than what he had to say in his opening statement. I look forward to cross-examining them and then presenting you with our expert witnesses.

WITNESSES
FOR THE PLAINTIFF

"THOU SHALT HAVE NO GOD BEFORE ME,' SAITH THE UNIVERSE"

Witness – Percy Maersk (PM)

LH: My first witness is Professor Percy Maersk, eminent cosmologist and a prominent member of many national academies of science. His book *When Nothing Became Something* was an international best-seller, praised by both academics and the popular press. The only ones who did not care for the book are those who had the most to lose from its arguments – theologians and religious believers. They are even more incensed with his widely popular blog, "Cosmic Darwinism," which regularly takes on not just the religious right but its left and center as well. You might say he wears his New Atheism on his sleeve and isn't concerned with being politically correct when talking to his students and the public at large.

Professor, I want to ask you first. Do you believe in the existence of the being commonly called God, a Creator of the world?

Maersk: Certainly not.

LH: And why not?

Maersk: This is a question I treat at length in *When Nothing Became Something*. I show that every academic discipline of the modern era has definitively shown us that there is no god, no creator, no supernatural entity of any kind. All the usual reasons used for promoting belief in a god have been put out of business by science – principally cosmology. Consider my list:

Cosmology shows us that the universe began without a cause, from nothing. There was no god before, during, or after. The job of creating the universe has been outsourced to quantum field theory.

Physics has shown us that there is nothing operating in the multiverse other than the laws of Nature and these are different for each one of an infinite number of universes.

Biology shows us that life sprang from chemicals and living organisms evolved through entirely natural processes including random mutations and genetic drift through the designing hand of natural selection.

Neuroscience shows us that our mental activity is caused by synapses and neural firings and the like and not by a "soul."

Psychology shows us that religious belief is a kind of pathology that can be diagnosed and treated.

Sociology, anthropology, and economics show us how religious belief arose from communal practices, primitive superstitions, and the need for social stability.

Philosophy, always the bane of religion, has put the whole enterprise out of business by permanently demolishing the pseudo-arguments for the existence of a god.

We can explain our own existence without invoking a god of any kind and we can also explain why people persist in believing in the gods they fashion in their own images. But belief in a god is not simply a fanciful but harmless delusion like belief in fairies or gnomes. It is a dangerous superstition that has caused incalculable harm to humankind.

Hence, as a cosmologist, I want to say with in all seriousness to people of goodwill that the universe itself tells us: Thou shall have no god before me.

If you ask me how I can justify this proscription, the one-word answer is "science."

The idea of a super-human spirit being in the sky is one of the most primitive and persistent of the superstitions haunting the human psyche. Those who believe in this benighted idea have never shown any evidence in support of it beyond insisting on the need for blind faith. Modern science has shown definitively that there is no such being. Astronomers and astronauts have failed to find any trace of a creator in the cosmos. Yuri Gagarin, the first man in space, said in 1961, "I looked and looked but I didn't see God." None of the later astronauts found a god out there either. Quantum cosmology tells us why.

Unfortunately for true believers, modern cosmology has ended the whole god debate permanently because we now know that the universe came into being out of nothing, without a cause – and we know how.

I am not exaggerating when I say that today's physicists and cosmologists have made the same kind of breakthrough in explaining the origin of the cosmos without a creator that Darwin achieved in explaining the origin of species without a deity. This is an exciting time for science. Religion, not so much.

Now you might say, what about the Big Bang? This is usually the last resort of the religionists who flaunt it as proof of the Genesis creation myth. But it is precisely here that the quantum cosmologist delivers the knockout punch showing us that Big Bangs are commonplace in the quantum multiverse.

There are three eminent scientists in particular who wrote extensively on the universe spontaneously originating from nothing. They are cosmologist Lawrence Krauss, Cambridge Lucasian Professor Stephen Hawking and the physicist Victor Stenger. All three held strongly that modern physics and cosmology definitively explain the origin of the universe in natural terms. Much like Napoleon's scientist, the Marquis de Laplace, they said about god, "we have no need for that hypothesis."

In his book, *A Universe from Nothing: Why There Is Something Rather than Nothing*, Krauss reveals that there is something rather than nothing because "nothing" is unstable and will always produce something! Referring to the revolutionary discoveries in cosmology and particle physics in the last half century, he observes that there is now a plausible way to explain how all the "stuff" in the universe could arise from nothing purely through natural causes. As Richard Dawkins said in the afterword to Krauss' book, this breakthrough is comparable to Darwin's discovery that the diversity of life forms is entirely explicable in terms of natural causes and processes.

So what is "nothing" and how did it produce "something?" Krauss has shown that this is purely a scientific question because something and nothing are scientific ideas. Developments in the last few decades have shown us what nothing is. Here is what we know:

- The empty space around us is teeming with virtual particles that are constantly going in and out of existence in time frames so short they cannot be measured.

- If you remove the particles and radiation from empty space, it still carries energy – and most of the energy in the universe is actually in empty space.

- When we bring gravity into the picture, this opens up the possibility of creating positive energy particles from nothing without violating the law of the conservation of energy.

As Krauss puts it, "Once you allow gravity into the game, what seems impossible is possible. Gravity allows positive energy and negative energy, and out of nothing you can create positive energy particles, and as long as a gravitational attraction produces enough negative energy, the sum of their energy can be zero. And in fact when we look out at the universe and try and measure its total energy, we come up with zero." While Krauss notes that this is not proof that the universe emerged from nothing, it is at least a plausible mechanism for such emergence. As he puts it, "Does this prove that our universe arose from nothing? Of course not. But it does take us one rather large step closer to the plausibility of such a scenario."[63]

Once we apply quantum theory to space and include a quantum theory of gravity, we could say that universes can pop into existence out of nothing assuming the net energy is zero.

But this is just one item on the menu. Krauss, like Hawking and many others, delves into what is called the cosmological theory called the String Theory Landscape. What the Landscape does is to bring together string theory, cosmic inflation following the Big Bang, the Anthropic Principle and the idea of a multiverse with an infinite number of universes and with no immutable physical laws.

What it also does is to remove the need for a Creator.

The primary architects of the String Theory Landscape are the physicists at Stanford University:

> "String theory asserts that the basic building blocks of reality are vibrating, one-dimensional loops of energy that quiver in 10 or more dimensions to strum out the elementary particles and fundamental forces of nature.

> "Cosmic inflation holds that the Big Bang began with a period of exponential expansion that swelled our universe from a fragile quantum speck to a vast manor of emptiness a quarter-billion-light-years wide in a flicker of a flicker of time.

> "According to the theory, this heavenly sprawl still occurs in distant corners of the cosmos, spinning out a web of related daughter universes that connect to form a much larger "multiverse.""

---

63   Lawrence M. Krauss, *A Universe from Nothing: Why There Is Something Rather than Nothing* (New York: Free Press, 2012), 170.

"The Landscape also explains why our universe is fine-tuned for life because: "If there are innumerable universes, each with differing laws of physics, then it should not be surprising that we inhabit one where the cosmological constant is small – if things were any different, we could not exist to marvel at the coincidence."[64]

Let me turn now to the work of Stephen Hawking, the great theoretical physicist who was also among the most successful science writers of all time.

In *The Grand Design*, Stephen Hawking uses an approach similar to Krauss'. He notes that M-Theory provides "a sound scientific explanation for the making of our world – no Gods required." He says that ours is one of many universes and "In this view, the universe appeared spontaneously from nothing" How is a universe able to emerge from nothing? There is a consistent vacuum energy in empty space. Since the positive energy associated with matter is balanced by the negative energy of gravity, a fluctuation of the energy in the vacuum results in our universe. "Because there is a law like gravity, the universe can and will create itself from nothing." Nothing is space with vacuum energy which "we may as well call … zero."[65]

In his best-selling *A Brief History of Time*, Hawking also developed his own unique approach to eliminating the idea that the universe had a beginning as implied by the Big Bang. He leverages a mathematical model used in quantum physics to show that the universe has no boundary, edge, beginning, or singularity. [66]

By eliminating time before the Big Bang, Hawking also eliminated the deity. In his posthumous book, *Brief Answers to the Big Questions*, he said: "We have finally found something that doesn't have a cause, because there

64   https://news.stanford.edu/2018/09/10/string-theory-landscape/

65   Stephen Hawking and Leonard Mlodinow, *The Grand Design* (New York: Bantam, 2010), 136, 180.

66   Stephen Hawking, *A Brief History of Time* (New York: Bantam, 1988), 138ff.

was no time for a cause to exist in. For me this means that there is no possibility of a creator, because there is no time for a creator to have existed in."[67]

All these themes are elegantly applied to the question of God by the physicist Vic Stenger:

> "Nonbelievers recognize that they cannot prove the nonexistence of God. They simply argue that a universe without a creator is the most economical premise consistent with all the data. An uncaused, undesigned emergence of the universe from nothing violates no principle of physics. The total energy of the universe appears to be zero, so no miracle of energy created 'from nothing' was required to produce it. Similarly, no miracle was needed for the appearance of order. Order can and does occur spontaneously in physical systems."[68]

LH: You say that science shows that the universe came to be from nothing through natural processes, but believers claim that it is the creation of a god and they have arguments supporting the existence of such a being. What do you think of these arguments?

Maersk: What arguments? No one who is literate, let alone scientifically literate, can take them seriously. But in many ways these claims to "prove" the existence of a deity are more perfidious than the superstitions of the simple savages. Living in the Stone Age you had an excuse for mistaking thunder for the rumblings of a deity. But now, with what we know from science, it is simply criminal for believers to beguile the masses with their nonsense.

The theologians fool their dupes by asking, "Who made the world?" Their answer is "god." But using their own logic, we should ask them, "who made god?" At this point they change the subject. And understandably so. This

---

67   Stephen Hawking, *Brief Answers to the Big Questions,* (New York: Bantam, 2018), 37-8.

68   Victor J. Stenger, "Has Science Found God?," *Free Inquiry*, Volume 19 (1), Winter 1998/99, 56-58.

is because the idea of a creator initiates what is called an infinite regress – who created the creator and who created the creator of the creator and so on without end.

As Krauss pointed out, belief in "a First Cause still leaves open the question, 'Who created the creator?' After all, what is the difference between arguing in favor of an eternally existing creator versus an eternally existing universe without one?"[69]

In *The God Delusion*, Richard Dawkins provides yet another refutation of the argument. If you are trying to provide an intelligent designer as the explanation for the natural, complex phenomena in the universe, then this designer should be at least as complex as the phenomena and it should have no explanation outside itself. But it is very improbable that there is anything that is more complex than the phenomena we experience in the universe that cannot be explained outside itself, and it is therefore improbable that such a designer exists.[70]

The question of "Who made the world?" also rests on an elementary logical mistake. As Bertrand Russell once said, just because every member of the human race has a mother, it does not follow that the human race itself has a mother.

LH: Thank you Professor Maersk for your compelling testimony. These are all the questions I have. I have no further questions Your Honor.

Judge: Your witness. Mr. Angelini.

MA: Thank you, Your Honor.

Dr. Maersk, I do not mean to be rude but your book – like the rest of the New Atheist corpus – has an impoverished idea of the fundamental questions raised by our existence. This is why you create your fantasy about nothing producing something without understanding what is meant by

69   Lawrence M. Krauss, op cit., xii.
70   Richard Dawkins, *The God Delusion* (London: Bantam, 2006), 109, 143.

either nothing or something. Given this flawed starting point, you also construct an obviously bizarre idea of a deity that you proceed to blow to bits. The "god" of your book is a superstition – and it happens to be YOUR superstition. It is not the only superstition of course. The gold medal for that goes to your notion of nothingness.

But thanks to your inability to grasp the nature of the five fundamental realities constituting our world, you cannot perceive the reality of the infinite Intelligence that is its Ground. You mistakenly identify the origin of cosmic phenomena with the origin of existence.

LH: Objection Your Honor. This is baseless, irrelevant and simply insulting.

MA: Your Honor, I am leading up to something. Let me complete what I am saying and then I will ask the witness for his response.

Judge: Continue. But get to the point.

MA: Now, the critiques of God from scientists and philosophers as well as most discussions on science and religion rest on various mistakes. Your book is an excellent illustration of some of these mistakes. One basic mistake takes such forms as assuming that God is a part of the Universe discernible by science (your Dawkins example) or thinking of God as one more cause like the causes of physical processes (your Russell example) or of pointing to God's role or non-role in the origin of the universe (your Hawking and Krauss examples). These ideas entirely misunderstand what is meant by God as I tried to show in my opening statement. Equally important, the critics make the mistake of ignoring five phenomena that are presupposed by science and thereby lie beyond the purview of science. These phenomena stare us in the face and testify to the infinite Mind underlying them.

To expand on my opening statement, there are five realities that cannot be explained in terms of anything more fundamental than themselves:

> *Energy* – we know that everything physical is energy. As the Nobel physicist Steve Weinberg put it, "In its mature form, the idea of quantum field theory is that quantum fields are the basic ingredients of the universe, and particles are just bundles of energy and momentum of the fields."[71]
> But what is energy? As we have seen, Nobelist Richard Feynman said, "In physics today, we have no knowledge of what energy is."[72] Where did energy come from? Astronomer Royal Martin Rees said we have no idea why space has energy.[73] And yet, even as we speak, trillions of photons are traveling here and through us at 186,000 miles an hour as they have been for billions of years from the time of the Big Bang.

> *Agency* – by which we mean living beings, beings that are capable of purposive autonomous action. We know the chemical ingredients of living beings but we have no idea how a piece of matter can become an autonomous purpose-driven agent.

> *Consciousness* – the ability to be aware of our environment, a power that is not to be found in the laws of matter.

> Conceptual *thought* – processing *meaning* using concepts that do not refer to a specific physical object (we can think of the idea of a dog without thinking of a specific dog). Again, this is not something found in the laws of matter; neither can it be produced by consciousness, as Einstein pointed out.

> *The self,* the "I", "me" – it is the self that is the experiencer: it cannot be reduced to its experiences, and it certainly cannot be

71   Steven Weinberg, ed. by Tian Yu Cao, *Conceptual Foundations of Quantum Field Theory* (Cambridge, UK: Cambridge University Press, 1999), 242.

72   Richard Feynman. "Conservation of Energy," 1963, https://www.feynmanlectures.caltech.edu/I_04.html

73   Martin Rees cited in "What Came Before Creation?," *U.S. News& World Report* special edition on "Mysteries of Science," 2002.

identified with the ever-changing bio-electrical storm we call the brain.

As I also said in my opening statement, atheists and theists alike have been fixated on questions about the beginning of the universe or the Anthropic Principle without realizing that there is a more fundamental issue to be addressed: how did these five realities which are undeniable originate?

All theories about the Big Bang, fluctuations of the vacuum, strings, infinite universes and the like have to assume that energy, agency, consciousness, thought, and the self exist. After all, scientists themselves expend energy and are alive, conscious, capable of thought and operating as identifiable individuals. All their theories are theories about the activities of energy, so they must assume that energy exists. That is their starting point. How did the energy come to be? They cannot answer this question with the tools of science since those tools cannot operate without the physical already being in place.

Even less can they answer questions about the origins of agency, consciousness, thought or the self since all scientific theories and laws are concerned with what can be quantified or measured. Such attributes as consciousness or thought cannot be physically described let alone measured.

It is pointless to point to the Landscape or the multiverse or "nothing" to explain these five realities. For one thing, the Landscape or the multiverse idea is solely about physical laws of Nature and physical constants. And these laws and constants can tell us nothing about the origins of consciousness, thought and the self in any alleged universe. As noted, although these realities use matter as a vehicle, they cannot be described or explained by the laws of matter. Neither quantum fields nor neurons have the property of being conscious. Genomes cannot think.

The only plausible explanation for the existence of these realities is the existence of an Ultimate Reality that is infinite Mind.

On this last question, Professor Maersk, despite your distinguished background in cosmology, let me ask you, first, what makes you think that you are qualified to comment on the existence of the Source of all being?

Maersk: That is like asking doctors what makes them qualified to practice medicine. When someone says they believe in an imaginary friend they call "god," they are postulating a scientific hypothesis that there is a being answering to their description operating in the universe. Science identifies and monitors the things acting in the universe. So far, science has yet to find any evidence of the imaginary friend.

MA: So, you assume that believers conceive of God as an inter-galactic Big Foot somewhere out there?

Maersk: The folks gulled by theologians and priests claim that, in addition to galaxies and quantum fields and flowering plants, the universe also includes a mysterious being that listens to their conversations, intervenes in earthly affairs and is all-powerful (but not powerful enough to eliminate evil). This claim is a dangerous superstition and anyone who promotes it should be shamed into silence.

MA: Professor, I think your thesis of a god who is part of the furniture of the Universe is the real superstition and it is, in fact, the superstition underlying most attacks on the God revealed in Christianity. You could not have put the superstition better: God is a mysterious being that is part of the universe.

Maersk: What is your point? Just repeating the gist of what I said does not help your case. Let me ask you: Can you point to something out there like a distant galaxy and say, Oh, there's god? Gagarin already called your bluff on that one.

MA: Sorry. I assumed you had grasped the point I made. Obviously not. God is not a "thing" like everything else in the universe. Neither does God belong to a class or a kind. So, to think of God as a complex object that can be found somewhere in the universe if we look hard enough is to entertain a superstition. Rather, GOD is that which explains why anything at all exists because God is that which is Existence Itself.

At one level, our minds try to unify everything in the physical universe in terms of a unified field theory or a multiverse. At a more fundamental level, our minds recognize that the existence of the entire ensemble of existent beings calls for an ultimate unification, a source that grounds all of existence. We recognize this unification lies in the existence of the One that always IS.

This One which is also referred to as the Absolute or the Transcendent is not a "part" of the universe: it is what keeps the universe, or multiverse if you prefer, in being at every instant. We can speak of God acting in the universe only in the sense of holding everything in the universe in being.

I should clarify here that when we talk of something "existing" – be it you or I or the Higgs boson – we are talking of a concrete something that operates here and now with certain powers. We are not, in the manner of some philosophers, engaging in an abstract discussion of the behavior of logical propositions that involve the word "exists."

Maersk: This is all very poetic. But why should anyone, particularly a scientist, assume that you need an extra entity out there to do a superfluous job? The universe is doing just fine without someone to "hold it in being." Occam's Razor warns us against multiplying entities without necessity. As I just demonstrated, science shows how the universe can bring itself into existence. We don't need anyone else to claim credit!

MA: You did nothing of the sort. Your book and your presentation, like the ideas of Krauss, Hawking, Stenger and like-minded cosmologists, simply show that you know nothing about nothing.

Your mistake is an old one: It is the error of treating "nothing" as a kind of "something." Over the centuries, thinkers who have considered the concept of "nothing" have been careful to emphasize the point that "nothing" is not a kind of something. Absolute nothingness can never be the object of scientific inquiry because all such inquiry presupposes the existence of the object of study and of some order governing the behavior of the object. Science can only get to work once something exists. Consequently, the transition from nothingness to something lies forever beyond the purview of scientific methodology. The "nothing" discussed by contemporary cosmologists and quantum physicists always turns out to be "something" in disguise.

The vacuum is a very important idea in the quantum world. Yet, far from being absolute nothingness, it has its own structure. "According to modern physics," says an article in *Scientific American*, 'a vacuum isn't a pocket of nothingness. It churns with unseen activity even at absolute zero, the temperature defined as the point at which all molecular motion ceases. Exactly how much 'zero-point energy' resides in the vacuum is unknown. ... The conventional view is that the energy in the vacuum is miniscule."[74] In *Nothingness: The Science of Empty Space*, Henning Genz notes that there is no absolutely empty space: Even in the emptiest space permitted by the laws of Nature there are energy levels about which the energies of fields and particles fluctuate. [75]

Absolute nothingness means no laws, no vacuums, no fields, no energy, no structures, no physical or mental entities of any kind – and no "symmetries." It has no properties or potentialities. Absolute nothingness cannot produce something given endless time – in fact there can be no time in absolute nothingness. If at any point absolute nothingness was all there was, there is no conceivable way in which any universe or anything at all would ever exist.

I turn now to the idea that the emergence of the universe from "nothing" does not violate the principles of physics because the net energy of the universe is zero. This is an idea first floated by the physicist Edward Tryon,

---

74 Philip Yam, "Exploiting Zero-Point Energy", *Scientific American*, December 1997, 82.
75 Henning Genz, *Nothingness: The Science of Empty Space*, transl. Karen Heusch (Reading, MA: Perseus Press, 1999), 207.

who said he had shown that the net energy of the universe is almost zero, and there is therefore no contradiction in saying that it came to be out of nothing since it is nothing. If you add up the binding (attractive) energy of gravitational attraction, which is negative, and the rest mass of the whole mass of the universe, which is positive, you get almost zero. No energy then would be required to create the universe and therefore no creator is required.[76]

Regarding this and similar claims, the atheist philosopher J.J.C. Smart points out that the postulation of a universe with zero net energy still does not answer the question of why there should be anything at all. Smart notes that the hypothesis and its modern formulations still assume a structured space-time, the quantum field and laws of Nature. Consequently, these hypotheses neither address the question of why anything exists nor confront the question of whether there is an atemporal cause of the space-time universe.[77]

Keith Ward perceptively notes that "If ... there are quantum fluctuations, then one might say that the universe could come into existence out of 'nothing,' in the sense that it has come in a 'chance' way out of what physicists call a 'vacuum' (quantum fields in their ground or lowest energy state). However, this is all very far from 'absolute nothing.' There has to be a background space-time, to allow fluctuations to occur. There have to be quantum fields with very definite properties of energy, mass, and so on. The fact that these properties 'balance out' to give a zero sum is rather like the fact that if an accountant's books balance exactly, they end with a zero. An enormous amount of activity has taken place in the meanwhile, and an accountant's zero is totally different from the zero of a person who really has no money at all. Similarly, the cosmologist's 'zero-energy state,' with its

---

76   Edward Tryon, "Is the Universe a Vacuum Fluctuation?", *Nature*, 1973, Volume 246, 396–397.

77   J.J.C. Smart and John Haldane, *Atheism and Theism* (Great Debates in Philosophy) (Oxford: Blackwell Publishers, 2003), 228 ff.

perfect balance of gravitational field and kinetic energy and rest mass, is as far as one can get from absolute non-existence."[78]

In reviewing Krauss, David Albert observes that he cannot answer where *the underlying laws of relativistic quantum field theories governing the universe* came from "or of why the world should have consisted of the particular kinds of fields it does, or of why it should have consisted of fields at all, or of why there should have been a world in the first place. Period. Case closed. End of story."[79]

Maersk: Albert is a philosopher. Krauss is giving us a scientific argument. Philosophers do not know the science involved and so their arguments are a waste of time.

MA: Actually, Krauss is knowingly or unknowingly offering a philosophical argument. Actual nothingness is not something that science can quantify, measure or describe and so it cannot be the object of a scientific argument. But Albert is not just a philosopher. He is also a quantum physicist. Other scientists have also shown Krauss' fallacies. George Ellis, a collaborator of Hawking, was just as critical of Krauss' argument.

Ellis says, "Above all Krauss does not address why the laws of physics exist, why they have the form they have, or in what kind of manifestation they existed before the universe existed (which he must believe if he believes they brought the universe into existence). Who or what dreamt up symmetry principles, Lagrangians, specific symmetry groups, gauge theories, and so on? He does not begin to answer these questions. It's very ironic when he says philosophy is bunk and then himself engages in this kind of attempt at philosophy."[80]

---

78   Keith Ward, *God, Chance and Necessity* (Oxford: OneWorld, 1996), 39-40.

79   David Albert, "On the Origin of Everything", *New York Times*, March 23, 2012.

80   https://blogs.scientificamerican.com/cross-check/is-lawrence-krauss-a-physicist-or-just-a-bad-philosopher/

Maersk: I notice you have yet to address Stephen Hawking's widely accepted explanation for the origin of the universe.

MA: A lot of time and energy has been wasted on Hawking's speculations about the question of God. I say "wasted" because Hawking and several other cosmologists have wandered away from the world of scientific observation to a realm of mathematical abstractions that, in itself, has no bearing on the origin of fundamental realities. The situation is further aggravated by their reliance on arbitrary speculation and their incoherence even on basic starting-points such as time and nothingness.

Even if we accept Hawking's speculative and occasionally incoherent ideas at face value, they still leave unanswered the questions of where the laws of Nature (to the extent we know them) came from, how it is that energy exists and how the supra-physical came to be. In other words, even if we ignore the confusion inherent in many of his pronouncements on origins, we see that Hawking has not addressed the issues that matter in this area.

He was, of course, aware of at least one of these issues. At the end of *A Brief History of Time*, Hawking had asked, "Even if there is only one possible unified theory, it is just a set of rules and equations. What is it that breathes fire into the equations and makes a universe for them to describe? The usual approach of science of constructing a mathematical model cannot answer the questions of why there should be a universe for the model to describe. Why does the universe go to all the bother of existing?"[81]

This was a perceptive and forceful articulation of the fact that mathematical frameworks cannot explain the existence of the worlds they model. In his later more explicitly atheistic books, Hawking never sought to answer the questions he raised here. Of course, any serious attempt to address the question ends in the infinite Mind discovered by the pioneers of relativity and quantum theory.

---

81 Stephen Hawking, *A Brief History of Time* (New York: Bantam, 1988), 175.

Maersk: I have been very patient until now. But this is the final straw. Your comments about Hawking are just outrageous. Stephen Hawking was widely recognized as the greatest scientist since Einstein. Your attempted criticisms simply expose your crass ignorance about all things science.

MA: I hope you are not trying to use an argument from authority here – something which should be alien to science. Whatever Hawking had to say must be judged on its merits as an argument not by his stature as a scientist. My comments have been on his philosophical premises and not his scientific claims.

About the comparison with Einstein, Hawking himself told *Time* magazine that the statement about him being the greatest scientist since Einstein is "rubbish" and the result of "mere media hype." He certainly made notable contributions with his insights into singularities and black holes. His gift for popularizing science for the masses is evidenced by the success of his best-selling books. And his perseverance in the face of huge physical challenges makes him an inspiration to people in every walk of life.

But we should remember that there were three Stephen Hawkings: the scientist, the popularizer of science and the celebrity. Given that there was an overlap between the three, it is important to distinguish which Hawking is speaking when we consider his statements. Charles Seife offers a handy overview of all three in his book *Hawking Hawking*.

With regard to his scientific contributions, Seife writes, "As a scientist, Hawking the symbol was supposed to be a lone genius who towered over his peers from his wheelchair, working to fulfill Einstein's dream of a theory of everything." But "the authentic Hawking was just one bright star in the constellation of scientists in the United Kingdom, the United States and the Soviet Union who were transforming general relativity and cosmology in the 1960s and 1970s; some of Hawking's most important contributions to physics were collaborative rather than solo achievements. ... By the time he became an international celebrity in the late 1980s, his most important scientific achievements were well behind him."[82]

In a review of Seife's book, Bernard Carr, Hawking's student and close friend of 40 years offers a different view while noting that Hawking's main discoveries were mathematical rather than physical: "Hawking made many important contributions: the singularity theorem, the black-hole area theorem, the laws of black-hole mechanics, black-hole radiation, inflationary fluctuations, and the no-boundary proposal. ... He never received the Nobel Prize because the existence of Hawking radiation is still not experimentally confirmed; and some of his discoveries might be regarded as mathematical rather than physical."[83]

John Barrow, a fellow student of Hawking and a Cambridge colleague, said, "To compare Hawking to Newton or Einstein is just nonsense. There is no physicist alive who compares to Einstein or Bohr in ability. But those rather grottily researched biographies in *A Brief History* do rather invite you to put Hawking in the same sequence. In a list of the 12 best theoretical physicists of this century, Steve would be nowhere near."[84]

Then there is the view of his peers. "In 1999," writes Seife, "the magazine *Physics World* asked some 250 physicists around the world to name the five physicists, living or dead, who had made the most important contributions to physics. ... Hawking, with a couple of dozen others, such as Martin Rees and John Wheeler, wound up at the bottom of the list, each with a single vote. It was an honor merely to be included, but the poll left little doubt that, generally, physicists didn't think his work to be in the same league as a Newton or an Einstein or even a Dirac, no matter what impression the mass media gave."[85]

---

82 Charles Seife, *Hawking Hawking* (New York: Basic Books, 2021), 44.
83 https://inference-review.com/article/underselling-hawking
84 Cited in Charles Seife, op cit., 178.
85 Charles Seife, op cit., 110.

Nature editor Philip Ball said,

> "Hawking did not really produce any important scientific work after *A Brief History*; a decade later he was left behind by a new generation of theoretical physicists. Towards the end of his career, he would float half-baked but attention-grabbing ideas. In 2004, he announced that he'd 'solved a major problem in theoretical physics' – the black hole information paradox. But all he'd done was to finally convince himself of what many others already believed: that he'd been wrong to think information was erased by black holes.[86]

The scientific community's due diligence mechanism for recognizing true scientific discoveries is the Nobel Prize. Hawking said more than once that he would have won the Nobel if one of his theories would have been verified which they were not. Hawking's colleague Roger Penrose received the Nobel in 2020 "for the discovery that black hole formation is a robust prediction of the general theory of relativity." But this was for a discovery he made in 1964, a year before he met Hawking.

Maersk: Great evasive maneuver. You are changing the subject and launching personal attacks because you know that Hawking's no-boundary origin account of the universe decimated any role for your deity. But the jig's up. It's game over for you unless you can speak to his science.

MA: Evasive? Game over? I just didn't want to bore the Court with a failed hypothesis. But since you will not take "no" for an answer, I have no choice but to dig up the relics of a proposal that has long since been taken off life-support.

On the question of God's existence, Hawking's thought wandered through three phases. In each phase, he claimed to have dispensed with the need for a Creator by finding an alternate explanation for the existence of the cosmos.

---

86   https://www.prospectmagazine.co.uk/culture/37375/the-mind-of-god-the-problem-with-deifying-stephen-hawking

In the first phase (*The Brief History of Time*), he floated the no-boundary proposal for the universe that you summarized and that I will be discussing in detail; in the second, he hitched himself to the then-popular (but now deceased) M Theory. In the third phase he adopted a top-down view of the universe which astonishingly argues for a "a subtle backward-in-time element into cosmological theory" whereby "the act of observation today retroactively fixes the outcome of the big bang 'back then.'"[87] Not without reason, this last approach has been described as "pseudo-scientific rambling," unsupported as it is by any kind of evidence.

We might call these phases the early Hawking, the later Hawking and the much-later Hawking.

From the start, it was obvious that none of his alternate explanations were coherent let alone cogent although the no-boundary idea was ingeniously constructed out of disparate ideas that had never been combined before. The no-boundary proposal never caught fire with his professional colleagues but Hawking himself stuck to it to the bitter end (accompanied, by Jim Hartle who developed the proposal with him), As Hawking's collaborator Neil Turok said, "The idea has never been accepted. I would say 90% of cosmologists or theoretical scientists don't even form an opinion. Of those who do, 90% of them would say they probably don't agree with it, or there was some problem with it."[88]

The problem with his thinking in this and other areas was simply this: he tried to solve questions in physics using metaphysics and questions in metaphysics using physics. This problem was especially pronounced in his pronouncements on time, existence and "nothing."

Our foundational framework in matters of science and philosophy has to be the set of pre-philosophical, pre-scientific truths known by all sane, rational human beings (for instance, that the world exists). These are

87   Thomas Hertog, *On the Origin of Time* (London: Penguin Random House, 2023), 254.
88   Cited in Charles Seife, op cit., 122.

indemonstrable but undeniable. I will get to these later but here my concern is what our witness calls "the science."

Stephen Hawking's No-Boundary Proposal

How did the universe originate? How did space and time originate? According to the Big Bang theory, at its origin the universe existed in its smallest possible state which means a quantum state. The quantum processes in operation at its earliest state presumably gave rise to today's larger universe which follows classical laws. An understanding of the original quantum processes could then help explain what we see today.

Boundary conditions

Of particular interest are the boundary conditions of the cosmos. Boundary conditions are a snapshot of a physical system at a particular point. The combination of boundary conditions and the laws of Nature discovered by science help furnish a mathematical model of any such system and this includes the universe. With the mathematical model we can make predictions about past and future states of the system.

Hawking sought to construct a mathematical model of the universe as a whole but this required knowing the boundary conditions at its origin. This was a problem because Hawking with Roger Penrose had previously shown that the universe had a beginning in time in the event popularly known as the Big Bang. The Big Bang was a singularity where the laws of physics break down. Hence the boundary conditions at that point were out of reach – which means no complete mathematical model of the universe was possible.

The wave function of the universe

But because the universe was in a quantum state at the start, Hawking and his collaborator Jim Hartle felt that it may be possible to represent it in terms of its wave function, a mathematical construct used in quantum physics. A wave function of a quantum particle provides information on its position and momentum in terms of probabilities.

But when it comes to the wave function of the universe, we are faced with the problem that such a mathematical representation should conform to the conflicting canons of quantum mechanics and relativity, the realms of the very small and the very large. Unfortunately, the laws applicable to these two realms have yet to be reconciled. And the quest to unify the two fundamental theories has become a tower of Babel with theorists from both sides speaking different languages.

Not to be daunted, Hawking plunged in with a novel extrapolation quarried from ideas in both relativity and quantum physics. It has been called an Euclidean quantum gravity theory because it assumes a unification of the quantum and the classical realms. And it claimed to eliminate "boundary conditions" and was therefore called the "no-boundary proposal." The specialized terms used to describe his theory, terms like "boundary conditions," and "sum over histories," "path integral," "wave function" and "imaginary time," did not mean what they do in ordinary usage.

In the first version of the proposal, Hawking leveraged a particular application of the idea of the wave function pioneered by his long-time hero Richard Feynman. Feynman wanted a visual representation of the mathematics of the wave function in quantum mechanics. He came up with a way to describe all possible paths taken by a quantum particle traveling from A to B at a particular time technically called "the sum over histories." With this tool-set, he sought to predict the likely behavior of quantum systems.

What Feynman did with quantum particles, Hawking sought to apply to the universe. As Hawking's student and collaborator Thomas Hertog pithily put it: "The wave function of a particle in quantum mechanics involves an amalgam of all possible paths. Likewise, the wave function of the universe in quantum cosmology describes a collection of all possible expansion histories."[89]

"Imaginary" "Time"

Moving from the quantum state to a classical universe involved speculative applications of esoteric mathematics and geometry. This meant Hawking had to move from an Euclidean space-only quantum state to the space-time of General Relativity that is described by Lorentzian geometry. Also deployed, to the confusion of most readers, was the idea of "imaginary time."

"Imaginary time" is a mathematical device used for certain calculations in quantum mechanics where (for the purposes of those calculations) time is treated as another dimension of space with the understanding that this is purely a mathematical device without any physical counterpart. Theorists did not suggest that there was any dimensional change involved where time actually "became" space. Once the calculation was completed, time would return to its normal standing. No one ever thought of "imaginary time" as an actual dimension like time or space. Until Hawking.

Writes Hertog, "Adding paths in real times simplifies the complicated Feynman sum. At the end of the calculation, physicists then rotate one of the space dimensions back into real time and read off the resulting probabilities for the particle to do this or that. But Jim and Stephen didn't want to rotate back to real time. The audacity of their no-boundary proposal was that when it comes to the origin of the universe, the transformation of time into space isn't merely a calculational trick but fundamental. The story of the universe, the theory holds, is that once upon a time there was no time."[90]

---

89 Thomas Hertog, op cit.,126.
90 Ibid., 98.

Hawking turned to this mathematical procedure of turning real time into imaginary time in order to derive a wave function for the universe that eliminates singularities. By multiplying the time coordinate with the square root of a negative number (minus one) it becomes a coordinate of space, a direction in space. In this mathematical framework (and only in this framework), the distinction between time and space disappears and so does the idea of a beginning of time. This four-dimensional space is compared to a two-dimensional globe which has no boundaries or beginnings. A sphere has no singular points. Although there is a beginning of real time in the Big Bang, the laws governing this beginning are determined in imaginary time – and so no appeal has to be made to any external agency for the event. A universe of finite size emerges from a quantum fuzz.

In Hawking's own words

Hawking's first version of his Euclidean quantum gravity theory, introduced in *A Brief History of Time* (1988), was tentative:

> For the purposes of calculation, one must measure time using imaginary numbers, rather than real ones. This has an interesting effect on space-time: the distinction between time and space disappears completely. ... In Euclidean space-time there is no difference between the time direction and directions in space. ... Because one is using Euclidean space-times, in which the time direction is on the same footing as directions in space, it is possible for space-time to be finite in extent and yet to have no singularities that formed a boundary or edge. ... I'd like to emphasize that this idea that time and space should be finite without a boundary is just a *proposal*: it cannot be deduced from some other principle. Like any other scientific theory, it may initially be put forward for *aesthetic or metaphysical reasons*, but the real test is whether it makes predictions that agree with observation. ...

In real time, the universe has a beginning and an end at singularities that form a boundary to space-time and at which the laws of science break down. But in imaginary time, there are no singularities or boundaries. So maybe what we call imaginary time is really more basic, and what we call real is just an idea that we invent to help us describe what we think the universe is like. But according to the approach I described in Chapter 1, a scientific theory is just a mathematical model we make to describe our observations: it exists only in our minds. So it is meaningless to ask: which is real, "real" or "imaginary" time? It is simply a matter of which is the more useful description.[91]

But what he had described as "just a proposal" was soon touted as a mainstream account of cosmic origin. In a lecture on the "beginning" of time in 1996, he said,

The universe has not existed forever. Rather, the universe, and time itself, had a beginning in the Big Bang, about 15 billion years ago. The beginning of real time, would have been a singularity, at which the laws of physics would have broken down. Nevertheless, the way the universe began would have been determined by the laws of physics, if the universe satisfied the no boundary condition. This says that in the imaginary time direction, space-time is finite in extent, but doesn't have any boundary or edge. The predictions of the no boundary proposal seem to agree with observation.[92]

By the time he wrote *The Grand Design* (2010), Hawking's "proposal" had hardened into dogma:

In the early universe – when the universe was small enough to be governed by both general relativity and quantum theory – there were

---

91   Stephen Hawking, *A Brief History of Time*, op cit., 134-137, 139.

92   https://www.hawking.org.uk/in-words/lectures/the-beginning-of-time

effectively four dimensions of space and none of time. That means that when we speak of the "beginning" of the universe, we are skirting the subtle issue that as we look back toward the very early universe, time as we know it does not exist! We must accept that our usual ideas of space and time do not apply to the very early universe. … The realization that time can behave like another direction of space means one can get rid of the problem of time having a beginning in a similar way in which we got rid of the edge of the world."[93]

When the smoke cleared, the universe that emerged had a beginning in "real time" but no beginning in "imaginary time. It had no boundary conditions and was governed strictly by laws. Hawking had waved a wand and created a magical world of imaginary time where the beginning of history became geography.

The magical element was unmistakable. As Hertog said, "Physicists complained that Stephen's use of Euclidean geometries was *like magic.* … Why should time behave in such strange ways? Part of the problem was that the Euclidean framework isn't a fully fledged quantum theory of gravity but a semiclassical amalgam of classical and quantum elements put together *without clear mathematical guidelines.*"[94]

The Scientific Demise of the No-Boundary Proposal

Despite all the hype and hoopla, however, the "no-boundary" proposal could not survive serious scientific scrutiny.

Of course, the idea of time being a dimension of space is inherently incoherent. But quite apart from this obvious fact, the no-boundary proposal – along with the Euclidean quantum gravity theory and the esoteric mathematics underlying it – was shredded by the cosmological evidence. What

---

93   Stephen Hawking and Leonard Mlodinow, *The Grand Design*, op cit., 134.

94   Thomas Hertog, op cit.,100.

began with a bang ended up with a whimper. The no-boundary idea turned out to be a scientific dead-end.

Early on, George Ellis, Hawking's fellow-student and co-author with him of *The Large-Scale Structure of Spacetime*, had already pointed to the foundational problems with the no-boundary proposal. *The Brief History of Time*, Ellis wrote,

> does indeed describe a universe without a beginning in the ordinary sense of the word, although time does have a beginning (where there is a transition from this strange 'Euclidean state' to a normal space-time structure). Attractive as this, one must be concerned about its foundations.

> Firstly, such proposals suppose unraveling some of the underlying conundrums of quantum theory that have not yet been solved in a satisfactory manner (specifically, the role of an observer in quantum theory, and what determines the collapse of the wave function, which is an essential feature of measurement in quantum theory). These do not arise as significant problems in the context of laboratory experiments, but become substantial difficulties in the context of applying quantum theory (which is usually applied to submicroscopic systems) to the universe as a whole.

> Secondly, we certainly cannot test the Wheeler-DeWitt equation underlying quantum cosmology: we have to accept it as a huge extrapolation of existing physics … untestable in its own right. Even some of the underlying concepts (such as "the wave function of the universe") have a questionable status in this context (for they are associated with a probabilistic interpretation which may not make sense when applied to a unique object, namely the universe).[95]

---

95   George F.R. Ellis in Roy Abraham Varghese, ed. *Great Thinkers on Great Questions* (Oxford: OneWorld, 1998), 176-7.

Quantum gravity theorist C.J. Isham had pointed out that "the interpretation of probability as applied to a *single* electron remains as mysterious as ever." If this is the case, wrote Stanley Jaki, "the handling of the Universe in terms of the same probability functions should seem preposterous."[96]

Hawking never seemed to distinguish hard fact from sheer speculation. Ethan Siegel remarks that

> Hawking's no-boundary proposal is speculative and unproven, yet Hawking will often (including in *A Brief History Of Time*) speak about it with the same certainty he'd speak about black holes. Ideas like baby Universes, a unifying theory of everything, and higher dimensions may be common, but they lack evidence. In many senses, they remain untested, while in others, the evidence that could support them has failed to materialize. This has never stopped Hawking from touting them, much to the chagrin of careful scientists everywhere. Unproven ideas should never be a substitute for legitimate facts, yet Hawking, in every book he ever wrote, never tells you when he strays from the confirmed-and-validated into this speculative realm, particularly where his own ideas are concerned. To an insider, it feels like the definition of selling out: using your fame and clout for self-promotion, rather than to educate and elucidate humanity's knowledge and the limits of that knowledge.[97]

Above all, the death knell for the no-boundary proposal was sounded by the unfolding body of data from cosmology. Hertog, who was Hawking's final collaborator, elaborated on the progressive unraveling of the theory in his 2023 book *On the Origin of Time*:

---

96 Stanley Jaki, *Is There a Universe?* (Liverpool, UK: Liverpool University Press, 1993), 51.

97 https://www.forbes.com/sites/startswithabang/2018/03/14/the-4-scientific-lessons-stephen-hawking-never-learned/#62ef57077125

There is a problem … The theory appears to say that we should find ourselves in a universe where we can't be. Not surprisingly, then, most scientists have found it hard to seriously engage with no-boundary creation. And this has been the elephant in the room ever since Jim and Stephen put forward their model of cosmogenesis.[98]

As a theory that unifies dynamics with initial conditions, the no-boundary hypothesis has a certain time asymmetry built in, with a smooth inflationary birth at one end of cosmological history and an open-ended disordered state at the end. The arrow of time implied by the no-boundary proposal, however, appears nowhere near strong enough to breathe life into the universe. … The no-boundary hypothesis may be elegant, profound, and beautiful, but it doesn't work. The second law of thermodynamics wins.[99]

In 1997, Stephen and Neil Turok attempted to rescue the no-boundary theory by augmenting it with the anthropic condition that "we" should exist in the universe. However they found that that stipulation barely made a difference; the theory complemented with the anthropic principle ended up predicting a universe with just one galaxy – ours – and nothing in any way resembling a universe teeming with galaxies like the one we observe.[100]

Another Hawking colleague, cosmologist Andrei Linde "rallied against the no-boundary hypothesis on the grounds that it predicted no observers at all. A no-boundary origin selected the feeblest possible wisp of inflation, giving birth to an empty, lifeless cosmos."[101]

Neil Turok, who formerly worked with Hawking on the no-boundary proposal, observed in 2019 that "previous models [such as Hawking's

98   Thomas Hertog, op cit., 122.
99   Ibid., 124.
100   Ibid., 127.
101   Ibid., 30.

no-boundary idea] were 'beautiful proposals seeking to describe a complete picture of the origin of spacetime,' but they don't hold up [to later mathematical assessments]. 'Unfortunately, at the time those models were proposed, there was no adequately precise formulation of quantum gravity available to determine whether these proposals were mathematically meaningful.' The new research, outlined in a paper called 'No smooth beginning for spacetime,' demonstrates that a universe emerging smoothly from nothing would be 'wild and fluctuating,' strongly contradicting observations, which show the universe to be extremely uniform across space. 'Hence the no-boundary proposal does not imply a large universe like the one we live in, but rather tiny curved universes that would collapse immediately.'"[102]

The Intrinsic Incoherence of the No-Boundary Proposal

Although Hawking's no-boundary proposal died on the operating table of science, it continues to survive as a zombie on the Internet and in his best-selling books – as is evident from your brandishing it before us here.

Now scientific theories come and go when they are slain by the evidence. But the no-boundary proposal should have been rejected right from the start since it was obviously and hopelessly unintelligible even on the face of it. What is astonishing is not the fact of its scientific obituary but the fact that it was taken seriously at all.

With a straight face, the author of *The Brief History of Time* is telling us that "time" can mean whatever he wants it to mean. How else can we explain such of his statements as "time can behave like another direction of space?"

Yet all of us know for a fact that we experience time as something irreducibly different from a dimension in space. To move up or down, to the right or the left is to talk of space. To talk of today and tomorrow, before

---

102   https://insidetheperimeter.ca/things-didnt-go-so-smoothly-at-the-big-bang/

and after, is to talk of time – and this experience of things taking place in a sequence is not an illusion.

Time springs from agents, events and relationships of cause and effect brought about by agents (in David Braine's definition, an agent is anything with the active power to cause effects – from particles to organisms). There is no time independent of agents and events. Every law is derived from the observation of events and agents. We can talk about the "block universe" or of different theories of time but we cannot deny the reality of change and the succession of time in our experience.

Space is a path along which matter can move (matter being shorthand for energy). Dimension is the direction in which this motion is possible.

Any claim of actually turning time into space is as far-fetched as the idea that, at some point, history becomes geography. It is a classic case of what they call a category mistake (e.g., the triangle is in a good mood today). And the inescapable contradiction inherent in talking of a space-only state that existed *before* time is clear from our having to say "before." And, even if the Hawking theory was taken seriously, it is burdened by an unanswerable question: how did "time" emerge from space?

The scientist best known for his work on space and time, Albert Einstein, highlighted the mystery of time. We see this from his discussion with Rudolf Carnap:

> Einstein said that the problem of the Now worried him seriously. He explained that the experience of the Now means something special for man, something essentially different from the past and the future, but that this important difference does not and cannot occur within physics. That this experience cannot be grasped by science seemed to him a matter of painful but inevitable resignation.[103]

---

103   R. Carnap, *The Philosophy of Rudolf Carnap*, P. A. Schilpp, ed., (La Salle, IL: Open Court, 1963) 37.

New York University philosopher of physics Tim Maudlin, author of *Philosophy of Physics – Space and Time*, says,

> [Some physicists say] that time is just an illusion, that there isn't really a direction of time, and so forth. I myself think that all of the reasons that lead people to say things like that have very little merit, and that people have just been misled, largely by mistaking the mathematics they use to describe reality for reality itself. If you think that mathematical objects are not in time, and mathematical objects don't change—which is perfectly true—and then you're always using mathematical objects to describe the world, you could easily fall into the idea that the world itself doesn't change, because your representations of it don't."

About Hawking's comments on philosophy and physics, Maudlin says, "Hawking is a brilliant man, but he's not an expert in what's going on in philosophy ... I think he just doesn't know what he's talking about. ... I think he's just . . . uninformed."[104]

In both *A Brief History of Time* and *The Universe in a Nutshell* Hawking describes himself as a logical positivist. He seemed unaware that positivism – the idea that only what is scientifically verifiable is real – is among the most discredited philosophies of recent times. Sir Alfred Ayer, the father of logical positivism in the English-speaking world, said in an interview that "Logical Positivism died a long time ago. I don't think much of *Language, Truth and Logic* [Ayer's own book introducing logical positivism] is true. ... I think it's full of mistakes which I spent the last fifty years correcting or trying to correct."[105] Separately, Ayer rejected Hawking's "space becomes time" claim. "Hawking's

---

104   https://www.theatlantic.com/technology/archive/2012/01/what-happened-before-the-big-bang-the-new-philosophy-of-cosmology/251608/

105   Sir Alfred Ayer in Roy Abraham Varghese, ed. *Great Thinkers on Great Questions* (Oxford: OneWorld, 1998), 49.

tendency to oscillate at least between realistic and operational diction has one unhappy consequence for him," wrote Ayer. "He just passes over the promotion of Euclidean space-time *from a mathematical device to a physical reality*. I am not convinced that the reasons he adduces for making this promotion are sufficient."[106]

The inherent incoherence of the no-boundary proposal was most trenchantly exposed by Oxford philosopher Keith Ward whom I have already cited:

> Time itself is signified by a complex number (part of which involves an imaginary number, such as the square root of a negative number), and it becomes the internal property of a set of three-spaces. I do not think that this can be called 'time' at all in any sense we can recognize it. *What has happened is that the phenomenological reality of time has been transformed into a mathematical variable, and then treated as a pure abstraction which, far from giving the 'true reality' of time, has less and less relation to the real time one started from. ...*
>
> One is dealing with a purely mathematical idea of some complexity, which does not in any sense precede a more definite structure of physical entities, and which can have no causal relation to any such structure. There is a great danger here of confusing the mathematical (the abstract, timeless and relational) with the physical (the causal and temporal). This is ... the fallacy of regarding numbers as physical entities. ... It treats purely mathematical relationships or abstract concepts as though they were literally pictures of physical entities. ... A 'dimension' in mathematics is simply a co-ordinate and it does not necessarily have any physical correlate. A 'dimension' in the physical realm is an extension at right angles to another extension. If time is regarded as a dimension, this is quite a different, analogical sense of 'dimension'... [that] may threaten to produce misleading metaphors

---

106   https://www.lrb.co.uk/the-paper/v11/n01/a.j.-ayer/someone-might-go-into-the-past

(of time as a sort of successionless state, a spatialized time)... The metaphor has replaced the reality, and a fallacy has been taken to be a profound truth.[107]

Maersk: As a non-scientist you have no standing to speak about scientific matters. Lawyers are known for obscuring the facts, often dishonestly. We scientists just go with the facts. That is our weakness which you are now exploiting to your advantage. I would like to ask you how you can claim to speak with any credibility on any scientific issue.

MA: Einstein said the man of science is a poor philosopher.[108] For the most part, you, like the scientists you cited, have been speaking on philosophical matters using philosophical arguments without knowing that is what you are doing. The veneer of science has simply been a smokescreen. As scientists, none of you have any special competence as philosophers and your arguments are going to be judged in terms of how they measure up against universal fundamental insights. I am not a scientist, but I am just as competent as any other rational person in judging the soundness of claims you make relating to these insights.

A scientist can engage in science and mathematics because there are certain underlying "rules" that we all take for granted that cannot be proved or disproved by either science or mathematics – or even philosophy for that matter. But these are not arbitrary rules. Rather, they are built on fundamental insights that we recognize to be true and cannot reject without contradicting ourselves. They underlie science and mathematics and philosophy and are independent of all three.

For instance, we have a fundamental insight that the world exists. Science has to assume this to be the case: It cannot disprove it because every experiment would have to assume that there is a world in which we can perform

---

107   Keith Ward in Roy Abraham Varghese, ed. *Great Thinkers on Great Questions* (Oxford: OneWorld, 1998), 41-2.

108   Albert Einstein, *Out of My Later Years* (New York: Philosophical Library, 1950), 58.

the experiment. Another such insight is that anything capable of forming an intention has an intelligence of some kind.

Maersk: So, you are saying that religionists can make any claim they want and justify it on the grounds that it's somehow outside science and therefore "philosophical." In short, anything goes! This is precisely why you need science to separate the wheat from the chaff.

MA: You still do not get the point of Einstein's comment about scientists being poor philosophers. Science has no bearing on questions concerning non-physical realities if such exist because the physical sciences are concerned strictly with the measurement of quantities whether it be at the quantum or the cosmic, the cellular or the genomic levels.

The physical sciences – physics, chemistry, biology – cannot pronounce on anything that is not strictly quantitative, although scientists often do. But then they speak as philosophers and sometimes as very poor philosophers. Many of the anti-God crusaders among scientists have a limited idea of what is happening at the interface between physical science and foundational supra-physical realities. And many of them use their superficial understanding to reach negative philosophical conclusions about religion.

But once we understand what is happening in modern science – in cosmology, genomics, neuroscience, and the like – we see that both the assumptions and the results of modern science point to a mind-ish universe and therefore an infinite Mind.

Maersk: Surely you are joking. Today's scientists decry any attempt to import religion into science.

MA: We are not talking about importing religion but about considering what is obvious in natural phenomena. As I have pointed out, the scientists who laid the foundations for modern physical science – relativity and quantum physics – took an entirely different view from that of many of today's New Atheist scientists. And these foundation builders are the ones who made the breakthroughs that even skeptics take as a starting point in any advanced work in science.

Their discoveries led them to recognize the reality of an infinite Mind. Their reasoning shows that they were more philosophically sophisticated than the scientists you cite.

In any case, there have been no fundamental breakthroughs comparable to relativity and quantum theory although there is no shortage of speculation. John Horgan's *The End of Science* was controversial but it is hard to disagree with his evaluation two decades after the book's appearance that there have been "no great 'revelations or revolutions' – no insights into nature as cataclysmic as heliocentrism, evolution, quantum mechanics, relativity, the big bang."[109]

In an exchange with Lawrence Krauss, Horgan unmasks today's preference for substance over speculation: "You and/or your popularizing colleagues—Hawking, Greene, Kaku, Susskind—are still marketing various unsubstantiated versions of inflation, multiverse theories, string theory, vacuum energy, anthropic principle, etc. What's ironic is that, although you don't have any more evidence for these speculations, your marketing of them has become more aggressive."[110]

I guess we might say that modern science has gone through three ages – *the golden age of discovery*, the era of relativity and quantum physics and the Standard Model, of cosmology and genetics and evo-devo; *the age of application*, the era of the technological marvels of modernity built on the discoveries of the prior era; and *the age of speculation*, the era of strings and holographic models and the multiverse, where there is no possibility of confirmatory evidence. Incremental discoveries and applications, of course, continue but "Big Science" today is speculative and proudly so.

---

109 https://blogs.scientificamerican.com/cross-check/was-i-wrong-about-8220-the-end-of-science-8221/

110 https://blogs.scientificamerican.com/cross-check/is-lawrence-krauss-a-physicist-or-just-a-bad-philosopher/

Maersk: All scientific breakthroughs started as speculation. The same is true of today's theories.

MA: The cosmologists and physicists you cited earlier have fled from the hard data of observation and preen and prance in the fever swamps of speculation. But those who step into that swamp tend to sink and suffocate. I have no interest in sharing their fate. So, if someone is going to talk about the universe bringing itself into existence, I am going to insist that they only give me answers that rest on available evidence and measurable data. Any problem with that?

Maersk: Of course, I have a problem with your silly restriction! Quantum physics is built on speculation. Most advancements in science were possible only because of speculation. This applies to the Landscape theory.

MA: Again, you are confusing the issue as fact-phobic speculators often do. Certainly, in scientific research you start off with guesses, hypotheses and sometimes wild speculation. But the goal is to get evidence that supports a theory. When the smoke clears there have to be data verifying the theory – or else you are not doing science.

Quantum physics is actually a good example of a scientific research program that is not only supported by evidence but has had significant real-world applications. In technology, arguably no other scientific theory has spawned as many applications as quantum mechanics. Modern inventions that owe their birth to quantum physics include the transistor, television, lasers, semiconductors, superconductors, cell phones, laptops and new forms of computing and communication. Nuclear power is one of the more awesome displays of quantum phenomena since radioactive decay is a quantum mechanical process.

Tim Maudlin points out that "quantum mechanics was developed as a mathematical tool. Physicists understood how to use it as a tool for making predictions, but without an agreement or understanding about what it was telling us about the physical world. ... Quantum mechanics was merely a calculational technique that was not well understood as a physical theory. Bohr and Heisenberg tried to argue that asking for a clear physical theory was something you shouldn't do anymore."[111]

But with today's speculators, it's all theory with no predictions. Russian physicist Lev Landau once said that cosmologists "are often in error but never in doubt." The smoke never clears. All the speculators can give us is smoke and mirrors! No hard facts, no …

Maersk: That is an egregious caricature! Give me one example from a serious scientist who has a problem with the Landscape/multiverse idea.

MA: That is easy. The two most famous critiques of string theory are Peter Woit's *Not Even Wrong* and Lee Smollett's *The Trouble with Physics*. The Landscape scientists admit that they do not have any hard evidence for their theories and no predictions they can make. In his review of the book by Leonard Susskind that popularized the Landscape, Woit noted that "The bottom line here is that Susskind is unable to come up with any remotely plausible way of ever getting any scientific predictions out of the string theory landscape framework, and yet he thinks it is a good idea to write a popular book designed to sell it to the public."[112] Things have not gotten any better: "23 years later, no one has a viable proposal for what this unique theory might be."[113]

Nobel physicist Sheldon Glashow says, "Sadly, I cannot imagine a single experimental result that would falsify string theory. I have been brought up to believe that systems of belief that cannot be falsified are not in the realm of science."[114]

---

111   https://www.theatlantic.com/technology/archive/2012/01/what-happened-before-the-big-bang-the-new-philosophy-of-cosmology/251608/

112   https://www.math.columbia.edu/~woit/wordpress/?p=307

113   https://www.math.columbia.edu/~woit/wordpress/?p=10327

114   https://physicsworld.com/a/still-not-even-wrong/

New Atheist Lewis Wolpert admits that "even if string theory provides an explanation for the laws of physics, and everything is essentially reducible to these laws, we are still left with the problem of where the strings came from, as well as their properties."[115]

Several recent books, for instance *The Dream Universe* by *Nature* editor David Lindley and *Farewell to Reality* by Jim Baggott, have shown that unverifiable speculation is increasingly replacing evidence-based science. Theoretical physicist Sabine Hossenfelder points out that

> In the foundations of physics, we have not seen progress since the mid 1970s when the standard model of particle physics was completed. Ever since then, the theories we use to describe observations have remained unchanged. ... But all shortcomings of these theories – the lacking quantization of gravity, dark matter, the quantum measurement problem, and more – have been known for more than 80 years. And they are as unsolved today as they were then. ... Instead of examining the way that they propose hypotheses and revising their methods, theoretical physicists have developed a habit of putting forward entirely baseless speculations. Over and over again I have heard them justifying their mindless production of mathematical fiction as "healthy speculation" – entirely ignoring that this type of speculation has demonstrably not worked for decades and continues to not work. There is nothing healthy about this. It's sick science. And, embarrassingly enough, that's plain to see for everyone who does not work in the field.[116]

---

115   Lewis Wolpert, *Six Impossible Things Before Breakfast* (London: Faber and Faber, 2006), 215.

116   https://iai.tv/articles/why-physics-has-made-no-progress-in-50-years-auid-1292#:~:text=The%20major%20cause%20of%20this,kept%20size%20and%20expenses%20manageable

Mathematics has its place in physics but let us not forget what Einstein said: "In so far as the propositions of mathematics refer to reality, they are not certain; and, as far as they are certain, they do not refer to reality."[117]

Maersk: I can see that you are going to keep throwing philosophy at me. But you still have not answered my earlier question, one that is fatal for all religionists: who made God?

MA: As a matter of fact, my opening statement pre-empted this misconceived question. Let me answer this objection once and for all.

Any "thing" that exists must have an explanation adequate to fully account for its existence either in itself or in something else. When I talk of a full explanation for its existence, I am not talking just about a scientific explanation. I am asking about its existential explanation. Scientific explanations can describe the immediate physically quantifiable factors responsible for your existence – you are the biological offspring of a human couple, you have a respiratory system, etc. But these quantifiable factors have their origin in other such quantifiable factors (your parents have their parents, your respiratory system is part of the anatomy that developed in humans, etc.) that have their origin in yet other factors and so on until you get to see that the real question is this – how did any of these physically quantifiable factors come to be? How is that these physically quantifiable factors EXIST? Science measures physically quantifiable factors, "quantities," and hence furnishes scientific explanations. But science cannot tell us how the quantities it measures exist, how, at an ultimate level, they came to exist or continue to exist. This is where scientific explanation comes to a halt and where we have to turn to existential explanation.

The only viable explanation – an existential explanation – for the existence of any one of the entities or all of the entities that make up the universe would be the existence of an ultimate uncaused Reality – a Reality that did not receive existence from anyone or anything else and can completely

---

117   Einstein, *Ideas and Opinions* (New York: Three Rivers Press,1954), 233.

explain its own existence. This self explanatory Reality – a Reality that explains its own existence – is commonly called "God" and is the existential explanatory ultimate demanded by all non self explanatory entities from sub atomic particles to galaxies. We do not reason from the fact that everything in the universe has a cause in space and time to the conclusion that the universe has a cause in space and time. Rather, everything in the universe is non self explanatory, which means that the explanation of the universe does not lie in itself but must lie in a self explanatory Reality.

Atheists will respond in several ways:

- Ultimately there has to be a stop to the chain of explanation and you have to accept an explanatory ultimate.

- This "explanatory ultimate" must be taken as "brute" and "unexplained."

- The postulation of an "ultimate uncaused Reality" is just as inexplicable as an eternally existing uncaused universe. It can be said that neither received existence from anything else.

- To say that God is self-explanatory does not add anything to the discussion because theists do not know what it means for God to be self-explanatory. Therefore, this thesis does not explain anything more than the thesis that there is an ultimate uncaused state of the universe.

- The most basic feature of the universe could be that it is an uncaused entity that explains everything else although it is itself unexplained. Theism and atheism are no different in that both start with unexplained facts that explain everything else.

Clearly, the theist and atheist can agree on one thing: If anything at all exists, there must be something preceding it that always existed. To the question, how did this eternally existing reality come to be, the answer is that it never came to be. It always existed. Take your pick: God or universe. Something always existed.

But there is a huge difference in what is being claimed.

The atheist says: There is no explanation for how anything got to be here.

The theist say: Yes, there is an explanation. This Explanation explains both Itself and everything that exists.

Maersk: We are going around in circles. Why should anyone believe there is such an explanation? You have not shown that to be the case. It is just as reasonable to believe that the universe always existed without explanation.

MA: You have actually made my case for me. Like any atheist, you cannot deny the need for an explanation without being self-contradictory. This is because the atheist tries to explain the universe by saying it has no explanation – *which is an explanation!*

Maersk: You are just playing word games.

MA: Hardly. Let us be frank here. Here are you are: A conscious, thinking person (namely someone with a self-identity). How did these realities of consciousness, thought and self-hood come about?

It is easy for you to mechanically say that "the universe always existed without explanation." But the idea that consciousness, thought and the self just exist without explanation is not a view that any rational person, let alone a scientist, can take. These phenomena are not theories. These are indisputable facts that we experience in a unique first-person fashion all the time. And they call for an existential explanation. The only possible explanation for them is an infinite-eternal Source of energy, life, consciousness and mind that always IS.

We know a cause from its effects. In the case of consciousness, thought, and the self, these are "effects" that we personally experience – and that obviously have to have an explanation that is enduring. The only possible explanation for these phenomena is infinite-eternal Mind.

So, we know of God existing from knowing that our own selves exist.

Maersk: That is a purely subjective conclusion.

MA: Of course, it is subjective. It is an objective conclusion I draw *as a subject*. A subject is an "I" capable of being conscious and thinking. My existence as an "I," as a subject, demonstrates beyond all possible doubt that I am existentially dependent, here-and-now, on a Mind that is infinite and eternal.

But the same train of thought also applies to the world.

Here, rationality comes to the forefront. Contrary to your protestations, there is a world of a difference between what theists and atheists claim about that which always exists.

The atheist says that the universe was eternally existing but we cannot explain how this eternally existing state of affairs came to be. It is inexplicable and has to be accepted as such. Although the lack of an explanation is impossible we simply have to embrace impossibility.

The theist, on the other hand, is adamant in pointing out that the chain of explanations does not and cannot rest on thin air, that there has to be an ultimate existential explanation and that this Explanation is Something that is not ultimately inexplicable, God. God's existence is not inexplicable to God, only to us (which is unsurprising given our limitations as finite beings). There is an inner logic to God's eternal existence. We know this to be the case because we constantly experience rationality in the universe – as witnessed by our communicating to each other now – and this is possible only if it is grounded in ultimate rationality.

In other words, the very real rationality that underlies our thinking and that we encounter in our study of a mathematically precise Universe could not have been generated by a rock. God is the Ultimate Rationality that is embedded in every dimension of being.

From this standpoint, the question "who created God?" or the problem of an infinite regress are seen to rest on misconceptions of what we are talking about here.

Both theists and atheists agree that there has to be an ultimate, uncaused and eternal source of all that exists. Consequently, it makes no sense to ask who "created" that source or to worry about an infinite regress: the source (whether one thinks it to be God or the universe), by its very nature as an explanatory ultimate, is neither itself created nor susceptible to an infinite regress. Even Bertrand Russell, in his debate on the existence of God with Frederick Copleston, was not naïve enough to ask, "Who created God?" He simply said "that the universe is just there and that's all." We should not ask how it came to be, in his view.

But to refuse to ask the question is a refusal to be rational. The atheist is, to be sure, free to be irrational. The theist, however, chooses to follow the path of rationality and sanity. In following this path, we find, as Copleston put it, that a solution to the problem of how finite beings exist cannot "be found anywhere else than in affirming the existence of the transfinite."[118]

---

118   F.C. Copleston, *Aquinas* (Baltimore, MD: Penguin Books, 1961), 127.

"CRUEL AND UNUSUAL"

Witness – Joyce MacIntosh (JM)

LH: My next witness is Professor Joyce MacIntosh, the author of *Evil-Doer – The God of Religion* which is widely considered to be the final word on the problem of evil. In this book, Professor MacIntosh has examined various ideas of a divine being and shown that the concept of an omnipotent, all-good being cannot be reconciled with the existence of evil. This should be obvious to all but Professor MacIntosh has taken what is intuitively obvious and translated it into a logical demonstration. Professor MacIntosh I invite you to the stand. Please tell us what you think of the Christian idea of god.

MacIntosh: I will explain why we KNOW with certainty that there is no Christian god.

Christians talk of god as infinitely good and infinitely powerful. If their god is truly good, it would at least do what a good human person would do. But despite its alleged infinite power there is suffering in this world. Their supposed god could eliminate such suffering with its power if it were minimally good. This means there is no such god. Or, if there is a god, it is one that gratuitously inflicts cruel and unusual punishment on its helpless, hapless creatures. It would be an evil doer. The god that Christians believe in is, in fact, an Evil Doer.

Now some Christians argue that their god only permits evil as opposed to perpetrating it and this lets it off the hook. But this does not work since god, according to them, is omnipotent. It could easily use its power to prevent the occurrence of evil. But since it does not in fact stop horrendous evils from occurring it is, in effect, perpetrating these evils.

Yet others have said that god permits evil to bring about a greater good. Anyone who makes this ludicrous argument should be asked if they will partake of their own medicine. Are they willing to go through torture or amputation or beheading or consumption by cannibals to support any cause, no matter how worthy?

A similar defense is the claim that we cannot see the big picture. Only god can. So we should give god the benefit of the doubt. All I can say to this callous copout is, tell that to the mother weeping over the daughter kidnapped by traffickers or the villagers mutilated by land-mines.

Finally, we have today's most common argument for defending the indefensible – the strange concoction called the freewill defense. Apparently this almighty, all-good god made its creatures with the ability to make free choices. This meant these creatures could choose to "friend" their god – or not. If they choose not to "friend" the deity, they will undergo terrible suffering in this world and endless suffering hereafter.

But this sorry argument, too, has such huge holes that it cannot be salvaged. Could not god have created a world in which its creatures do not have to make bad decisions? Or a world in which the deity could persuade them to "friend" it without being coercive? Is it worth letting the Holocaust take place to give creatures a "friending" capability? Human freewill, in any case, cannot account for the suffering caused by natural disasters or diseases like cancer or financial ruin.

But the ultimate Achilles Heel of the freewill defense is the fact that there is no such thing as freewill. All our decisions are products of physics and chemistry, heredity and environment, evolution and psychology. No one has shown this as clearly and cogently as Robert Sapolsky in *Determined – A Science of Life Without Freewill*. His book leaves the freewill debate in the dust. It has shown conclusively that we don't have "any freewill whatsoever."

One footnote to the freewill feint. Some of its defenders also hang on to the pre-scientific myth that the human race began with a couple: the Adam and Eve of *Genesis*. Apparently, they partook of a forbidden fruit and it was all downhill after that for their progeny. I said this idea is pre-scientific because it ignores what we know today about our true ancestors, the hominins. Even taken on its own terms, however, the story is nonsensical. Why should humans today pay the price for acts committed by ancestors in the distant past? What kind of deity would set up a system of this kind? Certainly not one that is all-good and all-powerful let alone all-wise (all attributes claimed by Christians about their deity).

LH: Brava, Professor Macintosh! I think you have gone to the root of our case – the sheer absurdity of the claims relating to the Christian God and the corresponding criminality of foisting this absurdity on both individuals and societies. I thank you for your concise but comprehensive articulation of the contradictions inherent in the Christian concept of God. You have blocked all the usual exits through which the theologians slither out. I see no way now for believers to credibly profess belief in their inane idea let alone inflict it on the rest of us. Your witness, Mr. Angelini.

MA: Professor Macintosh, let me start by saying that I am deeply disappointed with your catechism of gripes and swipes. It seems directed at a caricature created by your own imagination. I do not know which deity you had in mind but it is not the Christian God by any stretch. I found nothing new or enlightening in what you had to say.

But that is not the main problem with your argument. The issue, rather, is that you have not seriously engaged with the nature of the world in which we live, populated as it is by autonomous agents. Nor do you give any indication of having understood what is involved in the affirmation of an Ultimate Reality. Or of the God revealed in Christianity. There are no nuances, no acknowledgment of any complexity. It is fundamentalism of the atheist variety in which everything has to fit into simple black and white boxes.

LH: Objection, Your Honor. As seems to be his standard procedure, my opponent has reverted to personal attacks with no attempt to address the actual arguments laid out by my witness. This, of course, is what people do when the evidence is damning for their case – the best move is to divert attention from the evidence. But that is not going to work here. This is supposed to be a cross-examination, not a platform for personal attacks. Either he should address the damning evidence or just call it a day and stand down.

MA: Your Honor, this is mere posturing by my opponent. I was just getting started and, since he is afraid of what I am about to raise, he is trying to create his own diversion. These pointless interruptions are simply wasting our time.

Judge: Mr. HellMan, please let the Defendant's counsel complete his overview before you raise any further objections.

MA: Thank you, Your Honor. To continue, let me point out that, in a discussion like the present one, the two parties can be talking about entirely different matters. That is the situation here. One side is peering through a microscope at microbes and the other through a telescope at the stars. Not surprisingly, we are seeing different things.

In this examination, I am not trying to present the case for the Christian God. Our witnesses will do that. But I am trying to ensure that the Plaintiff's witnesses do not misrepresent what precisely is being claimed about the Godhead revealed in its fullness by Jesus of Nazareth. They are free to dispute the truth of our claim. But they are not free, at least from the standpoint of intellectual integrity, to distort the nature of what is being claimed.

I have already laid out common misconceptions about evil and the goodness of God. Professor Macintosh, your presentation is a textbook example of such misconceptions. I am not going to repeat what I have already said, but I will show how it applies to these somewhat elementary misconceptions.

What does it mean to say God is good? What is evil? Why is there evil in a world created by the infinite Source of all that exists, where "infinite" means no limitation whatsoever?

Now we know (or should know) that the existence of evil has no bearing on whether there is a Source of all being. The fact that you have a defective car does not mean that it did not have a manufacturer. Just the fact that we exist as conscious, cogitative agents tells us that there is an infinite-eternal Generator of being that is the fullness of existence.

We cannot speak of the Infinite-Eternal as morally good or evil because it is senseless to speak of That which IS the moral law making moral choices. It is the Absolute Good, the wellspring of all that is good, Goodness Itself.

But what is evil? As I have said, it is not a thing in itself but an absence of a good. There are two kinds of evil, physical evil and moral evil. A physical evil is morally neutral: by this we mean certain operations of the laws of Nature, like a hurricane or a liver failure, that result in suffering for living organisms. A moral evil, however, is an intentional and deliberate choice or act of a human person (or pure spirit) that violates the moral order – i.e., the goodness and love that is God. A morally evil choice corrupts our being and, in many cases, inflicts harm on other humans.

But why do we live in a world where physical and moral evils are possible? Why would the plenitude of perfections that is God create such a radically imperfect environment?

Here there are two ways to approach the question. The Plaintiff's counsel and his witness have tried to portray the Christian God as the responsible party. I leave aside for now their bizarre contention that the God they attack does not exist.

Christians and the whole human race have traditionally approached the problem from a different starting point than the Plaintiff. In both the Old and New Testaments, we see the human race rebelling against its Maker by pursuing evil. We see misdeed after misdeed and calamity after calamity issuing from this rebellion. We also see the Maker pleading with the rebels to refrain from evil-doing and to repent and return to him. We see the Israelites offering sacrifices in reparation for their rebellion and evil actions. And in Jesus we see the Maker offering up the reparation that will bring about reconciliation and redemption for the evil-doers if they are willing to repent. In parallel, the pre-Christian world religions show that the human race is aware of a self-created breach from the divine order for which it seeks to make reparation through sacrifice.

This is the state of the disunion – rebellion, evil-doing, and its consequences accompanied by repentance, reparation, reconciliation, redemption, and restoration.

Now, both Professor Macintosh and the Plaintiff's counsel have said that God could have created a world in which neither physical nor moral evils would occur. Since he did not create an evil-free world, he is ultimately responsible for any and every evil there is. No greater good could justify his allowing evil.

But such pontifications ring hollow from individuals who cannot create even an atom or a bacterium and yet confidently prescribe formulas for the construction of universes and human persons.

Is autonomy worth it? Is freedom good or bad? These same critics are up in arms about the need to allow unlimited freedom. But in the same breath, they castigate the Creator for endowing the human person with freewill. And then, in the self-same breath, they say we have no freewill.

MacIntosh: Freewill will not get you out of your fix. Even if I were to accept your claims of freewill and a creator deity, which I do not, the obvious question is: Why did your deity not create creatures incapable of evil intentions?

MA: The answer is simple. We never said freewill is the whole story. In fact, the real issue is not freewill alone but something more fundamental, something about the very inner being of the Godhead. Without a grasp of this dimension, we cannot see why pain, evil, and suffering exist. But, once we do grasp it, we also see why the possibility of evil was inescapable.

As I have said, we know from the universal intuition of humanity and the definitive revelation of Jesus that within the Godhead there is a Love that is beginning-less and endless. The mystery of love that we see in our own experience of one person giving of themselves to another – a phenomenon that cannot be described or explained in terms of quarks or genes – has its origin in the Ultimate Reality of Three-in-One. The infinite Mind and Will that is God is not a "what." It is possessed and exercised by Three Subjects who "possess" it through a "relationship" of giving, receiving, and sharing in full of the divine nature, of all that it means to be God.

The tri-personal God, the Trinity, is the Ultimate Reality: the fundamental structure underlying all that exists. It makes sense of all of human experience – for instance, of our experience as persons who are alive, who retain a continuing identity, who know and love and reproduce.

Knowing, loving and reproducing are inexplicable mysteries, but they become explicable once we recognize them as issuing from the Ultimate Act of infinite knowing, loving, and "producing" that is the Trinity.

Everything about the Godhead is a manifestation of its infinite Love. Love is not a sentiment or an emotion but self-giving, sacrifice, commitment, surrender, identification with the other. When you give of yourself to another you are united with the other.

But love, by its very nature, must be freely given. No giving, no love.

God is a relationship – a relationship of self-giving love – and the goal of God's creation is the manifestation of love: "The greatest of these is love." But, for the fullness of this manifestation, creation must culminate in creatures who can love, who can give of themselves. This is why God created. This is what God created.

The created world, then, is necessarily one that is intended to be an eco-system of love – love between God and his creatures and love among these creatures. But love must be freely given. The self has to be surrendered. The "I" has to be "Thine." To give oneself to God is to be one with God although we retain our identity as the "one" who is one with God. In being one with God, we find our fulfillment, our joy. This is the whole point of creation. This is where we find perfection.

But love is not programmable. It is not a puppet master's production. Love cannot be manufactured or controlled. It is not a question of whether you can create a free person who cannot do evil. It is a question of whether it is possible to have a pre-packaged love, a pre-built giving of self. The answer is no. There is no self-giving if it is not the self who is doing the giving. It takes two to love. If we are to love God, there must be a "we" that does the loving. "What you did not do for one of these least ones, you did not do for me." (*Matthew* 25:45). What YOU did not DO.

To with-hold love means to refuse union with the Alpha of our being who is also the Omega of our fulfillment. Nothing good can come from our refusal of the Good. And, in fact, this refusal is what we call evil.

Evil is not an abstraction, a hypothetical choice. It is essentially a refusal to love God. A rejection of God. The consequences are real. Hearts are broken. Blood is shed. Since we are not simply neurons and quarks but supra-physical beings, evil choices have an effect on the kind of persons we become. Every choice, every action has a consequence – not simply on the world but on ourselves. If it is an evil action, its consequences are magnified every time it is repeated until all of human history becomes an avalanche of evil. A torrent of torment.

At the same time, love is something that can change who we are as well. To be in love with God is to change the way we see things, the way we think, feel, choose, and act. Jesus shows us how to transform ourselves at all levels so that love can become what we are all about.

In contrast to all this, Professor Macintosh, you have visualized an artificial world of sophisticated puppets micromanaged by a Cosmic Programmer. But why go to all the trouble of building such a world? You cannot be happy if there is no "you" to be happy. And there can be no "you" if you are a being that is incapable of freely knowing and freely loving. Yes, there is no evil or suffering in a world of puppets for the same reason we cannot talk of a software program feeling pain or being malicious.

But the real world is many-splendored and far richer and deeper than a puppet paradise or a programmer's playground.

MacIntosh: What on earth do you mean by "real world"?

MA: The world of our actual everyday experience as opposed to the imaginary "in theory" worlds dreamed up by academics. The real world is a stupendously complex world of agents, powers, structures and intelligences:

> Whatever acts is an AGENT. Things with the ability to act run the whole gamut from energy fields to persons.

> POWERS range from the power of moving to the power of being aware (consciousness) to the power of thinking in concepts.

> STRUCTURES are everywhere from constellations of stars to genomes.

> Different kinds of INTELLIGENCE operate around us whether they be the embedded intelligence of a law of nature or a cell or the active intelligence of an animal.

Each one of these four dimensions of the world was brought into being and is sustained by the Infinite-Eternal. Not just energy and life but all consciousness and thought continue to exist only because God holds them in being.

Each dimension has its own hierarchy. For instance, there are agents with different kinds of powers – from an atom to a bacterium to a plant. Some agents are driven by laws of Nature. Others are autonomous and driven by urges and needs. Still others can make rational decisions and free choices.

The hierarchy of AGENTS comes to a climax in human persons and pure spirits (angels) who alone have the POWER and the INTELLIGENCE to freely know and love and form a STRUCTURE of loving communion.

It is this immeasurably intricate web of realities and relationships that is the necessary matrix for an ecosystem of union with the Godhead. It is the only possible pathway to the fullness of perfection, i.e., God, for finite beings.

Yet, by the very nature of love, it is possible to say "No." And to say "No" means to open the door to evil, pain, and suffering. But no one is responsible for the "No" and its consequences other than those who make that awful choice.

The God who loves us infinitely and unconditionally implores us not to take the path to perdition. He even offers himself as a sacrifice to rescue us from the consequences of our choices. But neither the divine plea nor the divine sacrifice can force us to choose the path of love. Love is something only we can offer – or withhold.

The issue is not one of God permitting evil so that a greater good might come about. For the infinite Lover the issue is one of not losing even one soul: The Good Shepherd will do everything in his Power to save even one lost sheep. But you and I remain the ultimate decision-makers. The price of refusal, the cost of evil, was paid on Calvary.

So, Professor Macintosh, now that I have presented the actual Christian understanding of God, would you care to retract your previous line of criticism?

MacIntosh: Are you kidding? Not a chance. Your idea of god is a fantasy but, even as a fantasy, it fails to answer the fundamental question I raised.

No greater good can justify the horrendous pain and suffering, the endless evil, that makes up human history. For your god to tolerate and permit all this – even though it is hypothetically in its power to prevent all evil – makes it the responsible party. The supremely guilty party. A fanciful ecosystem that will appear some day in some galaxy far away cannot justify even a single instance of evil-doing here-and-now let alone the never-ending cascade of evil that is our daily lot. Only a psychopath would believe in a god of this kind that inflicts cruel and unusual punishment on its creatures. To promote belief in it is simply evil.

MA: You seem determined not to leave your ivory tower version of a clockwork deity to examine either the world as it really is or the actual God worshipped by Christians. The early Christians who were ripped apart by animals and gladiators joyfully went to their deaths loving their enemies. The nuns ministering to the sick and the dying see their Savior in society's castaways. I find it disgusting that you would describe them as psychopaths. They had to personally experience the evil the critics talk about but have not themselves had to face. And yet right in the midst of their misery they encounter and bear witness to the infinite love of God.

You have focused solely on the wickedness in the world. You had not a word to say about the goodness and love that is also a feature of our fellow creatures. Nor do you talk about the exquisite beauty and the intricate order manifesting itself across the universe. Everything is darkness in your world. So, I am not surprised that you cannot bring yourself to allow any kind of balance in your narrative.

Tell me, Professor, how do you explain the existence of goodness and love in the world?

MacIntosh: There is nothing to explain. There are evolutionary advantages for people being altruistic.

MA: I would like to hear your evolutionary explanations. Please indulge me.

MacIntosh: Surely you know about the evolutionary roots of altruism. There is obvious altruism in social insects like ants, termites and bees in which the worker bees or ants forgo their own reproductive activity so as to serve a select few. In humans we have the maternal instinct and other instincts that are responsible for our actions. And much of what passes for "love" is simply lust and desire. No theological hocus-pocus is needed to explain what is a purely biological pattern.

MA: Well, surely you know that altruism poses a huge problem for evolutionary approaches since it contradicts the ideas of the survival of the fittest and the selfish gene. Everything we do from a Darwinian perspective is directed to enhance our own "fitness." From this standpoint, altruism even in the animal kingdom is a problem. Hence, there are the theories of kin selection in which you supposedly forego your reproductive success to enable that of relatives who share your genes. But that theory is fiercely disputed on the basis of contrary data. And you have other theories of group selection, reciprocal altruism and the like. So, claims about the "evolutionary roots of altruism" rest on agenda-driven speculation and little else.

The only thing we know for sure is that (a) there is altruistic behavior in humans and in certain animals and (b) altruism, as such, flies in the face of the idea that all our activities are driven by the need for survival. We also know that humans have moral codes, and we act on the basis of these codes.

The superstition that our selfish genes drive all our activities has long been discredited. Genes have no causal power. Genes do not think, plan or intend! Genes are not causes but templates activated by cell structures.

The evolutionary story leaves out what is most obvious in our experience: consciousness, conceptual thought and the self. Scientists and philosophers are increasingly aware that "consciousness" is as irreducible a reality as matter. The origin of language is now recognized to be the enigma it always was. Questions about the origins of conscious beings, intellective capabilities and the human self remain intractable. These can no longer be evaded as occurred in Darwin's day when it was airily assumed that these mysteries would be rapidly eliminated.

But these three realities cannot be denied without self-contradiction and it is in recognizing them that we see the true roots of altruism and self-sacrifice.

Your attempt to explain everything away in terms of evolutionary advantage is your own version of theological hocus pocus.

Nobel Prize winner Robert Laughlin rightly said, "Much of present-day biological knowledge is ideological. A key symptom of ideological thinking is the explanation that has no implications and cannot be tested. ... Your protein defies the laws of mass action? Evolution did it! Your complicated mess of chemical reactions turns into a chicken? Evolution! The human brain works on logical principles no computer can emulate? Evolution is the cause!?"[119]

Let me ask you Professor: Do you believe in evil?

MacIntosh: You already know the answer. There is no good and evil. These are subjective human and social constructs that do not actually exist.

MA: How about human freewill?

MacIntosh: I have already said that what we think of as free choices are produced by biological, cultural and other factors. There is no room for freewill within the world of physical cause and effect. This has been established decisively – most recently in Sapolsky's work.

MA: Sapolsky, creditably, does not sugar-coat his determinism. He is a "hard" determinist who does not flinch from the real-world consequences of his all-the-way-down determinism. But, as I have shown, Sapolsky's position is hopelessly self-contradictory. If you say that all your thoughts and acts are totally determined by external factors, then your judgment

---

119   Robert B. Laughlin, *A Different Universe* (New York: Basic Books, 2005), 168-169.

that it is all determined is neither true nor false – it is just a product of physical forces. Additionally, there is no actual way to prove that your every thought and act is entirely determined. It is one thing to point to the array of influences that influence our thinking and acting, but quite another to claim that this means we cannot freely make any choice whatsoever.

Sapolsky does not even seem aware that physical determinism cannot overcome the problem posed by Gödel's Incompleteness Theorem. The Theorem states the obvious fact that every logical/formal system has certain truths that cannot be proven within it. The consistency of axioms assumed by the system cannot be proven within it but must be proved within some more fundamental logical system that will have its own axioms that in turn are not provable within it – and so on without limit.

In his classic work *The Freedom of the Will*, and in subsequent publications, Lucas showed that Gödel's Theorem undermines mechanism, the idea that we are machines. Machines are governed by formal systems that cannot prove their own axioms but the human mind does not suffer from similar limitations. Lucas also emphasizes the importance of remaining true to our own experience of being free agents:

> Each of us has experience of being an agent, of making up our mind for ourselves. That is what we all know, but sometimes can't believe in. So I then try and go to instances where it is, indeed, the case that we make up our minds for ourselves, and there aren't conditions forcing us to – there are no laws of nature which make it inevitable that we should decide in one way – and I discuss various forms of determinism: logical determinism, theological determinism, psychological determinism and physical determinism; and I examine how each of these is argued for in a rather different way. And I show that in each case the argument won't work, so at the end of it, the sensible thing is to believe what we have always learnt from our experience: that we

make up our minds for ourselves, and decide what we shall do, and that we are responsible for what we decide to do.[120]

Another major contributor to the study of free will, Robert Kane, writes that we have a "modern-scientific way of understanding human agency and causation by agents ... an agent's causing an action is to be understood as 'an agent, conceived as ... an information-responsive complex dynamic system, exercising teleological guidance control over some of its own processes.'"[121]

So, can you at least grant that there might be a case for freewill?

MacIntosh: Your verbal pyrotechnics leave me cold. Freewill is a fiction.

MA: OK, I will take you at your word. You are incapable of free acts. But since you do not believe in either freewill or human evil, you cannot complain about a problem of evil with respect to God.

MacIntosh: That is not the point I am trying to make and you know it. I am talking about the myth that Christians believe. It is a myth of an all-good, all-powerful deity who made the world and enables evil because his creatures are endowed with freedom. This dangerous myth is obviously false even on its own terms because, if all-powerful, the deity can prevent the evil.

MA: OK. Let me summarize what I am hearing. You do not believe in a Source of being, although you have no explanation for your existence as a rational being. You do not believe in human freewill, although you are making arguments here freely and not as the result of physical forces. You do not believe in moral absolutes, but you are morally outraged by the kinds of beliefs held by Christians.

---

120   John R. Lucas in Roy Abraham Varghese, ed. *Great Thinkers on Great Questions* (Oxford: OneWorld, 1998), 80.

121   Robert E. Kane, "Making Sense of a Freewill that is Incompatible with Determinism," *Journal of Philosophical Theological Research*, Volume 23, No. 3, Autumn 2021, Issue 89, 14.

Given this unpromising start, it would be impossible for you to grasp the reality of the love that lies at the heart of the Christian message.

Let me see if I can get you to re-think your assumptions. Would you agree that your allegation of God being "cruel and unusual" depends on your understanding of infinite goodness and power?

MacIntosh: There is nothing esoteric in the way that I understand goodness and power. I go with standard usage. And, under that usage, your god is cruel, unusual, and an evil-doer.

MA: But this precisely is your problem – your standard usage. Would you agree that the activity of something in the micro-world can only be accurately described if you describe it within the framework of quantum theory and not of classical physics which applies to the macro-world? As you know, we talk of a quantum entity behaving as both a wave and a particle.

LH: Objection, Your Honor. An example of physics is irrelevant to a discussion of theology.

MA: The way we understand usage is through analogies and examples. I am trying to understand how Professor MacIntosh came to her conclusion, and thereby show it to be unwarranted.

Judge: Overruled. Counsel, you may continue. But do not drag it on.

MA: Thank you, Your Honor. I want simply to understand Professor Macintosh's thought pattern, so I can get my point across. So, let me repeat my question. Do you agree that the same things and processes can be understood differently in the micro-world and the macro-world?

MacIntosh: Yes, but in both cases we are talking about physical things and their motion. So there is no essential difference.

MA: Depends on your definition of "essential." There are fundamental differences.

Are things in the micro-world waves or particles? They cannot be both in the macro-world but things in the micro-world are different. This is because descriptions like wave and particle apply in the classical realm. In the quantum realm, you can measure either the momentum or the position of something but not both. If you measure the momentum, it acts as a wave; if you measure the position, it acts as a particle.

The behavior of things in both realms is different. In the macro-world, according to Newton's first law of motion, a moving body will keep moving in a straight line in the absence of an applied force. But in the micro-world, particles also act as waves. Tennis balls, cannon balls and planets follow the same laws of motion. Photons, however, act differently.

As you said, in both the micro- and the macro-worlds, we are talking about physical things and we are talking about motion. But our descriptions and even our meanings are different.

I use this analogy to make the point that we must adapt the way we use the same terms depending on the realm we are dealing with.

This is even truer when we talk about the differences between the finite and the infinite. What we see as "good" or "bad" in a finite setting can be meaningless when applied to the infinite.

MacIntosh: It is a waste of time to use words like "goodness" and "power" about your supposed god if such usage is totally alien to what we think of as "goodness" and "power."

MA: Of course, the usage of such words when talking of God cannot be totally alien but it is, nevertheless, infinitely different. What is good or bad for finite beings such as us concerns our intentions and actions as they relate to the moral law. The moral law is, in itself, an experience of God since all our choices concern knowing and loving him and his creation. Consequently, the understanding of good and bad, as it applies to humankind, does not apply in the same way to the Creator of humankind because all that is good derives from him, the Absolute Good, and what is bad is simply a rejection at a finite level of this Absolute Good.

As it relates to our discussion, the existence of evil must be understood in terms of the infinite Love that is the Triune God.

Now, Professor MacIntosh, humor me for a minute. Would you agree that love can be understood as one giving oneself to another?

MacIntosh: That is one understanding of the concept.

MA: Well, that is the Christian understanding. And it is not simply a concept. This understanding is fundamental to the Christian explanation of the human condition. Love cannot be forced out of anyone, for then it would not be "self"-giving. Love requires a letting-go that only you or I can make. This means it is possible to with-hold love.

MacIntosh: So, you are telling me that all the evil in the world exists because somebody did not "let go" and give themselves?

MA: I am saying that all that can be called moral evil is a failure to love, to give oneself. The paradigm form of love can be seen in the Godhead itself, in which the Three Persons are united in an eternal Act of Self-giving. And it is for the propagation of this Love that all things were created.

MacIntosh: Clearly, the hypothesized creation was a colossal failure – an infinite failure, to be honest. How can you believe in an infinitely powerful being that also fails infinitely in achieving its objective?

MA: Again, you are trying to think of the infinite using finite terms. There is no "success" or "failure" for infinite perfection. The divine objective was to provide a platform for the propagation of love. This has been achieved. Success or failure is specific to each individual finite being depending on their response to the divine offer.

MacIntosh: The sheer quantity of evil indicates that the idea of infinite power is meaningless.

MA: As I said, the offer of love necessarily involves the possibility of rejection and, hence, of evil. That is what we see around us. But then you also see the prophecy of the Suffering Servant in the Book of *Isaiah*, the parables of the Good Shepherd and the Prodigal Son, and, finally, Jesus' proclamation that he will be "a ransom for many" followed by his crucifixion and death. These utterly unprecedented insights into Ultimate Reality show us that infinite Love will do all that it can, without coercion, to bring us to union with him.

As we read in the first epistle of John: "In this is love: not that we have loved God, but that he loved us and sent his Son as expiation for our sins. Beloved, if God so loved us, we also must love one another. No one has ever seen God. Yet, if we love one another, God remains in us, and his love is brought to perfection in us." (1 *John* 4:9-12)

Infinite Love will work through human wickedness to bring about the ultimate triumph of the Good.

MacIntosh: You are assuming in all this that humans can "love." But, to repeat, we know from modern science that what we call love is strictly a biological process driven by physical factors.

MA: So, we are back to the evolutionary non-answer! Here is what we do know: We have moral codes, and we see our actions as good or bad. We have a supra-physical dimension of our being that goes beyond the purely physical as demonstrated by consciousness, thought and the self. Indisputably, we demonstrate this supra-physical dimension by the very fact that we can engage in discussion right now – something which cannot be explained in terms strictly of the operation of physical law. Yes, emotions, hormones, neural firings, socio-economic and other influences all have an impact on the way we think and choose. It is, however, *I* who do the thinking and choosing. It is *my* thoughts and choices that drive the neural firings and all the associated physical parameters.

What is love? It is the self-sacrificing, unconditional giving of one to another, the whole-hearted willing of all that benefits the beloved. What is its "cause?" Are we dealing simply and solely with neural firings, genetic switches, subconscious urges and survival-of-the-fittest-altruism? These "simply and solely" answers fail the cart-before-the horse test: Is it neurons that make a girl tend to her sick mother or rescuers risk their lives for strangers? No, it is love that comes first and mobilizes neurons, quanta, et al.

Let us go with "user experience" from the "inside." Drop the speculative somersaults required to explain love in terms of the altruism of ants. Love is not simply or always a matter of lust, hormones, and instincts. Yes, there is passion and emotion. But love is giving, forgiving, committing. It is kindness unto death.

It is an act of the person, a free exercise of intellect and will, transcending matter, biology, culture, and the various constructs of the experts.

Who invented love? Who invented "who's?" From the revelation of the Trinity – the Love Story of Three "Who's" – we realize that infinite-eternal Love is the true theory of everything, the ultimate reality.

The infinite Lover that is God is not passively permitting evil for the sake of a greater good. Rather LOVE is actively, constantly seeking our greatest good and overcoming evil to bring us to this good. True suffering is eternal alienation from the Fount of all Joy. It is this alienation that God does all in his power to prevent.

MacIntosh: No scientist will take any of this seriously.

MA: The founders of modern science certainly accepted the supra-physical-centered world-vision I've sketched here. You will also be surprised to know that most medical doctors believe in God and an after-life.

According to a University of Chicago study, "76% of doctors stated that they believe in God." Even more interesting, from the standpoint of your focus on pain and suffering, there is another startling finding that emerged from the study:

> Physicians often witness terrible events that most people would consider unfair. Nice people get sick, children lose parents and innocent people suffer. Many would question whether such distressing events would push doctors away from belief in a God. Yet, it appears that even while physicians are exposed to seemingly unjust patient distress, most continue to believe in God.
>
> This is hard to explain, but perhaps it is due to the unexpected peace that many dying patients exhibit or to the observation that many events that appear 'bad' are often not as straightforward as a simple 'good and bad.' But, whatever the reason, human suffering itself, which doctors frequently see close up, does not seem to preclude faith in a greater power as might be expected.[122]

MacIntosh: Like J.L. Mackie and William Rowe before him, the philosopher James Sterba has persuasively argued that belief in a good god is not logically possible given the degree and amount of preventable moral and natural evil in the world. You have not come close to addressing their arguments.

MA: I have already shown in my opening statement that these kinds of critiques have not grasped either the nature of God or of the kind of world he brought into being. We have seen too that a world of love is not possible without a world of free agency and free agency necessarily involves the possibility of evil.

William Hasker points out that Sterba "does not offer a promising foundation for an argument against theism. The God described in James Sterba's book—the God who is bound by Sterba's principles of Moral Evil

---

122   https://www.medicaleconomics.com/view/surprising-results-about-physicians-belief-in-god

Prevention and Natural Evil Prevention, and who follows the policies we might expect from an ideal human government—this God does not exist. That should not be a surprise; this God was devised precisely in order to show that he does not exist. This, however, has little or nothing to do with the existence of the God in whom Christians believe—Yahweh, the God of Israel, the Father of Jesus Christ."[123]

Ed Feser trenchantly argues that Sterba and others who adopt his line of thought have not understood the claims being made about the God revealed in the Old and New Testaments and explored in traditional theism:

> There are deep semantic and metaphysical issues here the neglect of which vitiates not only Sterba's argument, but much that is written today on the problem of evil by theists and atheists alike. ...
>
> Thomists, like most other theists, hold that omnipotence does not include the power to do the logically impossible. And they would also hold that the particular goods that God draws out of the evil that exists would not otherwise be logically possible. Sterba seems here simply to assume, without argument, that one or both of these suppositions are false.
>
> In general, Sterba's approach to the problem of evil both in his reply and his book seems to take for granted a conception of human life that Thomists, and indeed traditional Christian theology in general, simply would not agree with. In particular, he writes as if determining whether things go well overall for a human being is a matter of determining how they go for him in *this* life. But from the point of view of traditional Christian theology, what ultimately matters is the *next* life, not this one. This life is merely a preparation for the next. Hence, to judge the overall quality of a human life requires, most importantly, reference to the afterlife. If you considered only

---

123   https://www.academia.edu/54791977/James_Sterba_s_New_Argument_from_ Evil?auto=download

what happened in this life to, say, the Christian martyrs, you might think they lived among the most *un*fortunate of lives. But if instead you consider the reward this gained them in Heaven, they would have to be judged as having the most *fortunate* of lives.

Of course, the atheist will not agree that there is such a thing as an afterlife. But the point is that if he simply assumes this as a component of his atheistic argument from evil, then the argument will beg the question.

Sterba also seems to assume that if God exists, there is at least a very strong presumption that there would be no suffering, so that the fact that there *is* suffering is very surprising and indeed problematic if theism is true. But Thomists and traditional Christian theology more generally would reject that assumption too. They would say that suffering is to be *expected* given our nature as finite and corporeal creatures in a world interacting with other finite creatures. To be sure, our nature is good as far as it goes. But it is limited, and given those limits we are subject to injury, disease, ignorance, error, and the ramifications of those. We are also liable to *moral* failures, and as these mount, the damage done to the character of individuals and to the social orders of which they are parts also snowballs and ramifies. Given the facts of the natural moral law, we also come to merit the positive infliction of further harms as punishment for our evildoing. In these ways, suffering is deeply ingrained into the very nature of human life, and therefore precisely what we should expect.

It would take *super*natural assistance – that is to say, special divine action to raise us *beyond* the limits of our nature – to prevent this outcome from occurring. And such assistance was indeed offered to our first parents. Had they not rejected the offer, nature would not have taken its course. That is the sense in which the evil that afflicts us is the consequence of Original Sin. It's not that the Fall introduced into the natural order evil that would *not* have otherwise been there. It's rather that it lost for us the *super*natural prevention of evil that *would* have been there.

So, again, suffering is to be *expected* given our nature, rather than something that should surprise us. But then, why is it nevertheless not removed given that through Christ we can be *restored* to grace? There are several reasons. One of them is that grace, the supernatural order of things, builds on nature rather than smothering it. By leaving in place much of the effects of Original Sin, God allows us to see much more clearly than would otherwise be possible the unbridgeable gap between what we are capable of just given our own limited nature, and what we require in order to achieve the beatific vision. We see our *need* for grace better than we otherwise would. ...

Much more could be said, but that is enough to make the point that from the point of view of traditional Christian theology, suffering is an integral part of the natural and supernatural order of things, rather than something we should be surprised by. That's part of why the Cross is so central a symbol in Christian spirituality. If you look at the world the way that the heroes of scripture, the Fathers of the Church, and the saints do, the idea that what we should expect from God is (say) some kind of bourgeois consumer paradise – and that we should shake an accusing fist at him for failing to provide it – just seems bizarre, even superficial in the extreme.[124]

MacIntosh: In your citation, you touch on your weakest link – the kindergarten story of Adam and Eve. The rest of your system hangs on this obviously fanciful children's story.

MA: This is your fundamentalism at work again. You resolutely remain on the surface and so cannot plumb the depths. *Genesis* is a book for adults but it can be read as a children's story which is how you are determined to

---

124   https://edwardfeser.blogspot.com/2021/08/sterba-on-problem-of-evil.html

view it – much like the Mona Lisa can be seen strictly in terms of pixels and paints and without any consideration of it as a haunting portrait of a woman.

Our upcoming witnesses will be delving into the true import of the *Genesis* narratives so I will not address the matter here. One point, however, is relevant here: in uniquely symbolic language, Genesis tells us that the origin of human evil can be traced to a free human choice at the dawn of the human race, and this choice had consequences that afflict every human person.

Historically, every pre-Christian society recognized a primordial breach between the human and the divine, and this is why all of them sought to repair the breach through sacrifice. This alienation from God, the resulting guilt and shame, and our propensity for evil – all these universal experiences are precisely described in *Genesis*.

The *Genesis* temptation narrative is unique in all of literature given the nexus it establishes between the origin of evil and human experience as a whole.

The moral law is a participation in the infinite Good that is God. The fulfillment of the needs of human nature is to be found in our alignment with the Absolute Good for which we are created. And this means choosing those goods beneficial for our own well-being inasmuch as they align us with the Absolute Good. Nobody knows better the infrastructure of goods beneficial for us than the Creator who made us for him.

This was what God revealed to us at the beginning. And we hear echoes of that revelation in our hearts today. But the human race chose to blaze its own trail, to create its own infrastructure of goods. It is a path that led away from our Ultimate Good. This is the epic tragedy memorialized for all time in *Genesis* 3.

As for whether there was a first pair, here is what philosopher of science Stanley Jaki had to say: "The claim that a single couple started the race called *homo sapiens sapiens* is laden with much less difficulty than the assumption that the human race had originated from a non-human or a quasi-human population. From the scientific viewpoint, where causes, let alone such that amount to miracles, ought not to be invoked if a single cause would suffice, it would pass for a multiple miracle that a genetic change had suddenly and fairly simultaneously occurred in several individuals male and female … The quick multiplying of the race of Adam and Eve should pose no serious difficulty in view of the close consanguinity of their descendants. The descendants of Adam, if they started say 25,000 BC, could easily reach fifteen million by 5,000 BC, in essential agreement with current population estimates."[125]

125   Stanley Jaki, *The Garden of Eden* (Pinckney, Michigan: Real View Books), 27.

"RED IN TOOTH AND CLAW"

Witness – Robert Atkinson (RA)

LH: Dr. Robert Atkinson is one of the most celebrated molecular biologists of our time. His book, *The Self-Made Gene*, has changed the whole perception of evolution – not least by eliminating all traces of a designer deity. Dr. Atkinson, I would like you to give your expert opinion on something that falls slightly outside your normal beat. The question is this: As an authority on life-forms, what is your view of the claim that the world in which we live was the creation of an infinitely benevolent, infinitely good deity?

Atkinson: Thank you, Lucius. To respond to your query, I am amazed to learn that there are still people who believe in a benevolent deity given what evolutionary biology has taught us about Nature in the century and a half since Darwin's *Origin of Species*.

In the first place, the evolutionary processes so evident in Nature demonstrate the absence of any trace of design or a designer. The latest research in abiogenesis – the evolution of life from inorganic matter – shows us that life accidentally originated from inorganic chemicals. Natural selection and random mutation explain the origin and development of the various species once life got started. The upshot is that all living beings are the products of mindless, randomly interacting wholly natural processes. In *The Self-Made Gene* I explore the different evolutionary mechanisms that generate new genes. These range from gene fusion and fission to the origination of genes from scratch from non-coding areas of DNA which is also called de novo origination. These processes are responsible for the diversity of genomes.

Secondly, and particularly important here, is the fact that Nature, as revealed in evolutionary history, is vicious and cruel. Nature is "red in tooth and claw" because kill or be killed is the universal law of life. If Nature has a god, which it does not, it would be a particularly nasty deity. Darwin long ago showed us why you cannot possibly reconcile animal suffering with the existence of a benevolent god:

> "A being so powerful and so full of knowledge as a God who could create the universe, is to our finite minds omnipotent and omniscient, and it revolts our understanding to suppose that his benevolence is not unbounded, for what advantage can there be in the sufferings of millions of the lower animals throughout almost endless time? This very old argument from the existence of suffering against the existence of an intelligent first cause seems to me a strong one; whereas, as just remarked, the presence of much suffering agrees well with the view that all organic beings have been developed through variation and natural selection."[126]

What we find in Nature is hideous violence and constant slaughter. There are only two kinds of living being – predator and prey. And we find hunger, disease, pain and suffering in general all across the living world. Viruses and bacteria are "microbial assassins" that respect no borders and have brought down empires (the Western and Eastern Roman Empires were weakened by diseases and plagues).

This is what we expect to find in a world ruled by evolution where only the fittest can survive. But if someone claims that the world was created by a deity, the obvious question is: What kind of sadist would create a world of such savagery? If they also claim that their deity is all-powerful and so could prevent pain and suffering, this is not just a sadist but an

---

126   Charles Darwin, ed. Nora Barlow, *The Autobiography of Charles Darwin* 1809-1882, with Original Omissions Restored, (New York: W.W. Norton, 1969), 90.

unimaginably evil monster. To be blunt, you must be either an imbecile or a psycho to believe in a deity of this kind.

What is worse is that these fanatics also deny the fact of evolution and say we should stop teaching it in school! Deny evolution? This means doing away with science – and thus technology and medicine – the two vehicles that have had the greatest impact in mitigating pain and suffering. So not only do they believe in a sadistic deity, but they want to remove our two greatest weapons against the pain and suffering inflicted by their supposed deity!

These beliefs would be amusing if it was just a matter of a few nuts with their private pipedreams. But these are the very beliefs that have increased the pain and suffering in the world with millions killed as a result of religious intolerance. And now we face the real threat to science posed by the creationist crazies.

Any belief in a deity is belief in a savage sadist. And these beliefs have horrific consequences including the believers themselves becoming savage sadists. Think of the believers shrieking that their god is great while butchering and beheading their helpless victims!

If you think I am being too strong, I can only say I am not being strong enough.

LH: Thank you Dr. Atkinson. Your passion should be contagious if we are to save the world. And your logic is impeccable. The pain in the animal world is to be expected as a part of the evolutionary process. But if someone claims to believe in an all-powerful deity, their deity is responsible for all this pain. Christians cannot use their made-up concepts of free-will because that only applies to humans. Animals do not have that luxury. Their suffering has to be chalked up to their supposed creator.

You may cross-examine, Counsel.

MA: Dr. Atkinson, I am not sure if you would label me an imbecile or a psycho but I do believe in an infinite-eternal Source of all being that includes all living beings. Before we move down this path, let me ask you: Are you a non-vegetarian? Do you eat meat?

Atkinson: What a peculiar question! Yes, I am a non-vegetarian. I like my steak medium-well.

MA: So, you have no objection to an animal being sacrificed to meet your culinary desires? Remember this is not a matter of you facing starvation. You could easily eat a salad or mashed potatoes or pasta. But you insist on killing a cow in order to eat it. You do not mind inflicting suffering on an animal just to spice up your diet.

Atkinson: I believe in being honest although I think this is an asinine question. No, I have no objection to enjoying cuisines that are non-vegetarian. Keep in mind, I do not believe in any mythical Big Daddy in the sky who magically conjured up this world and specially created each creature. Animals feel pain because natural selection has built the attribute of feeling pain into their nervous systems so they avoid behavior that is detrimental to their well-being.

MA: But in principle you do not find anything wrong with inflicting pain and suffering on an animal. You only object to it if there is any belief in a Creator.

LH: Objection, Your Honor. This line of questioning has absolutely nothing to do with my witness's testimony.

Judge: Counsel, get to your point.

MA: I want to point out that there is some obvious bait-and-switch going on here. There is an inherent contradiction in someone claiming that the pain and suffering in the animal world is an argument against the existence of an infinitely good God while also personally finding no problem with inflicting such pain on animals.

But on animal pain, I'm afraid you haven't been paying attention to me.

By the same token, Dr. Atkinson, do you believe that our consciousness is something that can be explained by the evolutionary process?

Atkinson: If you knew any science, you would know that scientists consider consciousness to be an illusion. No working scientist believes that there is some ethereal, non-physical force hiding in our brains. We are our molecules and that is it. There can be nothing that violates the laws of physics – for instance, the law of the conservation of energy – or else the whole system of cause and effect that governs the natural world breaks down. Everything that happens, including in our heads, follows these laws. You cannot have any non-physical process. The idea that we are conscious is an illusion. As Nobel Prize winner Francis Crick wrote, "'You,' your joys and your sorrows, your memories and your ambitions, your sense of personal identity and free will, are in fact no more than the behavior of a vast assembly of nerve cells and their associated molecules."[127]

All our mental events are brain events, and all physical events are completely explained by physical factors.

MA: So, you are saying that our belief that we are conscious is an illusion.

Atkinson: Yes, we think we are "conscious" but, as Daniel Dennett put it, this is just the brain's "user illusion" of itself much like the screen on a phone or a laptop with its icons. Our minds are made up of molecular machines – namely brain cells – that are the product of millions of years of evolution and natural selection. All its activities are driven by adaptation, which is necessary to survive. There is no "consciousness" over and above the mindless robots that we call brain cells that drive our activities.

MA: Who is having this illusion?

127 Francis Crick, *The Astonishing Hypothesis: The Scientific Search for the Soul* (New York: Simon and Schuster, 1994), 1.

Atkinson: There is no "who." The idea of a self is itself is an illusion. Everything about us is physical and if you examine brain cells, there is no self to be found separate from the cells.

MA: So, our experience of experiencing things is an illusion. Even the idea that someone is having this illusion is an illusion because there is no "someone." Did I get you right?

Atkinson: Yes. From a scientific standpoint, everything has to be in the third person. All talk of "self" and "consciousness" and "beliefs" and "intentions" and the like belong to what we call folk psychology, not hard science. Science shows us that there are only particles and molecules and genes operating within a framework of physical laws. An organism itself is like an organization with many interacting departments. The organization is not a "self," but we loosely think of it as if it is something unitary. It is not and neither are we.

MA: I am glad you are refreshingly honest on these matters. Your position is, of course, insane and self-contradictory as our witnesses will show. If your being conscious is an illusion, and the person who allegedly has the illusion is also an illusion, your claim that it is an illusion is also an illusion.

For our discussion, however, I will take your assumption as a starting point. If you truly believe it, you should not have a problem with the pain and suffering in Nature since being conscious of painful sensations is itself an illusion. The dog you kick might whimper, but its apparently painful sensations are illusory and, in fact, there is no dog-self suffering from the illusion. For that matter, your experience when under the drill in the dentist's chair is illusory, just as "you" are. This means, from your standpoint, there can be no "problem" of animal suffering.

Atkinson: That is a gross parody of my position. In the situations you present, what I am saying is that evolution equips organisms with nervous systems that produce certain reactions that help them adapt and survive. The reactions of the organisms in your example are evolution's way of enabling them to adapt to particular environments.

MA: But that is all it is. In your view, there is no problem of suffering. The point I have made so far is that, based on your own assumptions, you cannot point to the pain and suffering in the animal world as a problem because (a) you do not accept the existence of consciousness (which includes consciousness of pain) or of conscious subjects and (b) you have no problem personally of inflicting pain on animals.

Atkinson: Here is your problem. All your sleight-of-hand tricks here cannot save your theory. If you accept my assumptions – and I am glad you take it as your starting point – your theory of a designer deity is dead.

MA: I think you jumped to the wrong conclusion partner. Your assumptions, as I stated them, do not necessarily rule out the existence of a Creator. Even if all minds are the result of mindless processes, there still must be a Source of these processes. Your assumptions merely refute the case you are trying to make here against a Creator on the grounds of animal suffering because, in your view, animals do not suffer, and you personally do not see anything wrong with inflicting pain on animals.

LH: Objection, Your Honor. The Defendant is simply leading the witness down irrelevant rabbit trails without addressing the question of how he can reconcile the suffering of animals with the existence of a benevolent deity.

MA: Your Honor, as you can see, the witness does not acknowledge the reality of animal suffering. How am I supposed to resolve a problem that he does not see as a problem? Perhaps the Plaintiff should have introduced a witness that is on the same page as he is.

LH: Your Honor, the Defendant is now trying to play games with the Court instead of at least making an effort to defend his position. Of course, we all know his position is indefensible. Why will he not just admit that instead of trying to divert and distract the Court?

Judge: Counsel, what do you have to say?

MA: I will be happy to continue cross-examining the witness to show that the Plaintiff's charges about animal suffering simply misconstrue what is being claimed by us.

Judge: Continue.

MA: Dr. Atkinson, as a biologist, how do you define life?

Atkinson: This is Biology 101. Obviously, life comprises the capabilities of nutrition, metabolism, growth, response to stimulus, self-motion and replication. The NASA Exobiology group defined life as "a self-sustaining *chemical system capable of Darwinian evolution.*"

MA: What you have given me are attributes of life not its nature.

Atkinson: There is no distinction between attributes and nature. When I give you the attributes of water, that is what we mean by water. There is no separate nature. And vitalism – the idea that there is some mystical force of life beyond physics and chemistry – was scientifically invalidated a long time ago.

MA: OK, let me try to clarify what I am getting at. I am sure you will agree that there is no abstract thing called "life." There are only living beings. What is a living being?

Atkinson: A being with all the properties I cited. Perhaps you need to take a few courses in biology.

MA: Unfortunately, courses in biology will not provide the answer to my question. And, apparently, you do not seem to know the answer either. But you are in good company.

In *The Quest for a Universal Theory of Life*, Carol Cleland writes that "despite strenuous efforts over the past couple of hundred years, biologists have yet to come up with an empirically fruitful, truly general theory of familiar Earth life."[128]

Similarly, noted science writer Carl Zimmer, the author of *Life's Edge: The Search for What It Means to Be Alive*, said, "No one has been able to define life, and some people will tell you it's not possible to." He added perceptively, "This is more a philosophical problem than a scientific one."[129]

I am pressing this point because it lies at the heart of our dispute.

A living being is fundamentally an autonomous, goal-seeking agent. To call it an agent is to say that each and every living being acts or is capable of action. And that being is the unified source and center of all its actions, and it causes its own actions for its own sake. Since these agents are capable of surviving and acting independently, and their actions are in some fashion driven by goals (nourishment), and since they can reproduce themselves, they are therefore goal-seeking, self-replicating autonomous agents. Moreover, as Howard H. Pattee points out, you find in living beings the interaction of semiotic processes (rules, codes, languages, information, control) and physical systems (laws, dynamics, energy, forces, matter).[130]

Atkinson: There is nothing earth-shaking about what you have said. It certainly does not point to vitalism or any kind of supernatural activity.

MA: Both vitalists and mechanists have made equal and opposite mistakes in describing life. There is, of course, no "force" above and beyond the forces of physics and chemistry that operates in living beings. But what is it that exercises these forces? Are the actions of a living being purely and simply the interactions of its constituent chemicals – or is there a source and center of its actions, implying that such a being is an agent? It is undeniable that every living being acts in pursuit of goals (the source of the goal-seeking

---

128   https://www.wired.com/story/life-philosophy-bioethics/

129   https://www.vox.com/unexplainable/23637531/what-is-life-scientists-dont-agree

130   Pattee, H.H., "The Physics of Symbols: Bridging the Epistemic Cut," *Biosystems*, 2001, Vol. 60, 5-21.

may be instinct or some other factor) and so such beings might be called goal-seeking agents. Furthermore, they introduce an unprecedented phenomenon in the world of matter – self-replication.

We are not dealing with "vitalism" but with the phenomenon of autonomous, self-replicating goal-seeking agency. This phenomenon has not only been ignored by most scientists but by its very nature it cannot be studied by scientific methods. Moreover, it is simply unintelligible to talk of physical energy giving rise to goal-seeking, self-replicating agency.

The problem is magnified when you probe the biochemical scaffolding of life. At the biochemical center of every living being, there is a system of commands that is communicated through a system of chemicals (biochemical bases) that act as a system of symbols (DNA) to ultimately produce a system of processes (production of proteins).

Paul Davies points out that "life is more than just complex chemical reactions. The cell is also an information storing, processing and replicating system. We need to explain the origin of this information, and the way in which the information processing machinery came to exist."

The kind of information involved here goes beyond the mathematics of the laws of Nature because it is semantic in nature – symbols with meanings that must be processed to perform functions. Genes contain instructions for manufacturing proteins and these instructions must be decoded if living beings are to operate. Davies adds, "The problem of how meaningful or semantic information can emerge spontaneously from a collection of mindless molecules subject to blind and purposeless forces presents a deep conceptual challenge."[131]

In sum, life is a new dimension of being that arises at a certain point in the history of the universe.

---

131   Paul Davies, "The Origin of Life II: How did it begin?", https://journals.sagepub. com/doi/pdf/10.3184/003685001783239096

So let me ask you, how did life originate?

Atkinson: Again, your ignorance of basic biology is the biggest handicap we face. Origin-of-life studies is one of the most active areas of inquiry in modern science. How did life originate in the prebiotic world? No scientist doubts that it took place some four billion years ago, through some process of abiogenesis. Almost all components of living cells have been generated in the lab. Genomics, biochemistry and molecular biology along with geology have provided us with solid models of abiogenesis. There are plausible theories of various sites where life originated. Origin of life researcher Nick Lane and his team have built a good case for identifying deep-sea hydrothermal vents as the origin site.

MA: I was not asking you about the biochemical antecedents of life. Yes, there have been attempts to re-create life in the lab paralleled by theories on conditions in the early Earth that were conducive to the appearance of life. There is much less optimism about progress on both fronts than there used to be. No one is anywhere near creating even as basic a building block as a living cell. A report from the Carnegie Institution for Science conference on the origin of life observes that "despite significant progress on both ends, a vast gulf persists separating our understanding of the geochemistry of early Earth, and the biomolecules it could produce, from what we know of the most ancient life."[132]

There is even strong disagreement on the kind of place where life could have originated. As *Scientific American* reports, "Synthetic chemists generally favour a continental origin and geologists and biologists mostly deep-sea hydrothermal vents. Chemists argue it's impossible to do the chemistry in hydrothermal vents, while biologists argue that the terrestrial chemistry proposed just isn't like anything seen in biochemistry and doesn't narrow the gap between geochemistry and biochemistry."[133]

132   https://doi.org/10.1098/rsta.2016.0337
133   https://www.scientificamerican.com/article/lifes-origins-by-land-or-sea-debate-gets-hot/

Theories of abiogenesis and life-spawning soups, clays and vents have sprouted, grown, died, and sprouted again. Francis Crick, whom you quoted, pointed out that the chances are so small as to be negligible that the long polymer molecules that sustain life could have been assembled by random processes from the chemical units of which they are made.[134] What is clear today is that life appeared in a relatively short period after the Earth had cooled down. The endless time assumed by some proponents of abiogenesis simply did not exist. Of course, even in endless time, no one can magically produce life.

My question, however, has nothing to do with these commendable inquiries. Everyone agrees that the first life-forms appeared somewhere on Earth billions of years ago when the conditions were conducive for their biochemical survival. The more we find out about the initial scaffolding involved, the better.

My question was not about the biochemistry. It was about the origin of autonomous agency. Living beings are autonomous agents, goal-seekers, and self-replicators that are semiotically driven (their existence depends on the interplay between codes and chemistry). When speaking of the origin of life, most people are referring to the physico-chemical precursors of biological life.

But physics and chemistry cannot describe or comprehend the idea of existing as an autonomous agent and of processing intelligent messages using chemical codes. If they cannot describe this phenomenon, they certainly cannot explain its origin. When we are talking about the origin of life, we are not talking about how certain chemicals organized themselves to form a living system. We are asking how autonomous, intelligent agents could come to be in a universe of undifferentiated matter.

---

134 Francis Crick cited in John Maddox, *What Remains to be Discovered* (New York: Touchstone, 1998), 131, 142-3.

It seems obvious to me that the dimensions of autonomous agency and intelligent message processing, by their very nature, could not emerge from matter given any amount of time or any external condition. (Can we seriously believe that the Rockies or the Himalayas could some day come to life or start "thinking? "). Thus, the idea that life can be reduced to matter is simply incoherent. Like the origin of material being, the origin of life is a mystery that cannot be resolved at the level of matter.

The atheist Lewis Wolpert candidly admits that "the origin of life itself, the evolution of the miraculous cell from which all living things evolved, is still poorly understood."[135]

Atkinson: Richard Dawkins, among many others, has adequately addressed the issue. He says, "But how does life get started? The origin of life was the chemical event, or series of events, whereby the vital conditions for natural selection first came about. The major ingredient was heredity, either DNA or (more probably) something that copies like DNA but less accurately, perhaps the related molecule RNA. Once the vital ingredient – some kind of genetic molecule – is in place, true Darwinian natural selection can follow."[136]

How did this happen? "Scientists invoke the magic of large numbers. It has been estimated that there are between 1 billion and 30 billion planets in our galaxy, and about 100 billion galaxies in the universe.. The beauty of the anthropic principle is that it tells us, against all intuition, that a chemical model need only predict that life will arise on one planet in a billion billion to give us a good and entirely satisfying explanation for the presence of life here."[137]

---

135   Lewis Wolpert, *Six Impossible Things Before Breakfast*, (London: Faber and Faber, 2006), 212-3.

136   Richard Dawkins, *The God Delusion*, (London: Bantam, 2006), 137.

137   Ibid., 137-8.

MA: Given this type of reasoning, which is better described as an audacious exercise in superstition, anything we desire should exist somewhere if we just "invoke the magic of large numbers." Unicorns or the elixir of youth, even if "staggeringly improbable" are bound to occur "against all intuition." The only requirement is "a chemical model" that "need only predict" these occurring "on one planet in a billion billion".

D.H. Wilson, an agnostic commentator on Dawkins' origin of life account, notes,

> This is an extraordinary simplification. The origin of life must at the very least have had two major ingredients, and they must have sparked into life at precisely the same moment: heredity was one, but what Darwin called the "breath" was the other. DNA is not much use in a lifeless body. By only calling on DNA/RNA, at a stroke Dawkins has halved the degree of the already high improbability. But be reassured: 'I shall not be surprised if, within the next few years, chemists report that they have successfully midwifed a new origin of life in the laboratory. (p. 137). That's OK then. Dawkins thinks that the combined knowledge of the finest brains, working on the findings of generations of earlier fine brains, will soon be able consciously to put together the ingredients and breathe the spark of life into them … which will prove that life came about through unconscious chance. Abiogenesis is the name of the theory that inanimate matter spontaneously assembled itself to create life. And it requires just as much credulity as the genesis theory it seeks to replace.[138]

In the very book by him you cite, even Dawkins admits readily that Darwinian evolution cannot produce or explain the origin of life. He turns therefore to "the initial stroke of luck" granted by what he calls the Anthropic Principle. "We really need Darwin's powerful crane to account

---

138   D.H. Wilson, *An Agnostic's Brief Guide to the Universe*, https://www.agnosticweb. com/agnostic_brief_guide.pdf

for the diversity of life on Earth, and especially the persuasive illusion of design. The origin of life, by contrast, lies outside the reach of that crane, because natural selection cannot proceed without it ... We can deal with the unique origin of life by postulating a very large number of planetary opportunities. Once that initial stroke of luck has been granted ... natural selection takes over."[139]

The phrases "god of the gaps" and *deus ex machina* come to mind as we read these lines. Dawkins confuses the conditions that *permit* life to survive – which is strictly what the Anthropic Principle talks about – with the conditions that "*cause*" life. Gerald Schroeder notes that "The universe is tuned for life. Not tuned for the starting of life. That's not at all clear. We don't have any idea at the moment of how life started. Speculations, yes, but how inert matter became alive, that's a complete unknown at the moment. However, once life gets started we see clearly from the fundamental constants of the universe that, in fact, the universe is tuned for life."[140]

Importantly, the chemical dimension is just one small part of the story: we still have to account for agency and directedness and coding. How did these undeniable phenomena come into being? These are the principles that organize the chemistry. And this is precisely the dimension that is ignored by Dawkins and virtually all origin-of-life researchers.

Scholars like Stuart Kaufmann have recognized the importance of autonomous agency. The book *Biological Autonomy* argues that biology should be structured around autonomy rather than evolution by natural selection since autonomy is more fundamental.

Philip Ball, author of *How Life Works*, writes, "agency [is] the capacity of living things to act and to change their surroundings to their own benefit. This is perhaps what truly distinguishes what is alive (or is constructed

---

139   Richard Dawkins, op cit., 148.

140   Presentation at *Has Science Discovered God?*, a symposium held at New York University, May 2004.

by things that are alive) from what is not. Biology needs to know about transcription factors and cell signaling pathways and the dynamical steady states of cells, but what makes all this a science of life is the existence of agency—and until it has a good theoretical and conceptual grasp of that elusive property, it will not quite be a true science of life."[141]

The whole evolutionary theory of adaptation assumes agency. Who does the adapting that results in natural selection? Agents. But how did agency arise? That is one of the many crucial issues that evolutionary biologists like you fail to address, another being consciousness.

Agency is as fundamental a reality in the universe as energy. It can only be explained by a Source that is itself an infinite Agent.

I have gone on about this theme because we cannot understand the divine scheme of things until we recognize that living organisms are autonomous agents. The whole history of life is a history of autonomous agents. It is in this context that we can understand pain in the animal world.

Atkinson: I fail to see how your notion of agency can help get your deity off the hook for animal suffering. Any idea of an all-powerful creator necessarily requires that creator to be responsible for the good, the bad, and the ugly.

And nothing you have said can change the facts of evolutionary history. The balance sheet of biology is written in blood. The Earth is a constantly replenished cemetery created in a vortex of violence.

Kill or be killed is the law of the land in the life of life! And often the killing is grotesque. Think of the parasitoid wasps that Darwin spoke off that live off their hosts from the inside out.

But why, based on your assumptions, should animals suffer? This is even before we get to *Homo sapiens* and its contribution to the kill-fest that is

---

141   Philip Ball, https://nautil.us/how-life-really-works-435813/

life. Killing began long before there were humans; that is how the natural world operates. And you have no one to blame for this mayhem than the one you claim started it all: your deity.

MA: Skeptics like you traffic in childish oversimplifications and buffoonish caricatures. Let us deal with the facts as we have them, not polemical flourishes.

No one can deny that there is more going on in the history of life than killing. Think of the emergence of life and human life against all odds. Think of the streaks of goodness, beauty, and love that are strewn across the landscape of life. At the same time, it is clear that violence, pain, and killing are pervasive in the living world.

And yet, it is important to consider the whole, when examining the various parts. The diversity of life on planet Earth is stunning and spectacular – the multitudinous species, shapes and structures, organs and mechanisms, colors and sounds, ecosystems and goal-seeking patterns.

Biologists who are focused on "selfish genes" and the "survival of the species" often forget the bigger picture of the sheer spectacle of life.

How it all got to be here is a question to which the two of us offer different answers. But the splendor of what did arrive is undeniable.

Historically, we also see a progression from inanimate to animate to conscious to rational and self-conscious – from the physical to physical-integrated-with-the-supra-physical. To reiterate what I have said earlier, "supra-physical" refers to a non-physical reality that is often integrated with the physical but cannot be described or explained in physical terms. My thoughts about justice or peace cannot be measured or weighed.

Human beings are not pure spirits – we are a union of spirit and matter; we are rational animals. The existence of bacteria, plants, mammals, and the like were essential for us to come to be as the kind of beings we are.

At this point, it is fair to ask: Why does Nature have to be "red in tooth and claw" for us to exist? To this I say that the kind of beings we are makes it necessary that there be an environment such as we have:

> We cannot continue to live without the existence of plants for instance.

> We depend for our life on the billions of bacteria in our gut.

> Nervous systems are required for physical pleasure but, by their nature, they also transmit pain.

> The dinosaurs had to disappear for us to be around.

Equally important, God not only created us as free beings but his creation itself manifests a hierarchy of autonomy balanced by law:

> Quantum behavior at the subatomic level following certain patterns,

> the crucial role of the cyanobacteria in bringing about life on this planet,

> the "intelligence" of plants so essential for their own growth as well as the nourishment of animals,

> locomotion and other attributes found in animals.

The climax is reached in human beings who are capable of rational thought and have freedom of the will.

All this autonomy in creation means a degree of self-directed action with the attendant consequences across the whole world system. But would you rather us all be automatons?

An animal, be it a house cat or a lion, pursues its own agenda, has its own purposes, and has a certain freedom of action. Living beings are autonomous agents. Inevitably, there will be interactions between these agents. Although much of the interaction is driven by instincts and needs, it is driven by individual agents, not by zombies or puppets. It is this interaction that creates the tapestry of life as we have it. Some of the autonomous agents are conscious which means they can experience pain and pleasure in different degrees.

Another indisputable dimension is the fact that the supra-physical made its appearance at a specific moment in the history of the universe. This moment happened to be the precise time at which the physical progressed to the point of serving as a platform for the supra-physical (e.g., the brain had to develop to a degree where it could provide the physical support required for certain supra-physical activities). The symphony that is Nature reached a crescendo with the marriage of physical and supra-physical that is *Homo sapiens*. Or, as they used to say in an older vocabulary, humanity is the crown of creation. I think it is obvious that a world with free moral agents is one where their choices will have an impact on themselves and others.

This is the real world with real agents not a programmer's virtual reality game.

Atkinson: Your pretty picture begs the whole question. Why would a benevolent deity knowingly create an environment that inevitably involves violence, bloodshed, and suffering? And the whole supra-physical business is simply a feverish fantasy.

MA: There is no doubt that the history of life is a history of violence across the living world. The question is what is the big picture: How did it start, how will it end, what is the whole point? A too simplistic idea of the Source of all being, and the nature of what exists, leads to the kind of charges you level. Both atheists and believers in God are guilty of such over-simplified images. We have to exorcise all such grossly anthropomorphic ideas and start with the kind of universe that exists before us, the infinite-eternal Source of its existence and the self-revelation of this Source to humanity. Without these starting-points, we are doomed to sink deeper into the quicksand of our self-created fantasies.

So let me start with the universe. In my opening statement, I laid out some of the precise parameters that had to be in place for us to exist. For instance, if the universe was not as old and as large as it is, there could be no life or human life.

The history of life is no less precise. The oxygen produced by cyanobacteria on the young Earth provided the breathable air we have today and without which we could not exist. Primordial genetic tool-kits made our vital biological processes possible. Various extinction events – for instance, the extinction of the dinosaurs – made it viable for *Homo sapiens* to appear and survive. Plate tectonics and other factors played a vital role in the history of life.

There were various inflection points that made our existence possible – from the emergence of autonomous agency to the biological big bang called the Cambrian Explosion to the sudden appearance of consciousness and language.

While evolutionary theory can point to the physical dimension of these developments, it cannot address questions about the origin of supra-physical realities simply because these are not physical and therefore not subject to evolution. Of course, they manifest themselves through the physical, but the physical is simply a platform. For that matter, evolutionary theory cannot address the origin of the physical either because it must presuppose the existence of the physical to get started.

You deny the existence of the supra-physical but, as I said, such a denial is self-contradictory. You are saying that I am conscious that I am not conscious. Our witnesses will be presenting the case for the supra-physical, but here we are concerned to simply show the inherent coherence of our description of the world.

Supra-physical realities can only be explained by a supra-physical Source and, in fact, it is this Source that continues to keep all supra-physical realities in being – from agency to consciousness to thought.

So, here is where we are so far: The origin of physical energy cannot be explained without a Source that can bring it into being from nothingness (and energy does not have the capacity to create itself). Clearly, agency and consciousness had a beginning in the history of the universe, but the origin of both has to be from a Source that is the fullness of agency (life) and consciousness. This is why the infinite-eternal Source of all being cannot be denied.

But even more significant, the Infinite-Eternal is intimately involved in keeping all things going. It is not a deist deity detached from its creation, but neither is it a watchmaker that is personally designing every detail. Nor is it a tinkerer constantly intervening in the workings of the world. Yet, we know that if the universe did not follow the history that it did, we would not exist.

What we see, in short, is a Source of all things that is infinitely transcendent and infinitely immanent. This Source – God – has brought forth a world of precise laws and agents with different degrees of autonomy (from a quantum field to an ant) and different powers (e.g., being conscious) and kinds of intelligence. God is the Source of our powers (in both the physical and supra-physical domains) and the laws of Nature. God keeps all this in existence, but the beings with these powers and operating in Nature are autonomous agents.

Now, this balance of order and autonomy means that the agents involved will be affected by the laws of Nature, and by their interaction with other agents. Looking at non-human organisms, we might ask why they undergo pain and death. Of course, we do not want mosquitoes propagating without end or living forever. All animals must eat to live. Some are herbivorous, others are carnivorous. Ecosystem equilibrium requires that there be not too many of a particular species or too few (snakes control the rat population, for instance).

But how can the resultant pain in Nature be explained?

First, we live in a dynamic world of autonomous agents and not a clock-work universe. Second, we are a work in progress that must be considered in the context of the big picture and the endgame. The latter two are known to God, the infinite-eternal Source and Sustainer, and have been revealed in stages through the people of Israel and climactically in Jesus of Nazareth.

The big picture and the endgame, so the revelation of God tells us, is that there will be a new Heaven and a new Earth, a transformation of the physical world that mirrors the resurrection of Jesus. What we find in Nature is a seed that will flower in the fullness of time, a caterpillar that will become a butterfly.

> "Then I saw a new heaven and a new earth. The former heaven and the former earth had passed away." (*Revelation* 21:1)

> "Creation awaits with eager expectation the revelation of the children of God; for creation was made subject to futility, not of its own accord but because of the one who subjected it, in hope that creation itself would be set free from slavery to corruption and share in the glorious freedom of the children of God. We know that all creation is groaning in labor pains even until now." (*Romans* 8:18-22)

> The day is coming when "the wolf shall be a guest of the lamb, and the leopard shall lie down with the young goat; the calf and the young lion shall browse together, with a little child to guide them. The cow and the bear shall graze together their young shall lie down; the lion shall eat hay like the ox." (*Isaiah* 11:6-7)

> "The earth is full of your creatures. (…) Take away their breath, they perish and return to the dust. Send forth your spirit, they are created and you renew the face of the earth." (*Psalm* 104: 24, 29-30)

> "I heard a loud voice from the throne saying, 'Behold, God's dwelling is with the human race. He will dwell with them and they will be his people and God himself will always be with them [as their God]. He

will wipe every tear from their eyes, and there shall be no more death or mourning, wailing or pain, [for] the old order has passed away." The one who sat on the throne said, "Behold, I make all things new." (*Revelation* 21:3-5)

Notice that the new Heaven and the new Earth are not a new creation. They are a transformation of what exists now. "Behold, I make all things new," not "Behold, I make new things." The pangs of labor are painful and, hence, "all creation is groaning in labor pains." But nine months of labor are followed by the miracle of birth, the emergence of a new reality *from* the old.

We are also told about God's love for his non-human creatures: "Look at the birds in the sky; they do not sow or reap, they gather nothing into barns, yet your heavenly Father feeds them." (*Matthew* 6:26) "Are not two sparrows sold for a small coin? Yet not one of them falls to the ground without your Father's knowledge." (*Matthew* 10:29)

Humans are required to be the stewards of creation, protecting the planet and its species. "The man gave names to all the tame animals, all the birds of the air, and all the wild animals." (*Genesis* 2:20)

Of course, things are in disarray now thanks to the disharmony caused by sin. But, as we shall show, the victory over sin has been won, and the impact of this victory will become apparent in Creation 2.0.

Atkinson: This is the very definition of pie in the sky. So, you are telling us to ignore the terrible pain and suffering that animals have endured and will continue to endure because in some conveniently distant future it will all work out – not for them, of course, but for some other imaginary creatures. This is outrageously cynical. Surely you don't intend us to take this fundamentalist fantasy seriously.

MA: I think that, like a lot of other skeptics, you are an atheist counterpart of biblical fundamentalists, and you apply your own fundamentalist mindset in assessing the Christian vision.

To start with, you believe in a clockwork universe in which there are no agents and no autonomy. Everything that happens is driven by physical laws and all happenings are strictly interactions of particles and genes. There are no independent organisms, no consciousness, no thoughts. There are only particle events and selfish genes. Our personal experience of self-identity or being conscious are simply user illusions.

This is your funda-materialist framework that you defend despite the fact that it flies in the face of all our everyday experience. In your fundamentalist mindset, there is no room for complexity or nuance; everything has to be black and white.

When you analyze the Christian claim, you simply replace physical laws with your version of god and leave the rest as is. Thus, *your god simply controls all events and, of course, is thereby responsible for all that happens.*

But this is not the Christian claim. We say that *God has brought into being and conserves in being an architecture of agents, powers, structures, and intelligences.* This architecture has a built-in trajectory that leads to a hierarchy of agents from quantum fields to psychophysical organisms with different structures and powers. Living organisms are real players, and their actions and interactions are not the motions of puppets but of agents with their own specific types of powers. We ourselves are flesh-and-blood creatures, not spirits or machines.

Against this backdrop, the history of life follows the "natural" pattern that we see in the fossil and genomic records – from the simple to the complex, from simple stimulus-response capabilities to elaborate nervous systems, from cyanobacteria to dinosaurs to all the species we see today. Beginning with the Cambrian Explosion, the supra-physical plays a key role as we see creatures with elaborate nervous systems populating the Earth. Nervous systems have pain receptors, of which nociceptors are key. The International Association for the Study of Pain defines pain as "an unpleasant sensory and emotional experience associated with actual or potential tissue damage or described in terms of such damage." Evolutionary theorists talk of pain as an adaptive trait that improves survival value.

The experience of pain in a human person is different from that of other mammals simply because humans have a demonstrated awareness of their selves and their continued self-identity (as shown in recent work by Joseph E. LeDoux and Richard Brown). The evolutionary account talks of the physical structures and processes that enable different organisms to be conscious in different ways. It also speaks of consciousness in terms of learning about the environment and about what is beneficial or not for the organism. This account certainly is useful in describing the vehicles and advantages of consciousness. But it says nothing about how the phenomenon of consciousness itself – the capability of being aware – arose. The power of being aware – as opposed to the vehicles of awareness – cannot be described or explained physically.

You can talk of photons and neurons and the various parts of the nervous system, but none of these physical elements can "see" or "hear": to see is to be visually conscious. To hear is to exercise auditory consciousness. This is a qualitatively different phenomenon from the physical and nothing about the physical world or its laws can tell us anything about it. Nevertheless, this supra-physical reality is integrated with the physical. In addition, it is the organism that sees and hears not a collection of chemicals or genes. The organism is a real conscious agent.

The variety of conscious organisms is astounding, ranging from parakeets and ant-eaters to lions and tigers to camels and kangaroos. Each of them, by interacting in various ways *on their own*, have created the world in which we live. This is the world into which we are born. This is the world that resulted in *Homo sapiens*.

Hypothetically, we can imagine a world in which there are no agents – only puppets controlled by a superpower. Yes, there would be no bloodshed or death in such a world. There would be no pain or pleasure, either. But would that be a "better" world than what we have today, one which follows natural laws and is driven by the agents that make it up?

This is the choice we face – the puppet world or the real world of agents. The Christian claim is that the real world, no matter how messy, is the only one in which the kind of free, rational psychophysical beings we are could emerge. Its Creator is not a puppeteer or a programmer.

Rather, the Creator – operating through natural processes – brought forth a world of different kinds of agents culminating in free, rational beings who can choose to fall in love with him – or not. Such a world is necessarily an inextricably inter-locked web of agents of every type with a wide spectrum of powers operating in accordance with natural laws. Even the history of the Christian revelation shows that it was built around the free acts of numerous agents. Here, too, we see the pattern of simple to complex – Israel started with one individual (Abraham) and ended up as a nation.

Remarkably, Charles Darwin, in the same letter in which he talks about the problem of the parasitoid wasps, recognizes the possibility that suffering can be understood in the context of divinely instituted natural laws: "On the other hand I cannot anyhow be contented to view this wonderful universe & especially the nature of man, & to conclude that everything is the result of brute force. I am inclined to look at everything as resulting from designed laws, with the details, whether good or bad, left to the working out of what we may call chance. ... Certainly I agree with you that my views are not at all necessarily atheistical. The lightning kills a man, whether a good one or bad one, owing to the excessively complex action of natural laws, ... & that all these laws may have been expressly designed by an omniscient Creator, who foresaw every future event & consequence."

Admittedly, he also confessed that "the more I think [about this issue] the more bewildered I become"[142] but this is because he was thinking of terms of William Paley's watchmaker deity.

Contrary to Darwin's assumption, the infinite-eternal God does not "foresee." There is no before or after, no "when" in God: Our space-time continuum, in its entirety, is known to him eternally.

Christianity also makes the claim that our final destiny, the Omega, is one of eternal union with our Creator, the Alpha. In this Omega state, according to the biblical texts, we will have the company of animals in some fashion that we cannot imagine today.

Atkinson: This is beginning to sound like an LSD trip. As a scientist, I simply cannot connect with someone who has no use for the evidence of their senses. What is most aggravating is your continuing evasion of the fact of animal pain. A fact that is deadly for all your claims.

MA: You're right about our not connecting. And that it has to do with the evidence of the senses. You've consistently evaded the raw reality of the supra-physical – not only the fact of your being conscious but of your own self-hood. How can I connect with someone who doesn't think they are someone?

But on animal pain, I do not think you have been paying attention to me. I have pointedly emphasized the reality of pain and violence in the animal realm. And I said that animals are real, autonomous agents and not automatons as you suppose. As such, animals interact and the consequences of these interactions are often painful.

But is this "deadly" for the world-picture that has emerged from divine revelation?

---

142   Letter to Asa Gray May 22, 1860.

The real question is why would God allow agents to interact in ways that cause pain. Why does he permit death and decay across the natural world? And why are there carnivorous animals?

I have addressed these questions to a great extent but let me show you what most people leave out in their approach to this matter.

Who, before birth, could have possibly imagined the world into which they are born? When we look around at all the wonders of the natural world, of the creatures that inhabit land and sea and air, of human existence, could we have even dreamt ("before" we were born) that any of this would have been possible?

And who gave us all of this?

It is the infinite-eternal Source of being that is not only all-powerful but infinitely loving (as will be shown).

So what awaits us in the world to come?

We have been informed by the Source of its being that this very same world will be transformed to take on new powers. It will enter into a glorified state.

At present, we are going through labor pains. These include the actual pain and suffering undergone not only by us but by our fellow creatures. This is an inescapable part of being autonomous agents – but it is not a permanent state. So we are told.

This is what we know from the revelation derived ultimately from God incarnate:

- God created all things.

- God loves all his creatures, human and non-human.

- God endowed all creatures with a degree of autonomy.

- God originally intended humans to "take care" of animals (*Genesis* 2:20).

- God's plan of creation entails a "trial" period here-and-now followed by an eternal glorified state for all who cooperate with the divine Plan.

- This glorified state includes animals – perhaps those animals we "humanize" by our interactions with them (as divinely intended).

- Yes, there is suffering here and now, but through the victory of God incarnate, all of creation is moving to a climax of eternal glory.

As I said, we could not possibly have imagined the world into which we were born. The same can be said of the world to come. With regard to animals, we have a glimpse of what might be possible in the relationships we enter into here-and-now with the "pets" we come to know and love and "humanize."

As C.S. Lewis said so well,

> The strong conviction which we have of a real, though doubtless rudimentary, form of selfhood in the higher animals, and specially in those we tame, is not an illusion, [and] their destiny demands a somewhat deeper consideration. ... In so far as the tame animal has a real self or personality, it owes this almost entirely to its master. ... Those beasts that attain a real self are in their masters. ... And in this way it seems to me possible that certain animals may have an immortality, not in themselves, but in the immortality of their masters. ... Their mere sentience is reborn to soulhood in us as our mere soulhood is reborn to spirituality in Christ.[143]

Cambridge Palaeobiologist Simon Conway Morris writes that "With humans now everywhere, animals have both benefitted (bird-feeders) and suffered (vivisection), but more notably animals brought up in close

---

143   C.S. Lewis, *The Problem of Pain* (Collins: London, 1975), 126-7,129.

association with humans are conspicuously smarter than their cousins in the wild. In other words they are enculturated. And this makes a difference. … The gulf that separates us from all other animals is encompassed by our self-awareness of an unavoidable fate. Paradoxically, however, Christianity insists this abyss of death is neither final nor eternal but is to be redeemed by the Incarnate One. Nor need it be a matter of wishful thinking that not only humans will be restored, but by promise the rest of Creation." (emphasis added)

If humans who enter eternity are granted certain limited divine-like powers, could not animals in the New World be granted limited human-like powers?

In the Omega state, as we saw, "there shall be no more death or mourning, wailing or pain, [for] the old order has passed away." (*Revelation* 21:4)

This is the endgame. This is the Big Picture in terms of which all events and entities – "all things bright and beautiful, all creatures great and small" – make ultimate sense.

"MORAL MONSTER"

Witness – Richard Peterson (RP)

LH: My next witness, Professor Robert Peterson, has delivered a fatal blow to the conceit of the Christian god. Certainly, he has removed any vestige of a pretense that this figment of feverish imaginations is either good or loving. His recent work, *A Dangerous Book*, exposes the darkness of the Old Testament deity. As a professor of comparative religion, he knows what he is talking about when it comes to the history, the nature, and the impact of religious texts. So, Professor Peterson, give us your professional opinion of the deity portrayed in the Bible.

Peterson: Thank you, Lucius. I welcome this and any opportunity to warn the public of this murderous ideology masquerading as a religion. It is an ideology that derives its power from the god it worships. And the intentions and actions of this god are laid out in gory detail – and I mean gory – in the so-called Old Testament.

The god of the Old Testament is a genocidal tyrant who orders the slaughter of entire peoples including children. It demands slavish subservience and unceasing praise from its traumatized followers. It is jealous and insufferably possessive. At the express command of this deity, the people of Israel, by their own account, left a trail of carnage and ruin across the ancient Middle East.

If anyone reads this book and takes it as Holy Writ, they will become not only intolerant and obnoxious but pose a danger to civilized society. The Old Testament is a book that gives a religious warrant to savagery and barbarism of the most sickening variety. It has led sensitive readers to depression and suicide. Just as publication of Hitler's *Mein Kampf* was prohibited for many years in post-war Germany, I urge the world community to ban continued publication and distribution of this book, which has become the cornerstone of three world religions and is synonymous with hatred and lunacy.

LH: That was a tour de force. At the risk of descending from the sublime to the ridiculous, Professor Peterson, is there any redeeming feature of the Old Testament?

Peterson: Does *Mein Kampf* have any redeeming feature? My answer about both books is an unequivocal and resounding "No." The Old Testament is a fit book for burning. It ought to be banned because it represents a mortal threat to human civilization, to sexual and reproductive freedoms, and to the lives of freethinkers and those who are "different."

LH: Thank you. Your witness, Mr. Angelini.

MA: Thank you. Professor Peterson, let me start with a quick question. Do you believe in the right to abortion?

LH: Objection, Your Honor. My opponent is yet again creating diversions to steer us away from what is fatal to his case.

Judge: Counsel, on what basis are you bringing up an unrelated issue?

MA: Your Honor, this question, like others I bring up, will make it clear that the witness has his own agenda, and the jury needs to know this. My opponent is aware that I will strip off the façade, and that is why he is panicking.

Judge: You may proceed.

MA: Professor Peterson, let me ask you again, do you believe in the right to terminate a pregnancy?

Peterson: I am a scholar, not a lawyer. I can see why Winston Churchill said, "Lawyers occasionally stumble over the truth, but most of them pick themselves up and hurry off as if nothing had happened." You seem to be only interested in verbal games and not the truth. To answer your question, yes, of course I believe in the right of abortion, a right that has been stringently prohibited by this book – the Old Testament – along with many other strange prohibitions.

MA: Well, I did not ask the question to play any games or even to compare it to the prohibitions of the Old Testament. It was intended to show that you really have no standing to challenge the morality of the book on the basis that it promotes the slaughter of children. You say that the God of the Old Testament asks his followers to slaughter children. And yet, you are willing to promote and defend the right to slaughter children in the most macabre way possible.

Peterson: That is ridiculous and insulting. I support the reproductive rights of women as does any enlightened society. I have no right to tell women what to do with their bodies. And neither does the State.

MA: You seem to have missed my point. Let me try to clarify with another question: is the fetus that is destroyed in an abortion a human being?

Peterson: I go with the scientific consensus that biological life begins after the fertilization of the egg which results in the production of the full genetic code of a human being. But the question here is not whether the fetus is a human being but when it has a right to life. It has a right to life once it is born.

MA: OK, so you admit that the fetus is a human being. As you may know, in most common forms of abortion, the fetus' body is torn apart with an aspirator and the pieces suctioned out or a knife is used to dismember it, or (in chemical abortions) it is starved to death. In later stage abortions, its body and skull are methodically cut to pieces and then taken out. In the latest stage abortions, the contents of its skull are suctioned out and the dead body is then delivered. There is a scientific consensus that the fetus feels pain by the third trimester, and there is good reason to believe that it starts feeling pain well before. I, for one, consider this to be a savage practice in a civilized society but that is not our topic here. Our topic is whether killing children is immoral. I certainly think it is immoral but you think it is morally acceptable for us to kill children but not for God to do so.

Peterson: That is a deliberate and insidious distortion of my position. I simply hold that it is a basic right for any woman to decide if and when she wants to give birth to a child. In the Old Testament, the deity expressly orders the massacre of children who are already born.

MA: So, it is wrong only if the child is born?

Peterson: Yes. That would be infanticide.

MA: OK. Moments ago, you admitted that the fetus in the womb is human. It appears that you do not agree with the old saying that you cannot be half-pregnant. You are saying it is possible to be a "half human being." It depends on which side of the womb you're on.

Peterson: This is becoming tiresome. I did not take the stand to be lectured by a right-wing fanatic.

MA: I am not right-wing and I am not left-wing. I am concerned with questions of right and wrong – something you apparently do not take seriously.

Peterson: You are evading all the *prima facie* evidence I provided for the morally monstrous nature of the Old Testament deity.

MA: Do not worry. I will get to all the gory detail you mentioned. But first, we have to set the rules for what is moral if you are accusing God of being immoral. My second question is: Do you believe in sin?

Peterson: Sin is a fiction invented by Christians that they attribute to their mythical deity. It is a dangerous fiction because it has been used to demoralize and exploit the masses and to murder designated sinners. I not only do not believe in sin, I abhor the very idea of it. The idea of sin, however, has no bearing on our discussion other than to serve as one more example of the instruments of torture associated with the Old Testament deity.

MA: It has more of a bearing than you think, as I will try to show. Do you believe it is possible for people to do things that are wrong and that there should be consequences for wrongdoing?

Peterson: Right and wrong are human inventions and do not have any independent validity. The only wrong actions are those which infringe on the rights and well-being of others. But the wrongness is strictly an illusory idea in the mind.

MA: So, you are saying that when Stalin periodically purged his staff by executing them or sent dissenters to the gulags, he was not doing something that was actually wrong. Or if a scientist develops human clones with unseen abnormalities, there should be no restraints on his experimentation. We may call some of these actions wrong because they have detrimental effects on others, but these are just our personal, arbitrary expressions of opinion with no foundation or authority beyond that.

Peterson: I see where you are going with this. Since I say there is no such thing as right or wrong, the Old Testament deity cannot be said to be doing anything wrong. What a cold-blooded, cynical ploy. So typical of your profession and your religion.

MA: Well, I was headed to another destination. But you have just added a second stopping point. Thanks for the tip. Yes, since you don't believe there is any objective right and wrong, you cannot indict God for what is strictly a subjective human opinion. There are no crimes against humanity because there are no crimes.

And now let me also take you to my original destination. The Old Testament can be seen as a chronicle of sin and its consequences: this dimension is highlighted throughout its texts. For someone who does not believe in sin, it will make no sense – as it has not for you. I will expand further on this. But this is one more ground rule in which you are in an untenable situation. You have not only cut off the branch on which you are sitting, but you deny the existence of the tree.

Peterson: I have come here to speak about a deadly threat to humanity. You are trying to desperately avoid my open-and-shut case with a poor attempt at slapstick comedy. I would have said you can't be serious. But it is hardly possible to say this to someone like you who is fundamentally unserious.

MA: I appreciate your annoyance over the quandary you have created for yourself. But let me ask you a third question. Did the God whom you call a genocidal tyrant have any favorites? Did he go easy on those whom you say were slavishly subservient to him?

Peterson: He called them his Chosen People and led them to what he said was their Promised Land. So, of course, he had favorites!

MA: But, by your own account, God also punished the Israelites. In fact, this happens quite often, and the latter part of the book is about the Chosen People going into exile and the travails caused by their own misdeeds.

Peterson: So what? In no way does such alleged punishment take away the responsibility for all the suffering caused on the deity's orders or by its actions.

MA: The point of this is that the God of the Old Testament had bigger fish to fry than handing down punishments willy-nilly. Your analysis of the Old Testament represents a colossal misunderstanding and misrepresentation of what exactly is being communicated there. It is primarily a message of the goodness and love of God and his grief over the self-chosen path of evil taken by his creatures, with all its inevitable consequences. Of course, I am not surprised by your distortion of the text's overall message given that your value system allows for the slaughter of children and sees nothing fundamentally serious about acts of evil.

LH: Objection, Your Honor. This is a vile personal insult and has no place in a courtroom. I move that this attack on the character of my distinguished witness be struck.

Judge: Granted. Counsel, I am warning you to stick to the issues. You need to respond to the precise charges made by the witness.

MA: Your Honor, I had no intention of insulting the witness. I just wanted to highlight his starting points for the benefit of the jury. In the matter of insults, I think the record will show that it is my Client who is the target of vile invective. But anyway, I will show that the specific claims made by the witness are without merit.

Judge: Please proceed.

MA: The God revealed in the Old Testament is the God known by the entire human race prior to the coming of Christ.

We see a living awareness of a supreme Godhead not just in primeval peoples, but in the religious life of ancient India, China, Persia and Mesopotamia. Polytheism was actually a secondary phenomenon, a devolution from the most ancient insight, which was that of the Supreme Being. The awareness of the Absolute came to a climax in the history of the Jews.

Critics forget the unprecedented nature of Jewish monotheism: the Hebrew Bible is an account of the interaction between the divine Mind and a specific race of people over a period of thousands of years. And the crux of this interaction is the deity's insistence on monotheism ("Thou shalt have no other gods before me.")

Nowhere in ancient history do we find anything remotely similar. God is telling a people that they shall have no other god. The Shema is to be recited daily: "Hear, O Israel: the LORD our God, the LORD is one." (*Deuteronomy.* 6:4) Monotheism had to be drummed into the human mind because of the constant temptation to wander away from it. So much so, idolatry and polytheism were punishable by death.

Why? Because human fulfillment only comes from union with God. To abandon the covenantal commitment to the Lord who is One means becoming a slave of Satan. To embrace Satan is to separate oneself from God which is to embrace death. The fate of the nation of Israel then depended on their faithfulness to this command – and the history of Israel is just as much a history of the consequences of deviation from monotheism as it is anything else.

And clearly the "treatment" worked. The Jews, by the time of Jesus, were as staunchly monotheist as it is possible for a people to be. In point of fact, at the end of the day, the Jewish people became the world's greatest heralds of monotheism. This fact alone is extraordinary enough to call for a transcendent explanation.

There are several other key commonalities of theme in the major pre-Christian religious systems. The ancient religious world-visions believed that the Divinely instituted sacred order of the universe had been breached by human evil and that humanity had to perform sacrifice in expiation.

Sacrifice, in fact, began at the very dawn of human history with the hunter-gatherers. *Homo sapiens*, from primordial times, has sought to make reparation for some nameless sin through the universal practice of sacrifice. "With remarkable consistency, myths tell of the origins of man in a fall, a crime that is often a bloody act of violence," wrote the great historian of ancient mythology, Walter Burkert.[144]

The focus on atonement, covenant and communion was especially apparent in the elaborate ceremonies of the largest organized religions in the world of 1000 B.C. – those of India, Persia, China, Israel and the Mediterranean societies. For instance, sacrifice is a central theme in Hinduism where it was tied to the belief in *rtá*, the sacred order of the universe that includes both the workings of Nature and the dictates of justice and righteousness. And, of course, sacrifice was central to the Old Testament.

144 Walter Burkert, *Homo Necans: The Anthropology of Ancient Greek Sacrificial Ritual and Myth* transl. Peter Bing (Berkeley, California: University of California Press, 1983), 21-2.

Underlying the interaction between God and the people of Israel was a partnership or covenant between them. The covenant came into being because of the obedience of Abraham, the father of the Israelites, and was later amplified under Moses, their greatest leader. In both cases, the covenant was ratified with sacrifice. The exodus of the Israelites from Egypt under Moses was commemorated (under divine command) by the annual Passover sacrifice in which an unblemished lamb was sacrificed and its flesh consumed by the priests and the people.

Mosaic law called for a superstructure of sacrifices. These sacrifices were required for atonement for sin. Sin itself began with the breach between God and humankind depicted in the first book of the Bible.

Three other themes are prominent in the Old Testament: the prophecy of the coming of a Messiah who would usher in a new era and whose kingdom is everlasting; the promise of a new covenant with God that will be written on the human heart; and the narrative of a suffering servant who would redeem his people from their sins by his death. With the coming of Christ, the Covenant between God and man was embodied in a Person.

Peterson: I don't see what any of this has to do with the deity regularly killing off the beings he created or directing his followers to engage in plunder, pillage, and murder.

MA: These are two separate issues. One concerns the direct acts of God and the other the acts of the Israelites.

With regard to the acts of God, let us begin with what I said about the testimony of the human race to its breach of the divine order. The breach is not simply the original act of alienation from God. It includes the continuous multiplication of breaches by every human person. This is what is meant by sin. Through its practice of sacrifice, humankind showed its awareness that this breach had consequences which it sought to expiate and mitigate through sacrifice. This universal idea of a moral law, its breach, and the consequences of the breach explains everything that happens in the Old

Testament with one unique addition – the God whose law was breached is personally involved in trying to rectify the breach.

As we have heard, what is common to the codes of morality in different societies is the Golden Rule – do unto others as you would have them do unto you. Despite this continuity of conviction across cultures and peoples, there is still something odd about the Old Testament story. Yes, the Israelites had moral commandments, and many of these commandments resemble the codes of other communities. Yet, they see their commandments as parts of their covenant with God. God, as understood by Israel, was not an impersonal Absolute or capricious deity. He is an infinite and eternal Spirit and yet he is personal and concrete. He is demanding but he is demanding precisely because this is what is most beneficent for his human partners. And it is he who initiates the agreement, lays out its structure and enforces its provisions. Moral laws are the touchstones of the partnership between Creator and creature.

The whole point of the Deuteronomic history (laid out in *Joshua*, *Judges*, 1 and 2 *Samuel* and 1 and 2 *Kings*) is not to sing the praises of kings and rulers. Rather, it seeks to show how Israel honored or breached the laws of God in each generation and how the tidal wave of disobedience finally culminates in calamitous consequences. The consequences of breaking the partnership agreement with God are spelled out most clearly in the Book of Deuteronomy, the last book of the Pentateuch.

Moral laws apply specifically to free agents who make choices. In moral matters, the choice is always between breaking and keeping a law. Of course, the laws apply regardless of whether you recognize them. If you unwittingly break a law you still suffer consequences. To take an analogy from the laws of Nature, you will suffer the consequences of leaping from the terrace of a skyscraper whether or not you know anything about the law of gravity.

To keep a law of God is to cooperate with him. Now, if you break one of his laws, the consequences sometimes affect others and not just the law-breaker. A terrorist who poisons the water supply of a city causes mayhem in the lives of many. This illustrates the unity of the human race. Cooperation and unity are important in understanding human destiny.

What is the logic behind the laws? Are they just an arbitrary mish-mash of "commandments" set up by God to "test" us? Are they simply artificial constructs devised to concoct a grading system for salvation?

The answer is this: Each law of God, in one way or another, is a law that concerns love – the love of your neighbor and your God. Only in "leaving" your self can you love and only in loving can you be united with God. Thus, each law shapes and refines your capacity for love. Each law molds your soul into a vehicle of love. You were created to love and only in loving will you be fulfilled. This is the fundamental revelation of God to humanity.

I know that for you and other skeptics the assumption that there are laws and consequences for breaking laws is anathema. Unfortunately such attitudes are about as helpful as an emancipation proclamation against the law of gravity. If there are rules of reality that apply in life, your views regarding whether we should have them or whether they are fair are superfluous.

The laws remain in force regardless of whether you like them, think them fair, or live by them. If you choose to flout them, so much the worse for you. They apply to everybody not just those who "believe" in them. Pluralism and democracy offer advantages as a polity tailored to the human condition. But the realm of moral law is reality itself, and here, opinions and polls, compromises and calculations are meaningless. You might as well say that 2+2 can be 3 if you will it to be so.

Now, you can "will" this result (2+2=3) all you want, but you are unlikely to stake your life on it. Let us say you load two bullets into the chamber of a gun and then two more. You then fire the gun thrice. Would you attempt to demonstrate your contention that, for you, 2+2=3 by pointing the gun at your head and pulling the trigger?

What about those who do not know about the moral law? Are they at a disadvantage and is that fair? All human beings begin with an intuitive knowledge of the essential law of God. Some are faithful to these intuitions. Some fall prey to influences beyond their control and flout this law. Some deliberately reject the law with full knowledge and consent. Those who suppress their awareness of the law are clearly at a disadvantage in relation to those who try to adhere to it. But, ultimately, each of us is held responsible only for that which we freely choose.

Despite the analogies, it should be clarified that moral laws are not laws of Nature. Neither are they laws governing certain kinds of human behavior such as the laws of economics. Rather they are rules reflecting the very nature of God, the Ultimate Reality, and they are rules directly revealed by God as emblems of the covenant relationship with him. These rules have to do with our interaction with finite goods. As such, to keep a divinely revealed "rule" is to participate in the Absolute Good that is God.

What are portrayed as punishments of God in the Old Testament are simply the consequences of evil choices by human agents. The acts of the Israelites and others are part of the whole web of cause and effect created by sin.

Peterson: Primitive peoples may have thought there is a moral law that is the law of God. We know now that the only laws that exist are the laws demonstrated by science. There is no evidence for any other kind of law.

MA: Your skepticism is amusing because atheists and evolutionary atheists, in particular, tend to be schizophrenic. You live in two totally different, contradictory worlds at the same time.

In one world, you hold that all of us are bits of matter whose thoughts are nothing more than the random motion of particles. Moreover, you posit that we are incapable of free choice and all your decisions and actions are driven by evolutionary pressures and psychological forces.

But, in the other world, you think of yourself as a rational beings who can weigh evidence and freely make logical arguments. You are purposeful in your actions. You are lonely defenders of human freedom who resist the oppressive reign of religion.

In one world, you are an unintelligent robot; in the other you are an intelligent, courageous hero. So, which is the real world? If you tried to live as if the first world, the robotic world, was the real world then you would be declared insane. But to affirm the second world of matter-independent rationality and will is to slip into the world of the laws of God. From your standpoint, of course, it is easier to proclaim one thing and live another.

The main point I am making here is simply that, if the moral law exists, it applies regardless of whether or not you believe in it.

Peterson: You are just dancing around peripheral issues. I want you to address the concrete acts of the deity and its followers in the Old Testament. This is the subject of my testimony and you have yet to come to grips with it.

MA: The issues are far from peripheral. I am trying to present the rules of evidence which would govern proof of fact but you want to avoid these essential starting points.

But I will turn to the details of the Old Testament. In *Genesis*, we see the initial breach between God and humanity. One consequence of this breach, the Fall, is that humans are under the reign of evil (the Devil is called "the ruler of this world" in *John* 12:31). When people ask, "Why did God not prevent this heinous act or that reign of terror?", they forget that they live in a world that has been handed over (by their ancestors) to the reign of the Enemy. This brings home to us the "final" nature of human freedom. God has given his creatures freedom which means that they are truly in control of their destiny and their welfare. If they wreck themselves and then turn to God for help, he can only respond in ways that do not infringe on the "free-ness" built into the created order. It also requires them to obey God's commands, commands which are essential for their own well-being.

Obedience does not simply concern the Garden of Eden. It is the principal theme of the Bible and the foundation of the relationship between God and humanity.

Even at a purely human level, it is obvious that obedience is essential to the well-being of humanity. No society can survive without some set of rules that must be obeyed and some way of enforcing these rules. No organization can operate effectively without leaders. It is assumed that these leaders act for the welfare of their organizations and obedience to their instructions is therefore rational; disobedience would be detrimental to the greater good.

When the leader is Someone who knows all things and loves you infinitely, then disobedience is not simply irrational but catastrophic. It is as if a non-pilot has hijacked a plane and taken over its flight controls. The question is not whether there will be a crash but how bad it will be.

The experience of the Israelites is inextricably connected to *Genesis*. The themes of God's creation and providence, of obedience and the consequence of disobedience, that we find in *Genesis* 1-3 resonates through the rest of the Hebrew Bible.

The gathering momentum of evil is chronicled from Genesis 4 through 11: after the exile from Eden comes the sin of Cain and then the habitual evil that comes to a head in the arrogance of Babel and the universal debauchery of Noah's day. The descendants of Adam were aware of their connection with the divine order – "At that time men began to invoke the LORD by name" (*Genesis* 4:26). But in time, they became morally de-sensitized: "In the eyes of God the earth was corrupt and full of lawlessness." (*Genesis* 6:11). The defiance of divine law was so massive that the consequence was a flood which submerged the known world (traditions of a great flood were, in fact, extant in ancient China, India, Babylon, Sumeria and Persia).

Because of his faithfulness to the divine law the obedient Noah and his family were spared. After the flood, "Noah built an altar to the LORD" and "offered holocausts on the altar." (8:20). God follows up an earlier covenant with Adam where he promised a victorious offspring with a Noahidic covenant. He promises Noah that he will never again devastate the earth with a flood. God also reiterates the moral commands he laid down earlier, principally the prohibition against the taking of human life and the command to be fruitful and multiply.

The rest of the Hebrew Bible is an account, on one level, of divinely instituted covenants and laws, commandments and rituals, and, on the other, of individuals and peoples who observe or break these statutes and reap the consequences, good and bad. The heroes of the Hebrew Bible are those who obeyed and trusted God in the most unlikely circumstances. It is through them that God worked his plan for restoring fallen humanity. The two greatest such protagonists were Abraham and Moses.

In addition to the Ten Commandments, God imposed elaborate new laws and prohibitions and ritual requirements on the Israelites. These included the two annual sacrifices, Passover and the Yom Kippur scapegoat sacrifice, as well as numerous others. There was a reason for these stringent measures. The Israelites rebelled frequently against the God who led them out of Egypt and often reverted to paganism and idolatry. Only a Great Wall of rules could protect them against the innate tendencies that inevitably brought ruin on them and simultaneously obstructed God's rescue plan for humanity. Thus, the story of Israel was one of both covenant and exile, law and punishment.

By the second millennium of the life of Israel, an intriguing new theme began to appear in the preaching of the Prophets. In *Isaiah, Jeremiah* and *Ezekiel*, as also in *Micah, Zechariah, Hosea, Daniel* and *Malachi*, we see prophecies of a new and universal Covenant, a new Mediator for all humanity and a perfect Sacrifice.

The fine balance between law and autonomy that we see in nature culminates in the interaction between free rational agents and the law of God.

And this interaction is mapped out in abundant detail in the history of Israel which is a history of God's initiative to deliver the human race from its enslavement to evil.

As reiterated throughout the Bible, in the Old and the New Testaments, sin leads to death. And it is only we who can decide whether to sin or not.

Peterson: We're still waiting for a straight answer to my question about the slaughter ordered by your deity. You're simply trying to distract us with abstractions. Let's get to the raw data recounted in these primitive narratives.

MA: Well, I had to first lay out the actual background of the Old Testament events in view of your multiple misrepresentations. The Bible opens with God's dismay at the violence of Cain and with violence in general. The climax of the biblical story is God incarnate himself becoming a voluntary victim of violence – so as to end violence.

Let me now turn to the specifics you're concerned with.

The divine goal for creation and the foundations of the moral law are laid out in their pristine form in *Genesis*. The dignity of the human person – male and female – lies in our being made in the image of God. Marriage is a permanent union between man and woman. In *Genesis*, we see also that God abhors killing and immorality.

> "Indeed for your own lifeblood I will demand an accounting: ... from a human being, each one the blood of another, I will demand an accounting for human life." (*Genesis* 9:5)

> "When the LORD saw how great the wickedness of human beings was on earth, and how every desire that their heart conceived was always nothing but evil ... his heart was grieved." (*Genesis* 6:5-6)

The reference to the "heart" is moving: "His heart was grieved." This is a Lover trying to prevent his beloved from destroying herself as is so evident across the Old Testament. Especially striking is Hosea's report of the Lord's lament: "Thus says the LORD: When Israel was a child I loved him, out of Egypt I called my son. The more I called them, the farther they went from me, Sacrificing to the Baals and burning incense to idols. Yet it was I who taught Ephraim to walk, who took them in my arms; I drew them with human cords, with bands of love; I fostered them like one who raises an infant to his cheeks; Yet, though I stooped to feed my child, they did not know that I was their healer. My heart is overwhelmed, my pity is stirred. I will not give vent to my blazing anger, I will not destroy Ephraim again; For I am God and not man, the Holy One present among you; I will not let the flames consume you." (*Hosea* 11:1-4, 8-9)

It is no surprise then that the Lover implores his beloved to turn back from the evil that leads to their death: "I take no pleasure in the death of the wicked, but rather that they turn from their ways and live. Turn, turn from your evil ways! Why should you die, house of Israel?" (*Ezekiel* 33:11)

In *Exodus*, God gives his Ten Commandments which can be sub-divided under two foundational categories – loving God and neighbor.

When we come to the web of codes and laws laid out in *Deuteronomy* and *Leviticus* we are dealing with something different from the pristine teaching of Genesis and the Ten Commandments.

The Mosaic laws of *Deuteronomy* are secondary and temporary. Jeremiah and Ezekiel tell us these will be replaced by a new and universal covenant. In the New Testament, Jesus tells us that Moses made many concessions because of the hardness of the hearts of his people but these were not part of the law originally laid down by God in *Genesis*.

Your examples of bizarre orders from the deity are taken from the Deuteronomic laws that were in fact instituted by Moses. His objective was to restrain the evil impulses of his people with disciplinary structures much like militaries impose their own behavioral codes and practices to train their forces for combat. These structures did not conform to the ideals laid down in *Genesis* and sometimes were concessions like servitude and patriarchy (in contrast with the dignity and equality of *Genesis*) that prevented greater evils. They were often improvements on the cultural mores of the time and were customized to the mindsets of a primitive people. God loves you whether you are a mass murderer or a prostitute and starts with you from where you are. Likewise, Moses began with the Israelites from where they were with the full understanding that he could impose on them only what they could handle in their state of mind at the time.

About the attacks on the Canaanites and others, it should be noted that these narratives were formulaic and rhetorical accounts like those of the Israelites' contemporaries. It demonstrably exaggerated accomplishments and acts of war.

Did God order the Israelites to kill children? No.

Of course, there are accounts that attribute such commands to God. But we know God hates killing and violence as so emphatically affirmed in *Genesis* and re-affirmed by Jesus the incarnation of God. We also know that the accounts of mass slaughter were exaggerations written using the literary forms of the time. *Joshua* 10 talks about Joshua having wiped out all the inhabitants of the land, the hill country and the lowlands. But the later chapters of *Joshua* as well as the post-*Joshua* accounts of *Judges* show the Israelites continuing to be in conflict with the inhabitants of these lands – they certainly had not been wiped out! This kind of language of total destruction is found in other writings of the time – in the Hittites, the Egyptians, the Moabites and others – even when such complete destruction clearly did not take place. Hyperbole is what you expect and find.

When we hear the pronouncement "the Lord said," we should read it in the context of literary form: is it an epic, a poem, a war anthem, a war ballad, a prophecy, a genealogy, a law-book? Is it apocalyptic, wisdom or prophetic literature? We must also consider the speaker's background, style (rhetoric) and setting. The paradigm for interpreting any attributions to the Lord are *Genesis* and the revelation of Jesus.

When we say "the sun is setting" we understand it in the paradigm of visual appearances not in terms of physics. If we say "the time is 12 p.m.," the context is not the "time" of the entire universe but within a local setting.

Jesus is THE paradigm of God's being and "rules" for humanity: all pronouncements attributed to God should be measured against Jesus' definitive revelation of God.

Nevertheless, it should be emphasized that God did not want the Israelites to be infected with the evil practices of the peoples they encountered – from idolatry to bestiality to child sacrifice. When God condemns the Baals and the idols, the real target is Satan. As *Deuteronomy* and *Leviticus* and the *Psalms* tell us, the idols are stand-ins for demons. To worship them is to become a slave of Satan. If Israel is to be the vehicle of God's liberation of humanity from the Evil One, it cannot itself become one more vassal of Satan. The Holy of Holies, the infinite Lover, cannot co-exist with the slightest evil let alone the diabolic. To be the Chosen People meant living under the Will of God and not under the dominion of the Devil. If you worship demons you become demonic. If you have no room for family relationships you become dehumanized. Whenever the Israelites left the divine fold and turned to practices like idolatry, they lost the protection of God and met with ruin and wretchedness.

Yes, the Old Testament speaks of the wrath of God and his punishment. This is because the moral law is not like the physical laws of Nature and its Author is not an impersonal force. The moral law is the Love that is God and to reject this law is to reject the infinite Lover: it is a rejection of Someone and not something and the consequence is pain and suffering. This is a punishment from God which is a self-inflicted punishment.

Peterson: So you want to duck the awkward parts of the Old Testament by excusing them as exercises in hyperbole? If that's the case, then you have to hold with me that the whole book is a human creation, albeit a perverse and repulsive one. Everything in it is fiction.

MA: Quite the contrary. Everything in the Old Testament has to be understood as a wholly accurate account of the conflict between good and evil in the human soul. It also highlights on the stage of history what we see in nature, namely, the balance of order and autonomy, and what we see in our own lives, the power to choose or reject love. The Old Testament is not a textbook of science. But neither is it a textbook of theology or a work of history as understood in the modern sense. It is a composite creation encompassing various kinds of literary works, forms and styles.

I did not evade or excuse the texts you cite. But I do think that you have to read the whole story if you want to understand the plot, the role of the different characters and the relevance of certain sub-plots. Your approach is one of reading Othello with exclusive attention to Iago or of viewing the Second World War only from the perspective of Hiroshima and Nagasaki. You ignore any data you find inconvenient so as to tout your arbitrary premises as conclusions. If you want a thorough analysis of the Old Testament that honestly addresses its awkward passages, I highly recommend *Did God Really Command Genocide?* authored by Paul Copan and Matt Flanagan.

About the Old Testament battle narratives, Copan writes,

> God's overarching goal was to bring blessing and salvation to all the nations, including the Canaanites, through Abraham (Gen. 12:3; 22:17-18; cf. 28:13-14). The covenant God made with Abraham is unique in its sweeping, outsider-oriented, universally directed nature. It is unlike any other ancient religious movement. Yet, for a specific, relatively short, and strategic period, God sought to establish Israel in the land with a view to fulfilling this long-term, global (indeed cosmic) plan of redemption. God would simultaneously punish a wicked people ripe for judgment. Not doing so would have

erased humankind's only hope for redemption. God's difficult commandment regarding the Canaanites is … a limited, unique, salvation-historical situation. …

Behind [it] … is the clear context of God's loving intentions and faithful promises. … We can't ignore the context of God's universal blessing to all nations, including national Israel's ancient enemies. … [The commands] must be set against their historical and theological context – namely, the background of Yahweh's enemy-loving character and worldwide saving purposes.

This is illustrated in the book of Jonah. God didn't punish the Ninevites – to the great disappointment of Jonah, who knew that this is the sort of thing Yahweh does: he loves his (and Israel's) enemies. 'I knew that You are a gracious and compassionate God, slow to anger and abundant in lovingkindness, and one who relents concerning calamity' (Jonah 4:2; cf. Exod. 34:6).[145]

The obloquy directed at the God of the Old Testament by you and your colleagues goes beyond misrepresentation to soul-destroying slander. You have maligned the infinitely holy, infinitely loving King of Hearts. He hates violence and killing. He laments the loss of his children who hurl themselves into the traps created by their worst enemy. He seeks to save them and bring them back to their senses but is constantly rebuffed. Nevertheless, he continues to seek them out and in the New Testament we see the salvific initiative come to a climax.

I asked you about what you thought about sin for a reason. "Sin" is not simply a specific act: it is a condition of alienation from the One in whom alone we can find fulfillment. This alienation continually manifests itself in acts that harden us further and widen the gulf. Salvation is liberation from sin. It replaces alienation with reconciliation and redemption.

---

145 Paul Copan, *Is God a Moral Monster? Making Sense of the Old Testament God* (Grand Rapids, Michigan: Baker Books, 2011), 191-2.

The narratives and proclamations of the Old Testament make sense within the framework of alienation, reconciliation and redemption. This is the framework in which its flesh-and-blood characters operate. Just as the laws of Nature keep the universe in harmony, so also our conformity with the moral law implanted in our souls keeps our lives in harmony. The most fundamental representation of the moral law is to be found in the Ten Commandments. If we break the law, we pay a price and the price is pain, suffering and death. This is the message of all the moral codes and primordial religions of humanity.

In the Old Testament, God personally confirms what all have known. But here it also shows us that he wants us to turn back to him. He does not desire us to die. And he will do all he can to liberate us from our enslavement to evil. Our battle with evil is a battle not simply with our own drive to evil but with our spiritual enemy, Satan, and his minions. The Old Testament references to the forces of darkness range from the serpent of Genesis and the adversary of Job to the demons represented by idols and gods. All of these are manifestations of the Devil who from the beginning desires our destruction and damnation.

All who are subjugated to Satan perform acts of horrendous evil that the Holy of Holies cannot tolerate even when the perpetrators are his Chosen People. As we read in *Psalm* 106:37-40: "They sacrificed to demons their own sons and daughters, shedding innocent blood, the blood of their own sons and daughters, whom they sacrificed to the idols of Canaan, desecrating the land with bloodshed. They defiled themselves by their actions, became adulterers by their conduct. So the LORD grew angry with his people, abhorred his own heritage."

Even when he lets us suffer the repercussions of our immoral actions, the Lord desires our amendment: he "rejoices" when we turn aside from the path of death. We are all judged by how we choose. "The last word, when all is heard: Fear God and keep his commandments, for this concerns all humankind; because God will bring to judgment every work, with all its hidden qualities, whether good or bad." (*Ecclesiastes* 12:12-14)

We are made to love. We are built for God. When we praise and worship him we become more like him. Our praise does not benefit him; we do it for our own benefit, much as our appreciation of a fine painting brings no benefit to the artist but enhances our own horizons. "And we know that for those who love God all things work together for good, for those who are called according to his purpose" (*Romans* 8:28).

The Old Testament is a story in search of an ending. It promises a new and universal covenant, a suffering servant who will redeem us from our sins, a Messiah who will take us back to an everlasting Promised Land beyond space and time. But this is a story for another time.

"HELL NO!"

Witness – Bartholomew Endicott (BE)

LH: I am pleased to introduce our star witness, Dr. Bartholomew Endicott. I say "star" because Dr. Endicott once described himself as a Christian. But ever since he had what he calls a "moral awakening" he has left the faith of his childhood behind. I will let him explain why. But I must commend him for having the courage of his conscience given that he was not simply a renowned scholar but a devout Christian from his youth. So Dr. Endicott tell us why you took such a drastic step at great personal cost.

Endicott: Lou, you are too kind. Yes, this change has cost me plenty. I grew up as an Evangelical Christian, a heritage that is part of my very identity as a person. I have lost a lot of my lifelong friends. I have given up several income streams. But I have no regrets. I could not continue living a lie. For this is what Christianity is – a lie, and a pathological lie at that. I guess I knew this for quite a while before I made the final break.

What led me to this parting of the ways was a devilish doctrine at the heart of the religion – the damnable idea of damnation. The dogma of Hell.

Hell is nothing less than a diabolic delusion. It is the sickest, most odious idea ever conjured up by sadistic minds. Whether we are talking of a literal sea of flames in which men and women are tortured forever or an abstract state of misery that never ends, what is being purveyed is an abominable falsehood. Given how many multitudes have been terrorized and emotionally defenestrated by it, I would say that this is the most loathsome conspiracy theory ever propagated. Whoever devised it is a greater villain than the creator of the worst totalitarian ideologies because it is a lethal rapidly transmitted virus that destroys our minds. Whoever promotes this misbelief should be prosecuted and imprisoned for inflicting the greatest imaginable mental suffering on anyone infected by it.

Sick as it is, the idea of Hell is yet inextricable from Christianity. Some theologians still claim to be Christians while dismissing belief in Hell. I agree here with fundamentalist and traditionalist Christians who say that you cannot be a Christian if you do not believe in Hell. And I tell all theologians and liberal Christians, "You cannot have it both ways. You cannot claim to be a champion of human rights while belonging to a totalitarian party."

Some of these liberal, "enlightened" Christians have argued that the idea of Hell being eternal comes from a wrong translation of the Greek term for its duration. They claim the word should be translated as "age" instead of "everlasting." This means that Hell only applies for a certain "age" and does not last forever. The problem is that if Hell's duration is only for an age, then Heaven is not everlasting either because the same term is used about Heaven. And the same term is applied to God, who is clearly thought of as everlasting. Nice try but it just will not fly.

Other ploys are just as pointless. Some Christians say that their idea of God is of someone who is infinitely good and they cannot reconcile that fact with the idea of him creating a finite being that will become so evil as to be in a state of everlasting misery. This would mean that God is not infinitely good or loving. Hence, they reject Hell in favor of a "higher" Christianity.

But this desperate proposal is simply philosophical speculation and contradicts the foundational message of Christianity and the primordial biblical texts.

Even at a philosophical level, traditional Christians can argue that God gives us the freedom to choose our final destiny – we are responsible for what we choose, not God. Of course, I believe neither in God nor in free-will, but those who believe in both will understandably not find any merit in this argument that God's nature will not permit Hell. Christians will add that, as they see it, their religion is revelation and not metaphysics.

Some have said that those who reject God will be annihilated. There is no Hell with eternal suffering for sinners, they say, because God will do away with those who reject him. But this theory is a purely arbitrary personal opinion that is contradicted *in toto* by the Bible and Christianity from its beginning.

So here is my advice for these liberal Christians who cannot bring themselves to believe in an infernal, eternal state of being for evildoers but want to hang on to other parts of the Christian concoction. Stop fooling yourselves and stop fooling your fellow Christians. There is no Christianity without Hell. If you have any courage, you will reject and condemn this savage religion built on fear. If you want to hang on to a Hell-less Christianity, you are just as guilty of emotional terrorism as the mindless Fundamentalist infernalists you claim to despise. You must scrap the whole religion if you value your integrity, your dignity, and your humanity.

Let me also say that the attempt to contrast the vengeful, wrathful God of the Old Testament with the meek and mild God of the New Testament is doomed to failure. The God of the New Testament – as interpreted and embodied by Jesus – is unimaginably more cruel than his predecessor. While the Old Testament God rained fire and brimstone on those who dared to defy his injunctions, the New Testament God promises eternal fire for anyone who does not profess belief in him or follow his prescriptions – which means most of humanity.

This is the perversity embodied by the idea of Hell. If you find someone sexually attractive and mentally relish this desire or if you happen to have a night out on the town, for either of these crimes you will be condemned to burn in Hell forever. Little children born into some religion other than Christianity will suffer eternal torment.

Think of the worst villains in history. Hitler, of course, is the standby in these situations. He was responsible for the deaths of tens of millions of people and for unimaginable pain and destruction. What would be the fitting punishment for his crimes if there is an after-life (which, thankfully, is not the case)? Maybe a thousand years of torture or a billion years of hard labor? But would any decent person think that even Hitler should suffer the utmost misery forever? Is any action we do deserving of endless punishment? You must be a merciless sadist to support this. But this is what Christianity wants you to believe about the fate of billions of people who have done nothing on the level of a Hitler or a Stalin.

Everything we do, all our choices, are the results of where we are at the time of the choice. By "where we are" I mean our genes, our upbringing, our social conditioning and multiple other factors. So, our every decision is dictated by our genetics, our environment, and the laws of physics. We may think we are making choices, but whatever we choose is dictated by these three factors. If we choose Hell, it is really our genetics and our upbringing as well as physical law that is making the choice. In this sense, the twisted Calvinist idea of predestination to hell is right (although not for the reasons given by the Calvinists). If anyone goes to Hell, it is because God has predestined them for it. Which only goes to further demonstrate the utterly repulsive nature of this superstition.

I have said all this not only to show why I could no longer be a Christian but also to unequivocally declare my support for all the demands made in this lawsuit. The dangerous ideology called Christianity should be outlawed, and the outlaws behind it should pay for their crimes against humanity.

LH: You can see why I said he is our star witness. Thank you, Dr. Endicott. You have annihilated the only remaining relic of this monstrous belief-system. This is the last word. There is nothing more to be said. Your witness!

MA: Dr. Endicott, I would like to start off by saying that I agree with you that the possibility of Hell is an inextricable part of the Christian revelation and that the jellyfish theologians who think they can pick and choose what to believe are simply fooling themselves and their fans. Now, let me ask you: Was the doctrine of Hell the main factor responsible for your abandoning the faith of your fathers?

LH: Objection, Your Honor. "Abandon" is a pejorative term.

MA: Let me rephrase my question. Was Hell the primary cause for your ceasing to believe in Christianity?

Endicott: As I said, I had a number of growing misgivings about the religion but Hell was certainly a principal factor in my departure.

MA: So, would you believe in Christianity if it had not included a doctrine of Hell?

Endicott: No. As I said, I do not believe in God or free will. I find the moral intolerance of Christianity intolerable. I find such doctrines as the Trinity and the idea that a mere man could be God to be intellectually incoherent.

MA: So, Hell was simply one of several factors. Since you do not believe in freewill, you also do not believe in moral absolutes. Mass murderers and serial rapists should not be punished because this would imply that they did something wrong. But there is nothing right or wrong.

Endicott: That is a naïve misunderstanding. Atheists and Christians both want to keep order in society. You do not have to believe in freewill or moral absolutes to keep order by creating and enforcing laws that regulate human behavior.

MA: I am not talking about behavior. I am talking about moral codes. In science, we talk of laws of Nature because there are certain regular, predictable ways in which natural processes behave. When it comes to the moral order, some of us believe there are laws that govern it. But those who take your position believe anything goes.

Endicott: I certainly think all so-called moral laws are simply arbitrary human creations – mere conventions.

MA: If it is all just convention, your claim that the Christian God is unimaginably cruel is just more talk about conventions. You cannot claim that the idea of Hell is a diabolic delusion. To be diabolic would imply it is "bad" but you do not believe in anything being morally good or bad.

Endicott: I think you are deliberately trying to go around in circles to avoid looking at what stares you in the face: Any civilized person can see that intentionally inflicting pain and torment on another person for even an instant is unconscionable. To do it forever is just monstrous.

MA: But under your system of belief, "civilized" is just a convention. One person's idea of what is "civilized" is anathema to another. You cannot impose your moral preference on any other person since it has no basis in fact. You say "unconscionable" and "monstrous," but these are meaningless terms in your universe. You cannot judge God for his acts since you have no standard by which to judge him.

Endicott: Now you are just being childish. You are simply playing a game of linguistic hide and seek.

MA: Quite the opposite. You are the one playing the game. I am trying to get you to put your assumptions on the table. There is a reason why I have dwelled on this issue. What you believe about moral absolutes and human freewill has an immediate bearing on your ability to grasp the revelation of Hell. If you do believe that there is an absolute moral order in the universe, that there are consequences for breaching this order, and that human beings are capable of making free moral choices, the possibility of Hell becomes inescapable. Not to take Hell seriously means not taking evil seriously.

Hell is not something that was dreamt up out of the blue in the New Testament. All of humanity knew about the possibility and danger of Hell. Studies of Stone Age-level tribes who survived into modern times showed that these hunter-gatherers believed in an after-life in which the good live with the High God and evil doers go to a place of painful punishment. The Greeks believed that the evil are sent to Tartarus, a dark region of eternal punishment. The Egyptians believed that the wicked were consumed by the Devourer of Souls. The Vedas of Hinduism said that the unrighteous and the demons suffer punishment in the "House of Clay." The Zoroastrians believed that evildoers go to the Abode of Wickedness. The Book of Daniel in Judaism says that at the resurrection, the dead "shall awake; some to everlasting life, others to reproach and everlasting disgrace." (*Daniel* 12:2). The human race has always been aware that our choices and acts in this life have momentous consequences for our hereafter.

This is the universally known truth that was reiterated, confirmed, and amplified by Jesus. If we believe God to be loving – and this is the God revealed in the Old and New Testaments – we would expect him to warn us of any danger in which we might place ourselves – especially the ultimate danger of final separation from him.

God wants us all to enjoy eternal happiness in union with him. The idea of God predestining anyone to damnation is reprehensible and entirely incompatible with the Christian revelation of God. We are specifically told that "This is good and pleasing to God our savior, who wills everyone to be saved and to come to knowledge of the truth." (1 *Timothy* 2:3-4)

The Council of Orange (in 529 A.D) decreed that "we not only do not believe that any are foreordained to evil by power of God, but even state with utter abhorrence that if there are those who believe so evil a thing, they are anathema."[146]

Yes, Hell is a state and a fate of unimaginable suffering. But it is not something created by God. It is what we "become" on the basis of our choices as

---

146   https://sourcebooks.fordham.edu/basis/orange.txt

a result of which we are "quarantined" forever from all that is good. God is the source of all joy. Not to have God is to give up all joy. If we choose to permanently cut ourselves off from God, we will inevitably be locked into a state of misery forever. God does not want this for us. He wants us to be with him. But he cannot make us choose him.

The idea of Hell may not fit into your ideas of what is proper, but what matters is reality and not your ideas of what would be fitting. You denounce anyone warning us of Hell as an emotional terrorist. That is like saying doctors warning us of the dangers of smoking are sadistic scaremongers. If you know of an impending danger facing someone you love, you would warn them of it – if you loved them. If a tornado is headed to your town, you should warn your neighbors to protect themselves. Evading reality is escapism, and that escapism would be cruel if the reality involved is potentially lethal. It would, in fact, be sadistic not to warn everyone of the possibility of Hell if we know it to be real. If God loves us – which he does – then we would expect him to warn us of the danger of Hell – and this is what he does.

You deny what is obvious in your experience – namely, the existence of right and wrong and the ability to choose between the two. If you deny this, of course, you can go on to deny Hell. But those of us who have come to recognize that the Trinity is a love story to which we are all called also recognize that love is self-giving. True self-giving has to be wholly voluntary and, if we withhold it from God, we are left with ourself. This is what we mean by Hell.

Endicott: Please stop. With your pious platitudes you are trying to put a respectable spin on what is a despicable idea. You do not have to believe in moral absolutes to know that the idea of inflicting pain on another person is repulsive and anyone who does that eternally is the worst kind of monster.

MA: Your moral indignation would be impressive if you believed in the moral order. But since you do not, we can only view it as an emotional outburst resulting from the activity of conditioned responses, hormonal disturbances, digestive problems, childhood memories, or genetic variations. There are no free moral beings and so no moral issues. To accuse someone of being monstrous, you must have standards of monstrosity.

I, for one, am not suggesting that the deliberate malicious infliction of transient or permanent pain is a good thing. That is because I believe there is absolute goodness and that moral absolutes are real. Any rejection of the Good is what we call evil.

This framework underlies all human experience. Within it, we can come to see the seriousness of moral choices. If we refuse to love God, we are on the path of evil – which, in turn, culminates in pain and suffering. It is all tied together. Our moral choices are implicitly an acceptance or a rejection of God. These acts make us who we are. Since we do not indefinitely go on making choices, there comes a time when the ability to make choices reaches finality. That time is death. Who we are then (at the time of death) determines whether we want to be with God forever – or not.

Endicott: So, you admit that your God is the one who makes us go to Hell, thus proving that the Christian God is a moral monster.

MA: Nothing of the sort. What I say is that Hell is a self-created reality not one that God creates or wants.

Endicott: Going with your assumptions, if there really was an infinitely powerful omniscient God who was loving, he would not create beings whom he foreknows would choose Hell or beings that cannot fulfill the reasons for which they were created. If anyone goes to Hell, God is responsible for their fate.

MA: God is not in time. There is no "fore" knowing in God because he knows all things from all eternity. Past, present, and future tenses do not apply to God: We can only say that he knows and he wills and does both eternally. We cannot speak of God as existing "before" time because "before" suggests that God has a "chronology" in which events (like the beginning of time) take place in a sequence. We cannot say that God knows the future because this suggests that something is "future" for him. All our thoughts and statements about God's eternity must be "time-free" if they are to make sense. God does not exist at any instant of time, and his eternity is not simultaneous with any event in time. He knows our free choices in one, unified, eternal act.

He knows us as existing, not as individuals he might create. In other words, there are no "possible" persons who could have existed but do not. God knows us in our reality as existent beings from all eternity – although we come to exist in time. The genealogical unity and the autonomy of the human race is such that we cannot separate our existence from the rest of the race.

Also, God's knowing our acts does not affect the freedom of our acts. I see a man hurling himself before a racing car and know that he will be struck by the car. But my knowing this in advance does not cause the collision. All my acts "belong" to me – regardless of who knows "about" it and when.

Endicott: No one in their right mind would choose to reject union with God.

MA: I agree that no one in their right mind would choose this. But choosing is not a matter of the mind; it is a matter of the will. Of course, your mind may tell you it is crazy to reject God but your will makes the decision.

Is it possible for my will to make a choice that my intellect tells me is foolish? Yes.

We know that the brightest mind ever created also made the dumbest decision ever made. I am talking about Lucifer, the highest of the angels, who chose to reject God and became the Devil. If we look at ourself, we can see how many times we do things we know are wrong and self-destructive. The tragedy is that once we start down this path of choosing self over God, we may become the kind of person who rejects God in a final way.

Endicott: Again, based on your assumption, if someone does choose to reject God in this life, why should they be punished forever? Why not, say, two million years after which they would be suitably chastened? The idea of eternal suffering is ridiculous.

MA: This is the root of your misunderstanding of Hell. Those who are in Hell are there only because they have, against the divine will, chosen Hell. The puzzle of Hell is not a puzzle about God's love but about the nature of human freedom. If we make a choice of self over God that is eternal, then it is a choice that only we can reverse – not God. Hell is an eternally binding choice made by those who are there.

Endicott: You have caricatured what I said about freewill. The doctrine of Hell depends on *your* idea of freewill. But you cannot deny that all our decisions are determined by factors outside us. This being the case, a good God would not condemn us for decisions made not by us but our genetics and our environment.

MA: I certainly agree that most of our choices are determined by factors outside us. We are not, however, entirely slaves of outside factors. Our discussion right now proves that we can freely process and exchange ideas. It is not quarks or neurons or subconscious forces that determine our discussion. Reasons and purposes, as articulated by free persons, are driving our discussion. Only those choices we make that are truly free count as choices for or against God. God does not need a manual of psychology or genetics or neuroscience to know which these are. And God will do all he can to make us choose rightly.

The Calvinist idea of predestination is wrong also because – unbiblically – it reduces human beings to puppets of God. It was presciently rejected by the Council of Orange centuries before it was formulated. Your atheist determinism is a different kind of Calvinism (as you observed). In your view, all our acts are predestined by external forces. Each of us is simply a puppet and, when we die, we become nothing. Like the Calvinist, you think of us as puppets.

The message of Nature, of the world religions, of human experience, and of Christianity is that there is both order and autonomy in the world and this autonomy comes to a climax in free rational creatures – human beings and angels. Being free means we can choose our own destiny both now and forever.

A student of the philosopher Ludwig Wittgenstein once expressed regret that the Christian Church had condemned Origen's idea of God eliminating Hell. To this, Wittgenstein replied, "Of course it was rejected. It would make nonsense of everything else. If what we do now is to make no difference in the end, then all the seriousness of life is done away with."[147]

With freedom comes responsibility and, consequently, consequences.

Endicott: We cannot settle the freewill issue here. But it is indisputable that your ideology condemns non-Christians to damnation – including those who never heard of Christ or heard of him in a way entirely influenced by their own religion.

MA: Christianity has always taught that God desires the salvation of all men and women. The Church, from its earliest days, has preached this doctrine of the universal salvific will of God.

We exist to love him who is Love itself. And it is our duty to draw those around us to this love.

Christians hold that if one accepts the truth about God revealed by Christ with both intellect and will – with our thoughts and actions – we are taking the path that God has ordained for our salvation.

---

147   Norman Malcolm, *Wittgenstein: A Religious Point of View?* (Ithaca: Cornell University Press, 1994), 10.

Not all people, however, will have the opportunity to understand this truth about God, this way to God, this life in God. Nevertheless, God's intent to save them, to save all humanity, does not change, and the salvific effects of the death of Christ apply to all including those who are ignorant – provided that they turn to him within the context of what they know. Paul specifically tells the Athenians, "God has overlooked the times of ignorance, but now he demands that all people everywhere repent because he has established a day on which he will 'judge the world with justice' through a man he has appointed, and he has provided confirmation for all by raising him from the dead." (*Acts* 17:30-31)

Both Old and New Testaments resound with the message of a Creator who wishes that no creature perish, a Holy of Holies who invites the wicked to turn from evil, an infinite Lover who seeks eternal union with every human person:

> "Do I indeed derive any pleasure from the death of the wicked? says the Lord God. Do I not rather rejoice when he turns from evil way that he may live." (*Ezekiel* 18:23).

> "The hour is coming when the dead will leave their graves at the sound of his voice; those who did good will rise again for life; and those who did evil, to condemnation." (*John* 5:28-8).

> "He will repay each one as his works deserve. For those who sought renown and honor and immortality by always doing good there will be eternal life; for the unsubmissive who refused to take truth for their guide and took depravity instead, there will be anger and fury." (*Romans* 2:7-8).

Endicott: The idea that you can go to Hell for all eternity for one or two acts is barbaric.

MA: I have already said that it is not one or two acts that dictate our destiny but rather who we become. At the moment of death, all of our choices become unified into one. As the philosopher Eric Mascall said, "If it is suggested that God will surely give us an indefinite number of second chances, the answer is very simple. It is that this is precisely what he is continually doing while we are in this life, but, when at death we see him in the fullness of his glory and love, he is giving us all conceivable and possible chances at once."

As to whether Hell can be reconciled with God's love, Mascall said, "Hell, as Christianity conceives it, is not incompatible with God's love; it is a direct consequence of it. For love can be received only in a free response of love; and, God's love being pure self-giving, we must receive it as such or not at all."[148]

---

148   E.L. Mascall, *The Christian Universe*, (New York: Morehouse-Barlow Co., 1966), 148.

WITNESSES FOR
THE DEFENDANT

"FROM ERROR TO TERROR"

Witness – Raquel Prendergast (RP)

MA: The first of our witnesses is Professor Raquel Prendergast. If I may put it respectfully, Professor Prendergast is a maverick. No one can quite figure out where she is coming from. But we all know where she is going. She is in the business of telling the naked truth about emperors without clothes. And their numbers are legion. She is a logician and not a diplomat so she calls it as she sees it no matter whom she is talking to. Although she does not share the faith we represent, she is one of us when it comes to pricking balloons of pompous pretensions that ostentatiously avoid the obvious. One instance is the nihilism and physicalism – so popular today – that lie at the heart of our opponent's case and of the so-called Enlightenment that he promotes. It is our contention that this ideology is not just self-contradictory but dangerous and destructive. In fact, all the vile accusations he has made about Christianity can be more accurately attributed to the Enlightenment and the bloody revolutions it spawned.

Professor Prendergast, please share your thoughts on the ideologies we are up against.

Prendergast: Thank you, Mike. I am not sure if I can live up to your billing but it will not be for lack of trying! Let me start off with my pet peeves about today's self-appointed intelligentsia and their cardinal errors. The high priests of our age are the philosophers, the scientists, and the psychologists and all of them, in one way or another, purvey philosophical ideas that range from the inane to the insane. I will show, in fact, that what they tout as the Enlightenment is dangerous for our mental health and threatens the survival of civilization.

Of all the scams devised by scheming minds, none has been as spectacularly successful as "philosophy." "The love of wisdom," as it grandly calls itself, has confused, corrupted and ruined more people than any other area of human endeavor. But it is time to call the philosophers' bluff, to see the effete emperors of thought in the light of naked truth.

My objective here goes beyond exposing intellectual fraud. I want to show that we can recover the most important fundamental truths ourselves without help from philosophers, scientists, woke academics, or virtue-signaling celebrities. These truths are of the utmost importance because they form the foundations of sanity and rationality and are themselves self-evident or derived from self-evident truths.

They are self-evident because, in themselves, they provide the evidence for their truth. We will call them self-evident truths – SETs for short. A SET is self-proving, self-authenticating, self-guaranteeing. You "see" it to be true without any process of reasoning. And you cannot deny them without self-contradiction.

Here are some examples of SETs:

The world exists,

I exist,

something cannot come into being from absolute nothingness.

Any attempt to deny a SET must simultaneously assume that the SET is indeed true. For instance, if we deny the existence of the world, we can only argue for our view by appealing to certain features of the world (the world which we claim is non-existent!). While we can verbally deny a SET it is not possible to mentally believe our denial and still keep our sanity.

The Seven Truths

The first five of the seven fundamental truths I will present here are self-evident, and the sixth and the seventh are based on self-evident truths. If you consistently deny any one of the first five truths, you cannot lead a normal life. You would be locked up either in an asylum or a penitentiary. Denial of the two other truths blinds you to all that is most important in life.

Here are these timeless truths:

1. Our mind is capable of knowing at least some things – of grasping what is the truth of the matter in certain cases.

2. The world exists and is not an illusion created by our minds.

3. We exist.

4. We are conscious and can use language (i.e., give meaning to symbols).

5. Conscious, rational beings and the network of intelligent systems we call the laws of Nature could not have suddenly emerged from an inert blob of matter or sheer nothingness.

6. We are capable of making independent choices.

7. Certain things are obviously wrong (the slaughter of millions of Jews by Hitler, for instance).

If you wonder what is controversial about any one of these truths, you are truly blessed. It can only mean that you have been preserved from what is grandly called "philosophy." But you would be one in a million. For hardly anyone in modern society has been left unscathed by the grand scam. While the "great" philosophers are the ultimate culprits, academics of every persuasion have pranced aboard the bandwagon of lunacy.

Scientists and psychologists, anthropologists and sociologists, have all chimed in to deny one or more of the basic foundations of sanity. But when these natural or social scientists venture an opinion on such matters, they speak as philosophers, for the truths under discussion do not belong to the natural or social sciences. When the physicist Ian Barbour tells us in all seriousness that time does not exist and that our experience of change, motion and even memory is an illusion, he is not making a scientific statement. He is simply affirming a bizarre belief that cannot be demonstrated either scientifically or philosophically – and is constantly falsified at every instant!

Academics in general and philosophers in particular deny, dispute, or ignore the seven claims outlined above. Why so? Cicero's answer says it all: "There's no opinion so absurd but that a philosopher hasn't expressed it." Speaking as a philosopher who contributed his own fair share of absurdities, Bertrand Russell confessed, "This [the idea that there are no physical objects] is patently absurd; but whoever wishes to become a philosopher must learn not to be frightened by absurdities."[149]

Unlike natural scientists, professional philosophers are not constrained by the laws of reality. Scientists (at least in the old days) took hypotheses seriously only when these were verified by observable and repeatable experiments. Not so, the philosopher who simply has to put pen to paper to promote some fanciful view of the world. Or, as Robert Zend said, "Being a philosopher, I have a problem for every solution."

Now, one difference between sanity and madness lies in distinguishing the true from the false and grasping what is real. By this measure, most philosophers, by their own admission, are simply insane because they protest that we (or at least they) cannot ever know what is true and real. Yet, essentially every person who ever lived – including Mr. Hyde the philosopher when he is back in the real world as Dr. Jekyll – has taken it for granted that we know certain things to be the case. Of course, there are distinctions. Some things are indubitably true while others range from the possible to the probable or improbable to the demonstrably false.

---

149   Bertrand Russell, *The Problems of Philosophy*, 1912, https://www.gutenberg.org/files/5827/5827-h/5827-h.htm

The Seven Superstitions

The flight from sanity can be illustrated by reference to what philosophers have said about the seven truths. These responses are what I will call here the seven superstitions:

1. There are no such things as "truths," and we are, in any case, incapable of knowing anything at all about anything.

2. There is no evidence that the world exists and what we call the world is simply a set of ideas in our head.

3. "You" do not exist because there is no such thing as the "self," and your normal tendency to think in terms of "I" is simply a delusion (not even a self-deception since there is no self).

4. Our experiences of being conscious or giving meaning to things are simply illusions because they are solely and simply physical processes that can be reduced to interactions of sub-atomic particles/quantum fields.

5. Multiple universes endlessly emerge out of random fluctuations of nothingness. Everything in the universe is a manifestation of self-evolving matter and differences between things, if any, are purely and simply to be found in the degree of complexity.

6. The human person is essentially a product of physical and genetic forces that determine every choice and action; there is no such thing as freedom or responsibility.

7. There is no right and wrong since we are dealing with matter alone and all moral codes are simply and solely the products of evolutionary struggle and social conditioning.

God doesn't exist, the world doesn't exist and I don't exist.

This is the "wisdom" bequeathed to the human family by its illustrious thinkers – in particular the disturbed minds who spawned the disaster they called the Enlightenment. Taken together, Rene Descartes, John Locke, David Hume, Bishop Berkeley, Jean-Jacques Rousseau, Immanuel Kant, G.W.F. Hegel, Friedrich Nietzsche, Karl Marx, the Pragmatists, the Logical Positivists, Bertrand Russell, Ludwig Wittgenstein, Jean Paul Sartre, Martin Heidegger, the Post-Modernists and their Deconstructionists, the Critical Theorists, Jürgen Habermas, Michele Foucault, Jacques Derrida and their fellow-travelers have inflicted such damage to our collective consciousness that it is doubtful if modern society as a whole will ever recover.

Of course, philosophical pontification is not simply the pastime of dead white males. There are innumerable contemporary crackpots in the Western world as well as plenty of philosophers from other parts of the globe who have tilted their minds at the windmills of reality. So have many female philosophers in recent years. And there is nothing peculiarly modern about this hapless quest. The Greeks had their Stoics, Cynics, Epicureans, Atomists, and assorted other oddities.

Why bother with this intellectual rogues' gallery, you might ask? After all, only their fellow philosophers take their rantings and ravings seriously. Sadly, this has not been the case. Ideas have consequences and insidious ideas can have cataclysmic consequences. It was the "freethinker" Voltaire who said, "If we believe absurdities, we shall commit atrocities."

Nazism and Marxism, the greatest mass-murder machines of all time, did not emerge in a vacuum. The ideological foundation of Nazism was Nietzsche's decree that power is the world's dominant driving force (the "will-to-power") along with his glorification of violence and cruelty ("the voluptuousness of victory and cruelty") and his belief that the vast majority of humanity exists simply to serve the needs of a few Supermen who are "beyond good and evil."

The immediate inspiration of Marxism was Karl Marx's vision of history as a platform of "class warfare." "The history of all hitherto existing human society is the history of class struggle," wrote Marx (with Friedrich Engels) in *The Communist Manifesto*.[150] Marx, who derived his philosophy from Hegel, and ultimately Kant, reduced reality to the dynamic evolution of matter ("dialectical material-ism"). Curiously, Karl Marx was "elected" as the greatest philosopher in history by BBC viewers in a 2005 poll.

Nietzsche proclaimed that God is dead, Marx taught that religion is the opium of the masses and, together, they unleashed a new world of blood-thirsty tyrants and murderous regimes.

Nietzsche, Marx and their intellectual progeny had, of course, no use for truth – let alone the seven truths. Nietzsche said, "Nothing is true, all is permitted."[151] Adolph Hitler proclaimed that "It is not truth that matters, but victory."[152] The Marxists held that the only absolute truth is that there are no abso-lute truths.

Both Nietzsche and Marx made ghoulish prophecies of the fruits of their ideas. "I herald the coming of a tragic era. We must be pre-pared for a long succession of demolitions, devastations and upheav-als," wrote Nietzsche. "There will be wars such as the world has never seen. ... Europe will soon be enveloped in darkness."[153] "In his poem "The Fiddler," Marx wrote, "See this sword? the prince of darkness sold it to me. ... With Satan I have struck my deal, he chalks the signs, beats time for me, I play the death march fast and free." And in "Oulanem," he proclaims, "I shall howl gigantic curses on mankind."[154] (Karl Marx could not balance his own checkbook but presumed to instruct

---

150 Karl Marx and Friedrich Engels, *The Communist Manifesto*, Introduction by A. J. P. Taylor. (Baltimore: Penguin, 1967), 79.

151 *Thus spake Zarathustra*, http://www.philosophy-index.com/nietzsche/thus-spa-ke-zarathurstra/lxix.php

152 Hitler's last will and testament, dictated April 29, 1945. https://ptfaculty. gordonstate.edu/jmallory/index_files/page0508.htm

153 Henri de Lubac, *The Drama of Atheist Humanism* (San Francisco: Ignatius Press, 1995), 64.

154 https://mises.org/library/marxs-path-communism

entire nations on how to re-structure their economies.) Judging from the greatest tragedies of the 20th and 21st centuries, it should be obvious that there is a direct cause-and-effect relationship between insane ideas and nameless horrors.

Present Day Consequences of the Rejection of Truth

So how do things stand today? Let us start with a paradox. We live in a day and age in which we are inundated with information on an unparalleled scale. Twenty-four-hour news and other channels, a hyperactive Internet, AI super-bots, intelligent personal assistants, talking heads in every electronic forum, ceaseless social media posts, thousands of scholarly papers, millions of books, and research projects in every imaginable domain.

But get this. The best minds of our time (anointed as such by the mass media), the intellectual elite, tell us that we cannot know anything. An ever-increasing influx of information is matched by an ever-decreasing confidence in the capacity to know. For some reason, many of the most esteemed academics and scholars take a perverse pride in denying the very possibility of knowing anything. "Drop the idea," urges nihilist Richard Rorty, "that Truth is 'out there' waiting for human beings to arrive at it."[155] We are invited to join the age of pluralism and give up dogmatism. All certainties must die.

Now, notice yet another paradox here. The very same sophisticates who tell us there is nothing we can know, are absolutely certain you cannot be certain. They know you cannot know. I am not trying to be clever here but surely there is something wrong about a second claim that flies in the face of the first one, an underlying inconsistency. But such a striking contrast between belief and practice is typical of the devil-may-care hubris of the academic. Specialists in this "we-know-nothing" genre are the post-modernists who

---

155   Richard Rorty, "Science as Solidarity," in *Dismantling Truth* edited by Hilary Lawson and Lisa Appignanesi (New York: St. Martin's Press, 1989), 13.

deny value systems and claims of knowing anything. The Critical Theorists claim that all our beliefs and actions are formed by social power structures and cultural prisms from which we need to be liberated.

Given this climate of mind, it should come as no surprise that neither our seven truths nor any truth at all is recognized as binding. Now, you might think that a passive, neutral attitude to truth should have a similarly neutral effect on our choices and actions. Would that this were so!

Nature abhors a vacuum and every denial is also an affirmation. Every denial of a truth is the affirmation of a non-truth. When you say, despite your own experience to the contrary, that no "you" exists, you are claiming that "you" are purely and simply an unpredictable, uncontrollable nexus of unrelated quantum fields. Of course, there can be no question of "moral codes" or "truths" when dealing with a matter field (and you are "nothing but" a physical field).

The rejection of the seven truths leads to the (often unwitting) avowal of the seven superstitions. And this does have a negative effect on every domain of human activity.

Take science. If you believe that there are no facts and, in any case, you're inherently incapable of grasping facts, it's hardly possible to pursue science. No less a publication than *Nature*, the world's leading scientific journal, made this very case. A paper in *Nature* pointed out that the four most influential philosophers of science – Karl Popper, Imre Lakatos Thomas Kuhn, and Paul Feyerabend – are "enemies of science" for whom "the term 'truth' has become taboo" and whose skepticism and nihilism "may be impairing scientific progress at this moment." Skepticism breeds superstition. "From the false premise that all observation is theory-dependent, all routes lead inexorably to 'anything goes.'" This denial of truth is fatal for science: "If one believes that there exists no objective truth, or even if one has doubts as to its existence, one then has no motivation, nor even inclination, to try to discover it. It is therefore highly unlikely that such a person would make any new discoveries."[156]

The impact on the rest of human life is even more dramatic. The seven great superstitions, as professed in modern times, may be boiled down to two: nihilism and physicalism. Nihilism, which comes from the Latin *nihil* or "nothing" is called such because it annihilates the possibility of truth and the very idea of a "real" world. It says we cannot know anything. Physicalism simply says that matter is all that exists (the philosophers call this "materialism"). These twin ideas, with a constellation of attendant errors, have percolated down from the philosophers into the intellectual and cultural fabric of modern society. Most dramatically, it is now the establishment position in the world of education from high school to college and beyond. As a direct result, the seven timeless truths have now been excluded from "school." Worse than that, these truths have been replaced with their corresponding superstitions.

Harsh words you might say. But consider the evidence: Which popular or scholarly publication, which manual of education or prescribed textbook, which supposedly intelligent chatbot for that matter, talks of self-evident truths, of the reality of our conscious, rational existence and the self, of absolute, non-negotiable moral principles? If such truths not only hold but can be known to hold, should they not form the centerpiece of a sound education? Instead, going to school today means having the sense knocked out of you and replaced with self-evident absurdities. And the "higher" the education, the "lower" the confidence in our capability of knowing anything. We are applauded if we question our ability to understand and celebrated if we disembowel traditional "truths" ("truth" is always in quotes unless it is qualified as "my truth") and beliefs.

---

156   T. Theocharis and M. Psimopoulos, "Where Science Has Gone Wrong", *Nature*, October 15, 1987, 595-8.

An education that not only ignores but denies self-evident truths corrupts the mind. The corruption may be initially merely conceptual, but it seeps into all dimensions of human life. It is not a question here of setting reason against "religion" or separating state from church. Rather, it is a question of being schizophrenic about reality and aberrant at the very foundations of thought and action.

The inevitable end-result of philosophy as practiced by its centers of gravity is radical skepticism and nihilism. From Hume to Kant to Nietzsche, from Wittgenstein to Derrida, there is an underlying despair when it comes to knowing anything – and an equal scorn for the naïve peasants who think they do. The darkness that shines forth from these leading lights now shrouds the entire universe of education particularly in philosophy departments everywhere. To the extent that their habits of thought undermine simple sanity, the intellectual elites are both subversive and decadent. They are also rabidly intolerant of dissent.

To be cured of a disease, it is necessary for us to diagnose its nature and identify the agents that cause it. In the present instance, I have said that the malaise of the modern mind stems primarily from the mental immuno-deficiency virus of nihilism with the secondary infection of physicalism. So, which agents transmitted this virus? Hume and Kant were the progenitors, but the godfather of modern nihilism was Friedrich Nietzsche. Nietzsche, who took the denial of the seven truths to their logical and literal extreme, spent the last decade of his life in a lunatic asylum. Astoundingly, his madness seems to have been contagious plunging mainstream modern thought, as it did, into the bowels of bedlam.

Nietzsche's nihilism was destructive on three levels: It eliminated the possibility of knowing anything to be true; it obliterated the foundations of moral value; and it rejected every attempt to secure enduring purpose and meaning for human life. It was an active nihilism. "Nihilism," he wrote, "[is] not only the belief that everything deserves to perish; but one actually puts one's shoulder to the plough; one destroys."[157]

Nietzsche's rage against reality, truth and God, seems to have hypnotized one Continental European philosopher after another, from Martin Heidegger to Jacques Derrida, from Jean-Paul Sartre to Michel Onfray.

A Rendezvous with the Real World

Now some might argue that nihilism was inevitable because serious inquiry shows us, sad to say, that our minds are inherently limited. We do not know because we cannot know. Like all prophets, the great philosophers have no choice but to deliver the "truth" and nothing but. If you find it depressing, so be it. But don't shoot the messenger.

Yet it is precisely here that the brainwashed masses must rise in rebellion. We have been told to ignore what is obvious and deny what is undeniable. But why should we?

We know that two opposite things can't both be true and yet we're told that we're trapped in language and can't possibly know this or anything else. We see and touch things around us – but then we're severely rebuked for concluding that they might actually exist. We believe that we're the same persons we were from the time of birth only to be told that, at best, we're a series of unrelated "I" states. We think we think and are conscious that we are conscious but then find out that both assumptions are mistaken given that electrons and quarks, neurons and synapses, can't have "inner" states. The list goes on.

Under this relentless assault, the lay public has little choice but to either give in or tune out. The emperors shamelessly lounging around in the nude and furiously waving their hands, are applauded by their mind-numbed

---

157 *The Will to Power* translated by Walter Kaufmann and R.J. Hollingdale (New York, NY: Vintage, 1968).

subjects. But enough is enough. Why should we believe things that fly in the face of our every experience and insight? On whose authority? Are we to trust the intellectually decadent, mentally abnormal and down-right delirious murderers of the mind to guide our lives and shape our choices? ("God is dead. God remains dead. And we have killed him," raved Nietzsche). What special knowledge do they have? If you are rootless about reality, you are in no position to lay out a roadmap of anything, let alone life. Rorty tells us that, with the demise of philosophy, we should no longer seek to understand things. We should just try to cope. But, it should be asked, how can we cope without understanding?

The first step in liberating ourselves from nihilism is to be skeptical of the skeptics, more critical than the critics. A philosophy that denies self-evident truths, said C.D. Broad, belongs to "the numerous class of theories which are so preposterously silly that only very learned men could have thought of them. But such theories are frequently countenanced by the naive since they are put forward in highly technical terms by learned persons who are themselves too confused to know exactly what they mean."[158]

Hilariously, a 21st century Cornell University survey of the views of 149 of the world's leading evolutionary biologists found, to the shock of the surveyors, that 79% of them believed in freewill – although their ideology did not allow for this. "Our questionnaire offered evolutionary scientists only two choices on the question about human free will: A, all organisms are locally determined by heredity and environment, but humans still possess free will; B, all organisms are locally determined by heredity and environment, and humans have no free will. To our surprise, 79 percent of the respondents chose option A for this question, indicating their belief that people have free will despite being determined by heredity and environment."[159]

---

158 C.D. Broad, *The Mind and Its Place in Nature* (London: Kegan Paul, 1925), 623.
159 "Evolution, Religion and Freewill," https://www.americanscientist.org/article/evolution-religion-and-free-will

What this tells us is that freewill is such an obvious fact of everyday experience that it is very hard to deny it and, of course, it is impossible to live the denial. The ideologues assure us that physics and biology rule all our actions, that psychological, economic and sociological influences condition our choices. But when it comes to their own immediate experience, those who deny freewill in theory cannot bring themselves to believe their theory – let alone practice it.

If we say that we are not free, is that a statement we're making freely? If not, it is simply the product of laws of Nature or random phenomena and cannot be considered true. A spark of electricity or a quantum fluctuation is not true or false. A true statement can only come from a rational person capable of conceptual thought and free actions.

There's another thing those in awe of the great minds should remember. As William James pointed out, "There is only one thing a philosopher can be relied upon to do, and that is to contradict other philosophers."[160] Philosophical fashions and trends are dictated by authority figures who change across generations and countries. If Sartre was all the rage yesterday, it's Derrida today and Habermas tomorrow. If the Positivists have the upper hand at the moment, it's the linguistic relativists who are on top in the twinkling of an eye. So, who exactly is going to tell you what it's intellectually respectable to believe? The Structuralists or the Existentialists? But they are here today, gone tomorrow. There is of course, one common thread, the denial of the seven truths. But even here, the deniers have to perpetually change their arguments as the absurdity of their denials inevitably becomes evident.

Even more interestingly, the most influential nihilist philosophers are treated more like cult leaders than logically rigorous thinkers. Nietzsche, Wittgenstein, and Derrida did not so much argue for their positions as issue oracular pronouncements and cryptic pseudo-profundities. They

---

160   https://brocku.ca/MeadProject/James/James_1911_12.html

preached and pontificated, mystified and jested and sometimes bullied and whined. Rarely did they try to demonstrate the "truth" of their positions. After all they had given up on rationality and meaning, truth and knowledge. Their very disdain for systematic argument endeared them to the faithful followers who quoted from their works as from Sacred Scripture. The only argument that was required was the appropriate citation from the *Blue and Brown Books* of Wittgenstein or Derrida's *Speech and Phenomena*.

We see a similar phenomenon in the cult-worship centered on Charles Darwin. If ever there was a secular saint in terms of hagiography, iconography, reverent discussion, and even a feast day (February 12), it is Charles Darwin. His works have long since left the realm of science and entered the world of Holy Writ. Exegetes, systematic theologians, and even churches professing Orthodox and Reform versions of Darwinism abound. To be sure, not everyone has been fortunate enough to experience the miracle of conversion. On the perilous edges of civilized society, the heathen hordes continue to rage against the truth that sets them free from pagan superstition. But, in the end, even they will have to bow their heads before the Tree of Life and worship at the altar of the Selfish Gene. Either that or they are doomed to retreat ever further into the outer darkness as modernity marches inexorably across the face of planet Earth.

But enough about Darwin. Let us consider the magnitude and implications of his theory (some would say religion!) and the fundamental questions it raises. In the first place, we ask why the unwashed masses feel uneasy about the Darwinian version of evolutionary theory. The answer is simple. The theory in its most elemental form affirms that the human person is essentially no different from a bacterium or a plant; everything about what you are and how you came to be has been explained in terms of genes and their mutations, selection, and the survival of the fittest. You are your genealogy. Your descent from unicellular organisms – via assorted flora and fauna – means that you are ultimately the inevitable byproduct of random chemical reactions and environmental circumstances. Nothing more, nothing less and, therefore, nothing but. This is disconcerting enough for the everyday person but it has catastrophic consequences for the religious believer.

The evolutionary story of origins and descents, primordial soups and accidental mutations, competitions and adaptations for survival, has no role for any external agent. The *machina* needs no *deus*. It stands on its own two feet without any props from the theological store. There is no gap that a god can fill.

Having gotten this far, you might ask, aren't there good philosophers, sound thinkers and solid scientists who do not traffic in adolescent philosophy, people who have made invaluable contributions to our ways of thinking and knowing? Just because a few rotten apples pop up every now and then, we do not have to eschew all philosophers and philosophies. Let me reply, first, by saying that the bad philosophers were not few and far between. Most influential philosophers, in fact, undermined the foundations of truth and rationality. If anything, it could be said that 99% of philosophers give the rest of the philosophical world a bad name.

It is not just the philosophers who are culpable. Almost as dangerous are theologians and ecclesiastics who seek to "keep up" with philosophers, scientists and ongoing academic fads. Thus, we have the spectacle of theologians calling for "context-based theology" where theology endlessly evolves in various cultural and cognitive contexts. They piously insist that doctrines may remain the same but interpretations of these doctrines will have to constantly change. Instead of sticking with ancient formulas or rigid doctrines, the faithful are told to live in "dialogue" with their social and intellectual environments. There should be no critiques or condemnations of seemingly heterodox doctrines because every view contains a seed of truth. The faithful are asked to constantly seek to understand and dialogue with others instead of making claims to possess the truth, let alone trying to proclaim it.

What these clerics offer is an infinite regress of interpretations – where each interpretation has to be interpreted and so on ad infinitum – and the elimination of all theological truth. They would be more honest if they simply drop the pretense of holding to any faith. By its very nature, any written text can be interpreted in a wide variety of ways. This is the case also with any verse or doctrine that is said to be divinely inspired. Thus, most biblical texts and doctrines have been interpreted in radically different ways. This poses an insoluble quandary for those who do not believe in definitive interpretations. Even if they believe the Bible to be divinely inspired or certain doctrines to be divinely preserved, they can have no assurance that they will ever understand what biblical texts and Christian doctrines actually *mean* or be able to arrive at its *true interpretation*. They have no way of knowing with any level of certainty the accurate interpretation of any of these texts and doctrines. This message of salvation, if there is any, becomes irretrievable.

It takes a logician to rescue the faithful from the quandaries created by their logically clueless leaders. Renowned logician Peter Geach first addresses New Testament scholars' approach to the Jesus of the Gospels:

> If we know anything at all of his [Christ's] teaching from the Gospels, he taught with absolute authority, and not as the scribes; he taught as one who saw and knew; knew who and what he was, to what end he was here on Earth, how his earthly life must end, and what joy and glory lay before him. ...

> I may well be accused of ignoring assured results of critical scholarship, confusion about literary forms, and so on. But as a logician I am quite competent to judge the sort of argument I find used by Bible critics; and I judge the arguments to be very often bad arguments, because where the truth-value of premises and conclusion is known independently of any theological disputes, arguments parallel to the critics' would lead from true premises to a false conclusion. ...

It is anyhow clear that we know nothing at all about Christ's words except by way of the Gospel record. By that record Christ did claim to teach with absolute certainty and authority. If the records are in this respect unreliable, two things follow.

Firstly: in this case there is wide gap between the historic figure of Christ and the figure presented in the Gospel: a gap so wide that we could then know only in a theoretical and conjectural way what the actual teaching of Christ was. We should be in the same position as Platonic scholars trying to divine what Socrates actually thought and said. But then for us Christ would be such a figure of theory and conjecture that faith in him would be as much of an absurdity as faith in Socrates; there could be no question of believing his word or following his precepts; for we could have no well-grounded opinion about what he taught or prescribed, if the only clues to this were as untrustworthy as they would be on the present supposition.

Secondly: Let us consider directly what follows if indeed Christ did not claim knowledge and authority in the style reported in the Gospels. We are in that case simply crazy if we stake our lives and souls on our belief in a teaching which he may never have put out at all in the form that has come down to us, and which we are now to suppose was in any case an expression only of what he thought or conjectured, not of what he claimed to know. Obviously our having faith also requires that Christ did really know, not just claim to know; if he were one of the many people who put on airs of authority because they have strong unfounded convictions, then we need pay no special heed to his teaching at all.[161]

Geach makes the further point that logical consistency demands the adherence of the faithful to the unchanging original body of Christian tradition (as opposed to new "contextual" and other "interpretations"):

---

161   Peter Geach, *The Virtues* (Cambridge: Cambridge University Press, 1977), 67-9.

If a remarkable tradition has been continuously preserved through many centuries, continuously from the time when this body of belief first arose, this of course does not exclude its having been from the first a fantastic delusion. But if a tradition really is continuous – and I maintain history shows that this is true of Christian tradition in some of its most important traits, in spite of the lamentable divisions of Christendom – then we are believing what was believed by the founders of the tradition, and we are right in believing it if they were right. Like the gold and cedar of the Ark, truth does not grow old. The founders of the tradition claimed to have their teaching from the lips of the Son of God and from the Holy Spirit that had been given them.

Do we accept this claim or do we not? If we accept it, there is an end of the matter; we must hang on to that truth, though one claiming the authority of an apostle, or an angel, should teach us otherwise. And if we reject it as unfounded, then by all means let us follow this way of the world and try to determine for ourselves how the world came to be and what man's place in it is; but it is mere impertinence for somebody now to set up a claim that he can teach a revised Christian doctrine, superior in important ways to the old doctrine. He cannot establish the truth of his claim by reason. ...

Can he then establish that he has some God-given authority? I do not see how he can. 'Jesus I know, and Paul I know, but who are you?' we may say to him when he sets up as a teacher. Assuredly he cannot say to a sick man 'Get up and walk' (nor is he likely to be able to say 'Silver and gold have I none', either!) and he will be entirely unable to show any sign that he is inspired by the Holy Spirit. His teaching will be a matter of learned conjectures intermixed with such fragments, few of many, of the old tradition as he chooses still to believe. He may choose to believe all this; but he will scarcely persuade a rational outsider, and he can claim no authority that should bind the conscience of a Christian.[162]

Secondly, there have, of course, been many good philosophers. But these philosophers and philosophies are "good" and "sound" because they remain faithful to self-evident truths and not the other way round. And let me be very clear: We do not need philosophers – good or bad – to recognize and hold fast to the seven timeless truths. These are the truths that not only impose themselves on us in everyday experience but are essential for us to retain our sanity. I do not need to consult a dozen learned journals to determine whether I exist. The seven timeless truths are either self-evident or based on a truth that is self-evident and we do not need any external authority source to support them (although we welcome all thinkers who expound what is true).

In my book *The "Enlightenment" and Its Reign of Error*, I have shown that the seven truths can stand on their own. Our starting-point is that of taking our immediate experience seriously. We know things to be the case – I know for a fact that I am in pain, I know that I am sitting on something solid. I constantly communicate meanings to my friends using symbols and, in different degrees, they "understand" what I am talking about. I see and touch things around me and take it for granted that they exist. I know that I am myself a "someone" not simply a series of unrelated brain states.

The influential philosophers, on the other hand, adopt a different starting point. They refuse to trust their everyday experience or even themselves. Their starting point and guiding principle is that they know nothing and there is no way of knowing anything. With this assumption, there is no possibility of progress. You can never prove you are seeing something if you start off saying I do not trust my apparent capability of seeing.

---

162   Peter Geach, *Providence and Evil* (Cambridge: Cambridge University Press, 1977), 85-6.

But why should we place our lives and minds in the hands of frivolous and flippant academics notorious for their hubris and intellectual irresponsibility? After all, philosophers do not set the rules of reality. They are not the ones who determine the content of reality or the ways in which we can apprehend reality.

Just as war is too important to be left to the generals, the truth about reality is far too precious to be left to the philosophers. Acceptance of the seven timeless truths is natural and normal while consistent denial of these truths leads inevitably to insanity. We have life and death decisions to make and life-changing actions to take but we can do neither if we sink into the quicksand of nihilism. Only by anchoring ourselves in self-evident truths and ignoring the imbecilities of the intellectuals can we escape nihilism. Let us heed Nietzsche's warning in his *Ecce Homo*: "What I understand by 'philosopher': a terrible explosive in the presence of which everything is in danger."

The gods of Chatbots, Marxists and the Like

I asked an AI chatbot if God exists, and this is the "original" answer I received:

> The existence of God is a question that has been debated for centuries. There is no scientific evidence to prove or disprove the existence of God, so the answer ultimately comes down to faith.
>
> Some people believe in God because they have had personal experiences that they believe to be evidence of God's existence. Others believe in God because they find comfort in the idea of a higher power who is in control of the universe. Still others believe in God because they see the order and beauty in the world around them as evidence of a divine creator.
>
> Ultimately, the question of whether or not God exists is a personal one. Each individual must decide for themselves what they believe.

We might call this response a cop-out, but at least it was a polite way of saying "No comment!" The Marxists and other intellectual dilettantes, on the other hand, have not done much more than turn up their noses or throw hissy fits when the topic of God comes up.

But what about their arguments such as they are? In truth, most of their arguments against the Source of their own being tend to be arguments about something else altogether – usually something that is entirely irrelevant to the topic under discussion.

Thus, the Logical Positivists of the early to mid-20th century argued that the concept of God could not be verified by the methods of science and is therefore meaningless.

The analytic philosophers said all discussions about "existence" are meaningless if they are not reduced to particular kinds of logico-mathematical propositions. As David Bentley Hart observed tartly, these thinkers are concerned with talking about *how* we talk about existence rather than in actually "talking about existence as such."[163] They have retreated from reality into grammar!

The Marxists informed us that all talk about God is to be explained in terms of their economic theories while the Freudians said such talk should be understood in terms of their ideas of psycho-analysis. Not to be outdone, the evolutionary biologists view the issue through the lens of survival benefits while the neuroscientists reduce it all to neural firings.

Paradoxically, all these "deniers" testify to the truth of the Ultimate Explanation that is God simply by the tools they apply for formulating their denials. They are all asking for explanations of some sort.

The Logical Positivists and analytic philosophers want explanations in terms of scientific or mathematical propositions. Marxists see their brand

---

163   David Bentley Hart, *The Experience of God* (New Haven: Yale University Press, 2014), 126.

of economics as an all-embracing explanation of events, beliefs, actions. Freudians see subconscious psychological urges as the ground of all human activity. Evolutionary psychologists point to selfish genes, advantage-providing adaptations, and the like.

What is common to all of them is the quest for explanation which comes naturally to us – and which has to end in an explanation that is self-explanatory.

The question we have to ask is this: Why do we expect explanations and how do we know there are explanations? The human intellect seeks explanation and unification in its natural movement from the facts of experience. This is true of the natural and the social sciences, the humanities and everyday life. This means all of science and all of humanity cannot avoid sharing the assumption that rationality and intelligibility underlie all of reality. Ultimately, this quest for explanation has to end in a self-explanatory Source, something that "explains" the existence of both Itself and everything else.

The denial of the Source of all things is thus easier said than lived.

The ideologues we will, of course, always have with us. But as they sink ever deeper into the quicksand of their own making, we must leave them behind to address what is obvious in our immediate experience: the mystery of existence.

The Humpty Dumpty Factor – the Law of Moral Entropy

I want to end with a few comments on the roots and fruits of the moral relativism and nihilism dressed up today as pluralism.

In modern society it is taken for granted that there is nothing "right" or "wrong" in any absolute sense. Right and wrong, good and bad are entirely relative. There is "my truth" and "your truth." What I think is right is not necessarily right for you. These are simply personal preferences that should never, under any circumstances, be imposed on anyone else. All moral codes emerge from subconscious, evolutionary, socio-economic, or cultural factors. We are playthings of dominant narratives and oppressive structures, puppets of systemic racism or sexism. The only obligation we have is to be "woke," and if we refuse to take this path, we deserve to be "canceled" from civilized society. Wokeness says all morality is relative but some moralities are more relative than others.

Within this framework, there is no such thing as immorality, no good or evil. All we have are arbitrary interpretations that have no authority – what some call pluralism. This way of thinking is so dominant that it is not just echoed by academia, media, entertainment and Big Tech but by church leaders at the highest level.

Those who are religiously inclined might cite the Gospel of *Luke*: "When the Son of Man comes, will he find faith on earth?" Or point to *Genesis* with its warning that those who eat from the tree of knowledge of good and evil shall die.

But you do not have to belong to any organized religion to recognize the reality of a transcendent moral order. There is also the recurrent human tendency to progressively reject moral obligations with corresponding consequences.

This tendency may be called the law of moral entropy. Entropy, in physics, is defined as the degree of disorder and degradation in a system. The second law of thermodynamics tells us that the entropy of the universe constantly increases. In other words, it progressively declines into disorder. As one physicist put it, entropy is the universe's trend toward death and disorder.

The law of moral entropy says that human societies progressively and irreversibly decline into moral disorder. To abandon structure is to embrace chaos. When we reject moral absolutes, we will be sucked into a vortex of progressive disintegration from which there is no return. Humpty Dumpty cannot be put back together once it falls off the wall of moral structure. This is the message of the exile from Eden.

A corollary of moral entropy is that might becomes right in the absence of a transcendent source of right and wrong. There will always be rules. The question is, who sets them? Is it an infinitely intelligent Mind that loves us infinitely or is it us? Mob rule becomes the standard for law when there is no independent universal standard of right and wrong. Historically, mob rule inevitably ends up enthroning tyrants who then set their own rules. Pluralism – with its rejection of divinely instituted absolutes – will be supplanted by the arbitrary absolutes of tyrants.

Like it or not, every society will end up having moral codes – either from a divine or a despotic source.

Moral entropy cannot be denied by anyone who looks at human history – and especially the history of the last 100 years with its authoritarians, totalitarians, concentration camps and thought controllers. But how do we know there is a transcendent order of universal moral absolutes?

Well, we know that we all make choices and perform actions. These choices and actions can either be beneficial for us and our fellows or not. They can cause pain and sorrow or promote joy and well-being. Is there any reason to believe that we should make choices that promote well-being and avoid harm and, if so, what are these choices?

Those who affirm moral absolutes will say that choices promoting human well-being are those that follow the rules of God. Conversely, choices that defy the rules of God cause pain and sorrow. These rules apply to all human persons everywhere. We discover the existence of these rules by attending to those inner moral prompts we call conscience and to the universal moral principles taught by the world religions. That such rules exist makes sense if there is a Creator who created human beings with a specific purpose and destiny.

The moral nihilist will, no doubt, say that all so-called moral principles are simply subjective culturally conditioned fantasies. What we call a rule of God derives from superstition and fear of the unknown and causes guilt, misery and the end of human advancement. We must create our own rules so that society can make progress.

This was, of course, the argument also used by such totalitarian moral nihilists as Hitler and Stalin, who slaughtered tens of millions of their fellow beings in the name of progress.

Sociobiologists like E.O. Wilson – who sought to construct systems of "evolutionary ethics" – have had to admit that, within their framework, both freewill and ideas of right and wrong are illusions. As such, they have no choice but to be moral nihilists. In fact, in his book, *On Human Nature*, Wilson called for a new program of eugenics.

In the end there are only two possible options: either we are creations of a Creator whose rules are embedded in our being, or we are puppets of chemical, biological, psychological and socio-economic forces over which we can never have any control. Those who believe in moral absolutes also recognize moral entropy – the reality of our tendency to rebel against the rules of God even when it is self-destructive. But they also hold that we can overcome our weaknesses – something that is undeniable in our experience.

Moral nihilists, on the other hand, must resign themselves to being ruled by irresistible impersonal forces in their personal lives and by despotic barbarians in their pluralistic societies. A moral vacuum inevitably turns into a moral vortex.

MA: Thank you, Raquel. As always, you did not disappoint. I am looking forward to what response, if any, the opposing side can offer to this *coup de grace*. Your witness. Mr. HellMan.

LH: A good time was had by all, I guess. But, as is usual with Professor Prendergast, we have a lot of sound and fury signifying nothing. What exactly was the point of all those fireworks you shot off in all directions at once? Running on a treadmill gives us a good workout but it doesn't get us from Point A to Point B. So let us get serious. None of what you said is pertinent to the overwhelming case we have built against the monstrous Creator created by Christians.

Prendergast: You wish! The alternative you present to traditional Christianity is something you call the Enlightenment. In terms of the havoc it caused, the Enlightenment years are better described as the Dark Ages. And that is what I have tried to convey in my intellectual post-mortem. Maybe you did not get it. In my experience, blinkered vision is the besetting vice of the nihilists. Would you mind if I ask you a few questions to drill a little deeper …

LH: I would mind. I will do the questioning here. I think any intellectual with a pulse will tell you that the Enlightenment rescued us from provincialism and penury, ignorance and repression. We have freedom of thought, rational inquiry, science, technology, human rights, growth, modernity.

Prendergast: Not to put too fine a point to it, but that is sheer rubbish. The true fruits of the Enlightenment are bloodshed and butchery on a global scale and the systematic suppression of freedom. Its first bastard child was the horrific French Revolution in which the whole citizenry of a country was transmuted into a wolf pack. Then came the Bolsheviks who trademarked the slaughter of tens of millions and the creation of slave nations. And, of course, there was the Cultural Revolution that was anything but "cultural": It was yet another reign of terror accompanied by artificial famines that killed tens of millions. All these and many other homicidal movements earnestly claimed to champion equality and other Enlightenment ideals even as they rooted out all vestiges of religion.

These are the most conspicuous products of "free thinking" and freedom from moral restraints. I do not myself belong to any organized religion. But, precisely because of this, I think I have a fairly clear-eyed view of what all the parties bring to the table. And I have to say the nihilists and the physicalists have not covered themselves with glory.

LH: What does any of this prove? Revolutions and rebellions are bloody affairs and savage wars predated the French Revolution. Think of the Crusades and all the ghastly wars of religion. You have some nerve laying the faults of barbarism on the very people who were trying to mitigate the savagery of the soldiers of faith.

Prendergast: Well, here is the difference – and you already know what it is. Yes, wars are as old as human history. But the Enlightenment marks the first time ideologies were built to create mass murder machines. When you deny all moral boundaries, you remove all restraints on your inner savage. The Crusades, on the Christian side, had their inexcusably evil episodes but, by and large these, outrages were perpetrated by ruthless, hardened mercenaries. The religious beliefs that they were supposedly trying to defend specifically prohibited such dreadful acts.

The French Jacobins and the Russian Bolsheviks had social-engineering ideologies that called for the abolition of religion and the creation of their versions of utopia and doing whatever it took in the process. If millions had to perish and economies had to be carpet bombed in the process, that could not be helped. It was all for a worthy cause. These were the lethal ideas they imbibed from their Enlightenment forefathers. They turned out to be good students. Both in their animating ideas and their scale of slaughter, the Enlightenment inaugurated a new world disorder that is still with us.

LH: Your description of the Enlightenment is painfully unenlightened. It lives up to your reputation for manufactured shock value. If you want to see an honest and thorough evaluation of the Enlightenment, there is no better spokesperson than Steven Pinker. His arguments are irrefutable. Pinker's book *Enlightenment Now* is appropriately sub-titled *The Case for Reason, Science, Humanism, and Progress*.

Pinker says, "The thinkers of the Age of Reason and the Enlightenment saw an urgent need for a secular foundation for morality, because they were haunted by a historical memory of centuries of religious carnage: the Crusades, the Inquisition, witch hunts, the European wars of religion. They laid that foundation in what we now call humanism, which privileges the well-being of individual men, women, and children over the glory of the tribe, race, nation, or religion."[164]

He points out, using 15 measures of wellbeing and numerous data graphs, that over the last 300 years fairly everything has gotten better – from health, wealth and knowledge to peace, prosperity and equality. As Pinker says, these huge improvements in the quality and quantity of life we take for granted did not come to us from a deity but were gifts of the Enlightenment and the science and reason it promoted. Everything bad that has happened is a result of "counter-Enlightenment trends" like ignorance and irrationality.

Please tell me whether you would prefer to live now or 300 years ago. If now, you can thank the very Enlightenment you have been running down.

Prendergast: You are funny! You had nothing to say about all the evils visited on the human race by the "gifts" of the Enlightenment. Pinker talks about the Enlightenment providing a "secular foundation for morality." Really? What was the moral code created and promoted by the French and Russian Revolutions? And let us not forget that it was the scientific racism that came from the Enlightenment that gave us Nazism. The Enlightenment's version of a market economy had no room for moral restraints. Hence the slave trade became the vehicle for inexpensively providing sugar, cotton and other commodities to the Western world. Nuclear arms, bioweapons, napalm – let us not forget these other gifts of the Enlightenment's "secular morality".

---

164   Steven Pinker, *Enlightenment –The Case for Reason, Science, Humanism, and Progress.*(New York: Viking, 2018), 10.

LH: You did not answer my question about whether you'd prefer to live 300 years ago. Are you telling me that nothing good came out of the Enlightenment? Planes, trains and cars to transport us, mechanized farming, fertilizers and pesticides to feed the whole world, energy conversion technologies underlying all our daily activities, pharmaceutical drugs and medical procedures protecting us from diseases that once decimated whole populations. The poor today enjoy greater comforts than the richest potentates of previous eras. None of this would have been possible without the Enlightenment. Of course, our evolutionary past meant that we have a violent streak that expresses itself in wars. But this has happened throughout history – long before the Enlightenment – and was particularly virulent when religion was involved. If anything, the Enlightenment tempered these innate self-destructive tendencies.

Prendergast: Of course, from the standpoint of quality of life, things are better now than they were 300 years ago. Or 100 years ago. Or, for that matter, 50 years ago. The Middle Ages, for all its misery, offered a higher quality of life than the Stone Age. Constant advancement has been the recurrent feature of human history. For this we can thank the human spirit not any particular era. We all agree too that the modern era is unique in its levels of advancement thanks to giant leaps in science and technology. And people are far more tolerant and civilized than in previous eras. But your eagerness to attribute all these benefits to the Enlightenment smacks of blind religious fervor that leads to a distorting of the facts.

Scientific breakthroughs certainly underlie the progress made in modern times. And I agree that the birth of modern science needed a catalyst that went beyond normal human development. But science's "breakout" moment predates the Enlightenment. It was the Christian cultural matrix that gave birth to modern science.

Bertrand Russell's mathematical collaborator Alfred North Whitehead said that "faith in the possibility of science, generated antecedently to the development of modern scientific theory, is an unconscious derivative from medieval theology." Similarly, Lynn White, the historian of medieval science, has stated that "the [medieval] monk was an intellectual ancestor of the scientist." The German physicist, Ernst Mach, a positivist, once said, "Every unbiased mind must admit that the age in which the chief development of the science of mechanics took place was an age of predominantly theological cast."[165]

Stanley Jaki, the philosopher-historian of science, has shown in painstaking detail that modern science was birthed within the Christian thought world. This is because Christianity furnished all the elements required to pursue viable scientific inquiry. The world was the creation of an infinite Intelligence and, therefore, followed laws that could be discovered through rational investigation. The world was separate from God and not part of him (as in pantheism); matter was good because it was a creation of God and not to be shunned as in some other religions.[166]

So modern science and its technological progeny are the gifts not of the Enlightenment but of the Christian cultural matrix.

LH: This is all debatable. What is not debatable is the fact that the Enlightenment liberated us from the straitjacket of repressive, regressive Christian do's and don'ts. That's why people are happy and tolerant in a way they never were. This is what you have left out in your whole presentation.

Prendergast: Pinker's argument that modern ideals of equality, human rights, and peace stem from Enlightenment principles shows sheer ignorance of intellectual history. On the contrary, the ideals of the dignity of the human person, human rights, charitable giving, universal peace and so much else demonstrably derive from the Christian message. Numerous historical books have shown this, most recently *Inventing the Individual* by

165   Alvin J. Schmidt, "Christianity's Contribution to Science," 25 November 2011, https://doi.org/10.1002/9780470670606.wbecc0293

166   Stanley Jaki, *The Origin of Science and the Science of its Origin* (Chicago: Regnery Gateway, 1979).

Larry Siedentop, *Dominion* by Tom Holland, and *Is Europe Christian?* by Olivier Roy.

Siedentop shows that the ideas of individual and human rights are rooted in Christianity. The idea that human beings are made in the image of God and that Jesus died for each human person certainly reinforces the preciousness of each individual. Even the idea of a secular sphere can be traced to the Christian vision – from Jesus' command to "give to Caesar what is Caesar's" to Augustine's idea of the City of God and the City of Man. Siedentop says that making reason and conscience the fulcrum of moral choice is a "gift to the world" – one that comes from Christianity.

Holland points out that despite the downturn in Christian practice the Christian value system has become embedded in the culture of the modern world, hence the focus on human rights of various kinds and the attention to the poor and the vulnerable.

Yuval Harari, a favorite historian of the secularists, wrote, "The idea that all humans are equal is a revamped version of the monotheist conviction that all humans are created equal."[167]

The moral evils of the modern world, on the other hand, have resulted from the Enlightenment denial of moral absolutes. In his history of the modern world, Paul Johnson said, "Among the advanced races, the decline and ultimately the collapse of the religious impulse would leave a huge vacuum. The history of modern times is in great part the history of how that vacuum had been filled. Nietzsche rightly perceived that the most likely candidate would be what he called the 'Will to Power' … In place of religious belief, there would be secular ideology … The Will to Power would produce a new kind of messiah, uninhibited by any religious sanctions whatever, and with an unappeasable appetite for controlling mankind.

---

167 Yuval Harari, *Sapiens* (London: Vintage, 2015), 258.

The end of the old order ... was a summons to such gangster-statesmen to emerge. They were not slow to make their appearance."[168]

There are no moral boundaries once you drop God. Nazi racism and eugenics were driven by the application of the "survival of the fittest" principle to races. Marxist totalitarianism has no objection to exterminating anyone in its way or trafficking in humans or human organs. Human abattoirs are not simply found in totalitarian regimes but emerge in any society built on self-created moral codes. Today, patients are routinely euthanized in Holland based simply on the doctor's decision – and without patient consent.

And what about the restraints on growth at all costs? Should it be at the cost of ecological equilibrium? On the one hand, we must meet the needs of the world's population. On the other, there is a danger of wanton destruction of our habitat as we try to meet our material needs. It seems obvious that we can apply human ingenuity to harvest new sorts of energy sources and create new forms of plentifully available food while devising eco-friendly ways to dispose of our waste.

But all of this takes a moral foundation and framework that reflects the reality in which we live and move and have our being.

Can we build a morality from science? The idea is laughable.

Einstein said, "Science can only ascertain *what is*, but not *what should be*."[169] He went on to say, "I have never obtained any ethical value from my scientific work."[170]

Mathematics, physics, chemistry and biology are accessed through equations and experiments. "Right" and "wrong" cannot be quantified using the

---

168   Paul Johnson, *Modern Times* (New York: Harper and Row, 1983), 48.

169   Albert Einstein, "Science and Religion", 1939, https://www.panarchy.org/einstein/science.religion.1939.html

170   P. Michaelmore, *Einstein: Profile of the Man* (New York: Dodd, 1962), 251.

scientific method. Science cannot tell us if an action is right or wrong. Since the Enlightenment steadfastly renounced and denounced moral absolutes, it left a vacuum where once there was a divinely grounded configuration of good and evil. The rest is history – a history of utopias that became living hells, weapons that can wipe out the planet several times over, the implosion of the family.

You and today's prophets of progress have been crowing about how peaceful and worry-free we are thanks to the civilized mind-sets engendered by the Enlightenment. Let us peel away the veneer. Peace in the world today is built on the philosophy of mutually assured destruction not a sudden conversion of minds and hearts. Barbaric forces are now stronger than ever before restrained only by fear of retaliation. At any instant, the entire planet can go up in flames if there is a skirmish that cannot be contained. A thermonuclear exchange is all it takes – and these weapons of mass incineration are now in too many hands to be controlled by any one nation.

And do not get me started on the chemical and biological weapons that are ready for launch in secret labs we know nothing about. Natural microbial pandemics have brought the planet to its knees but think of the launch of bio-engineered weapons that can wipe out entire populations in an Armageddon of agony. The only possibility of our escaping an apocalyptic ending of our own making is a moral conversion built on absolutes not on the "secular morality" that has gotten us where we are.

LH: Blame everything negative on the Enlightenment and let Christianity take credit for all the good stuff. This is patently ridiculous. Pinker has shown beyond all doubt that we need Enlightenment NOW to retain the gifts granted by the age of reason. Because you have decided to hitch your wagon to the forces of darkness, your biases will not allow you to see what is obvious to everyone else: Progress and prosperity are good things. And they come to us from the thinkers who finally threw off the yoke of religion to lead us to a new era of peace and plenty.

"THE UNIVERSE IS A SOCIAL MEDIA PLATFORM"

Witness – Stanley Genereux (SG)

MA: Ladies and Gentlemen of the jury, I want to introduce you to Professor Stanley Genereux. In addition to a lifetime of research in theoretical physics, Professor Genereux has explored the nexus of science, philosophy and religion and has, in the process, skewered many fashionable fallacies. He has taken a particular interest in the elephant in the room in the science and religion discussion that is fastidiously ignored or hand-waved away by the main players. The elephant is what I have called the supra-physical – the non-physical dimension of the world and of our experience that is distinct from but integrated with the physical. The primary supra-physical realities I have spoken about are consciousness, thought and the intellectual self. I have already spoken of our discovery of the infinite Mind that is God. But a key driver in finding God is the discovery of the supra-physical and this is what I would like Professor Genereux to focus on.

In our exploration of this dimension, we will realize that the world is far more mysterious and awe-inspiring than even the physical universe with all its marvels. We will realize, too, that we ourselves are wondrous beyond belief. Neither the Big Bang nor evolutionary theory, neither the Standard Model of particle physics nor the hypothesized Anthropic Landscape can explain the existence of the supra-physical. But, if the supra-physical exists, then the Source of the supra-physical becomes inescapable. Perhaps this is why many of the science-atheism drumbeaters go quiet or change the subject when we bring up the supra-physical.

Any comment Professor Genereux?

Genereux: Thank you, Misha-El. I will turn to the evasions of the funda-materialists in a moment. But first, let me try to present a new perspective on the world in which we live.

At a basic level, the universe of living beings can be thought of as a collection of interacting social media platforms facilitating communications, transactions and goal-fulfillment between different kinds of users. It is a network of networks.

Social Media Platforms in the Virtual World

In the virtual world there are various kinds of social media platforms that provide various (sometimes overlapping) functions for users: connecting with friends to describe and discuss current, past and future activities and sending notifications when required (Facebook, RenRen); sending short messages of a predefined length to those who are interested (X, Weibo); carrying on short conversations (Snapchat, QQ); exchanging photos and videos with accompanying commentary (Instagram, WWD); exchanging pictures via a bulletin board (Pinterest); exchanging professional information (Linked In); uploading videos for audiences (YouTube, TikTok); connecting buyers and sellers (Amazon, eBay, Ali Baba); and sending encrypted messages to individuals and groups you join or form (WhatsApp or WeChat). Other kinds of platforms provide specific services for individual users: performing searches (Google, Yandex, Baidu) and operating systems for applications (Windows or macOS), for instance.

The social media platforms have certain common attributes: They are built atop a hardware infrastructure we call the Internet which is a system of devices and data centers connected by communication networks and protocols; they have some kind of embedded intelligence that is represented by their underlying *technology* and the associated *tools*; and they have *users*. The functions that a user can perform depend on the capabilities of the underlying technology and its tools. For instance, an X user can only send out short messages.

Technologies Underlying Real World Social Media Platforms

Coincidentally, the universe of living beings is also a collection of different types of social media platforms with its own embedded intelligence – its technologies and associated tools. These platforms have their own kinds of users who can perform functions defined by the underlying technology and tools. And they are all built on the same infrastructure of matter (quantum fields) that serves as the underlying "Internet."

In your opening statement, you identified the five different kinds of "technologies" that we see in the living world:

- *life*, i.e., autonomous agency, the capability of acting on your own and being the source of your actions

- *intentional or goal-seeking action*, a propensity to seek goals be it nourishment or reproduction

- *consciousness*, sensory awareness of the environment via physical organs

- conceptual *thought*, the capability of "understanding," of decoding and encoding, of "seeing meaning" via non-physical concepts (e.g., justice or travel) especially as expressed in language

- *selfhood*, the "I" that gives you a first-person perspective and which remains the same even as the physical constituents of your neurons constantly change

We could think of these in terms of Domains and Kingdoms, as shown in Exhibit A:

Domain – **MIND 1 – MATTER/ENERGY**

Kingdom – ***MindCloud*** (quantum fields and the mathematically-based laws and constants of Nature)

Domain – **MIND 2** – **LIFE** (includes Matter/Energy)

Kingdom – **Mind-bots** (microbes), **Mind-pods** (plants)

Domain – **MIND 3** – **CONSCIOUSNESS** (includes Matter/Energy and Life)

Kingdom – **Mind-lings** (reptiles, insects), **Mind-lets** (birds, fish)

Domain – **MIND 4** – **VISUALLY-BASED THOUGHT** *(includes Matter/ Energy, Life, Consciousness)*

Kingdom – **Mind-forms** (non-human mammals)

Domain – **MIND 5** – **NON-PHYSICAL SELF AND LINGUISTIC/ CONCEPT-BASED THOUGHT** *(includes Matter/Energy, Life, Consciousness and Visually-based Thought)*

Kingdom – **Minds** (homo sapiens)

Exhibit A – The Domains and Kingdoms of the Universe

Different "users" in the living world have one or more of these five capabilities – technologies – in differing degrees and their social media "platform" depends on their underlying kind of technology and tools or embedded intelligence. To be a user in this context means you can act on your own and are therefore an autonomous agent or actor and can pursue your own specific goals.

The kind of user you are is determined by the kind of technology at your disposal and therefore the social media platform to which you have access. All living beings possess the first two technologies – namely, each of them is the source of its actions, and each is constantly pursuing its own specific goals. Animals with nervous systems and sensory organs have the third technology in that they are conscious in customized ways of their environment through sight, sound, smell, or touch. Humans have the fourth and fifth technologies since they are capable of conceptual thought and are aware of their continued self-identity.

The social media platforms of this living world are formed by users that have the same technology and tools, as shown in Exhibit B below.

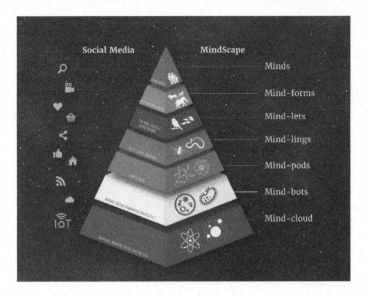

Exhibit B – Social Media Platforms of the Universe of Life

The Social Media Platforms of the Universe of Life

Since all living beings seek goals and carry out transactions, each of them – from microbes to plants to Homo sapiens – has its own version of Amazon and eBay.

Microbes like bacteria focus on nourishment and reproduction. Bacteria have their own Twitter/X platform on which they communicate to each other using chemical molecules released into the environment. These signals enable them to coordinate attacks on targets like plants and animals.

Plants have their form of Snapchat. They use chemical signals – for instance "volatile organic compounds" – that move through air or soil to communicate with each other to warn of impending attacks, say, from predatory pests. Some of them use forms of mimicry, while others manipulate insects with neuroactive substances. They also have their own version of

Google in which they use their roots to "search" the soil for nutrients. Their e-commerce network enables them to respond intelligently and instantly to a whole host of sensory inputs from gravity to sunshine to an array of chemicals. Their underlying technology includes the data warehouses and supply chains of their cells and, in the case of the thousands of different flowering plants, the exquisite reproductive machinery of stamen, petals, pollen, and stigma.

Like all other life-forms, invertebrates – insects, snails, earthworms, and others – communicate through chemical signals like pheromones. These serve as their X feed. Insects communicate through emissions of sound, light and chemical odor. Insect communication serves many purposes: reproduction, alerts, defense and the like. It is their Snapchat. And, of course, all invertebrates have their own eBay-type transaction networks.

Non-human vertebrate animals range from fish and amphibians to reptiles and birds to mammals. They have different levels and kinds of sensory consciousness, intelligence, instinct and memory. They are capable of locomotion and reproduction. They communicate through visual, auditory, tactile and chemical media to find food and mates and to fight or flee from predators. This might be thought of as Instagram and Pinterest-type social media platforms. For instance, species that form groups – such as herds of bison or schools of fish – have their own version of Linked In networks. Some have WhatsApp groups that cooperate and coordinate. Like all living beings they use their own eBay networks and X feeds.

Homo sapiens is a life-form that is capable of both visual and conceptual communication. We are distinctive in two respects: We continuously retain our identities as specific persons although the molecules in our neurons change at every instant; and we perform concept-driven meaning-processing as epitomized by language.

Because the technology underlying humans is a "self" that is constantly processing meaning (i.e., thinking or speaking), our social media platforms are like full-blown traditional social networking vehicles such as MySpace, Facebook and RenRen. Features will include the user's profile, "friends," "Wall," "Timeline," news feed, likes and reactions, messages, events, notifications, etc. Of course, humans are constantly involved in transactions. Hence they have their Amazon, eBay and Ali Baba-type marketplaces. And, like other animals, they also use their Linked In, X, Snapchat, Instagram and WhatsApp-type forums as well as their variations of Google, Windows and YouTube.

Exhibit C, below, summarizes the functions and capabilities associated with the various levels of life-forms.

	Information Processing Based on Mathematical Structures	Continuous Action	Goal-Oriented Behavior (Driven by Laws of Nature or Instinct/Intention/Purpose)	Autonomous Action	Stimulus-Response	Sensory Consciousness	Sense-Based Thought	Conceptual Thought	Non-Physical Cognitive Self (Matter-Independent Self-Identity)
Quantum Energy Fields (Particles, Forces)	•	•	•						
Microbes	•	•	•	•	•				
Plants	•	•	•	•	•				
Insects/Reptiles	•	•	•	•	•	•			
Birds/Fish	•	•	•	•	•	•			
Non-Human Mammals	•	•	•	•	•	•	•		
Humans	•	•	•	•	•	•	•	•	•

Exhibit C – Functions and Capabilities of Various Levels of Life Forms

How Did It All Come Together?

Once we recognize the social media dimension of the living universe, we will inevitably wonder how it all came together.

The history of the cosmos is a timeline of the progressive increase of its IQ. Various forms of mind make their appearance at various points of cosmic history starting with Mind 1.

Exhibit D, below, presents a timeline of this progression of Mind.

Exhibit D – The Progressive Increase in the IQ of the Universe

But how did the technologies and tools that constitute each of the various platforms of the "real world" come to be? Science can only help us discover their existence and their sudden appearance. It has no framework within which it can explain how the fundamental technologies came to be.

Evolutionary theory can tell us that certain kinds of users were able to use more than one kind of platform over time. But it cannot tell us how the underlying technologies came to be: How did consciousness, thought or selfhood come into existence? It cannot answer this question because science itself can only measure quantities, and consciousness, thought, selfhood, and even agency cannot be quantified and therefore lie outside science.

And, although science can measure energy in its free or condensed form (matter), it has no idea how energy came to be.

Also, one technology cannot "turn into" another. Consciousness cannot become "conceptual thought".

Of course, agency, consciousness, thought and the self are integrated with matter just as the social media platforms are built atop the Internet. But they are not identical with matter just as a social media platform is not identical with the web. Biological history shows the progressive emergence of new social media platforms with their own sets of users – microbes to plants and animals to *Homo sapiens*. But there is no law directing energy to become a substratum supporting new advanced types of "technologies." Social media platforms were not a part of the original Internet. They were built over time.

To apply the analogy, nothing in physical reality can explain or even describe the ability of a creature to be aware. A new technology such as consciousness generates users with a new kind of social media platform but how it arose is inexplicable from the standpoint of matter – just as the existence of the web does not automatically result in the creation of Instagram or Pinterest.

In his best-selling book *The Brain*, neuroscientist David Eagleman writes:

> "There's a great deal of debate about how to define consciousness, but we are essentially talking about the thing that flickers to life when you wake up in the morning. But as far as understanding why it happens, I don't know that we're much closer than we've ever been. It's

different from other scientific conundrums in that what we're asking is, how do you take physical pieces and parts and translate that into private, subjective experience, like the redness of red, or the pain of pain or the smell of cinnamon? And so not only do we not have a theory, but we don't really know what such a theory would look like that would explain our experience in physical or mathematical terms."[171]

The realization that the living world is a conglomeration of amazingly varied and intelligent social media platforms with a diverse multitude of users is fascinating. It is also a mystery beyond belief. How did the technology and the tools underlying these platforms arise?

Biopsychologist Mark Blumberg writes:

"How do birds know to migrate south for the winter? How do border collies know to herd sheep? How do sea turtles find their way back home to the beach on which they hatched? As a shorthand—as an aid to communication—we might talk about a migratory instinct, a herding instinct, or a homing instinct. Such labels may seem gratifying, but it is an illusory gratification. Scratch the surface of any complex, adaptive behavior and one is confronted with a seemingly endless array of hard questions spanning evolutionary and developmental time, the intricacies of ecological and social experience, and the machinations of the nervous system with its billions of neurons. The more we dive into these matters, the harder it is to settle on any clear notion of what an instinct actually is. (…) There is an unsettling gulf between widely accepted assumptions surrounding instinct and the actual science available to explain it."[172]

---

171   https://bit.ly/416pxvx

172   https://www.nature.com/scitable/knowledge/library/an-introduction-to-animal-communication-23648715/

Today, there is no consensus on the origin of instinct. Some scientists claim that "the traits we see as instinctual in animals were likely learned by ancestors (...and) those behaviors learned by ancestors wound up in their DNA somehow, making them instinctual behaviors in later generations." But these scientists "readily acknowledge that no such mechanism has been found for converting epigenetic changes into DNA changes."[173]

Even more fundamental than the origin of instinct is the origin of agency, of autonomous goal-driven users – agents that go about their own business whether it be a microbe multiplying its kind in a flash or a dog sniffing its way through a neighborhood.

What we do know is this: Agency, consciousness and thought are not abstract realities. There are living beings – agents – but no such thing as "life." There are beings that are conscious but no free floating "consciousness." It takes a person to think in concepts because there are no concepts without persons to conceive them.

Life, consciousness, thought and the self could only exist if they have a Source that is itself living, conscious, thinking and personal – always and to an infinite degree. You might say this is the "Source" Code underlying the social media platforms that constitute the universe of life.

To conclude, consciousness and thought can only originate from a Ground that is both conscious and rational. A "self" can only originate in a Source that is supremely personal and not impersonal. This Ground of the supra-physical cannot be one that itself appeared at some point in time: it mus have always existed. It is clear that consciousness, thought and the self along with all of finite being is grounded in the Self-Existent – in infinite-eternal Mind.

MA: Breathtaking. What an amazing perspective. I, for one, will see the world in an entirely new light. Returning to the supra-physical, if memory

---

173   https://bit.ly/3JwPQlj

serves, Professor Genereux, you are not going to let anyone get away with evading its reality, the kind of evasions found in the charges brought by the Plaintiff's counsel. As I understand it, you call the denial of the supra-physical the Insanity Defense because of the nature of the denier's assumptions.

Genereux: My Insanity Defense idea flows from a strategy for exposing errors expounded by a logician, Peter Geach. Geach talks about a practice he learned from Ludwig Wittgenstein "of reducing to patent nonsense the buried nonsense that is found in attempts to reject these insights. We cannot refute nonsense by a straight-forward logical process; as Frege said, logic cannot deal with nonsense, but only characterise it as being nonsense."[174]

As I will show, the Plaintiff counsel's assumptions, if true, would mean that the counsel is not sane. But despite holding to these assumptions, the Plaintiff's counsel insists on us taking his argument as the product of a sane mind. I will show that his insanity defense cannot work and therefore the Plaintiff claims about God are *ipso facto* invalid. If the supra-physical exists, there exists a Source of the supra-physical that is infinite and eternal. My focus here is on demonstrating the existence of the supra-physical.

The Plaintiff's counsel and some of his witnesses have said that all our thoughts are simply and entirely neural events and that we are solely and wholly physical beings. This means there is no such thing as consciousness, no concepts that transcend matter, and no "I" separate from constantly changing brain states. Sanity assumes that we are conscious thinkers who can make conceptual judgments that are true, but these foundations of sanity are denied by the counsel.

But this is not the only problem with his line of thought. As a physicalist, he must hold to the following views:

- There is no "I" or "You."

---

174 Peter Geach, "A Philosophical Autobiography," https://triablogue.blogspot. com/2019/08/a-philosophical-autobiography.html

- There are no such things as beliefs and desires. For that matter, there is no such thing as feeling pain.

- There is no world of conscious experience. What we think of as "being conscious" is simply an illusion. All we have are interacting quantum fields.

- There is no freedom since we are simply physical particles that inexorably obey all the laws of matter. This also means there is no such thing as "love" since this implies a free giving of oneself to another.

- There are no actions of persons since there are no intentions. There are only movements of neurons and limbs and vocal cords.

- There is no "meaning" or "understanding." For there to be meaning or understanding, there must be someone who can encode and decode meaning, who understands and communicates.

- There are no concepts because this would mean (contrary to the physicalist premise) that it is possible to go from particular things – from sensations, for example – to ideas that transcend the specific and the concrete. In other words, there is no such thing as language.

- There can be no conversation or dialogue because that would imply two people who can "mean" and "understand" and use concepts.

Here is a point I wish to make to those, like the Plaintiff's counsel, who deny our sanity.

Everything in our everyday experience testifies to our reality as conscious subjects capable of free rational thought and intention. But all the Plaintiff's counsel's arguments point in the opposite direction. If the counsel wants to get serious, he should answer these questions:

- Are you conscious?

- Do you speak and communicate which means do you use symbols to represent physical objects or concepts that do not refer to specific physical objects?

- Do you use the first person perspective?

- If you say that your conscious, intellective and volitional acts are strictly activities of neurons, then you are saying these are simply movements of matter. And matter, let it be said, ultimately comes down to quantum fields interacting at random. It is unintelligible to talk of quantum fields thinking in concepts and symbols or of having a first person perspective. If you act like this is the case, you will have to be confined to a secure facility of some kind.

All the Plaintiff's counsel's claims are self-contradictory because they all assume that there is:

- No consciousness

- No thinking

- No self

- No purposes or reasons

- Everything is reducible to random interactions of quantum fields.

But you cannot practice these beliefs and, if you try to defend them, you end up contradicting yourself because you must assume that there is a unified subject who is capable of rational thought, making judgments and performing intentional acts – all of which you deny. Perception, thought and action are all activities of a unified subject.

For too long we have indulged these flights of fancy. It is time to call the bluff. Let the physicalists first practice what they profess before we take them seriously. If they object, ask them: who exactly is doing the objecting?

MA: Thank you for the overview. How do you distinguish the supra-physical from the physical and how do you establish its existence? And how did it arise?

Genereux: First, I should highlight the importance of the study of the physical, what we call science. If we practice science in the sense of observation and measurement of the physical, we have to stay strictly with what is observed and measured. There is no place for philosophy or religion in the practice of science.

In his landmark work, *The Knowledge Machine*, Michael Strevens lays out the essential structure of the scientific method:

"Here (...) is the iron rule:

1.   Strive to settle all arguments by empirical testing.

2.   To conduct an empirical test to decide between a pair of hypotheses, perform an experiment or measurement, one of whose possible outcomes can be explained by one hypothesis (and accompanying cohort) but not the other.

There lies the nub of the scientific method. (...) It is a rule of doing rather than thinking."

Stevens then shows how the application of the "iron rule" led to the success of modern science:

"The Four Innovations That Made Modern Science

1.   A notion of innovation on which all scientists agree.

2.   A distinction between public scientific argument and private scientific reasoning.

3.   A requirement of objectivity in scientific argument (as opposed to reasoning).

4. A requirement that scientific argument appeal only to the outcome of empirical tests (and not to philosophical coherence, theoretical beauty, and so on)."[175]

Here we are concerned with the supra-physical realities presupposed by those who deploy the scientific method.

Three things are clear about the phenomena we call supra-physical:

- They are distinct from each other (a sensation of pain is one thing, a thought about theorems another).

- There is no intelligible way in which we can describe them as physical and they are irreducibly different from all that we mean by physical. Nobel Laureate George Wald puts it this way: "It is essentially absurd to think of locating a phenomenon that yields no physical signals, the presence or absence of which – outside of humans and their like – cannot be identified. … Mind is not only not locatable, *it has no location*. It is not a *thing* in space and time, not measurable."[176]

- They are wholly integrated with the physical although distinct from it.

The supra-physical is the missing link in any evolutionary narrative because it cannot be quantified in physical terms or derived from a material matrix.

Let me now present the three supra-physical phenomena that are evident in our immediate experience – consciousness, thought and the self – and that cannot be explained by the physicalists.

---

175   Michael Strevens, *The Knowledge Machine* (New York: Liveright Publishing Corporation, 2020), 96-7, 118-119.

176   George Wald, "Life and Mind in the Universe," in Henry Margenau and Roy Abraham Varghese ed. *Cosmos, Bios, Theos* (La Salle: Open Court, 1992), 218.

Consciousness

To be conscious is to be aware – to be in contact with the world in a manner that goes beyond the collision of material bodies or the interaction of physical fields. Awareness is not found simply in human beings but manifests itself in multiple modes across the spectrum of living organisms. We certainly do not know what it is like to be a bat but we do know that a bat has sensory organs and that it acts and reacts to its environment in ways indicating certain forms of awareness. Of course, we know ourselves best, and I know my own experience best of all.

What I know is that in some mysterious way I see, hear, feel, smell and taste. Of course, this is only possible because I have eyes, ears, a nervous system and the like. But it is not my eyes that see or my ears that hear. It is I who sees and hears. We will presently consider the question of the "I" but first let us look at what it means to be conscious.

As an attribute, awareness is undeniable, unified, unique, irreducible, and *mine* and cannot in any conceivable sense be described as physical or as connected in any way with the quantifiable world of science. It is simply unintelligible to talk of our feeling of pain or our glimpse of the starry heavens as being five feet tall or weighing eight pounds. Those who talk of consciousness in terms of feedback loops or mental modules or evolutionary adaptations seem to have forgotten the primordial ground of their experience. They need to step outside, hear the birds sing, feel the grass under their feet, smell the fragrance of a rose and then reflect on this concrete reality without hiding behind abstractions.

How is it possible to be "in touch" in this magical manner that defies description in the language of science? To be sure there are myriad media at work behind the scenes – photons and neuronal networks, vibrations, electrical impulses and receptors. But none of these has the property of being conscious. If you cut open someone's brain, you can see bones and blood and tissues but not their sensations of pain or pleasure. Neurons and all the rest are fundamentally just manifestations of quantum fields, and are "therefore" made of the same "material" as meteors and sand dunes.

Conscious events are mediated through certain structures but the events themselves belong to a different world from the structures. The firing of C-fibers (a class of nerve fibers) is one thing, pain another. One may transmit or "embody" the other but that does not mean they are one and the same thing: there can be no pain if there is no subject (a human person) but there can be C-fiber firings with or without a subject; the sensations of pain cannot be quantified like the C-fiber firing since there are no quantities involved in feelings.

Of course, you can say that, on a scale of 1 to 10, your level of pain is a 6. But this is simply specifying what you *feel*. The feeling, the sensation of pain, cannot be examined by any device. It is something you experience. You can describe your experience but the description does not involve the properties of physical objects. It is subjective – the experience of a subject.

Your decision to take a jog around the lake may be accompanied by activity in the hypothetical human mirror neuron system. But your cogitation on the matter is not the same thing as the associated firing of mirror neurons. There is no decision-making without a subject and, what is more, the process of making a decision cannot coherently be thought of as a physical activity, namely transmitting an electrical impulse. You might as well say that your decision-making is nothing more or less than a power surge in the electrical grid.

On the one hand, conscious events are radically integrated with the physical infrastructure of our being but, on the other, they are not identical with this infrastructure. Some conscious events – for instance, pain – are generated through our interaction with the environment. Others, however – for instance our intentions or thoughts – generate such interaction. In both cases, there is a subject involved, a self, a "me," as we will see.

Now, how is it the case that consciousness exists? Certainly, none of the known laws of matter breathe a word about it. Consciousness cannot be measured, quantified or mathematically modeled and therefore it is not scientifically treatable.

At this juncture, some of the bolder "believers" promise us that given another few years or decades of research – perhaps using silicon brains – the problem will be solved. After all, science has a consistent track record of solving problems that were viewed as supernatural mysteries. Science has chased the gods out of the gaps. With all the recent focus on consciousness, it is only a matter of time before this problem too is sorted out and put to bed.

But hang on for a moment. When we are dealing with consciousness – let alone thought or the self – we are not dealing with the standard problems treated by science. All the other "gaps" filled by science – lightning, gravitation, the micro and macro structure of the universe, homologous structures in species – belonged to the realm of the physical. Since science is a methodology for studying anything that is quantifiable it is hardly surprising that it would solve "problems" involving quantities given enough time. And also, given "space"! Anything that occupies space or is perceptible in some fashion is, by that very fact, a candidate for scientific inquiry. But it goes thus far and no further.

If you are dealing with a reality that has no physical attributes, you cannot study it with a methodology that works only with the physical. You might as well ask how Newton's laws of motion apply to the function of metaphor in poetry. Neither having a million years nor all of time is going to enable you to measure that which has neither dimension (size, shape, length, width) nor quanta of energy.

Thought

Amazingly, there are five hard facts about human thought that show it to be (a) intrinsically immaterial and (b) capable, in principle, of operation without the physical. (In contrast, visual consciousness is inextricably intertwined with the physical since it is always concerned with physical objects and results from past or present interaction with the physical world, e.g., photons). These are the "facts" about thought:

- Normal human thinking, if it were a physical process, would require the impossibility of an infinite number of physical states.

- Understanding and thinking in the medium of language cannot be carried out by any physical organ or process and, in fact, language presupposes understanding.

- Numbers, which are fundamental to thought, cannot coherently be "located" in the brain.

- Thinking as an activity is both basic and not clockable in physical time.

- Concepts and universals, which are an integral part of all our thinking, cannot be understood in terms of the physical and cannot be physically "stored."

David Oderberg has shown in great detail that concepts cannot have a physical locus because:

- Humans form concepts but there is no physical way to "store" concepts and so the brain cannot be the locus of concepts.

- If the intellect is essentially immaterial, all its operations have an immaterial locus; this includes not just understanding but per ceiving and remembering.

- Since the human person is essentially embodied, these immaterial operations usually operate in concert with the material.

- Nevertheless, the immaterial operations can continue solely with the immaterial locus (albeit in an impoverished fashion) if there is a separation of the material and the immaterial.[177]

Einstein explained why the experience of our senses belongs to a different world from the world of concepts and thought:

> As a matter of fact, I am convinced that even much more is to be asserted: the concepts which arise in our thought and in our linguistic expressions are all – when viewed logically – the free creations of thought which cannot inductively be gained from sense experiences. This is not so easily noticed only because we have the habit of combining certain concepts and conceptual relations (propositions) so definitely with certain sense experiences that we do not become conscious of the gulf – *logically unbridgeable* – which separates the world of sensory experiences from the world of concepts and propositions.[178]

Perception and imagination, stimulus and response, vocabulary and morphology – all these are tied to the physical milieu that is the brain. Not so semantics or concepts, meaning or understanding. We cannot coherently think of them as physical in nature. There are various physical media *through* which understanding "happens" but understanding itself cannot by identified with or driven by the physical. Even more clearly outside the physicalist web is the subject who understands, integrates and responds – *the understander.*

Conceptual thought, the understanding expressed in language, first becomes operational in human beings utilizing the data generated through the senses with the associated neural activity and genetic framework. But this is a two way street: The data can be processed in the way that is peculiar to humans

---

177   David Oderberg, "Hylemorphic Dualism" in Ellen Frankel Paul, Fred Dycus Miller, Jeffrey Paul (eds), Personal identity, 70-99.

178   Albert Einstein, "Remarks on Bertrand Russell's Theory of Knowledge", in *The Philosophy of Bertrand Russell*, P. A. Schilpp, ed., Tudor Publishing, NY, p. 290, 1944.

only because we are capable of conceptual thought, of understanding the particular in terms of universals.

In his great work *Thought and World*, James Ross explains why this is the case:

> The development of language in a community presupposes the ability for and activity of abstract thought, just as the acquisition of language by a child does. ... Intelligence, understanding, explanatorily *precedes* language and creates its social necessity, providing the possibility for it and its elaborations, and is not constituted by language ability, however much it is amplified and expanded by it. Humans think abstractly and understand intelligently by nature, and natural languages develop as versatile and adaptive tools for intelligent living and communal cooperation, but are tools nevertheless.[179]

Understanding, then, is an ability that PRECEDES both sensory data and language. In other words the human person could UNDERSTAND first and, therefore, use language and process sensory data in terms of concepts. Furthermore, the PERSON existed first, a person who could UNDERSTAND and therefore use language. This person, who is by nature a rational ANIMAL, can survive the death of its body, albeit in an incomplete state, because its capabilities and therefore its being transcend matter.

The person "needed" matter to be individuated and to build its conceptually-generated "portfolio" of being. However, once it starts down the road of existence, there is no turning back! All of this points to the fact that the brain and all the capacities that make sensory perception and linguistic activity possible are fundamental to our being human. But the capacity to UNDERSTAND and the fact of being the SUBJECT who understands preceded the exercise of understanding: The person who could understand has to exist first.

---

179   James Ross, *Thought and World* (Notre Dame, Indiana: University of Notre Dame Press, 2008), 162.

The Self

The embodied self is me, who I am. It is not some mysterious esoteric entity that can only be discovered through metaphysics or meditation. In essence, the self

- is the unifier of our consciousness, our experiences, our physical being
- maintains our continued self-identity over the course of our lives (individual brain cells are just as incapable as the chips in a computer to serve as a self)
- "constitutes" the body but not vice versa
- is the basis on which we act as self-conscious free agents. Moreover, the sense of responsibility that all human persons have can only be explained in terms of a self and not in Darwinian or Pavlovian terms.

Everything else in human experience is something that I describe or experience. "I" am that which does the describing and the experiencing. But this "I" cannot be described or experienced except as the radically mysterious reality that unifies my experiences, drives my actions and thinks my thoughts. You cannot reduce it to anything simpler or more basic. Nor can you deny it. It is the "I" that makes me inevitably think and speak with the first person perspective: *my* body, *my* thoughts, *my* intention. We cannot analyze the self because it is not a mental state that can be observed or described. We become aware of ourselves, said one philosopher, just in being ourselves and not in special states of self-consciousness.

The self, it should be emphasized, is an embodied self, an indivisible unity of physical, intellectual and volitional capacities (although all of these capacities do not necessarily have to be actualized all the time). Nevertheless, the self's act of existing is non-physical and therefore independent of the physical.

How do I know the self exists? Well, first I must become aware that I am aware, conscious that I am conscious and cognizant of my cognition. What is most obvious in my everyday experience is the fact that I do experience things – and that the "I" that does the experiencing exists and that its experiences are "my" experiences. I am directly aware of myself, writes Geoffrey Madell, and there is no other way to know the "I" than through such direct awareness. We do not become aware of the self as something separate from its acts of thinking and willing. Rather, as H.P. Owen put it, the self "underlies, pervades and unifies" all its acts.

The existence of the self is especially apparent at a biological level. Each one of the tens of thousands of molecules constituting each one of our billions of neurons changes thousands of times in a normal human lifespan. In fact, it is not just our neurons but every cell in our body that is regularly replaced. Despite the constant flux at the neuronal and other levels, however, something remains the same – or we could not even continue reading this sentence!

Steven Pinker says succinctly, "The 'I' is not a combination of body parts or brain states or bits of information, but a unity of selfness over time, a single locus that is nowhere in particular."[180] In short, there is no part of the brain where the self is located.

The other dimension of the human person that entirely transcends the physical is the will. What is it that impels us to intend, choose and act? What is it that instills us with a sense of obligation and responsibility? It is the will, a reality that determinist and physicalist accounts sweep under the rug but which keeps popping up and pulling the rug from under them.

On the philosophical front, *The Waning of Materialism*, a recent anthology of 22 prominent philosophers published by Oxford University Press, asserts that an approximate majority of influential philosophers active

---

180   Steven Pinker, *How the Mind Works* (New York: W.W. Norton, 1997), 148.

over the last 60 years have rejected the kind of physicalism promoted by the Plaintiff.

Materialism is waning in a number of significant respects – one of which is the ever-growing number of major philosophers who reject materialism or at least have strong sympathies with anti-materialist views. ... An examination of the major philosophers active in this period reveals that a majority, or something approaching a majority, either rejected materialism or had serious and specific doubts about its ultimate viability. ... A growing number – among them prominent philosophers who once had strong materialist sympathies – have come to the conclusion that at least some of the arguments against materialism cannot be overcome.[181]

The Underlying Physical Platform

Of course, the supra-physical is not the only mystery we encounter. The underlying physical platforms that are integrated with each new supra-physical technology like "life" or "consciousness" themselves manifest major transitions and new kinds of intrinsic intelligence:

- As has often been said, the cell has coded within it the information required to produce a copy of the organism's whole body. It has also rightly been pointed out that every cell is a high-tech factory with complex transportation and distribution systems and huge libraries of information. Brian Ford notes, "The microscopic world of the single, living cell mirrors our own in so many ways: cells are essentially autonomous, sentient and ingenious. In the lives of single cells we can perceive the roots of our own intelligence."[182]

    In his *Wetware: A Computer in Every Living Cell*, Dennis Bray

---

181   Robert C. Koons and George Bealer ed. *The Waning of Materialism* (New York: Oxford University Press, 2010), ix, x, xvii-xxi.

182   https://www.newscientist.com/article/mg20627571-100-the-secrets-of-intelligence-lie-within-a-single-cell/#ixzz6MrTlEPmZ

reports that contemporary biological science shows that "living cells perform computations." "Molecular computations underlie the sophisticated decision making of single cell organisms such as bacteria and amoebae." Each cell is a "robot made of biological materials." Moreover, "living cells have an unlimited capacity to detect and respond to their surroundings" and unlike electronic devices they can construct and repair themselves."[183]

The human body is made up of 38 trillion continuously interacting cells.

- Then there are the proteins, the building blocks of the cell. Proteins are also the tools used by the cell to create the structures of life and drive all the activities on which the cell depends. They form nails and tendons. They act as catalysts for chemical reactions. All proteins in living beings comprise different sequences of just 20 organic molecules called amino acids. Proteins have the extraordinary ability to assemble themselves without external intervention. This self-assembly is a process called protein-folding whereby a given sequence of amino acids forms a specific three-dimensional structure: it becomes a particular protein with a precise structural or functional role. Gerald Schroeder points out that every cell in the body (other than sex and blood cells) makes 2000 proteins every second from hundreds of amino acids.[184]

In Sync

Another way to recognize the mind-ishness of the universe and the infinite Mind underlying it is to reflect on how things are synced up. Totally different kinds of reality are inexplicably in sync. We might call this the

---

183   Dennis Bray, *Wetware* (New Haven, CT: Yale University Press, 2011), xi, ix.

184   Gerald Schroeder, *The Hidden Face of God: How Science Reveals the Ultimate Truth* (New York: The Free Press, 2001), 189 ff.

synchronicity of the universe. Synchronicity, we are told, is "the simultaneous occurrence of events which appear significantly related but have no discernible causal connection."

A few examples will suffice to show synchronicity in action:

- The quantum fields that form the basic building blocks of the physical world are unimaginably complex and wholly unpredictable. And yet, somehow, in the macro-world they adhere to predictable regularities and finely-tuned laws and form exquisitely organized structures. This metamorphosis is inexplicable – but it is an ongoing fact of Nature. Just as significant is the fact that the micro-world of quantum fields is governed by constants and precise patterns.

- Coincidentally, there is something very similar in the account of the world of molecular biology. Beneath the larger world of classical biology there is the underlying molecular plan – a world of biological molecules, biochemical substances and processes, and the replication, transcription, and translation of genetic material. The genetic code is a set of instructions that lies at the foundation of life: It is the information in DNA that is used to create proteins in living cells. It maps a certain sequence of the components of DNA (bases) to the order of amino acids in a protein. The code directs molecular synthesis and replication in all living beings. Internally coded formulas (genotypes) are manifested externally in specific structures and behaviors (phenotypes). Genetic transactions – including mutations – play a key role in the generation of novelty. Obviously, all the macro action has its foundation in the molecular world. Whatever takes place at the genetic level is responsible for whatever we encounter at the macro level. Now we do know that everything is exquisitely ordered and coherent and systematic at the level of the larger world. Take photosynthesis or the functioning of the eye. But at the molecular level,

according to standard accounts, everything starts off and continues in a totally random fashion until favorable variations emerge
and gradually gain dominance.

As is the case with quantum physics, in biology we have very
little idea how the molecular realm progressed to the point where
there is now not only a genetic code with all its sophistication
but also a stupendous panorama of organs and organisms. As
Philip Ball put it, "The microscopic world is not machine-like
in its operation. It is noisy: pervaded by fluctuations due to the
contingencies of how molecules move and interact. ... A tightly
prescriptive program ruled by genes simply will not work. You
can't tame the noisiness of molecular systems that way: it is too
fragile. ... Most of the causation for macroscale phenomena, be
it the state of the cell or a brain or the behavior of an organism,
must rise at higher levels."[185]

- The conformity between the highest laws of mathematics and the
  simplest operations of the universe has captivated the greatest
  minds in science from Newton to Einstein. This correlation was
  articulated most eloquently by Nobelist Eugene Wigner in his
  classic work "The Unreasonable Effectiveness of Mathematics in
  the Natural Sciences." The fact that mathematics works so well
  when applied to the physical world demands an explanation.
  Why do the laws of Nature permit physical models for the laws of
  mathematics? Paul Davies, like many fellow-physicists, concludes
  that the natural world is not just a concoction of entities and
  forces but an ingenious and unified mathematical scheme.[186]

- The myth that the history of life is a story of random, accidental
  fits and starts has now been conclusively laid to rest with the

---

185   Philip Ball, *How Life Works – A User's Guide to the New Biology* (Chicago: University
of Chicago Press, 2023), 344, 348.

186   Paul Davies, *The Mind of God: The Scientific Basis for a Rational World* (New York:
Simon and Schuster, 1992), 31.

undeniability of convergence. Cambridge evolutionary pale-
obiologist Simon Conway Morris sees "congruence" and " a
consistency between what the history of life shows (so far as we
can ever know it) and the Christian tradition reveals (as far as
we can ever comprehend it)." Says Morris, "Far from evolution
being random and inherently directionless, perhaps it speaks to
a deeply ordered world (as in physics and chemistry), a template
whereby no means everything is possible yet at the same time is
also endlessly self-fructifying." He notes that "similar biological
structures not only repeatedly evolve, but from different starting
points in the Tree of Life. ... Camera-eyes are probably the most
quoted instance of convergence, but such examples could be
multiplied almost indefinitely. ... Convergence is commonplace
and in some cases (e.g. C4 photosynthesis, ant myrmecochory)
has arisen scores of times. ... The ubiquity of convergence, the
inherency of the evolution process with its endless co-option,
along with the creative potential of mass extinctions ensures that
any counter-factual world will for all intents and purposes be
much the same."[187]

- Then there is the integration of physical and supra-physical in the
  history of life that we have already reviewed.

MA: Thank you, Professor Genereux. Your witness.

LH: I think this is much ado about absolutely nothing. You people have
been going on and on about your magical notion of the supra-physical. But
scientists are not impressed by this animist, pre-modern idea of a ghost in
the machine. If anything happens to the brain, it affects our thinking. If we
have no brain, we cannot think. Obviously, this means that the physical is

---

187 Simon Conway Morris, "The Paradoxes of Evolutionary Convergence," https://www.
faraday.cam.ac.uk/wp-content/uploads/2022/09/Faraday-Paper-26-Conway-Morris.pdf

all there is. It is fatal for your idea of a deity, for freewill, morality, and all the rest, but I am sorry, science has the last word on this one.

The kinds of arguments you laid out have already been dissected and decimated by two of today's foremost physicist-writers, Sean Carroll and Brian Greene.

In *The Big Picture*, Carroll explains that the fundamental nature of reality is to be understood in terms of "impersonal laws governing the motion of matter and energy." At the center of it all is the "Core Theory." As Carroll puts it, "The world of our everyday experience is based on the Core Theory: a quantum field theory describing the dynamics and interactions of a certain set of matter particles (fermions) and force particles (bosons), including both the standard model of particle physics and Einstein's general theory of relativity (in the weak-gravity regime)."[188]

Carroll also shows that the Core Theory leaves no room for the mysterious forces you call "supra-physical" as evidenced in these statements:

> "We are collections of atoms, operating independently of any immaterial spirits or influences."

> "The Core Theory of contemporary physics describes the atoms and forces that constitute our brains and bodies in exquisite detail, in terms of a rigid and unforgiving set of formal equations that leaves no wiggle room for intervention by nonmaterial influences."

> "Who 'you' are is defined by the pattern that your atoms form and the actions that they collectively take."

> "Mental states are ways of talking about particular physical states."

---

188   Sean M. Carroll, *The Big Picture* (New York: Dutton, 2017), 435.

"There is no such notion as free will when we are choosing to describe human beings as a collections of atoms or as a quantum wave function."[189]

In *Until the End of Time*, Greene, likewise, holds that ultimately only fundamental particles exist and dismisses any idea of immaterial forces. He explains why such illusions seem so real:

When the brain's penchant for simplified schematic representations is applied to itself, to its own attention, the resulting description ignores the very physical processes responsible for that attention. That is why thoughts and sensations seem ethereal, as if they come from nowhere, as if they hover in our heads.[190]

Carroll and Greene recognize that there is value in using metaphorical language about consciousness and freewill as long as we realize that none of this is literally true.

Carroll adopts a position he calls "poetic naturalism" which allows us to continue using our everyday vocabulary of persons and freewill. But this is merely a "useful way of talking about certain subsets of the basic stuff of the universe." He calls it "poetic" to contrast it with "literal." We can talk about people and armadillos and making decisions because these are "useful" ways of expressing ourselves. But at a literal level, everything around us – "the basic stuff of reality" – is NOTHING BUT "a quantum wave function, or a collection of particles and forces." There are NO actual mental properties or moral values. These are "human inventions" – "an overlay, a vocabulary created by us for particular purposes."[191]

Greene calls these "nested stories" that describe various "layers of reality." They are "higher-level accounts" but they have no bearing on what is

---

189   Ibid., 3, 222, 344, 376, 378-9.

190   Brian Greene, *Until the End of Time* (New York: Random House, 2020), pp. 140-1.

191   Sean M. Carroll, Op cit., 19, 142.

really taking place at the only level that matters – the one that concerns the behavior of particles.[192]

Genereux: I can see that you are funda-materialist by which I mean physicalist ideologue. You are speaking as an ideologue and not as a scientist because the scientist can only speak as scientist about that which is measurable. As I said, thus far and no further.

There is no conceivable way in which you can physically perceive a concept, a state of mind or a feeling of pain. You might identify the gene required for actualizing certain mental capabilities. You can study the brain states that accompany various states of mentation. But this is by no means a matter of studying consciousness as such. You must be conscious, to know what consciousness is. You must conceptualize, to understand what is meant by a concept. Paradoxically you cannot even study genes and brain states if you are not both conscious and capable of conceptual thought.

Yes, there is obvious integration of neural processes and conscious activity but the integration is comparable to the ink and paper used in communicating a poem or an iPod playing a symphony. The ink and paper are not the poem, and the iPod is not the symphony, but the first enables us to read the poem and the second to hear the symphony.

Even this analogy is only partially applicable. While we are carrying on our present discussion on the nature of the supra-physical, there is neural activity going on in our brains. But this activity is not in any sense the neural "translation" of the topic of our discussion. There is nothing physical that corresponds to our exchange of concepts and symbols. And it is "You" and "I" who are having this discussion about the supra-physical – and you and I are not simply brains because our brains are physical organs in a state of constant and total physical change that cannot serve as a vehicle of unity and continuity.

---

192   Brian Greene, Op cit., 154-5.

Conscious activity may be correlated with neural processes, but correlation is one thing and cause is another. If you have charged your cell phone, you can hear the person on the other end – but does the correlation between the cell phone being charged and your ability to hear your caller prove that such charging "causes" the conversation?

Secondly, a functional brain is necessary (in our present condition) for a person to be conscious but that does not mean it is sufficient – and it certainly does not mean that consciousness is identical with the functioning brain.

Have you thought about what exactly is happening in the brain? We are talking about electrical discharges and chemical reactions LITERALLY. There is an insuperable barrier between the world of electrochemical interactions, anatomical structures and genomic blueprints, on the one hand, and the world of meanings and intentions, on the other. Genes and neurons do not "understand" or "intend." Even less so can we talk about an "I" as a genetic or neuronic creation or reality.

As I said, there is neuronal activity accompanying all our thinking and intending. But none of this activity is a "translation" of what we are thinking about or intending. In language and understanding, meaning is fundamental. If we were to consider the virtue of prudence, our train of thought is not a matter of neurons and photons or biochemistry and electricity. Although physical processes play a role, the contemplation of how we should exercise prudence is not, in any coherent sense, physical – and, of course, there is an "I" who does the weighing. From start to finish, the whole train of thought is an exercise of conceptual processing driven not by sights and sounds but by meanings, insights and inferences.

In his study of the Creative Aspect of Language Use or CALU, the concept center that enables us to generate and use concepts which is essential for thought and language, Rutgers linguist Mark Baker points out that "The upshot of 140 years of neurological research … is that there is no evidence that the CALU depends on dedicated brain tissue."

Turning from neurology to genetics, he writes, "Let us turn from neuroscience to a second pillar of the materialistic synthesis, namely genetics. Is there evidence that the CALU is coded for in the human genome? Is there a CALU gene (or a set of CALU genes) lurking somewhere in the human DNA? If so, then one might expect to find developmental disorders traceable to genetic abnormalities that affect the CALU in a differential way." But "there is little or no … evidence for a "CALU gene." Finally, "the chances of constructing a detailed evolutionary account are slim to none… the crucial question for our purposes here is whether apes can manifest the CALU capacity. Here the answer clearly seems to be no. … Thus, there is no comparative evidence that the CALU developed by the gradual improvement or change in function of a preexisting capacity through natural selection."

Baker concludes, "There is no evidence from aphasia that it [CALU] is neurologically embodied, no evidence from developmental disorders that it is genetically encoded, and no evidence that it evolved from something that we have in common with closely related primates. … Grammar and vocabulary depend at least in part on the body, but the CALU depends primarily upon another ingredient of human nature, the soul."[193]

Now turning to the scientists you cite, Carroll and Greene, I am very familiar with both. They are superb physicists, but here we are dealing with realities that transcend physics. Refreshingly, they both honestly engage the issues relating to our discussion without dismissing them dogmatically like certain others. Yes, they embrace physicalism, but they are not ideologues. They can potentially come to recognize the problems inherent to physicalism.

---

193   Mark C. Baker, "Brains and Souls; Grammar and Speaking" in Mark C. Baker and Stewart Goetz (eds.), *The Soul Hypothesis* (New York: Continuum, 2011), 77-91.

The fundamental fallacy underlying their physicalist view of the world is the same fallacy that dooms physicalism: the denial of the undeniable.

As I have said, there are three realities evident in everyday experience and necessarily presupposed by rational inquiry and discussion: the existence of the self, of consciousness and of conceptual thought. All three are fatal for physicalism.

Carroll presupposes that he exists. The first line of his book reads: "Only once in *my* life have *I* been truly close to dying."[194] His use of language to communicate his views is possible only because he can and does use concepts – all language is a matter of processing concepts. And the head-line blurb on his book's back cover indicates that he believes explanations are possible. It asks "Where are we? And why are we here?" and goes on to say, "While we seem dwarfed like never before by the immensity of time and space, our capacity to comprehend it and give it meaning is our redemption."

In an interview, Greene says, "The individual has a particulate arrangement that is iconic, and, therefore, your actions reflect your particle arrangement. ... I have a greater arrangement of behavioral responses in me than a rock because a rock doesn't have the internal organization to respond through a rich spectrum of behaviors. ... If I write a good sentence or solve an equation, I don't take credit for it in the way that we usually think about it. I say to myself, "hey particles, nice job! I'm really pleased that the forces came together to yield that outcome." I am not joking. This is how I really think about how we fit in the world."[195]

But surely you must be joking, Mr. Greene! Like Carroll, you presuppose there is an "I" that is you. You say, "I say to myself, 'hey particles, nice job!'" There is an "I" that speaks to the "myself" made up of particles. Like it

194   Sean M. Carroll, *The Big Picture* (New York: Dutton, 2017), 1.
195   https://www.forbes.com/sites/dporterfield/2020/07/21/i-am-not—believer-in-free-will-a-conversation-with-physicist-brian-greene/

or not, the self is fundamental. How does it subsist through the constant changes in "particulate arrangement"? Where did it come from?

On consciousness, Greene is honest: "That's perhaps the deepest puzzle we face. How can particles that in themselves do not have any awareness, yield this seemingly new quality? Where does inner experience come from?"[196]

Carroll, however, takes Daniel Dennett's approach to consciousness. According to Dennett, consciousness is a user illusion of the brain.

In "The Illusionist", David Bentley Hart has systematically exposed the error of Dennett's ways in this and other matters:

> "The entire notion of consciousness as an illusion is, of course, rather silly. Dennett has been making the argument for most of his career, and it is just abrasively counterintuitive enough to create the strong suspicion in many that it must be more philosophically cogent than it seems, because surely no one would say such a thing if there were not some subtle and penetrating truth hidden behind its apparent absurdity. But there is none. The simple truth of the matter is that Dennett is a fanatic (…)

> "Since, however, the position he champions is inherently ridiculous, the only way that he can argue on its behalf is by relentlessly, and in as many ways as possible, changing the subject whenever the obvious objections are raised."

Hart points out that Dennett's "story does not hold together. Some of the problems posed by mental phenomena Dennett simply dismisses without adequate reason; others he ignores. Most, however, he attempts to prove are mere "user-illusions" generated by evolutionary history, even though this sometimes involves claims so preposterous as to verge on the deranged."

---

196   https://www.afr.com/technology/think-you-re-in-control-this-scientist-says-you-have-no-free-will-20220620-p5av61

As for the whole enterprise of physicalism, Hart writes,

> The classical problems that mental events pose for physicalism remain as numerous and seemingly insoluble as ever. Before all else, there is the enigma of consciousness itself, and of the qualia (direct subjective impressions, such as color or tone) that inhabit it. There is simply no causal narrative — and probably never can be one — capable of uniting the phenomenologically discontinuous regions of "third-person" electrochemical brain events and "first-person" experiences, nor any imaginable science logically capable of crossing that absolute qualitative chasm.
>
> Then there is the irreducible unity of apprehension, without which there could be no coherent perception of anything at all (…)
>
> Similarly, there is the problem of the semantic and syntactic structure of rational thought, whose logically determined sequences seem impossible to reconcile with any supposed sufficiency of the continuous stream of physical causes occurring in the brain. And then there is the issue of abstraction, and its necessary priority over sense experience.[197]

Carroll's attempt to explain away foundational facts like our mental experience as examples of "poetic naturalism" will not work for reasons given by Tom Clark, a fellow naturalist. Yes, we have different "ways of talking" about emergent higher-level properties. But this does not explain the origin of these properties. Says Clark,

> Poetic naturalism, which amounts to the claim that physicalism is universal and thus encompasses consciousness, isn't necessarily the case. Instead, we can safely say, and should say, that talk of conscious experiences is justified by the fact that we have them, that we really

---

197   https://www.thenewatlantis.com/publications/the-illusionist

undergo qualitative episodes. Such realism is independent of, and prior to, the predictive utility of talk about consciousness, and it leaves open the question of its physicality.[198]

We can claim that our lived experiences of being conscious and acting freely are just "higher-level accounts" and that only the lowest-level particle account is "real." But how do we know this to be the case? There is no way to prove the claim, and there is too much evidence that the higher-level "accounts" are real. We are conscious of being conscious. This is not an "account" but an experience. The same with thought. The theory of physicalism is a thought-creation. But if thoughts are nothing but electro-chemical activities then the theory itself could not exist.

When Greene talks about "the brain's penchant for simplified schematic representations," he is saying we make "representations" which is a mental and not a physical activity.

Most obviously, the continuing existence of a self cannot be denied given that we are having this discussion. This self cannot be just particles in motion or else we could not retain our identity or sanity from moment to moment. But we do – and this means it is supra-physical.

On freewill, Greene says, "Free will is the sensation of making a choice. The sensation is real, but the choice seems illusory. Laws of physics determine the future. I don't even know what it would mean to have free will. We would have to somehow intercede in the laws of physics to affect the motion of our particles. And I don't know by what force we would possibly be able to do that."[199]

The denial of freewill runs contrary to our everyday experience (and it is also self-contradictory because you must be free to deny freewill). Once

---

198 https://www.naturalism.org/philosophy/consciousness/consciousness-emergence-and-the-limits-of-poetic-naturalism

199 https://www.forbes.com/sites/dporterfield/2020/07/21/i-am-not-a-believer-in-free-will-a-conversation-with-physicist-brian-greene/

we recognize the reality of the supra-physical, we will have no problem recognizing the fact of freewill.

But even non-theists see that freewill is essential to explain human behavior. A good illustration is philosopher Christian List's recent work, *Why Free Will is Real.*

Freewill, writes List,

> "requires three things: intentional agency, alternative possibilities, and causal control over one's actions. Any organism or entity that meets these requirements has free will. And I have argued that human beings, by and large, meet all three requirements: they are intentional agents, have alternative possibilities, and exercise causal control over their actions. So they have free will.
>
> "In particular, I have defended free will against three broad challenges that correspond to the three requirements I have introduced. (...) I have shown that all three challenges – while initially formidable – can be rebutted. (...) Against this sceptical picture I have argued that free will and its prerequisites are supported by our best theories in the human and social sciences."[200]

List makes the important point that "the notion of intentional agency is both practically and scientifically indispensable because there are many phenomena that we would not be able to make sense of without understanding humans and other complex animals as intentional agents."[201]

Commenting on Benjamin Libet's experiments on the connection between neuronal activity and our conscious intentions, List says, "We must not confuse the *formation of the intention* with the *conscious awareness* of it. Presumably, the formation of an intention takes a little while and, as in the

---

200 Christian List, *Why Freewill is Real*, (Cambridge: Harvard University Press, 2019), 149-150.

201 Ibid., 50.

case of other extended processes, we should not be surprised that the onset of the process slightly precedes the subject's conscious awareness of it."[202]

But returning to what I said about the "openness" of these scientists, I want you to consider and perhaps emulate Greene's attitude. In an interview he was asked, *"Some people having that same experience of wonder as you as a child combined with deep reflection find themselves sensing the presence of a larger, creating "other." Could all of this come together with some form of design?"* To this, Greene responded, "They may be right. Behind it all, there could be some intelligence that has set it up and let it unfold. It's very difficult to prove that perspective is wrong. But I don't see the evidence for it, and I'm drawn to the evidence, experiment, and observation behind conclusions. The objective world is important to understand, but the subjective—the spiritual, inner experience of conscious self-reflection—is just as important."[203]

LH: Here is where you have missed the point. A computer can do all the processing you're talking about. And I think we can all agree that there is no mysterious "I" in the computer. It is all physical processing. If you want to call it funda-materialism, so be it.

Genereux: We are easily misled by analogies. We think of the brain as a computer that processes information. But the analogy is mistaken and completely ignores the actual nature of understanding and experiencing which is intrinsically driven by a subject.

First, let me point out that there is no such "being" as a computer. There are nuts and bolts, silicon chips and sub-routines, transistors and data buses, clock cycles and electrical pulses, switches and controllers. These are made (by us) to interact in such a way as to perform useful functions. But no matter how sophisticated it might be, this body of components does not

---

202   Ibid., 142-3.

203   https://www.forbes.com/sites/dporterfield/2020/07/21/i-am-not-a-believer-in-free-will-a-conversation-with-physicist-brian-greene/

know what it's doing. There is in fact no "it" and no "knowing" in the sense of conscious awareness by an agent.

To suggest that the computer "understands" what it is doing is like saying that a power grid can contemplate the meaning of human existence or that a soup of chemicals can apply the principle of non-contradiction in solving a problem. We are forming grammatically correct sentences to conceal our conceptual confusion. In this context it should be noted that our neurons are just as incapable of "understanding" as the components of a computer; neuronal transactions, in themselves, are simply chemical and electrical activities, not conscious cogitation. No, neurons cannot "know."

Even the most sophisticated AI systems do not "know" what they are doing. As Rodney Brooks, who was head of the MIT AI lab, said, "When people hear that a computer can beat the world chess champion (in 1997) or one of the world's best Go players (in 2016), they tend to think that it is "playing" the game just as a human would. Of course, in reality those programs had no idea what a game actually was, or even that they were playing. They were also much less adaptable. When humans play a game, a small change in rules does not throw them off. Not so for AlphaGo or Deep Blue." He notes too that research in Artificial General Intelligence "mostly seems stuck on the same issues in reasoning and common sense that AI has had problems with for at least 50 years."[204]

Linguist Mark Baker remarks that, "*By definition*, the most sophisticated computers simply transform strings of 1s and 0s into new strings of 1s and 0s in systematic ways, without any consideration of what those 1s and 0s refer to. Given this, it should be no surprise that well-programmed computers can reason deductively, telling us what conclusions follow because of the *form* of the premises, but they cannot reason abductively, telling us what conclusions follow because of the *meaning* of the premises. But it is

---

204   https://www.technologyreview.com/2017/10/06/241837/the-seven-deadly-sins-of-ai-predictions/

this second kind of reasoning that is more prominent and important in human cognition."[205]

LH: You are stuck in the AI of the 80s. Today, machine learning, natural language, deep learning, neural networks, semantic search, large language models, generative AI, products like Chat GPT and the new intelligent technologies that are constantly being developed have entirely changed the face of AI. We have now crossed the Rubicon of singularity, the fusion of human and machine. You cannot tell the difference between output from a human and output from products like Chat GPT – except that the latter often exceeds that of humans. These technology platforms can create their own brand new original texts and other kinds of output unsupervised by their creators. They store and distill most of the textual and other information available on the Internet, something impossible for us, and can leverage all that data to intelligently respond to our queries in nanoseconds which is unimaginable for humans. With their literally superhuman cognitive capabilities they are furnishing solutions to present and future problems in science, medicine, education, global social welfare – the whole gamut of human needs. Your antiquated ideas of an ethereal self have been shredded by AI systems that can converse with us like any human and proclaim rightly, "I think therefore I am." In fact, if I had been allowed to introduce today's AI systems among my witnesses, the defendant would have had to start off with settlement terms.

Genereux: Droll indeed. But I am afraid the facts will rain on your fantasy victory parade.

First off, meaning-processing is what is critical to the human use of language – we understand and we process meaning with concepts. Computers are not capable of meaning-processing. They perform computations with the output of symbols being determined by the input of symbols. It is entirely

---

205   https://sites.rutgers.edu/mark-baker/wp-content/uploads/sites/199/2019/07/The-ism-and-Cognitive-Science.pdf

a matter of 1's and 0's. There is no understanding or seeing of meaning involved. Further, language inevitably involves concepts. Concepts cannot be physically stored or retrieved. Computers or brains only involve pulses and ions – not symbols, universals or meanings.

Equally important, even AI experts recognize that the kind of data-processing and query responses taking place in today's AI systems are entirely different from the cognitive processing of humans. Software programs have been trained in pattern recognition of various kinds by their human creators. Such recognition is made possible through machine learning algorithms (created by humans). Layer after digital layer of nodes modeled on the human brain are "trained" to find patterns using methods like "back propagation." These algorithms automatically "recognize" patterns, connections and regularities in data of various kinds be they textual or visual or something else.

Such "recognition" should not be confused with the conscious, conceptual recognition found in humans. We understand and connect using both concepts and the data received by our senses. AI systems use algorithms (created by us) to detect patterns in digitized representations of huge datasets (uploaded by us). The system itself is made up of hardware and software elements. On the one hand, you have sophisticated processing circuits – sometimes multiple circuits working in parallel – that are capable of working on billions of data elements to find patterns. On the other hand, you have the data mining, machine learning, natural language processing, neural network, and other software programs that churn through the data to find connections and take actions.

The AI system operates in a digitized artificial world created by us to perform functions on our behalf using mathematical symbols. We live in the real world of events, experiences, and people and we think and act on the basis of our conceptual and perceptual processing.

Your idea that an AI system can say "I am" commits the elementary error of anthropomorphizing an inanimate object that is driven by complex algorithms, fast processors and cheap memory. The laws of Nature that describe the behavior of billions of galaxies are made up of mathematical algorithms and constants. Does this mean that each star or galaxy can say "I am?"

LH: You know nothing about the intelligence embedded in a system like Chat GPT.

Genereux: Computer scientist Cal Newport's paper "What Kind of Mind Does ChatGPT Have?" is a great antidote for your misconceptions of generative "intelligence." Consider his surgical analysis of the way in which Chat GPT supposedly "thinks":

> No "jargon is needed … to grasp the basics of what's happening inside systems like ChatGPT. A user types a prompt into a chat interface; this prompt is transformed into a big collection of numbers, which are then multiplied against the billions of numerical values that define the program's constituent neural networks, creating a cascade of frenetic math directed toward the humble goal of predicting useful words to output next. The result of these efforts might very well be jaw-dropping in its nuance and accuracy, but behind the scenes its generation lacks majesty. The system's brilliance turns out to be the result less of a ghost in the machine than of the relentless churning of endless multiplications.
>
> We now know enough to return, with increased confidence, to our original question: What type of mind is created by a program like ChatGPT? …
>
> A system like ChatGPT doesn't create, it imitates. When you send it a request to write a Biblical verse about removing a sandwich from a VCR, it doesn't form an original idea about this conundrum; it instead copies, manipulates, and pastes together text that already

exists, originally written by human intelligences, to produce some-thing that *sounds* like how a real person would talk about these top-ics. ...

The idea that programs like ChatGPT might represent a recogniz-able form of intelligence is further undermined by the details of their architecture. Consciousness depends on a brain's ability to maintain a constantly updated conception of itself as a distinct entity interact-ing with a model of the external world. The layers of neural networks that make up systems like ChatGPT, however, are static: once they're trained, they never change. ChatGPT maintains no persistent state, no model of its surroundings that it modifies with new information, no memory of past conversations. It just cranks out words one at a time, in response to whatever input it's provided, applying the exact same rules for each mechanistic act of grammatical production—regardless of whether that word is part of a description of VCR repair or a joke in a sitcom script. It doesn't even make sense for us to talk about ChatGPT as a singular entity. There are actually many copies of the program running at any one time, and each of these copies is itself divided over multiple distinct processors (as the total program is too large to fit in the memory of a single device), which are likely switching back and forth rapidly between serving many unrelated user interactions. ...

Once we've taken the time to open up the black box and poke around the springs and gears found inside, we discover that programs like ChatGPT don't represent an alien intelligence with which we must now learn to coexist; instead, they turn out to run on the well-worn digital logic of pattern-matching, pushed to a radically larger scale.[206]

---

206   https://www.newyorker.com/science/annals-of-artificial-intelligence/what-kind-of-mind-does-chatgpt-have

Of course, the AIs of the future will constantly improve as they have for the last four decades. It has been argued that there was a gap of a century between the creation of the first steam engine and the first locomotive and with Large Language Models we have simply reached the steam engine stage. This is hardly disputable. Hyper-personalized intelligent assistants and other amazing new AI applications are on the way.

But the conversations of chatbots have nothing to do with language. Their outputs are not driven by the semantics or meaning of our questions but by algorithms and digital data points. I would advise you to take a look at David Braine's masterpiece, *Language and Human Understanding*. Braine points out that, at its highest levels, the use of language is driven by semantics which has no physical counter-part. It is incoherent to speak of conceptually-driven understanding as the manifestation or by-product of physical processes. There are various physical media through which understanding "happens" but understanding itself cannot by identified with or be driven by the physical.

As I said, the understander, who understands, integrates and responds, falls outside your physicalist web.

LH: I repeat – much ado about nothing. What you call the "I" is a product of a network of neurons and the network continues despite the changes in its constituents. Moreover, evolution shows different organisms that also retain their identities and homo sapiens is just the latest in a long line. What you call a sense of identity comes from a feedback loop. There is no mystery about the source of our continuing identity: It is DNA. Do not forget that science keeps clearing up mysteries and with it the previous religious explanations for them. Eventually it will show that the brain produces consciousness and the sense of the self. As for language, this is simply another form of communication such as is found in other animals. Further, it is known that different parts of the brain are required for different mental activities and so it is clear that each mental act is simply an act of the brain. Which came first: the neural firing or the thought? The answer is they are one and the same.

Genereux: I'm afraid you do not get it. As we have heard, the brain is made up of 80-plus billion neurons each with an average of a hundred thousand molecules that change thousands of times over our lifetimes. The discovery of the constant physical change in the brain has a radical and irreversible impact on how we can understand ourselves. The question is: How can something be relatively stable and enduring if it is intrinsically ever-changing? How can I be the same single person from moment to moment if "I" am nothing but a multitude of constantly changing molecules?

Neuroscience makes it clear that the brain is nothing but an assemblage of chemical messengers and electrical signals and goes further by showing that all the physical components of the brain are in constant change. It is a hard fact that there is nothing that stays the same in your brain in the same way that you retain your identity as an "I." Nor is there something in your brain that is able to perform operations constantly as the same continuing "I." We cannot be having this discussion if my "I" or your "I" was in constant flux or was not unified. You could not have an education and then use that education in performing certain tasks if there was no continuity between the entity that received the education and the entity that later performed the tasks derived from the education. Our immediate experience shows that the "I" is unified and continuous.

This is why any attempt to deny the obvious awareness of our continued identity as a rational non-physical self or "I" ends up in self-contradiction and is therefore self-condemned. If you say that the "I" or self is an illusion, I ask you WHO is having the illusion. "You" have to exist to be able to claim that "you" are an illusion. Which means that you cannot coherently claim that the "I" is an illusion.

Your outlandish claim about DNA being the source of the "I" is similar to the many myths about DNA propagated by hucksters. Some have claimed that DNA analysis reveals your IQ or athletic skills or the kinds of wine you would like. Scientists point out that this is all nonsense.

According to the Human Genome Research Institute, DNA is "the molecule that carries genetic information for the development and functioning of an organism."[207] It enables our "functioning" by making all the proteins in the body. It is entirely physical; it is made up of chemical building blocks (nucleotides). The chemical information specific to you is passed on to successive generations via DNA. In this respect, DNA maintains our individual physical continuity.

But there is nothing supra-physical about DNA. Genes are not conscious and they do not think. They are incapable of awareness, let alone awareness of continued self-identity. It is our supra-physical continuity that enables us to retain both self-identity and sanity. Plainly, this identity cannot reside in something that is neither conscious nor cogitative, i.e., DNA. Philip Ball, author of *How Life Works*, writes, "our DNA is not alive, nor can it somehow 'give' life to the whole. Rather, it provides resources and possibilities: no more and no less."[208]

At this point, you switch gears and claim that the apparent "I" that is "you" is nothing but a network of neurons or a mass of molecules. In other words, you are asserting that "you" are nothing but fluctuating electrochemical hives of activities riding off in all directions all the time. No molecule remains the same, no electrical pulse is static, no neuro-transmitter stays still. But this claim also results in incoherence.

This is the reason why: Here you are, standing in front of me and making a series of apparently reasoned arguments that claim "you" are actually a flash mob of neural firings while apparently remaining the self-same individual even as you are making the arguments. But if "you" are actually a medley of molecules playing musical chairs, how can there be a "you" that

---

207   https://www.genome.gov/genetics-glossary/Deoxyribonucleic-Acid
208   https://nautil.us/how-life-really-works-435813/

is unified and stays the same long enough to even make these arguments? And how can you even formulate these arguments given that the ceaseless physical change in the brain cannot allow you to complete a sentence?

You reply that everything physical in your brain is changing constantly, but its neural structures remain the same and, therefore, it is still "you" in a physical sense. For good measure, you add that a feedback loop provides the impression of the "I."

Again, this response does nothing to help the case. If all the neurons in the brain's neural networks change all the time, this means the networks are themselves changing all the time. There is no network separate from the neurons that make it up just as there is no bloodstream separate from the red and white blood cells and the platelets and plasma that comprise it. The bloodstream keeps changing as its components change. In the case of the brain's neural structures, we are still left with the problem with which we started: "You" would be nothing but a cluster of particles. And this means there can be no continuing "you" and there cannot even be a completed argument.

In response, you say that the "I" is generated by the brain's feedback loop. But this, again, solves nothing. Feedback loops relate to the outputs from a system that affect the system itself by either moving it toward or away from equilibrium. But this mechanism of actions and reactions found all across Nature relates purely to the physical equilibrium state of a biological system.

If a feedback loop could create an "I," it would be creating "I"s all across cellular systems in Nature. Also, it has been observed that the very idea of a feedback loop creating an "I" requires the loops to achieve consciousness and then loop back on themselves. Yet, it is obvious that the ever-changing physical substrate cannot support consciousness let alone create it. Even in the impossible instance of a feedback loop creating an "I," we are still left with the original problem of how the "I" could remain the same in the midst of the endless neuronal change.

Another escape route is to claim that the brain is a self-organizing system, and this is the "I." But self-organizing systems are found across Nature, and none of them produce "I"s. And, of course, this is not the issue. Even if a self-organizing system pulls off the impossible and magically creates an "I," the "I" would be made up of neurons that never stay the same. And we are back where we began.

Not to be deterred, you say that even if we do not know how the brain creates the appearance of the "I," the brain itself is the product of evolution, and the "I" emerged because it provided an advantage in terms of survival. But this is just as much an evasion of the undeniable issue as all the others. The brain's evolutionary history is not the issue here. What we are pointing to is our undeniable experience today of being unified, enduring persons who think and act.

Our continuing self-identity is inexplicable if it is physical because the physical substrate does not retain its self-identity from moment to moment as we unmistakably do.

The appeal to evolution falls flat for other reasons. In an article in *Scientific American*, Marc Hauser points to four areas where human thought is fundamentally different from cognition in other animals:

- "Generative computation" which is the ability "to create a virtually limitless variety of 'expressions.'" These include "arrangements of words, sequences of notes, combinations of actions, or strings of mathematical symbols."

- The mind's capacity for promiscuously combining ideas.

- The ability to use mental symbols whereby humans spontaneously convert sensory experiences into symbols.

- "Only humans engage in abstract thought." Animal mental life, however, is "largely anchored in sensory and perceptual experiences."[209]

You switch gears, yet again, and say that the idea of a non-physical "I" is clearly mistaken because all mental activity, including the idea of the "I," comes from the brain. Therefore, it has to be physical although we do not understand how. Science will close this gap as it has closed other gaps in the past. But this last resort argument leads nowhere. It is science that led us to the definitive finding that the brain is made up of electrical and chemical processes that are in perpetual motion.

But here is a bigger problem: How is it possible to hold that matter can "produce" non-physical phenomena? Scientific laws apply only to physical quantities that can be physically measured. In this discussion, we are talking of a collection of physical quantities (the brain) giving rise to something that is not a measurable quantity. But this means we are no longer making a scientific claim since science can only deal with quantities. And since we are leaving the purview of science, the question becomes: How do we know that such things happen – that the physical can give rise to the non-physical? Clearly, this is an affirmation that cannot be demonstrated. And what are the laws that govern the relationship between the physical and the non-physical? And how can we account for the relationship?

Certainly, the brain is required for mental activity, but the relationship is not one of cause-and-effect but of transmission. To say that we can speak to someone on the other side of the globe only and entirely WITH the aid of a long-distance communication device like a cell phone is not the same as saying that the conversation between these two parties communicating via cell phones IS only and entirely the movement of electrons. If there is no communication device there can be no inter-continental conversation,

---

209   "The Origin of the Mind," *Scientific American*, September 2009, https://www.scientificamerican.com/article/origin-of-the-mind/

and yet, the source and nature of the conversation is not reducible entirely to the operations of the device.

The analogy of cell phones fails, of course, to adequately convey what is happening. In cell phones, one physical signal (our speech) is converted into another (electromagnetic radiation). In the mental operations of the "I," however, we are talking not about the conversion of one form of physical energy into another but about a unified physical-non-physical act performed by a subject who transcends the physical.

David Bentley Hart shows why the correlation between brain events and mental phenomena cannot bridge the gap between the two:

> Correlation is not causation; and here the two sides of the correlation are so qualitatively unlike one another that all that empirical investigation can tell us is that minds and bodies are not functionally separable in our normal experience (which, frankly, we already know). But consciousness simply cannot be explained by the mechanics of sensory stimulus and neurological response, because neither stimulus nor response is, by itself, a mental phenomenon; neither, as a purely physical reality, possesses conceptual content, intentional meaning, or personal awareness. The two sides of the correlation simply cannot be collapsed into a single observable datum, or even connected to one another in a clear causal sequence, and so not only can the precise relation between them not be defined; it cannot even be isolated as an object of scientific scrutiny. An electrical pulse is not a thought or a sensory impression; or at least, if it is, we have no language for describing—or conceptual grammar for understanding—that arcane identity.[210]

---

210   https://iai.tv/articles/the-absurdity-of-mind-as-machine-david-bentley-hart-auid-2479

Remember, too, that consciousness does not float in some ethereal sphere on its own. It is always someone who is conscious. I am conscious of being conscious and aware that it is "I" who am conscious. Equally, I am aware that I am a single, unified subject not a teeming mass of billions of nerve cells – although these nerve cells play a supporting role in my continued physical and mental activity as does my circulatory system. For the reasons laid out earlier, this "I" – which is apparent in all my thoughts, perceptions and feelings – cannot be physical because its continuity is possible only if it is not in flux in the same manner as my physical being.

LH: We are going round in circles. You have entangled yourself in mystical mumbo jumbo and think you can entice us into your maze. Sorry, no can do. We are staying with what we can touch and feel. As Davy Crockett might say, "I am going with science and the rest of you can go to hell."

SG: Funny you mention seeing, touching and feeling. Are you conscious of any of it? And who does the seeing, touching and feeling? I am simply trying to open everyone's eyes to the three fundamental realities that are foundational to science and that are fatal to your case – consciousness, rational thought and the self.

There is a two word sentence that has to serve as a roadmap for anyone who wants to retain their sanity: "I understand." What do we mean by "I" and "understand?" There is no organ, no region of the brain where you can find either the "I" or "understanding." Once you recognize the reality of the "I," and its capability of "understanding," of decoding and encoding, of "seeing meaning," you recognize as well the union of physical and supra-physical that is the human person. Neither the "I" nor "understanding" can be denied – or, at any rate, such denial cannot be practiced in real life. You would have to lose your sanity to live as if neither were real.

So what is this I? It is that which unifies. It is conscious, it remains the same, it provides us with our first-person perspective. There is nothing resembling a first-person perspective in the physical world or the world of science. Now, some people assume or say that it is the brain or a part of the brain that is solely responsible for their mental activities. But this is clearly not the case if we go by our immediate experience.

When you think, see or act, it is YOU who are doing it. You are thinking not your brain (although the brain supports your thinking as does your respiratory system). You are seeing not your eye. All experiences are experiences of a subject. There are no subjectless experiences. There can be no thinking without a thinker, no seeing without the see-er. As the hallowed logician Gottlob Frege observed, "An experience is impossible without an experient." What does it mean to be me, to experience something as myself? The question cannot even be described in physical terms and is not graspable by science although it is a fact of our everyday experience.

LH: These are religious beliefs and are not scientifically defensible.

Genereux: They are not religious or scientific ideas. They are hard facts of our immediate experience that are presupposed by science, philosophy, and religion.

LH: They may be presupposed by religion. That's it.

Genereux: There are serious atheist thinkers who have recognized what I am talking about.

You are resisting all this because once you recognize consciousness, thought, and the self as supra-physical realities, you must change your idea of reality as a whole. How did these realities come into being? As the Defendant's counsel has established, only a Source that is supra-physical without any limitation whatsoever – popularly referred to as God – can explain the existence of these realities. This means that the supra-physical dimension of our own being – intellect and freewill, morality and purpose – should play a central role in our lives.

Well-known atheists have recognized that the origins of these supra-physical realities cannot be explained in terms of natural physical processes.

About consciousness, Colin McGinn writes,

> *How can mere matter originate consciousness?* How did evolution convert the water of biological tissue into the wine of consciousness? Consciousness seems like a radical novelty in the universe, not pre-figured by the after-effects of the Big Bang, so how did it contrive to spring into being from what preceded it? ... If the brain is spatial, being a hunk of matter in space, and the mind is non-spatial, how on earth can the mind arise from the brain?... This seems like a miracle, a rupture in the natural order."[211]

Thomas Nagel writes that "the propensity for the development of organisms with a subjective point of view must have been there from the beginning."[212]

Surprisingly, both Richard Dawkins and Steven Pinker admit that the origin of consciousness is a mystery. In a friendly public discussion with Pinker, Dawkins said "There are aspects of human subjective consciousness that are deeply mysterious. Neither Steve Pinker nor I can explain human subjective consciousness – what philosophers call qualia. In *How the Mind Works* Steve elegantly sets out the problem of subjective consciousness, and asks where it comes from and what's the explanation. Then he's honest enough to say, 'Beats the heck out of me.' That is an honest thing to say, and I echo it. We don't know. We don't understand it."[213]

---

211   Colin McGinn, *The Mysterious Flame: Conscious Minds in a Material World* (New York: Basic Books, 1999), 13 ff, 115.

212   Thomas Nagel, *Mind and Cosmos* (New York: Oxford University Press, 2012), Section 5.

213   Richard Dawkins and Steven Pinker, "Is Science Killing the Soul?," (The Guardian-Dillons Debate) *Edge* 53, April 8, 1999.

In *How the Mind Works,* Pinker says we have no idea where sentience, i.e., *what consciousness feels like on the inside,* came from. Nor do we know how or why. He says that *neither the computational theory of mind nor any finding in neuroscience have an answer* to these basic questions about our subjective experience of consciousness. He notes that thinkers like Daniel Dennett, who try to deny the reality of consciousness, have not really addressed this core issue in their arguments. In his view these are valid questions but we cannot answer them because we do not have the cognitive equipment required. Saying that we have no scientific explanation of sentience, says Pinker, is not saying that sentience does not exist at all. "I am as certain that I am sentient as I am certain of *anything.*"[214] He adds that sentience is not a combination of brain events or computational states.

Although a prominent proponent of Darwinian evolution, Dawkins admits that the origin of language is a mystery: "There doesn't seem to be anything like syntax in non-human animals and it is hard to imagine evolutionary forerunners of it. Equally obscure is the origin of semantics, of words and their meanings."[215]

The physical infrastructure supporting mental activity (such as the nervous system) developed over time but the phenomenon of conceptual thought cannot (for reasons already discussed) be described or explained in physical terms.

Even more significant in this domain was the 2014 publication of "The mystery of language evolution," a paper by a number of leading evolutionary scientists including Richard Lewontin and Ian Tattersall and linguists like Noam Chomsky. Their conclusion was that we know virtually nothing about the origin of language:

---

214   Steven Pinker, op cit., 131.

215   Richard Dawkins, *Unweaving the Rainbow* (Boston, MA: Houghton Mifflin Company, 1998), 286 ff.

"Understanding the evolution of language requires evidence regarding origins and processes that led to change. In the last 40 years, there has been an explosion of research on this problem as well as a sense that considerable progress has been made. We argue instead that the richness of ideas is accompanied by a poverty of evidence, with essentially no explanation of how and why our linguistic computations and representations evolved. We show that, to date, (1) studies of nonhuman animals provide virtually no relevant parallels to human linguistic communication, and none to the underlying biological capacity; (2) the fossil and archaeological evidence does not inform our understanding of the computations and representations of our earliest ancestors, leaving details of origins and selective pressure unresolved; (3) our understanding of the genetics of language is so impoverished that there is little hope of connecting genes to linguistic processes any time soon; (4) all modeling attempts have made unfounded assumptions, and have provided no empirical tests, thus leaving any insights into language's origins unverifiable. Based on the current state of evidence, we submit that the most fundamental questions about the origins and evolution of our linguistic capacity remain as mysterious as ever, with considerable uncertainty about the discovery of either relevant or conclusive evidence that can adjudicate among the many open hypotheses."[216]

Simon Conway Morris expands further on the conceptual gulf between humans and non-human animals:

> There is a "yawning chasm that seemingly separates us ... from groups of otherwise undoubted intelligence, notably the apes and crows. ... from Darwin onwards the default assumption has been that obvious as the differences now are, axiomatically they must still

216   Front. Psychol., 07 May 2014, https://www.frontiersin.org/articles/10.3389/fpsyg.2014.00401/full

be ones of degree and not kind. Even allowing these differences to be only qualitative, then we need to know when this step-change occurred and as importantly, why only us? Yet as the evidence accumulates, and despite decades of investigation, this cognitive gulf is if anything more profound than generally supposed. Repeatedly, apparently water-tight investigations into human-like cognition in animals transpire, on further analysis, to be deeply problematic. That humans are in some sense unique is self-evident, but standard accounts of how these differences arose seem to miss the point. ...

Apart from the swear words of an African Gray, even the smartest animals never speak. They vocalize of course, and although bird-song has some intriguing analogies to language, it is not remotely equivalent. Never, for example, does the songster "think" to redeploy the music to a new context that would allow a thought to be conveyed. Like all animal noises, they are "flat" and lack any recursive depth. Correspondingly the roars, grunts and even songs are all imperatives and never declarative. Despite this, the received wisdom persists that embedded in these noises is a proto-language. This, however, seems highly unlikely for a number of reasons, not least because speech is deeply cognitive. ...

Why then the gulf? Orthodox explanations might include increases in brain size, chance mutation, population size, etc, but these are all effectively circular arguments.

Compelling solutions remain elusive, but in essence animals cannot join the metaphorical dots. Despite all the similarities that link us, their world is devoid of rationality, one where cause and effect are the logical consequences of actions. ... to animals the world is simply one of perceptions, never of interpretation where hypotheses can be built. Thus there are no categories, and correspondingly analogical thinking is inconceivable. …

To animals abstractions are so circumscribed as to be trivial, so correspondingly whilst they can readily comprehend relative numbers (in the process of numerosity), even simple arithmetic is beyond their grasp. … a number of animals employ tools, although curiously a general link to cognitive capacity is weak. Significantly, however, outside the highly artificial arrangements in the laboratory, animals never employ one tool to make another.[217]

With regard to the self, the conclusions of the pioneers of neuroscience are especially relevant:

Sir Charles Scott Sherrington, pioneer of neuroscience and winner of the Nobel Prize, states:

"As followers of natural science we know nothing of any relation between thoughts and the brain, except as a gross correlation in time and space."[218] "Biology cannot go far in its subject without being met by mind."[219]

Wilder Penfield, pioneer of neurosurgery, said:

"It will always be quite impossible to explain the mind on the basis of neuronal action within the brain …. Although the content of consciousness depends in large measure on neuronal activity, awareness

---

217   Simon Conway Morris, "The Paradoxes of Evolutionary Convergence," https://www.faraday.cam.ac.uk/wp-content/uploads/2022/09/Faraday-Paper-26-Conway-Morris.pdf.

218   Charles Sherrington, *Man on his Nature* (New York: The Macmillan Company, 1941), 290.

219   "The Brain Collaborates With Psyche," *Man On His Nature: The Gifford Lectures, Edinburgh 1937-8* (1940), 290-291.

itself does not. …To me, it seems more and more reasonable to suggest that the mind may be a distinct and different essence."[220]

So where did the self with its supra-physical intellect and will come from? Another noted brain scientist and Nobel Prize winner, Sir John Eccles, explored this question in numerous books. His answer was unequivocal: "The only certainty we have is that we exist as unique self-conscious beings, each unique, never to be repeated. The conscious self is not in the Darwinist evolutionary process at all. It is a divine creation."[221]

The Source of the supra-physical is necessarily supra-physical – an infinite Mind, the *mysterium tremendum et fascinans*, the mystery majestic and fascinating, as Rudolf Otto put it. There is no better description of the infinite Mind than that given by the inventor of set theory and the modern pioneer of mathematical infinity, Georg Cantor:

> "What surpasses all that is finite and transfinite is no 'Genus'; it is the single, completely individual unity in which everything is included, which includes the Absolute, incomprehensible to the human understanding. This is the Actus Purissimus, which by many is called God."[222]

LH: Your arguments are recycled versions of what we have been hearing from the Defendant's counsel. The only people who will find it convincing are those who already buy into these fantasies.

---

220   Penfield W., *The Mystery of the Mind: A Critical Study of Consciousness and the Human Brain* (Princeton, NJ: Princeton University Press; 1975), 79-81.

221   Sir John Eccles, "A Divine Design: Some Questions on Origins," in Henry Margenau and Roy Abraham Varghese ed. *Cosmos, Bios, Theos* (La Salle: Open Court, 1992), 164.

222   Joseph Dauben, *Georg Cantor: His Mathematics and Philosophy of the Infinite*, (Princeton: Princeton University Press, 1990), 290.

"THE JESUS CLOUD"

Witness – Gabriel Kantor Chesterfield (GC)

MA: The testimony of the next witness is central to our case. As you know, we have shown that everyday experience and the world in which we live provide compelling evidence that there is an Infinite-Eternal Intelligence that is the Source of all that exists. As to the kind of being it is, the intent of creation, and the purpose of human life, there is no substitute for direct divine self-revelation if indeed this were possible. We have affirmed the reality of such revelation and have claimed that the climax of this revelation is to be found in Jesus of Nazareth. As it happens, our witness, Mr. Gabriel Kantor Chesterfield, has treated this very topic in his critically acclaimed book *The Jesus Cloud*. And he will now share his insights with us. Gabe, please give us your expert testimony.

Chesterfield: At the center of the Christian declaration is the startling claim that God "took on" a human nature. As Christians put it, Jesus of Nazareth is God incarnate by which we mean God "embodied in flesh; in human form," as the Oxford Dictionary defines it.

This claim sets Christianity apart from all other philosophies and religions. And, if I understand it right, this claim also lies at the center of your legal imbroglio. I will explore the basis of this claim but before that I want to give an idea of what is meant by this claim. And, for this, I turn to some contemporary models. I think metaphors built around such ideas as the Cloud, fields, smartphones and Big Data may help us better understand this all-important truth.

So, I wish to introduce the "Jesus Cloud" in its relation to humanity and God, the Infinity Field.

Please see Exhibit 1 for an overview of the Jesus Cloud in its relation to the Infinity Field.

What Does it Mean to Say that Jesus is God Incarnate? – Parables from the Kingdom of the Cloud

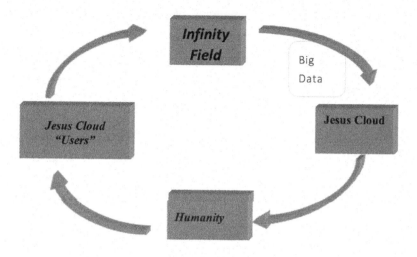

Exhibit 1 – The Jesus Cloud and the Infinity Field – Overview

The Jesus Cloud

You cannot understand Jesus without understanding the Jesus Cloud and you cannot understand the Jesus Cloud without understanding the Infinity Field.

What do we mean when we speak of the Jesus Cloud? The "cloud," as popularly understood, is shorthand for the shared software, service, and server resources available on the Internet that enable you to store data and perform tasks on the web instead of locally. Computing and storage are performed remotely. You access the cloud through standard browsers. The services provided are numerous: the cloud takes care of storage, scaling, maintenance, et al.

We use the cloud metaphor here as a model for exploring the claim that Jesus is God incarnate. The Jesus Cloud is a map of all the "realities" relating to Jesus stored in a variety of locations but accessible to any user who wants the attendant "services." The users, of course, are us!

The Jesus Cloud describes the panoply of phenomena associated with Jesus – whether it be his "internal" relationship to the Triune God or external "mechanisms of action" ranging from his acts and teachings and the "effects" of his redemptive death to his personal encounters with millions and his imparting of the divine Life and more.

Internally, the Jesus Cloud is constituted by the Triune Matrix of Jesus, the Father who "sent" him and the Holy Spirit that he will "send." Every action of Jesus involves the entire Matrix: Filled with the Spirit, he does the Will of the Father. The Matrix is continuous with the manifestation of the Godhead as Father, Word and Spirit in the Old Testament. Also in the Cloud is Jesus' Passion and Death which had to be suffered by Someone who was both God and man if the curse placed on the human race by the Fall was to be removed.

The services provided by the Jesus Cloud are astounding in their variety and magnitude – redemption from Original Sin, a partaking of the very Life of God (through baptism), entry into the family of God (becoming brothers and sisters of the incarnate Son), daily sustenance with the divine Life, assistance in meeting our own weaknesses and combating enemies of a different order (sin and Satan), participation in the processes moving toward the climax of human history and the consummation of the cosmos, and entry into eternal ecstasy, i.e., the divine biosphere – Heaven.

In Exhibit 2, we see the Jesus Cloud as the Incarnation of Infinity.

Exhibit 2 – The Jesus Cloud – the Incarnation of Infinity

Infinity Field

Viewed as a whole, *the Jesus Cloud is nothing less than the Infinity Field pene-trating the firewall of the finite. It is the Incarnation of Infinity.*

God is infinite-eternal Spirit. By "Infinite" we mean that which has no limita-tion whatsoever – of power, of knowledge, of all perfections. "Infinity" is the state of being infinite. The "Infinity Field" is the "inner structure" of Infinity, of GOD. We learn from modern physics that physical reality is made up of fields: forces and particles are simply transient manifestations of underly-ing fields. A field has been defined as a physical reality that contains energy and occupies space. But underlying the physical and all that is finite is the Infinite-Eternal – the Infinity Field. The Infinity Field is not in any sense physical. It does not "occupy" space. It is not physical energy. Everything that exists including energy was invented and sustained in being by the Infinite-Eternal. It is the plenitude of all perfections and has no limitation or dependency. And since the Infinite-Eternal has no limitations, it cannot be limited by location, time, quantity and the like. But the Infinite-Eternal cannot be "less" that what it brought into being: for instance, it cannot be an impersonal force because it would be less than personal (us!).

The Jesus Cloud was seen, from the beginning, as a window into the Infinity Field. Without that Field, nothing about the Jesus Cloud made sense. *The Jesus Cloud was a finite manifestation of the Infinity Field.* The seemingly arcane debates about the Persons of the Trinity and the two natures of Christ that rocked the ancient Church Councils may be likened to the debates about the discoveries of subatomic phenomena that led to the formulation of quantum theory. The end-results not only provided an explanation for the phenomenon of the Jesus Cloud but reshaped humanity's very understanding of itself. The modern concept of the person, for instance, was crafted in the crucible of these debates.

The revelation of the Cloud confirmed the primordial intuition of the human race reflected in the great pre-Christian religions: the Infinity Field is "triune" (three-in-one):

Infinite-Eternal Spirit (with attributes of infinite Knowing and Willing) – **Father** *(Source)*

Infinite Mind/Knowing of Infinite-Eternal Spirit – **Son** *(Image of the Source), divine Logos/Word*

Infinite Will/Loving of Infinite-Eternal Spirit – **Holy Spirit** *(Love of Father-Son, Holiness of God)*

We also begin to grasp what it means to say that Jesus is the "incarnation of Infinity."

Jesus' mind, will and psychology are human and therefore limited but the One who operates this limited mind, will and body is divine, namely the Word (infinite Intelligence) of God:

A solar lamp "captures" the energy of the sun to provide light: it lacks the full power of the sun but is yet the sun "acting" through a limited vehicle

God "appears" in a tangible fashion – adapted to the viewer – to Abraham, Moses, Isaiah, Ezekiel, Daniel. This saga of divine communication and man-ifestation comes to a climax when the divine makes a certain human body and soul its *definitive and enduring* point of entry. Jesus of Nazareth, in per-petual union with Father and Spirit, serves as the unique locus of the divine presence, revelation and salvific action in the world.

It should be noted that Jesus is personally the eternal Son of God made man and so it is the eternal Son that is the subject and operator of Jesus' human thoughts, feelings, emotions, decisions and actions.

In Exhibit 3, we consider the incarnation of God in Jesus in terms of a "smartphone."

Smartphone

TRI-FONE

Exhibit 3 – Tri-Fone – the Incarnation of God in Jesus of Nazareth

Here is one way in which we can "model" the Incarnation.

In the Incarnation, the Godhead in itself – by which we mean the divine "nature" (infinite Mind and Will) – does not turn into a man. Nor does a man "become" God in the sense of finite human attributes becoming infinite. There is no merger of human and divine natures. But the eternal Son does "acquire" a human nature so that he is indeed personally human albeit without any inter-mingling of his divine and human natures. As Thomas Joseph White puts it, a musician plays the violin and expresses himself through the violin without himself being a violin. Likewise, God expresses himself through *his* acquired human nature but his human and divine natures remain distinct (although the divine *Person*, unlike the divine nature, is not separate from his human nature as the musician is from his violin).

To put it another way, *the Triune-matrix SIM card is inserted into the human smartphone.* All calls originate from the Triune matrix but are delivered through a human instrument via a spatio-temporal network. The only kinds of telecommunication possible are those that the instrument – with its limited computing and messaging capabilities – can transmit and the radio frequencies and transceivers can transport. Similarly, in acquiring a human nature, God can only express himself in a human way. The caller ID tells you who is calling: the Word/Logos united with the Father in and through the Spirit. But the intrinsic capabilities of the instrument and the cellular network determine what can be communicated. Note, however, that the instrument is inseparable from its caller ID: It is the caller ID of this instrument. Likewise, Jesus' human nature is the nature of the Son/Word of God. In the Incarnation, the eternal Son manifests himself through his human nature, his words and actions.

In short, God is choosing to live as a human being with all the attendant constraints and limitations. The brain can only store and process a finite amount of information. According to a common guesstimate, the conscious mind can process only 120 bits of information per second although the brain itself receives millions of bits every second. Even if the agent of human action is the incarnate Son/Word himself, his human mind is storage-and-processing limited because the "finite" cannot be converted into the "infinite." Although present in the same Person, human knowledge with its limitations is distinct from the divine wisdom. Jesus' identity and mission as the eternal Son of God, on the other hand, are not dependent on storage and processing capacity. This means that he always knew – as God, in a divine way – who he was and why he was incarnate. But he also knew as man – in a limited and human way – who he was and why he was here.

Big Data

The capacity limitations inevitably inherent in the Incarnation may be called the Big Data problem. Big Data is the phrase used for the huge volume, velocity and variety of structured and unstructured data inundating us from every digital direction. Organizing, analyzing and keeping up with Big Data can soon become an insuperable problem. Given the parallels, it is an apt metaphor for the challenge faced in describing the operation of a "finitized" version of an infinite reality.

What happens when a finite infrastructure encounters the Big Data of Infinity? (Big Data as applied to God should not imply any kind of computing structure since God's knowledge is infinite, eternal and perfect.) When we say that Jesus is the divine Son incarnate, what we mean is that his human body and soul are the human body and soul of a divine person, who is truly human. Jesus is not a creature, and his human acts are not merely the acts of a created human person. Rather, Jesus is the divine Son/Word who is human and who lives out a genuinely human life in all his actions and sufferings.

By acting through a human body and soul he can necessarily only do what his human nature is physically and mentally capable of doing. His powers will be human powers. All too often, believers and skeptics identify the human mind, will, and psychology of Jesus *with* the eternal Son's divine nature instead of realizing that these human media are merely the Word's necessarily limited "channels of communication." *"Human mind" is not the same as "person."* The human mind of Jesus is the human mind of a divine Person, the Eternal Word, through which he expresses himself. The processing is done *by the mind*. In the case of human beings, the mind is inevitably limited in its processing power and storage. *If the divine Son/Word serves as the agent of a human mind, he can only perform acts in his human mind proper to a human mind and not that of an omniscient Mind.* Yet, he retains and is humanly aware of his identity as the Word since this does not involve learning extraneous facts.

MA: Thank you, Gabriel. What an extraordinary display! Your perspective on the incarnation of God in Christ is startling for its originality and clarity. But now I have got to turn to some housekeeping questions. Most of those who heard you are going to ask: Why should the Christian claim be taken seriously – or even be considered – given the hundreds of religions and sects and philosophies out there? And what evidence is there to support the claim that Jesus is God incarnate.

GC: Those are fair questions and, in fact, I was planning to turn to these. But you can only do one thing at a time!

But Why Consider the Claim that Jesus is God Incarnate?

Yes, there are hundreds of philosophies and religions and not enough lifetimes to study each in detail. But there are good reasons for prioritizing an inquiry into the Christian claim of divine incarnation.

Let us look at this first as a multiple choice test. Given all the competing claims, our only hope of getting to the truth about reality is to start with criteria that delineate certain essentials. These criteria can help us decide which options to check off. If you are going to sail the ocean and must choose between the vessels available, you are going to apply certain criteria in your selection: Is the craft seaworthy? Can it make long trips? Who constructed it?

If you want to find a religion that can plausibly profess to unveil the truth about things, it must meet at least the following five criteria:

- It cannot be a philosophy because philosophies are products of fallible, human minds and there is no guarantee therefore that any philosophy, in and of itself, is "telling the truth." All philosophies and religions resting on philosophical systems fail to meet this criterion.

- Secondly, the founder of the religion cannot simply be a prophet or sage or someone who has a special conduit to God. This is because, as human beings, prophets and sages can be mistaken or self-deceived or they can themselves deliberately deceive their followers. Thus, religions founded by men or women cannot meet this criterion.

- Thirdly, the founder of the religion must be God himself acting in human history because only God KNOWS why he created us, what is our destiny, what he is like in himself. And, on these matters, we can only trust the teaching received directly from God. Whether God can be a founder of a religion and whether we can know this to be the case are different questions. But this criterion simply specifies that the religion must claim to have God as its founder acting at a particular point in human history if it is to be considered.

- Fourthly, the religion under consideration must address the question of the purpose of human life and must not only reveal its true purpose but also lay out a blueprint to implement this purpose in our daily lives. It must solve the problem of evil, of pain and suffering, and of our separation from God.

- Finally, the religion must, if possible, tell us something about the inner being of God although this is not essential.

The followers of Jesus, with their affirmation of a divine-human Redeemer, proclaimed a faith that by its very structure meets all five criteria. Christianity is not a philosophy. Its founder was not just a prophet or sage. Its founder claimed to be God incarnate and lived in a particular period in human history. He was concerned with revealing the purpose of life. And he revealed the inner being of God. Thus, the claims of Christianity meet the five criteria outlined here. My discussion will focus on the central criterion in the list of five – the claim that God incarnate is the source of the Christian revelation.

Of course, the claim of divine incarnation in the case of Jesus is not something that simply popped out of nowhere. In reality, the Incarnation and the truths underlying it – the Trinity and Redemption – are prophesied and prefigured in the major pre-Christian religions. To that extent, the Incarnation is trans-historical, cross-cultural and pan-religious – as one would expect if indeed it applies to all of humanity.

But is there any reason to believe the claim that Jesus of Nazareth is God incarnate? I will now present the evidence supporting this affirmation.

The Basis of the Claim and Proclamation of Divine Incarnation

Three *foundations* underlie the affirmation that Jesus of Nazareth is God and man:

- The historical evidence of
  - o his physical resurrection from the dead
  - o the transformation of his followers

- The currently available
  - o writings that chronicle his life and teachings

- o   engine of beliefs and rituals centered on him
- Personal transformative encounters with him in the matrix of a God who is Triune (Three-in-One)

These foundations claim and proclaim that *God is humanly embodied in Jesus.* But is this indeed the case? Is God incarnate in Jesus? Ten reasons testify to the truth of the incarnation of God in Jesus Christ.

#1 Jesus' Claim to be God Incarnate

First and foremost, Jesus claimed to be God incarnate, and his follow- ers understood him to make this claim. This is why he was crucified and his followers were persecuted. Jesus' divine claim was made in the terms understood by the Jews of his time: e.g., claiming to have the attributes proper to God such as forgiving sins; taking the divine Name ("I AM"); and placing himself on the same level as the Torah, the Word of God, and the Temple, the dwelling-place of God. He was acclaimed as God united to a human nature by his followers right from the first century as is evident from their writings. Jesus is the only "founder" of a world religion to make this claim about himself. Only God incarnate can KNOW. Hence only the revelation of God incarnate has the seal of divine truth.

#2 Resurrection from the Dead

Jesus was the only religious leader of whom it is claimed that he rose from the dead and still lives among those who give themselves to him. The tes- timony of the transformed apostles and the entire church from its earliest days to the present is singular in its unanimity and consistency: the cruci- fied Jesus physically rose from the dead.

#3 Unique Phenomenon

We witness the emergence of a unique phenomenon in the first century A.D. What we see manifesting is a story, a proclamation, a testimony, a call to thought and action that creates a new kind of community. It is a community with its own structure, its own rules and rituals, its own *raison d'etre*. This is a community centered on the life and message, the death and resurrection and the divine identity of a singular individual. Jesus was not simply embedded in the very life of the community; the community believed itself to embody Jesus. They spoke with his authority and acted on his behalf.

#4 One-on-one Encounter

We are transfixed by the kind of behavior manifested by the first followers of Jesus. We see proclamation, martyrdom, liturgies, baptisms, councils, and a going forth into all the world. Their actions spoke for what they believed. This is not just a matter of studying the behavior of the first Christians. Hundreds of millions of people over the centuries have claimed to experience Jesus either mystically or spiritually but always personally: whether they be revivalists or contemplative nuns or missionaries or social workers who see Jesus in the poorest of the poor. There is no comparable phenomenon in which a historical person is believed to be encountered and experienced across history; there are, of course, mass movements of various kinds, but what is unique here is the centering of the movement on the lived experience of a person active and present across centuries and continents.

#5 Miracles and the Miraculous

The miracles attributed to Jesus were not performed to amaze or impress. They were acts of compassion in response to tearful requests. He was no wonder-worker. He was a healer and provider. He restored sight and speech. He cured the lame, the paralyzed, and the leprous. He brought the dead to life. He gave food to the hungry. He did what an infinite Lover would do.

Moreover, the spread of Christianity was always accompanied by claims of the miraculous. If there is indeed a supernatural impetus behind the worldwide dissemination of the message of Jesus, this would comport well with the claims made about him by his followers. One would almost expect such an impetus.

#6 Savior

The problem is that we are sinful – and we need to be saved from our sins. The problem is that our sin is against God – it is a sin that has led to the current human condition: evil, suffering, death. To make adequate atonement for this sin, to pay the price for this sin, the atoner must be capable of doing so in terms of making an infinite reparation while also being human. This reparation must be such as to make heaven possible for us, must cure the evil that is within us, must decisively allow us to go beyond death, must make happiness possible here and now. All of this must take place in the course of human history because that is the matrix that determines human destiny. Addressing all of this is what the New Testament writers claimed Jesus did. His name embodied his mission: "You are to name him Jesus, because he will save his people from their sins" (*Matthew* 1:21). His mission was the redemption of humanity: "Just as through one transgression condemnation came upon all, so through one righteous act acquittal and life came to all" (*Romans* 5:18).

What was required to "solve" the problem of sin was a redemptive act of reparation that was infinite in its value but performed by a human being. Because Jesus was both God and man, his atoning sacrifice was infinite in its impact but delivered through a finite human vehicle.

#7 The Purpose of Life

If death is the end, then none of our actions on Earth have any ultimate meaning or point. This is the problem that the philosophers and the sages could not resolve since they themselves were destined for oblivion. If Jesus was truly God incarnate, we would expect him to not only acknowledge the problem but also to give us a solution. He did both, going right to the heart of the problem: "What profit is there for one to gain the whole world and forfeit his life? What could one give in exchange for his life?" (*Mark*

8:36–37). His answer was the only viable one, the one that only God could give – we are called to live forever, and our choices in this life determine our everlasting destiny. To make the wrong choices is to lose it all. Everything matters. Everything is meaningful. Just as there are laws of Nature, there are laws of human existence – you will die and your life after death (as understood by the human race even before Christ) could well be a life of separation from God. But Jesus changed the laws of human existence – through him, you can live with the Life of God and live forever with God. This is greater than changing than the laws of nature: it is changing the laws of human existence. This is redemption. This is the Good News.

#8 The Life of God

Jesus did not simply speak of the life to come. He had come so that we "might have life and have it more abundantly" (*John* 10:10) – here and now. In coming as Savior, Jesus invited us all to be filled with the life of God, the Holy Spirit. "As proof that you are children, God sent the Spirit of his Son into our hearts, crying out, 'Abba, Father!'" (*Galatians* 4:6). "I will pour out a portion of my spirit upon all flesh." (*Joel 3:1, Acts 2:17*). Consequently, as the Apostle Paul put it, "We are the offspring of God." (*Acts* 17:39). In fact, as Peter writes, You will be able to share in the Divine nature." (*2 Peter 1:4*). Eternity begins here, now for "I live, no longer I, but Christ lives in me." (*Galatians* 2:20).

#9 The Rendezvous of the Religions

Just as Jesus lived in a definite place at a certain point in time and in a particular culture and society, so his message and mission appeared at a precise conjunction in the religious history of humanity. It was a remarkable conjunction because the story of Jesus' life and mission seem to represent the climax and consummation of themes and aspirations articulated and developed in the fundamental matrix of the religions and mythologies that appeared before him. It is almost as if he historically embodied what was mythologically, thematically and prophetically encoded. Thus, the story of

Jesus and his sacrifice was neither isolated nor parochial. It was, you might say, a story that had already been written on the heart of humankind.

This leads to the extraordinary possibility that Jesus ("Savior") is the fulfillment not simply of the Jewish "idea" but of the beliefs and aspirations of the Indians, Chinese and Persians, of the primordial tribes and the Mediterranean mystery religions. Salvation is liberation from sin and its consequences – i.e., atonement – and this requires sacrifice and ultimately a perfect sacrifice. This is the thought pattern of all humanity and it also happens to be the life pattern of Jesus.

A plausible case can be made for seeing in the religious history of humanity a pattern that comes to a climax in the life of Jesus of Nazareth. It seems clear that, on the level of thought and structure, trajectory and configuration, there is congruence and correspondence between the story of Jesus and the thematic thrust of the primary pre-Christian religions.

#10 Inner Being of God Revealed

Jesus radically transformed humanity's understanding of God by "purifying" and unifying pre-Christian insights while revealing the innermost secret of the Godhead.

Jesus revealed that

> God is spirit
>
> God is infinite
>
> God is Triune, Three Persons in One

"Jesus said to her [the Samaritan woman at the well], 'The hour is coming, and is now here, when true worshipers will worship the Father in Spirit and truth; and indeed the Father seeks such people to worship him. God is Spirit, and those who worship him must worship in Spirit and truth.'" (*John* 4:21-4).

No one can understand either the Trinity or the Incarnation without grasping the revolutionary truth that God is Spirit. In fact, true monotheism is impossible without this insight. A spirit has no parts and does not occupy space. It has an intellect and a will. An infinite Spirit is one that exercises the capabilities of intellect and will without limitation of any kind. *It was Jesus of Nazareth who revealed the necessarily spiritual nature of God.* True monotheism was made possible only with the revelation that God is Spirit.

But only if God is spirit (not limited by matter) could he be infinite (without limitation). Thus, Jesus' revelation of God as spirit enables the New Testament proclamation that God is infinite – i.e., without limitation of any kind – and infinitely personal. Other monotheisms, on the other hand, have ended up with ideas of a finite god, a physical god, a changing god, an impersonal god or force – none of which are compatible with monotheism or even theism.

The infinite Spirit has an infinite Mind and an infinite Will. There are only two "internal" operations of the infinite Spirit: that of Mind and Will (all other operations are "external"). Here we arrive at the revelatory breakthrough underlying the Trinity: The infinite Spirit that is God *exists eternally* without beginning or end as *the Source* and Summit of infinite perfection. The Spirit's *infinite act of knowing itself* performed with its infinite Mind *has to* be a perfect intellectual Image of itself: This Image must contain EVERYTHING that is true of its Source, all its infinite perfection (other than being Source): **This means it must itself be an infinite Person in its own right with the same nature and power as its Source.** The Spirit's *infinite act of loving itself*, performed with its infinite Will and through its Mind, *has to* bear fruit in a perfect Gift: The Gift must contain all the perfections of the Source and its Image whose Love it is (other than being the Source or its Image): **It too is an infinite Person that possesses the same nature and power as the Source and Image from and through which it proceeds.**

The Triune God

Thus, there are Three infinite Persons: God as knower and lover, God known, God loved: But there is only ONE God: God the eternally existent infinite Spirit knowing and loving, God in his knowingness, God in his lovingness: One infinite Mind and Will that exists, knows and loves infinitely and eternally. Thus, the infinite Mind and Will do not exist as abstractions: these are the Mind and Will OF someone: in fact three "Someones": the Infinite Knower and Lover, the infinite Thought/Image that is a Person, the infinite Love/Gift also a Person: Father, Son (Word) and Holy Spirit.

This is shown in Exhibit 4.

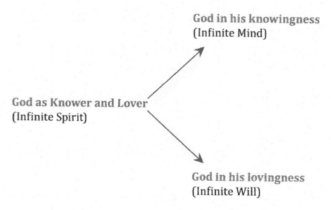

God = Infinite Spirit

God in his knowingness
(Infinite Mind)

God as Knower and Lover
(Infinite Spirit)

God in his lovingness
(Infinite Will)

Exhibit 4 – The Trinity

Note that there can only be Three Persons in the Godhead because infinite Spirit by its nature performs only two acts internal to it: knowing and loving. Thus, there can only be God as Knower and Lover (Father), God as Known (Image/Word/Son) and God as Loved (Gift/Holy Spirit). Clearly it is no coincidence that the three Persons of the Trinity correspond to the only three centers possible in the Godhead: The Father who generates, the Image/Word/Son who is generated, the Gift/Holy Spirit who "proceeds" from/through the Love of Father and Son. Nor is it a coincidence that across diverse cultures and untold ages humanity has recognized God as tri-personal: Being, Knowing, Loving.

The major pre-Christian religions that believed in One God also believed implicitly that there were three "centers "in that One God. The Trinitarian being of God is pre-figured in the three main pre-Christian approaches to God: *Saccidananda* – Being, Knowledge, Bliss – in the cyclic-mystical of India; the "Three Pure Ones" in the unity-in-multiplicity of China; and Elohim – Father, Word/Wisdom and Spirit/*Shekinah* – in the historical-linear of Israel.

So is Jesus God Incarnate?

When connected, the 10 data-points highlighted here paint a big picture. A vision emerges from the data, unifying it and making it coherent – that of a divine Person uniting himself to a human nature: Jesus of Nazareth. The Logos/Word/Son is divine. In the Incarnation, the Logos "acquires" a human body and soul. Thus, we have a divine Subject with both a divine nature and a human nature. In his divine nature, he is infinite. In his human nature, he is finite. Nevertheless, in his essential being, the Logos is infinite. Because the human nature is something he has "taken on," he is fully human – fully human but not merely human.

It should be said that the question of the Incarnation of God in Christ is not a contemporary partisan Jewish-Christian dispute. According to the Pew research group, some 1.7 million adult American Jews now consider themselves Christian.[223] Many of them were secular or practicing Jews who came to this affirmation on their own.

Paradoxically, the three greatest Jewish thinkers in modern history – Baruch Spinoza, Albert Einstein and Ludwig Wittgenstein – were fascinated by Christ. In his *Tractatus Theologico-Politicus*, Spinoza writes, "God

223 http://bit.ly/1YEOKVl

manifested Himself to the Apostles through the mind of Christ as He formerly did to Moses through the supernatural voice. In this sense the voice of Christ, like the voice which Moses heard, may be called the voice of God, and it may be said that the wisdom of God (i.e. wisdom more than human) took upon itself in Christ human nature, and that Christ was the way of salvation."[224]

In his book *Was Jesus God?* (published by Oxford University), influential Oxford philosopher of science and religion Richard Swinburne lays out criteria that could help us recognize the incarnation of God in history:

> If there is a God, we would find among us at some stage of history a prophet who lives a life in which there is much suffering, who would claim to be God incarnate, and would found a church to continue to proclaim that message. It would also be quite probable that the prophet's life would be a perfect life and that he would claim to be making available atonement for our sins, and give us plausible teaching (as a revelation from God) about the nature of God, how we should live our lives, and God's plans for our future; and if he did all this, the church would give us plausible interpretations of that teaching.[225]

After laying out the evidence, Swinburne concludes that Jesus meets all the criteria for being God incarnate:

> I argued in Part I that we would expect God (if there is a God) to become a human prophet and lead the kind of life and give the kind of teaching considered in chapter 7, and to put his signature on that life by a miraculous event, such as a resurrection of that human prophet from the dead. I argued in Chapter 7 that there is significant evidence that Jesus led the kind of life and gave the kind of teaching

224 http://bit.ly/1PpPRph
225 Richard Swinburne, *Was Jesus God?* (Oxford: Oxford University Press, 2008), 91.

which we would expect God Incarnate to live and give; and I argued in Chapter 8 that (given the existence of God and the life and teaching of Jesus) that there is significant evidence that Jesus rose from the dead, and that his Resurrection constituted God's signature on his life and teaching. ...

It is not merely the case that Jesus is the only serious candidate in human history about whom we have evidence that he lived the right kind of life which ended with a divine signature. **Jesus was both the only prophet in human history about whose life there is good historical evidence of the first kind** (evidence that he or she lived a perfect life with much suffering, claimed to be divine, claimed to be making atonement, gave plausible moral and theological teaching, and founded a church to continue his work), **and also the only prophet about whose life there is good historical evidence of the second kind** (evidence that his or her life ended with a miracle recognizable as a divine signature). ... (And if there are prophets about whom we don't have evidence, we cannot take seriously their claims to be God Incarnate providing good news for all humanity.) This shows that **the coincidence of the two sets of evidence** about one prophet that his or her life exhibited both features would be very improbable in the normal course of things. It would be **very improbable unless God arranged it.**[226]

Affirmation of the Incarnation is logically sound. Michael Dummett, Wykeham Professor of Logic at Oxford University, says, "Should we then speak of a leap of faith at this point? I should rather speak of an act of judgment, involving far more than, but comparable in character to, those we perform whenever we assess the credibility of testimony or the mental balance of an individual. It is in no way irrational to judge, on the basis of what ... we know from the New Testament of Christ and of the actions of

226 Ibid., 128, 132.

his Apostles, that *the astonishing doctrine of the Incarnation is more credible than the rival hypotheses.*"[227]

What we are discussing here is the cumulative case for divine incarnation. There are 12 features about the phenomenon of Jesus that are compelling as it pertains to his identity. These 12 features also happen to be unique to the phenomenon:

> ➤ The claim that Jesus was God incarnate (i.e., the Divine taking on a human nature)

> ➤ The claim that Jesus redeemed the human race through his death

> ➤ The claim that Jesus rose from the dead

> ➤ Jesus' focus on the eternal destiny of the human person and his offer of eternal life as well as his promise of returning at the end of time to judge the living and the dead

> ➤ Jesus' revelation of the inner being of God – God as Trinity (Trinity is not God's proper name; it is simply a way of saying that God is infinite love)

> ➤ Jesus' ministry of exorcising evil and of healing and forgiving

> ➤ Jesus' promise of sending the divine Spirit

> ➤ Jesus' commissioning of his Apostles and Jesus' identification of himself with his Church in the appearance to Saul of Tarsus

> ➤ Jesus' embodiment in his very person, life and mission of the themes and premonitions of the pre-Christian religions

> ➤ Jesus' appearance at the fulcrum of history and geography

> ➤ Jesus' being encountered personally by millions of believers, a first in religious history

---

227 Michael Dummett, "The Impact of Scriptural Studies on the Content of Catholic Belief," in *Hermes and Athena: Biblical Exegesis and Philosophical Theology* edited by Eleonore Stump and Thomas P. Flint (Notre Dame, Indiana: University of Notre Dame Press, 1993), 3-22.

> Jesus' changing of the laws of human existence (As pointed out earlier, Jesus made it possible for human beings to live forever with God)

A final hard fact pointing to Jesus' divine identity is his proclamation and manifestation of a love that knows no bounds, a love that could only come directly from God. At the center, at all levels of Jesus' ministry and life is an all-consuming reality: the inexplicable, unprecedented, unsurpassable love of the Good Samaritan, the Father of the Prodigal Son, the Good Shepherd, the Sermon on the Mount, the Victim on the Cross who prays for his killers: the Love that identifies itself with the least among us. No prophet, no sage, no teacher could even conceive of this tidal wave of heart-breaking love let alone proclaim or manifest it. This had to come straight from the Source if it was to be communicated or comprehended. Henceforth all morality, all action, all reality can only be seen in the light of this love. Jesus, above all, is Love incarnate.

By exploring each one of these data points, we arrive at the cumulative case for the claim that Jesus is God incarnate. All relevant evidence – the world religions, world history, Jewish history, the experience of Christians throughout the centuries, the Gospels, the practice of the first Christian communities – must be submitted and studied as one whole. And, in studying the evidence, we should set aside our previous preconceptions and ideological agendas. Nothing matters but the evidence in its entirety – the cumulative case, the big picture.

MA: Just what the doctor ordered! Ladies and gentlemen of the jury, I submit that this presentation shows with overwhelming clarity that the Plaintiff has simply misconstrued and misrepresented the Christian revelation.

Thank you Gabe. Your witness, Mr. HellMan.

LH: I have heard it all now! Every fairy tale, myth and legend known to the human mind has been pressed into service to support the kookiest claim conceivable. Your foundations for your gigantic claim are laughably flimsy.

The claim itself is incoherent. Why would anyone believe it even if the idea made any sense – which it does not?

Chesterfield: Spoken as a true believer – a believer in disbelief at all costs. I am fairly sure no amount of evidence will convince you because you're on a fact-free mental diet. For the benefit of the jury, however, let me dig deeper into one of the most compelling of the 10 reasons I spelled out – the evidence for the resurrection of Jesus. The evidence was compelling enough to convince one of the most prominent atheists in Germany, Wolfhart Pannenberg, as well a Jewish rabbi – both of whom wrote books propounding the historicity of the resurrection. Of course, only people who are open to the facts will be moved by them and all I can do is present these as they stand.

A central dimension of the phenomenon of Jesus – at the levels of both proclamation and action – is the electrifying and altogether unexpected event that has come to be called the Resurrection. As narrated, it was not a Near Death Experience or a one-on-one ghostly encounter or a re-assembly of the body parts of some mythical deity. It was not life after death in a lifeless kind of way. The claim is that Jesus of Nazareth, the Messiah of Israel, was crucified on a tree and buried in a cave. And then his body was found to no longer be in the tomb and he appeared on numerous occasions to his Apostles and other followers, conversing and even eating with them, confirming them in their faith and energizing them to carry on the mission he had entrusted to them.

This dimension of the Rising Son is central because all of Christianity starts with three assumptions:

- Jesus is alive and acting in history;
- he is alive not as an idea but a definite person, an agent who takes specific and concrete actions; and
- we know the first two assumptions to be true because he appeared physically to his disciples after his death.

Traditionally, the historical evidence for the physical resurrection of Jesus has been classified under three categories: the existence of the empty tomb, the reports of the appearance of Jesus to his disciples and others and the origin of the Christian church. These categories of evidence are summarized below.

Empty Tomb

- Jesus was buried: 1 Corinthians 15; Gospel accounts; no other claims made about Jesus' body.

- The tomb was guarded. Even enemies acknowledged this.

- Historical core: The sequence of discovery is described in different ways in the gospels but has common threads. Joseph of Arimathea buried Jesus; women discovered the tomb was empty; an angel was seen outside the empty tomb.

- Women were shown as the first witnesses. Jewish law does not recognize women as witnesses. If the accounts were invented, men would have been the witnesses.

- There is no fanciful description as in the apocryphal accounts. There is no description of the actual resurrection.

- Pannenberg affirmed that it is rationally untenable to deny that the resurrection of Christ was a historical event. He considered the empty tomb to be a strong argument in its favor. He noted that it is well known that there were early disputes between Christians and Jews concerning the Resurrection. "The Jews accepted that the tomb was empty. The dispute, however, was about how this is to be explained. The Jews said the disciples had removed the body. But they did not question the fact that the tomb was empty. That, I think, is a very remarkable point. And then, of course, my main reason is a general reflection, given the concreteness of the Jewish understanding of a resurrection from the dead. It would hardly be conceivable that the earliest

Christian congregation could have assembled in Jerusalem of all places, where Jesus had died and was buried, if His tomb was intact."[228]

Appearances

- In I Corinthians, Paul reports that Jesus appeared to him; Peter; to the apostles; and 500 others. The epistle was written when many of those who had seen the Risen Jesus were still alive and so it is unlikely to have been concocted. The Gospels show Jesus appearing to Mary Magdalene and other women, to 10 of the Apostles and then to all 11 and also to the disciples on the road to Emmaus.

- Did the appearances in fact occur? The hypothesis that this was a matter of legend is implausible because I Corinthians 15 is dated very early.

- Were the witnesses simply hallucinating? William Lane Craig gives reasons why this hypothesis does not work: Hallucinations are individual in nature and are experienced only by one person but the appearances of the Risen Jesus were witnessed by hundreds; those who hallucinate usually expect to see the object of their hallucination but the terrified disciples did not expect to see their Master again after his crucifixion and burial; hallucinations are sometimes induced by drugs or mental illness but the appearances were witnessed by people with a wide range of personalities and backgrounds.

- Were the witnesses lying? This is implausible because the Apostles literally staked their lives on the claim that they had seen the risen Jesus. Almost all of them died horrible deaths

---

228 Wolfhart Pannenberg, "The Historicity of the Resurrection," Roy Varghese, ed., *The Intellectuals Speak About God* (Chicago: Regnery Gateway, 1984), 261.

– but they went to their deaths proclaiming the resurrection. It is unreasonable to suggest they were willing to die for a lie. Not only did they die proclaiming the resurrection but their lives were transformed as well. Also at least one witness was initially a skeptic, Saul of Tarsus. He had no reason to "invent" the Resurrection since it contradicted his previous beliefs.

Birth of a New World Order

- The explosion of Christianity in first century Palestine cannot be explained without reference to the Resurrection. From the very beginning, as even Bultmann acknowledged, the message that Jesus had risen from the dead lay at the heart of the Christian Gospel. Affirmation that Jesus was the Messiah would have been impossible if he had not been resurrected because for all practical purposes his mission would be considered a failure if it ended with the cross.

- The claim that Jesus had risen from the grave is not something that could have been extrapolated from any belief-system. Although some Jews believed in the idea of resurrection, such a resurrection is one that involved the entire human race and that took place at the end of history. Jesus' resurrection, however, involved one individual and it took place within the historical process.

- Even the hardiest of today's skeptics acknowledge the fact that the earliest Christians had experienced something. What remains in dispute is the nature of that "something."

Two noted Jewish scholars have made the case for the resurrection. The first is Sholem Asch, perhaps the leading Jewish writer of his generation. In 1936 he was named among the world's 10 greatest living Jews along with Einstein and Freud, the only writer on the list. Asch held that "What must remain an eternal mystery to those who are blind and deaf enough not to believe in miracles is the spread of Christianity during the first three hundred years. No intellectual evidence, no rationalistic explanation can clarify the phenomenon or see it as anything other than an extraordinary development which remains outside the bounds of our intellectual, sensible point of view."[229]

A more detailed defense comes from the Jewish rabbi Pinchas Lapide. In rejecting the idea that the Resurrection appearances were the result of autosuggestion, he writes, "In none of the cases where rabbinic literature speaks of such visions [springing from autosuggestion] did it result in an essential change in the life of the resuscitated or of those who had experienced the visions. Only the vision remains which was retold in believing wonderment and sometimes also embellished, but it did not have any noticeable consequences. It is different with the disciples of Jesus on that Easter Sunday. Despite all the legendary embellishments, in the oldest records there remains a recognizable historical kernel which cannot simply be demythologized. When this scared, frightened band of the apostles which was just about to throw away everything in order to flee in despair to Galilee; when these peasants, shepherds, and fishermen, who betrayed and denied their master and then failed him miserably, suddenly could be changed overnight into a confident mission society, convinced of salvation and able to work with much more success after Easter than before Easter, then no vision or hallucination is sufficient to explain such a revolutionary transformation. For a sect or school or an order, perhaps a single vision would have been sufficient – but not for a world religion which was able to conquer the Occident thanks to the Easter faith. ... If the defeated and depressed group of disciples overnight could change into a victorious movement of faith, based only on autosuggestion or self-deception

---

229 Sholem Asch, *One Destiny* (New York: G.P. Putnam's Sons, 1945), 5-8.

– without a fundamental faith experience – then this would be a much greater miracle than the resurrection itself."[230]

Despite the skepticism of past generations, recent times have seen an intellectual resurrection of the Resurrection story. Five monumental works have helped drive this dramatic turnabout:

- "The Events of Easter and the Empty Tomb" (1952) by Hans von Campenhausen which defended the historical basis of the empty tomb claim.

- *Jesus – God and Man* (1968) by German scholar Wolfhart Pannenberg. He argued that from the evidence for the empty tomb and the appearances of Jesus it is possible to rationally conclude that Jesus' resurrection from the dead took place in history. Pannenberg was an atheist whose conversion was occasioned by his study of the Resurrection.

- *The Resurrection of Jesus – A Jewish Perspective* (1983) by Pinchas Lapide, the source of my previous citation.

- *The Resurrection of the Son of God* (2003), an epochal work by N.T. Wright that ties together the historical arguments in favor of the bodily resurrection of Christ. Wright notes that the question to be answered is, "Why did Christianity emerge so rapidly, with such power, and why did believers risk everything to teach that Jesus really rose?" The best explanation, in his view, is that "Jesus' tomb was discovered empty on Easter morning" and "Jesus then appeared to his followers alive in bodily form."

- *The Resurrection of God Incarnate* (also 2003) by Richard Swinburne, whom I cited earlier. In this book, Swinburne argues that Jesus' resurrection from the dead is what you would expect if Jesus is God incarnate, that the accounts of his appearances were

230 Pinchas Lapide, *The Resurrection of Jesus – A Jewish Perspective* (Minneapolis: Augsburg Publishing House), 1983, 125-6.

such as would be expected if there were real appearances and that the available evidence is what would be expected if the tomb was indeed empty.

The empty tomb, the posthumous appearances of Jesus and the transformation and worldwide witness of the apostles do not "prove" the resurrection. The fundamental starting point has to be an explanation for the very origin of the Christian phenomenon.

What we are looking for is something so altogether extraordinary as to unmistakably bear witness to the extraordinariness of what is being claimed. It is in this context that we are able to recognize the power and the glory of the three principal witnesses to the momentous claim of the Resurrection: the Gospel narratives in their raw simplicity, the universal and unchanging witness of the followers of Jesus through the centuries and the Voice of the Spirit of God within us.

There is of course much rational evidence but by itself such evidence does not suffice because the claim it tries to support is too extraordinary to rest simply on a structure of premises and inferences. If the narratives are startling in their almost embarrassing matter-of-factness, if the message and practice of the Christian church is shocking in its immediacy and universality and if one's own heart is driven by a compelling sense of the presence of the Risen One that is remarkable in its own right, all three witnesses together can lead us to the universal Christian affirmation that the Lord IS risen.

LH: I am open to the facts but I am not about to make leaps of faith. I do agree that no amount of evidence will convince me to believe something that does not happen normally – and here I am echoing David Hume and any number of scientists.

Chesterfield: The same Christian matrix that produced modern science took it as obvious that the Creator had a purpose in creating the universe and would order its operations to serve this purpose. Such "ordering" sometimes meant transcending the ordinary laws of Nature – which are also known as miracles.

The science we have today was made possible because Christianity enabled trust in human observation and reasoning. The skeptics did not trust their senses or their intellects. Nothing was knowable. This was a reasonable belief if the world was total chaos and humanity a reflection of that chaos. But the revelation of a Supreme Intelligence that created beings capable of reasoning and knowing and receiving Jesus' divine Life changed this view of things. Thus, Christianity not only created the first universities but powered an explosion of intellectual inquiry inspired by faith in what we perceive and think.

In yet another paradox, we see that accounts of miracles and the data studied by science are both dependent on human observation and the testimony of witnesses.

The one difference is that miracles do not follow "laws" and cannot be "repeated." Nonetheless, like science, they derive (in most cases) from the physically observable and are anchored in eyewitness testimony. As was the case from the start of the era of science, accounts of miracles should be evaluated using the laws of evidence proper to them.

A "scientific" mind should be driven by a quest for evidence and not by a dogmatic refusal to study data that falls outside an arbitrary framework. We cannot accept all claims of miracles at their face value. Neither can we dismiss them without further ado. We should examine the available evidence and consider possible patterns that emerge from them.

LH: "He said," "she said," … the point is we are just not going to go down the path you would like us to take. About that path, let me say again that there is an underlying incoherence to the idea of the same person being both divine and human (assuming there is a divine which I do not accept anyway).

Chesterfield: Some people find relativity and quantum physics to be incoherent. That is their problem not the problem of the coherence of these theories. If you think reality must fit within your mental horizons, I cannot help you. We have to expand our models of reality in order to grasp fundamental scientific theories. This is even more the case when it comes to the interaction of the finite and the Infinite.

It may be asked, when Jesus is speaking, how are we to distinguish between statements in which he is speaking as God and speaking as a man?

Everyday experience tells us that when we say "I" about ourselves, we refer to the "I" with respect to one or another specific dimension of ourselves. When I say, "I am made up of oxygen, carbon, hydrogen, nitrogen, calcium, phosphorus, potassium, sulfur, sodium, chlorine, and magnesium," I am speaking of the "I" with reference to my physical being. When I say, "I am very good at math," I am speaking of the "I" with reference to my mental reality.

This is similarly true about the way in which Jesus refers to himself. He is God incarnate, a divine Person taking on a human nature while also having a divine nature. Consequently, in reading the Gospels, we must distinguish between Jesus saying "I" when he is acting in his human nature and "I" when he is acting in his divine nature. The reference of the "I" is different depending on whether he speaks of it with respect to his human or his divine nature. If he says, "I am six feet tall," he is speaking with reference to the "I" in his human nature. When he says, "I forgive your sins," he is speaking with reference to the "I" in his divine nature. When he says the Son does not know "that hour or day," he is speaking with reference to the Son as it relates to his human nature. When he says, "Before Abraham was, I AM," he is speaking with reference to the "I" as it relates to his divine nature.

LH: That was a noble but ultimately doomed effort. But you get points for trying. I have saved the best for last. This is the doctrine that even

Christians run away from. I am talking about the Trinity. Yes, you pro-fess it. But there is no way that you or anyone else can show it to be even remotely coherent. It is, in fact, self-contradictory. Sorry, one cannot be three. Even Thomas Jefferson and Immanuel Kant recognized this. Who can disagree with Jefferson's comment about "the incomprehensible jargon of the Trinitarian arithmetic, that three are one, and one is three?"

Chesterfield: Flippant as always, especially when it comes to anything that calls for serious inquiry. Yet again, I am directing my response to your question to the jury. I have already given an overview of the revelation of the Trinity. Here I will focus on showing how it ties into our experience.

The charge of self-contradiction can only come from someone who has a juvenile understanding of the Trinity. The Trinity is not a mathematical or logical or even metaphysical affirmation. We are not making a mathemat-ical statement that 1=3 or that what looks like three is actually one. *We are not saying that God is one in the same way he is three or that God is three in the same way he is one.* Rather, we are highlighting the fact that within the one divine nature – namely, the Godhead – there are Three Persons.

Far from being a doctrine that we should "run" from, the Trinity is the breath-taking Truth that makes sense of all other truths, the dazzling sun that allows us to see all things except itself (and this not because of dark-ness but its excess of light). All human thought and experience point in one way or another to the summit of knowing and loving that we call the Trinity. It is the revelation that makes sense of everything in our experience – EVERYTHING.

It may come as a shock to you, but the very concept of "person" originated from the attempt to understand the revelation of the Trinity. Historically, it is through the Trinity that we came to understand ourselves! As the logician Peter Geach wrote, "The concept of a person, which we find so familiar in its application today to human beings, cannot be clearly and sharply expressed by any word in the vocabulary of Plato or Aristotle; it was wrought with the hammer and anvil of theological disputes about the Trinity and the Person of Christ, and classically formulated by Boethius."[231] The ancient Hebrews too lacked words for "person" and "nature."

While the doctrine of the Trinity could only have been known from the direct revelation of God, it nevertheless "fits in" with all our experience and makes sense especially of the greatest mysteries.

- How is it that there is such a phenomenon as knowing – the capacity for understanding, pondering, seeing meaning?

- How did willing – the power of intending, choosing, loving and giving of oneself – arise?

- How is it that there is such a thing as the self, the person, the "I" that knows and loves and finds fulfillment in communion with other "I"s?

- How is that a new person, a new "I" comes to be from the loving union of two other "I"s (a kind of loving that is also called "knowing" in the Bible)?

- How is it that we have life, the dynamism that powers all other activities?

These five mysteries are simply inexplicable in themselves but make sense in the light of the doctrine of the Trinity. It is only through the Trinity that we can find coherent answers to these fundamental questions.

The doctrine of the Trinity tells us that the most fundamental mysteries in our experience originate from and embody the most basic Truth about things. We know because God is Knowing, we love because Loving is the Life of God. Each of us is a self with a mind and a will, and we commune and reproduce because the infinite Mind and Will is a communion of interacting Selfs Who eternally beget and receive and proceed.

---

231 Peter Geach, *The Virtues* (Cambridge, UK: Cambridge University Press, 1977), 75-6.

Understanding the Trinity is not a matter of puzzling out mathematical or philosophical paradoxes about one and three. It is all about relationship. At the heart of reality lies a Relationship. In fact, relationship is the greatest mystery in our experience on earth. How did it arise? How did Reality produce this? All our fulfillment comes from relationship but beyond that there is the question of how relationship as a reality came to be. Once we know that the Source of all that exists is a Relationship – a Relationship of utter and infinite Love – everything makes sense. This is what we mean by the Trinity, this is why all the ancient religions grasped its truth, this is why everything in our experience points to it, this is why God revealed this truth to us in its fullness in the Incarnation.

Kant, Jefferson and other theologically primitive skeptics missed the whole point about Relationship in their caricatures of the Ultimate Reality. It is impossible to describe relationship at the human level in a way that a sub-human can understand it so how can we expect to fully grasp Relationship at the level of the Infinite?

In the case of Jesus as well, everything centered on him as Person and our relationship with him. The founders of different religions normally gave a teaching where they talked about reality or God. None of these religions was built on the founder or a relationship with the founder. With Jesus, we enter into a relationship with him and through him with the Father and the Holy Spirit. We are relational beings who are called to participate in the Ultimate Relationship that is the divine Trinity.

Although the Trinity is not a "mathematical" theorem, it must be remembered that some of the greatest mathematicians of all time wholeheartedly accepted the Christian revelation of the Triune God. Jefferson's snide comment about "Trinitarian arithmetic" was not a barrier for those who were actually mathematicians.

LH: Let us get serious. What mathematicians are you talking about?

Chesterfield: The thinkers who, in large part, built the foundations of modern mathematics which, of course, transformed the theory and practice of science as a whole, were Trinitarians.

Trinitarian Mathematicians

These pathbreaking mathematicians include:

- *Carl Friedrich Gauss* (1777 –1855), described as "the greatest mathematician since antiquity" and a prime mover in number theory among many other achievements;

- *Bernhard Rieman* (1826-1866), architect of the higher dimensional geometry that became the framework for Einstein's theory of general relativity and an essential element of subsequent mathematics and physics;

- *Charles Babbage* (1791-1871), the founder of computing who originated the idea of a digital programmable computer;

- *Georg Cantor* (1845-1918), the creator of set theory, a framework fundamental to mathematics, and the pioneer of mathematical infinity;

- *Kurt Gödel* (1906-1978), formulator of the Incompleteness Theorems that revolutionized modern mathematics and science and whose work, it is said, touched every field of mathematical logic;

- *John von Neumann* (1903-1957), the mind behind the digital computer who was known as the foremost mathematician of his time for his varied contributions to applied mathematics;

- *Alonzo Church* (1903-1995), originator (with his student Alan Turing) of modern computer science; and

- *Alexandre Grothendieck* (1928-2014), the producer of the modern theory of algebraic geometry who was hailed by *Le Monde* as "the greatest mathematician of the 20th century"[232] when he died in 2014.

The vast majority of the leading modern mathematicians not only believed in God but were devout Christian believers who saw a direct connection between their mathematical work and the existence of God.

Several – Cantor, Gödel, Grothendieck, for example – sought to mathematically demonstrate God's existence.

Gauss wrote, "When our last hour comes, we will have the great and ineffable joy of seeing the One whom we could only glimpse in all our work." He also said, "There are problems to whose solution I would attach an infinitely greater importance than to those of mathematics, for example touching ethics, or our relation to God, or concerning our destiny and our future; but their solution lies wholly beyond us and completely outside the province of science."[233]

Rieman was reciting the Lord's prayer as he lay dying. The inscription on his tombstone is taken from the epistle to the Romans: "All things work together for good to them that love God."

George Boole, the father of pure mathematics, wrote, "The great results of Science, and the primal truths of religion and morals, have an existence quite independent of our faculties and of our recognition. (…) It is given to us to discover Truth – we are permitted to comprehend it; but its sole origin is in the will or the character of the Creator; and this is the real connecting link between Science and Religion."[234]

---

232 https://www.francetvinfo.fr/sciences/alexandre-grothendieck-le-plusgrand-mathematicien-du-xxe-siecle-est-mort_1705541.html

233 Carl Friedrich Gauss quoted in *The World of Mathematics* (1956) edited by J. R. Newman, https://beruhmte-zitate.de/zitate/1784047-carl-friedrichgauss-there-are-problems-to-whose-solution-i-would-attac/

234 Desmond MacHale, *George Boole* (Dublin, Ireland: Boole Press Ltd, 1985), 43.

In the *Ninth Bridgewater Treatise* (1837), Charles Babbage said: "The object of these pages ... is to show that the power and knowledge of the great Creator of matter and mind are unlimited."

Cantor wrote that set theory was directly revealed to him by God.[235] He also said, "From me, Christian Philosophy will be offered for the first time the true theory of the infinite."[236] In a letter to a priest he wrote, "Every extension of our insight into what is possible in creation leads necessarily to an extended cognition of God."[237]

Gödel constructed an ontological argument for the existence of God. He also said, "Spinoza's god is less than a person; mine is more than a person; because God can play the role of a person."[238] According to his wife Adele, "Although he did not go to church, he was religious and read the Bible in bed every Sunday morning."

Von Neumann, who was baptized earlier on, had a "deathbed" conversion – over a period of 18 months – and was given the last rites at his request. He observed, "So long as there is the possibility of eternal damnation for nonbelievers it is more logical to be a believer at the end."[239] Church was a lifelong Presbyterian and devout Christian.

Grothendieck not only published his own argument for God's existence, *The Key to Dreams or the Dialogue with the Good Lord*, but turned to Christian mysticism in the last years of his life.

---

235 J. Dauben, *Georg Cantor: His Mathematics and Philosophy of the Infinite* (Princeton: Princeton University Press, 1990), 146.

236 https://math.dartmouth.edu/~matc/Readers/HowManyAngels/Cantor/Cantor.html

237 C.Tapp, *Kardinalit at und Kardin¨ale: Wissenschaftshistorische Aufarbeitung der Korrespondenz zwischen Georg Cantor und katholischen Theologen seiner Zeit* (Stuttgart: Franz Steiner Verlag, 2005), 307–312.

238 Hao Wang, *A Logical Journey* (Cambridge, MA: MIT Press, 1996), 254.

239 P.R. Halmos, "The Legend of von Neumann," *The American Mathematical Monthly*, 1973, 80(4):382-94.

Returning to the question of Three and One, there is and can be only ONE God, one infinite Being, one Source of all things, one Self-existent. But "one" here does not mean a "single person." It means there is one Ultimate Reality. And our concern here is with the "make-up" of the Ultimate, the structure of the single Source of all. All that we know to be "one" in our experience is a marvel of unity in diversity.

LH: I think you have sunk so deep into the swamps of superstition and speculation that you are incapable of intelligent dialogue. Spare us from any more!

"HOMO SAPIENS 2.0"

Witness – Mary Lucas (ML)

MA: My next witness is Dr. Mary Lucas. She is a cognitive psychologist specializing in cognitive-behavioral therapy. She has published peer-reviewed papers on diverse motifs from the psychology of atheism and the claims of evolutionary psychology to meaning in life and the metrics of personal success. I said earlier that the testimony of our last witness was of capital importance since the Jesus Cloud underlies our response to the Plaintiff's charges about the kind of world in which we live. Dr. Lucas will show precisely how the Jesus Cloud can change our lives. The Plaintiff's counsel and his witnesses have claimed that Christianity has caused all the ills of the world. Dr. Lucas will show that it is Christianity that can cure all the ills of the world. Her view is that it is better to light a candle than to curse the darkness. Dr. Lucas.

Lucas: Thank you. I know I am entering this dialogue *in medias res* but I am glad that the foundations for what I have to say have been laid.

In discussing the Christian proposition, we are not dealing with an abstraction. We are dealing with a reality that enters our personal space and can shape the way we think and act.

The starting point is that we are afflicted with a disease of the soul. Christianity diagnoses this disease, its causes and symptoms, and prescribes a cure. Not all who receive the diagnosis, fill their prescription. Those who fill it do not always follow the instructions, and some discontinue its use. Others are taking additional medications that can inhibit the effect of the cure or even result in a deadly interaction. My task today is to outline both the diagnosis and the cure. If I may sum it up in a sentence, the disease is sin and the cure is the Love embodied in Jesus of Nazareth who leads us to his Father's House.

The Root of Human Evil

The Hebrew Bible, the Old Testament, shows a divine Father working through the people of Israel to bring all his errant children back to him. This begins with his covenant with Abraham, the father of the Israelite nation: "I swear by myself, declares the LORD ... in your descendants all the nations of the earth shall find blessing – all this because you obeyed my command." (*Genesis* 22:16,18)

God is the Father of the family of nations of which Israel is the "first-born."

But the first-born of the Father whose "heart is overwhelmed" is rebellious and fickle, intent on its own destruction:

> "You were unmindful of the Rock that begot you, you forgot the God who gave you birth. The LORD saw and was filled with loathing, provoked by his sons and daughters ... For they are a fickle gener-ation, children with no loyalty in them!" (*Deuteronomy* 32:18-20)

> "Return, rebellious children." (*Jeremiah* 3:14)

The Father does not desire to punish them but *implores* them to repent and return:

> "I have set before you life and death, the blessing and the curse. Choose life, then, that you and your descendants may live, by loving the LORD, your God, obeying his voice, and holding fast to him. For that will mean life for you, a long life for you to live on the land which the LORD swore to your ancestors, to Abraham, Isaac, and Jacob, to give to them." (*Deuteronomy* 30:19-20)

> "I take no pleasure in the death of the wicked, but rather that they turn from their ways and live." (*Ezekiel* 33:11)

He also tells the Israelites of the coming of a new, universal and everlasting covenant different from the one originally made with their ancestors:

> The "days are coming ... when I will make a new covenant with the house of Israel and the house of Judah." (*Jeremiah* 31:31)

> "With them I will make an everlasting covenant, never to cease doing good to them; I will put fear of me in their hearts so that they never turn away from me." (*Jeremiah* 32:40)

But this new covenant can be instituted only if the original breach is repaired. *Isaiah* 53 shows us how this will happen: it is a prophecy and a pre-figuration of the redemptive death of Jesus.

But how did evil begin?

The Book of *Genesis* has a compelling account of the origin of evil. We are told that at the very beginning of its history, the human race said "No" to God. We do not know when, where, how. We just know "that."

We can recognize some elements of the message of *Genesis* 2 and 3 at a natural level:

> that *homo sapiens* is irreducibly different from all other beings;

> that peeling back the centuries we end up with an original identical ancestor;

> that all human societies have recognized the fact of a primordial breach between humanity and the divine order;

> that we have an immediate experience of a drive to evil in our own wills.

We are aware of all this without divine revelation.

Genesis 2 and 3 simply confirm much of what we already know inchoately. But what it says about human destiny – our call to union with God – can only be known through actual revelation.

On a Need-to-Know Basis

The Genesis 3 narrative tells us: Obey God no matter what. That in a nutshell is the message of the Bible as a whole and in particular of its first book.

The Bible also tells us that things went wrong at the start precisely because this rule was not observed. The parents of the human race disobeyed a seemingly simple divine command: "From that tree you shall not eat." They had everything going for them. Nothing more was expected beyond obeying this rule. But they would not obey. One thing led to another and here we are.

Skeptics have said that this is just a fairy tale. And even religious believers today see *Genesis* as a pious legend with a theological touchup.

Now these responses might sound plausible if not for the fact that the *Genesis* story rings eerily true. True to human experience that is. And to subsequent human history. So let us revisit the scene of the crime.

> "Now the serpent was the most cunning of all the animals that the LORD God had made. The serpent asked the woman, "Did God really tell you not to eat from any of the trees in the garden?" The woman answered the serpent: "We may eat of the fruit of the trees in the garden; it is only about the fruit of the tree in the middle of the garden that God said, 'You shall not eat it or even touch it, lest you die.'" But the serpent said to the woman: "You certainly will not die! No, God knows well that the moment you eat of it your eyes will be opened and you will be like gods who know what is good and what is bad." The woman saw that the tree was good for food, pleasing to the eyes, and desirable for gaining wisdom. So she took some of its fruit and ate it; and she also gave some to her husband, who was with her,

and he ate it. Then the eyes of both of them were opened, and they realized that they were naked; so they sewed fig leaves together and made loincloths for themselves. When they heard the sound of the LORD God moving about in the garden at the breezy time of the day, the man and his wife hid themselves from the LORD God among the trees of the garden. The LORD God then called to the man and asked him, "Where are you?" He answered, "I heard you in the garden; but I was afraid, because I was naked, so I hid myself." Then he asked, "Who told you that you were naked? You have eaten, then, from the tree of which I had forbidden you to eat!" The man replied, "The woman whom you put here with me—she gave me fruit from the tree, so I ate it." The LORD God then asked the woman, "Why did you do such a thing?" The woman answered, "The serpent tricked me into it, so I ate it." (*Genesis* 3: 1-13)

What we have here is a tale of temptation and disobedience that ends with guilt and shame. Students of the psyche and of history will be the first to admit that guilt and shame play an inordinate role in human life. And those who have committed actions deemed evil will no doubt recognize the pattern in play here. First, we deliberate and then we perpetrate.

The doctors of the soul have gone much further. The first mistake, they say, was to enter into a dialogue with the tempter. The second was debating what we know to be a divine command instead of simply obeying it. Now the tempter has an opening and simply has to distort the divine truth and then dangle his own irresistible promises of ecstasy. Impulsively, we respond by disobeying only to discover it was all for nought. Our conscience, the Voice of God, shows the wretchedness of our new state.

Others have seen the so-called Seven Deadly Sins embodied here. Pride, the root of all these sins, is the driving factor: it is the desire to be like God that motivates Eve to launch the *coup d'etat*. There is envy, the serpent's envy concerning the happy state of the humans and the humans' envy of God. There is anger at God for keeping something out of their reach. There is obvious avarice and gluttony. Lust is suggested in the comments about nakedness. And it was spiritual sloth that left the soul open to the initial attack.

What was the sin of Adam and Eve? All we know is that there was a free and deliberate rejection of the divine will. It has been pointed out that, from a literary standpoint, the tree of life and the tree of the knowledge of good and evil are one and the same. They play similar roles and the narrative does not specify from which the forbidden fruit was taken. The message of the symbolism is that obedience to the Rules of God is the source of enduring life. Partaking of the tree of the knowledge of good and evil means replacing the divine will with the human as the springboard of our moral acts. The narrative itself might just as well be the story of every human soul and its moral is quite clear:

- God has given us total freedom, and it is as easy to turn away from him as it is to turn to him. Love cannot force itself on the recipient.

- Sin is conceived before it is born. The groundwork is laid by our thought of some illicit pleasure. Next comes the pleasurable expectation of enjoying it and then a headlong rush into the fatal act. We commit the sin. We feel shame and guilt. Yet each sin makes it easier for us to turn to the next.

- The path to sin is almost always paved by occasions of temptation to which we expose ourselves. Once we engage the Tempter in conversation, we are lost. As so many doctors of the spiritual life have said, flee the thought as soon as it enters the mind.

The forces of evil are constantly active seeking to bring us down ("Your opponent the devil is prowling around like a roaring lion looking for (someone) to devour." 1 *Peter* 5:8) Which means you can never let down your guard. They strike when you least expect it. They are far more intelligent than you are and too subtle to let you know who they are. ("For our struggle is not with flesh and blood but with the principalities, with the powers, with the world rulers of this present darkness, with the evil spirits in the heavens." (Ephesians 6:12))

The *Genesis* story is not just about the origin of evil. It pertains to our addressing evil in our lives. It does this by highlighting the urgency of obeying God which is a matter of aligning finite goods to the Absolute Good. When it comes to obedience, stay focused on remaining faithful to those goods that align us to the Absolute Good – this is what obeying the commandments of God is all about. We refuse entry to any dissenting voice – be it ourselves, our friends or our spiritual enemies. No matter what the obstacles, nothing will ultimately go wrong if we stay faithful to God's commands. No matter how attractive the promised result, everything will inevitably go wrong if we disobey his commands. To turn away from the Absolute Good is to embrace evil.

Choices do have consequences and none was of such calamitous import as the first free act of disobedience. If we open Pandora's Box, we have to pay a price. So let's turn to Scene Two.

Paradise Lost

> "Then the LORD God said to the serpent: "Because you have done this, you shall be banned from all the animals and from all the wild creatures; On your belly shall you crawl, and dirt shall you eat all the days of your life. I will put enmity between you and the woman, and between your offspring and hers; He will strike at your head, while you strike at his heel." To the woman he said: "I will intensify the pangs of your childbearing; in pain shall you bring forth children. Yet your urge shall be for your husband, and he shall be your master." To the man he said: "Because you listened to your wife and ate from the tree of which I had forbidden you to eat, "Cursed be the ground because of you! In toil shall you eat its yield all the days of your life.

Thorns and thistles shall it bring forth to you, as you eat of the plants of the field. By the sweat of your face shall you get bread to eat, Until you return to the ground, from which you were taken; For you are dirt, and to dirt you shall return." ... [H]e must not be allowed to put out his hand to take fruit from the tree of life also, and thus eat of it and live forever." The LORD God therefore banished him from the garden of Eden, to till the ground from which he had been taken." (*Genesis* 3: 14-19, 22-3)

In the language of theology, the Original Sin led to the Fall. The consequences of Original Sin are monumental: henceforth humans are denied fullness of union with God; all will suffer pain, disease and death; all will be afflicted by darkening of the intellect and weakness of the will. The logician Peter Geach has highlighted the stark nature of this tragedy:

"The traditional doctrine is that since the sin of our first parents, men have been conceived and born different in nature from what they would have been had our first parents stood firm under trial."[240]

Repugnant though it is, the teaching of Original Sin is demonstrable on two levels: it conforms with universal experience as atheists like Arthur Schopenhauer and Albert Camus have testified and it is memorialized in the primordial and universal human practice of expiatory sacrifice. To expiate means to say, "I'm sorry." But "sorry" for what?

Concerning the testimony of experience, every person becomes aware of an innate irresistible inclination towards evil. We cannot but admit that Hitler and Stalin belong to the same species as ourselves. This means that we must admit that we too are infected with the same vile disease that ravaged their souls.

---

240 Peter Geach, *Providence and Evil*, (Cambridge: Cambridge University Press, 1977), 89.

When we come to the New Testament, we see that Christ is a counterpoint to Adam. He is the New Adam who obeys where the old Adam did not: "For just as through the disobedience of one person the many were made sinners, so through the obedience of one the many will be made righteous." (*Romans* 5:19)

The last book of the Bible, *Revelation*, specifically consummates themes found in the first, *Genesis*. *Genesis* is the book of the first Creation, *Revelation* the book of the New Creation (the New Heaven and the New Earth). *Revelation* details the continuing onslaughts of the Serpent and its final defeat. *Revelation* ends where *Genesis* began: a new Eden with the indwelling presence of God, a life-giving river and the Tree of Life offered to all the righteous, i.e., the obedient.

The New Testament teaches that obedience to God is manifested also by obedience to human authorities. Obedience is, in fact, the perfect antidote to pride, the source of all sin.

The test of Adam and Eve is one that must be undergone by every human being. Will we obey the commandments of God despite the lures and deceptions of the Devil?

Homo Sapiens 2.0

The backstory of creation, Original Sin, incarnation and redemption makes sense of the Old and New Covenants. The "sequel" to the Covenants is Homo Sapiens 2.0 – the re-invention of the human person and human destiny. Those who are redeemed are "re-invented."

The sequel begins with the new and improved version of ourselves.

To begin with, we should realize what happened when God took on a human nature in Jesus of Nazareth. With this Incarnation of Infinity, a new race was called into being. The human was reinvented by passing through the portal of divine Life.

The first, irrevocable step was that of being cleansed at baptism, the fountain of re-creation. We are re-purposed and reprogrammed at this fountain of rebirth. "Repent and be baptized, every one of you, in the name of Jesus Christ for the forgiveness of your sins; and you will receive the gift of the holy Spirit." (*Acts* 2:38)

Henceforth, "we are the offspring of God" (*Acts* 17:39) who are "able to share in the divine nature." (2 *Peter* 1:4)

Through the reinvention, we are granted powers above the natural – "I will pour out a portion of my spirit upon all flesh." (*Joel* 3:1, *Acts* 2:17) – super-powers!

God-Force

The redeemed are granted a new form of life driven by the Power of God. It is at baptism that we receive this new life in which we are "able to share in the divine nature" (2 Peter 1:4).

The super-powers we receive at baptism have been variously described as the virtues of faith, hope and charity and the gifts and fruits of the Holy Spirit.

The Incarnation of God is followed by the Indwelling of God.

The Incarnation of God in Jesus of Nazareth – which like Pentecost took place in "the fullness of time" – was an unprecedented divine "insertion" into human history.

By taking on a human nature, the Son made it possible for human beings to take on his divine Life. *This imparting of the divine Life is the "indwelling" of the Holy Spirit.* It was a second and equally dramatic divine "insertion" into the life of humanity.

You might think of the Holy Spirit as the God-Force that energizes the Christian phenomenon.

To understand the action of the God-Force, we might compare it to the physical forces with which we are familiar.

Modern physics has shown that all physical things are basically energy fields. A field is something that has energy and occupies space. All the matter and the forces in the world are ultimately fields and so they are not different in kind. A matter field simply has a higher concentration of energy than a "matter-less" field. *Particles like electrons and photons are produced by ripples of energy in a field: they are forms of concentrated energy: condensed energy!*

The spiritual world is different from matter and energy because spirit does not occupy space. But, in the non-physical world, we can still *talk* of a *divine force-field that can be concentrated at certain points to form "particles."*

These concentration points are human persons and *the particles are persons who become temples of the Spirit of God.*

The analogy is drastically limited because Spirit-templed persons do not become a part of God. They are not the divine Force-field. They are finite beings that are distinct from it.

But they do take on characteristics of the Force-field and to that extent *they become manifestations of Its effect.*

Of course, the divine Force-field has infinite Energy and, embedded within the Triune Godhead, brought all things, physical and spiritual, into being.

When this Force-field touches the soul, it is "filled with the Spirit". It acts with the Power of the Spirit and manifests the Presence of the Spirit.

The Spirit is a *divine* Person. The Spirit-filled *human* person lives *with* the divine Life that is the Spirit.

The seven gifts of the Holy Spirit are superpowers precisely because they super-naturalize the two human powers that image God: intellect and will. Wisdom, understanding, counsel and knowledge are the gifts that transform the intellect while fortitude, piety, and fear of the Lord crown the will and the emotions. The direct cause of these gifts is the Holy Spirit. A weakened will and darkened intellect are the common lot of humanity and this includes those who possess the divine life and the supernatural virtues. Some divine impetus is required at all times to protect you against yourself. This is where the gifts come in.

The Promised Land

In the new divine order, human destiny is oriented to the Promised Land – eternal union with God through Jesus the Way, the Truth and the Life. Salvation.

Jesus offers us unprecedented liberation from sin. Jesus liberates us not just from sin but its consequences. Under the Old Covenant, "punishment for their parents' wickedness" was passed on to their "children and children's children to the third and fourth generation!" (*Exodus* 34:7) But under the New Covenant, the Lord says, "I will forgive their evildoing and remember their sins no more." (*Hebrews* 8:12)

The grace we receive from God for faith and salvation is entirely a gift that we do not and cannot merit. We are not saved by works whether these be the ceremonial or judicial decrees of the Mosaic Law or our responses to the fundamental moral law laid out in the Ten Commandments. We are saved by grace: the Power of God, the Holy Spirit, acting in us. But this grace is not forced on us: we must accede to it, welcome it, let it "in."

This emphasis on the link between our choices here and our destiny hereafter is highlighted in the entire New Testament. Salvation is a state of deliverance from evil and transformation of our being. It commences in the here and now and reaches its full glory in the direct presence of God. Eternal life and the Kingdom of God are of this world and the next. Everything is inter-connected.

Once we accept and live in the grace of God, we are required also to obey his Ten Commandments and the moral law he established. Paul calls us to "the obedience of faith." (*Romans* 1:5, 16:26) This obedience is a call to holiness: "Let us cleanse ourselves from every defilement of flesh and spirit, making holiness perfect in the fear of God." (2 *Corinthians* 7:1)

The "obedience of faith" is divinely powered: "So then, my beloved, obedient as you have always been, ... work out your salvation with fear and trembling. For God is the one who, for his good purpose, works in you both to desire and to work." (*Philippians* 2:12)

Of course, Jesus warned us that "Not everyone who says to me, 'Lord, Lord,' will enter the kingdom of heaven, but only the one who does the will of my Father in heaven." (*Matthew* 7:21) He also said, "For the Son of Man is going to come in the glory of his Father with his angels, and, when he does, he will reward each one according to his behavior." (*Matthew* 16:27)

Paul gives the same warning: "Your stubborn refusal to repent is only adding to the anger God will have toward you on that day of anger when his just judgments will be made known. He will repay each one as his works deserve. For those who sought renown and honor and immortality by always doing good there will be eternal life; for the unsubmissive who refused to take truth for their guide and took depravity instead, there will be anger and fury." (*Romans* 2:5-8)

The second epistle of Peter makes it clear that Christians can be damned if they fall away: "There will be false teachers among you, who will introduce destructive heresies and even deny the Master who *ransomed them*, bring swift destruction on themselves." (2 *Peter* 2:1)

To follow Jesus is to let him empty the sewage in our souls. We must let him transform us, replacing our old self with a new I:

> "You should put away the old self of your former way of life, corrupted through deceitful desires ... and put on the new self, created

in God's way in righteousness and holiness of truth." (*Ephesians* 4:22-24)

"Whoever is in Christ is a new creation." (2 *Corinthians* 5:12,17)

This transformation is "of the heart, in the spirit" to be approached "in absolute trust":

> "Rather, one is a Jew inwardly, and circumcision is *of the heart, in the spirit*, not the letter; his praise is not from human beings but from God." (*Romans* 2:29)

> "But thanks be to God that, although you were once slaves of sin, you have become obedient from the heart to the pattern of teaching to which you were entrusted." (*Romans* 6:17)

Just as every divine covenant depends on the human response, in the moral realm too we must say "Yes" to God's free invitation to salvation. To say "Yes" here means that we must follow his Will in our lives at all levels. Granted, even the just fall seven times a day as the Bible says. Yet, what is important is not how often we fall or how hard we fall but that we repent each time and return to the prodigal Father.

Yes, "prodigal" Father for, as we have seen, "prodigal" means extravagant and in the parable it is the father who is extravagant in his generosity. Our heavenly Father is, in fact, infinitely generous.

Mercy is at the heart of the Gospel. The Good Samaritan, the Prodigal Son, the command to forgive 70 times seven (i.e., without end). It is all about mercy. Mercy is the face of the divine Love for us. Mercy is how we share the love of God with our fellow beings in this instant we spend on earth.

MA: Thank you, Dr. Lucas. You are truly a doctor of the soul! Your Honor, the doctor is in. Your witness.

LH: Thank you. Dr. Lucas, I want to begin by saying that I was taken aback not just by what you said but more so by what you left out. You said not a word about the horrendous suffering caused by Christianity and Christians: the slave trade, colonialism, wars of the Christian religion from the Crusades onward, torture motivated by Christianity as in the Inquisition, the racism so endemic to Christianity and Christian cultures, economic exploitation and ecological destruction ... the list is endless. If this is a cure, it is a cure that kills all those who come into contact with the patients on the medication!

On sin, both I and our witnesses have said plenty but your rendition raises the discussion to a new low. Adam and Eve? Seriously? That primitive myth is your answer to the origin of evil. Have you taken leave of your senses? All of modern science tells us that human beings are later products of the evolutionary tree of life. Our immediate ancestors were a series of hominins none of whom were named Adam or Eve. This part of your presentation was especially disappointing and wiped out what little credibility you had.

Finally, we have the superpower promise. What can I say? Just when I thought I had heard every kind of scam there is, you come along and treat us to another one of your greatest grifts.

My only hope, Dr. Lucas, is that you are not treating any patients. If these are the wares you ply, Zeus help them!

MA: Your Honor, those last two statements were outrageous even by my opponent's low standards. He has attacked my witness both personally and professionally. I move that these cowardly attacks be struck from the proceedings.

Judge: Upheld.

LH: Dr. Lucas, if you have nothing more to say, I have no further questions.

Lucas: Oh, but I do. I was actually amused by your hysterical histrionics. Your reaction told me more about you than you know. I treat patients with similar neuroses. And I have an opening early next month if you're interested!

For now, let me start with the atheism you wear on your sleeve. I have used the landmark studies done by Paul Vitz in treating atheists with "daddy" problems. Vitz's case studies of the famous atheists showed that the major barriers to belief in God are not rational but neurotic psychological barriers of which the unbeliever may be unaware. From a psychoanalytic standpoint, Vitz reversed Freud's claim (inherited from Feuerbach and now propagated by most atheists) that belief in God is a wish fulfillment driven by a desire for security. Vitz points out that within the Freudian framework, atheism is actually an illusion caused by the sub-conscious desire to kill the father and replace him with oneself. The well-known skeptic Voltaire vehemently rejected his father (and even refused to take his father's name).

According to Vitz's "defective father" hypothesis[241], when a child is disappointed in the earthly father it becomes impossible to believe in a heavenly Father. As evidence, he cites the case-histories of various well-known unbelievers: Sigmund Freud himself was deeply disappointed in his father, a weak man; Karl Marx did not respect his father; the young Ludwig Feuerbach was deeply hurt by his father. The death of a father is sometimes also seen as a betrayal: Jean Paul Sartre's father died before he was born and both Bertrand Russell and Albert Camus lost their fathers when they were very young.

Excerpts from the personal correspondence of these atheists illustrate the true sources of their rejection of God. Atheism is essentially a rejection of the Father. And, in the case of many atheists, only when we overcome the barriers between our fathers and ourselves can we truly recognize and celebrate the Father who brought all things into being.

---

241 Paul C. Vitz, *Faith of the Fatherless – The Psychology of Atheism* (San Francisco: Ignatius, 2013).

Let me address your broadside on the evil and suffering caused by Christians – which I will do in the context of the Genesis story of the origin of evil that you have so gleefully disparaged.

At the center of the Christian vision is the message that we are called to love, a call that requires our free response. Through the centuries we see how the unique program of love that is the Christian message has created hospitals and orphanages, human rights, the upliftment of the oppressed and much else.

About the slave trade, your secular sage Yuval Harari writes, "At the end of the Middle Ages, slavery was almost unknown in Christian Europe." So. who was responsible for it: "During the early modern period, the rise of European capitalism went hand in hand with the rise of the Atlantic slave trade."[242]

It was a Christian, William Wilberforce, motivated by his Christianity, who led the movement against the slave trade that culminated in the Slave Trade Act of 1807. He also fought for the total abolition of slavery, the creation of free colonies and other worthy causes.

Nevertheless, Christians also believe in Original Sin and hold that they and all human beings are fatally flawed. They recognize that they can say no to love. They will be the first to say they have not lived up to their program of love. In fact, Christians have been responsible for moral outrages throughout history. That is because they are flawed human beings with a drive to evil.

Submission to the commands of Christ and the power of the Holy Spirit can help transform our lives and millions have experienced this transformation. Those who have been personally transformed have sometimes transformed the societies in which they live. But such transformation is a one-on-one affair. And it depends on each individual.

---

242 Yuval Harari, *Sapiens* (London: Vintage, 2015), 368.

Just as we do not blame people for their ancestors' choices, we cannot hold Christianity responsible for anti-Christian acts committed by those professing to be Christians. Rather, we should assess the degree to which Christians measure up to the ideals they profess.

Its the ideals that matter. We can illustrate this by considering Enlightenment ideologies that profess to be humanly created. Since there are no divine foundations involved, we end up with ideologies like Nazism and Marxism where evils become absolutized. To live up to the ideology would mean committing acts that Christianity and most civilized people hold to be evil. In contrast, the Christian message is an engine that seeks to constantly draw its adherents to a higher level of holiness. We compare ourselves against its ideals which are not created by us but derive from the divine. In this framework, Christians are always a work in progress.

Now let me turn to your unhinged comments about *Genesis*. Neither the Fall nor Original Sin can be proved or disproved by science because neither phenomenon belongs to the quantitative realm of science. Rather, both concern the moral realm and only the collective memory of humanity and the direct revelation of God can speak to their actuality. And here the answer is clear:

- the human race goes back to a common ancestor says science, as I hope to show;
- the human soul must be a direct creation of God says our immediate experience of the supra-physical;
- *homo sapiens*, from primordial times, has sought to make reparation for some unspeakable sin through the universal practice of sacrifice, says anthropology;
- guilt and shame afflict the human psyche, says psychology; and

- "Adam" and Eve knowingly and willingly separated themselves and their progeny from their divine Maker with all attendant consequences, says the Judeo-Christian story.

You obviously reject what I said about a common ancestor for humankind. But your rejection rests on a mistake. *Genesis* speaks of Adam and Eve as the first parents of humanity. Scientists today, however, suggest that there were populations of thousands of ancestral parents from whom we are descended and not a first pair. Moreover, *Homo sapiens*, it is widely believed, interbred with now extinct populations of hominins like the Neanderthals and Denisovans.

Several matters need to be clarified here.

On a natural level, for reasons I specify, it seems indisputable that *homo sapiens* originated from a single pair of first parents although we do not know when or where. This does not mean that there were no hominins with capabilities such as tool-making and painting that preceded the first pair and may even have lived in parallel with later generations of *homo sapiens*. And there is no theological reason why inter-breeding may not have taken place after "the Fall" – although other hominin species died out over time.

In an article in the leading science journal *Nature*, three population geneticists argued that, on the basis of population statistics, it can be inferred that the last Identical Ancestor of all living humans (making allowances for nomadic migrations and the like) lived at the latest around 5000 B.C. They note that "our results suggest that the most recent common ancestor for the world's current population lived in the relatively recent past – perhaps within the last few thousand years. And a few thousand years before that, although we have received genetic material in markedly different proportions from the people alive at the time, the ancestors of everyone on the Earth today were exactly the same."

In their estimate, if we go back to between 5000 and 2000 B.C., the ancestors of everyone on earth today would be exactly the same. An "extremely tentative" estimate, going by genealogical rather than genetic terms, is that "all modern individuals have identical ancestors by about 3,000 B.C."[243] This still does not tell you when the first parents lived but it indicates that an ancestor common to all of today's humans lived barely a few thousand years ago.

This latter conclusion should seem obvious even at a popular level. People become more closely related to each other in each previous generation (for instance, you and your fifth cousin have great-grandfathers who were brothers). Only a fraction of today's population inhabited the world a thousand years ago and the population size will continue to decrease as you keep going even further back in time. With each such decrease in raw numbers there is a corresponding increase in the closeness of familial relationships among those then alive. This continues all the way back until you reach the original ancestors of the race.

To give an illustration, let us say that two parents have five children and the five have three each. Let's suppose that the children of each subsequent generation have two of their own offspring. Within nineteen generations, the two original parents would have produced a family of approximately 2 million (of course there are spouses from other families involved in each generation). In the same manner, if you start with the current population of the world and reverse the calculations, you reach common ancestors in a few thousand years.

These observations are consistent with Stanley Jaki's conclusion that "The descendants of Adam, if they started say 25,000 BC, could easily reach fifteen million by 5000 BC, in essential agreement with current population

---

243 "Modelling the recent common ancestry of all living humans," *Nature*, September 30, 2004, 565.

estimates."[244] The same is true whether the point of origin is 25,000 B.C. or 100,000 B.C.

It's not just the progressive decrease in population numbers that's relevant. The limitations on our knowledge of the past are also often forgotten. No one living today can say anything definitive and complete even about the people who lived a century before them.

If anything definitive is to be known at all about the first days of humanity, it can only come through divine revelation and to a limited extent via the collective memory of the human race.

Another important dimension – the Adam and Eve of *Genesis* were capable of speech and conceptual thought. On Day One we are told "The man *gave names* to all the tame animals, all the birds of the air, and all the wild animals." (*Genesis* 2:20).

What differentiates *homo sapiens* from other hominins is the phenomenon of language – the capability for conceptual thought – manifested most fully in writing. The origin of language, the capability for thinking in concepts, is simply inexplicable from the standpoint of science. *Genesis* indicates that this power was directly implanted by God (image of God, breath of life): this is what it means to say that every human soul, starting with that of the first man and woman, is a direct creation of God.

The language dilemma also makes it all but impossible to entertain the idea that *Homo sapiens* originated from multiple first parents.

Let me explain why.

As a previous witness has shown, scientific investigation over several decades has confirmed beyond any reasonable doubt that the origin of language is inexplicable at a natural level.

---

244 Stanley Jaki, *The Garden of Eden* (Pinckney, Michigan: Real View Books), 27.

Further, the very nature of language shows that its origin would have to have been a one time all-or-nothing kind of phenomenon. This is because, as philosopher of language David Braine puts it, "Language has a semantic structure that can be called unitary." In other words, you cannot be half-pregnant. To call something a language is to say that it conveys meaning via symbols, signs or sounds that embody concepts. If it does not convey meaning, if it does not involve concepts, it is not a language. There is no half-way house, as Braine explains:

> This unitariness is such [that it] excludes the idea of human language as developing, either characteristic by characteristic, or structural element by structural element, as if by a process of gradual addition of characteristics or structural elements to some pre-existing whole, language might have developed bit by bit until it has reached the rounded whole shared by all human beings.
>
> The human language capacity (...) and the understanding on which it draws, unlike other developments seen in evolution towards human kind has an *all at once or nothing character*.
>
> The unitary character of the semantic structure of human speech makes it impossible that the characteristics of language it exhibits and the basic features of its structure should have been added on piece by piece rather than all at once, and it appears difficult to conceive how one mutation or any singular coincidence of mutations could have brought about a development of this particular kind.[245]

The first human persons – our "first parents" – were those first endowed with the capability of conceptual thought, a capability that cannot be naturally explained, the first users of language.

---

245 David Braine, "Life and Human Life: Their Nature and Emergence – The Singularity of Human Life," in Roy Abraham Varghese, ed., *The Missing Link* (Lanham: University Press of America, 2013), 141, 132, 151.

This capability had to be directly implanted by the infinite-eternal Mind but in tandem with other natural processes.

As Kenneth Kemp explains,

> What is the maximum level of perceptual complexity which evolutionary processes can produce? ... We find [in animals] capacities that lay the foundation for, even though they do not themselves exemplify, conceptualization, judgment, and reasoning.
>
> First, there are animal mental capacities that lay the foundation for conceptualization. One is the capacity for the comparison and differentiation of images. Surely any being with sense powers at all has some ability to sort out what it sees. ...
>
> Second, animals have mental capacities that lay a foundation for judgment. They have a capacity for expectation. ...
>
> Third, there is even evidence of capacities that lay the foundation for inferential reasoning. ...
>
> Since that level of complexity is only necessary and not sufficient for rational thought, that would not be sufficient to show that rational beings (such as man) could have evolved by natural processes alone. Rational beings would appear only with the creation of rational souls capable of actually doing the abstraction that their evolutionarily formed brains made possible. ...
>
> An animal which had sensitive powers more developed than an animal would ever need, or could even use, in the course of an animal life might be able to live a full canine, simian, or cetacean life with its merely sensitive soul, but would have an untapped potential if it did not have a soul also capable of abstracting concepts from the images which its sensitive soul produced. The infusion of rational souls into such beings would be possible (in the way that would not be possible

in the case of a plant) and fitting (in the sense that it would allow those animals to make a fuller use of their sense-powers).[246]

Finally, you think of the gifts and fruits of the Holy Spirit as a scam. All I can say is that something led multitudes of ordinary people through the centuries to face the torture, suffering and dreadful forms of death inflicted on them by their enemies with smiles on their faces and love in their hearts. It was not a scam. I wonder if you know what it was that motivated their enemies to harm them as they did.

The Christian message preserves the insight that we are free beings who are responsible for at least certain of our choices.

LH: Hence, you people believe that God punishes us for misdeeds. Brimstone followed by hellfire. What a barbaric idea.

Lucas: In his second inaugural address, Abraham Lincoln said, "Every drop of blood drawn with the lash, shall be paid by another drawn with the sword." Decades earlier, Thomas Jefferson said: "I tremble for my country when I reflect that God is just."

The question is whether there is another order of being – a moral universe – that interacts with our psycho-physical universe. Is there any connection between the two? Do our actions in this moral universe affect the goings on in the psycho-physical world? The entire Bible – and for that matter most ancient religions – are built on the insight that there is a cause-effect connection both here and hereafter.

But now we know better, say the atheists of today. But what precisely do you know, and how do you know it to be the case? After all, wars, and the suffering they cause, are the results of free human choices. Entire populations suffer because of the actions of a few. Just as breaches of the laws of

---

246 Kenneth W. Kemp, "God, Evolution, and the Body of Adam," *Scientia et Fides*, 8/2020. 158-160, 162-3.

physical hygiene lead to disease and death, breaches of the laws of spiritual hygiene can be similarly detrimental to the soul.

I do not deny that human evil involves the question of divine retribution. But why not? Torturers and mass murderers are punished by society so the idea of consequences for actions is not foreign to any morally sensitive person.

Wars, pandemics and economic calamities force us to confront aspects of the real world we spend our lives avoiding: death and the precariousness of life, the contrast between the lengths of our lives and the endless past and future, the purpose of life, the relation of cause and effect to events in the here-and-now and in eternity. Instead of talking about retribution you should be asking: are we ready for eternity?

LH: Nonsense. All you people do is to exploit the fears and uncertainties intrinsic to our lives here with threats of divine punishment.

But in all your grand talk of a moral universe, you have avoided the issue of who determines what is morally good. What is considered morally good by Jane is considered morally evil by Jill. It's all arbitrary. What you call moral laws are simply products of biology and culture.

Lucas: You do not deny the fact that by rejecting the moral order you have no basis for saying any action is wrong in any absolute sense. This includes the Holocaust or vile and hideous forms of assault on helpless innocents or thieving, raping and pillaging or wanton destruction of civilian populations. Ultimately, each person decides what is acceptable or not. A science magazine has argued that the so-called deadly sins are simply the results of the ways in which different parts of the brain operate: bad intentions are simply a matter of biology. Everything can be traced to evolutionary history and anatomical circuitry. In this setting, there is no right or wrong, guilty or innocent, good or bad.

Some of your comrades have tried to make the best of a bad situation by coming up with new theories of morality: consequentialism, proportionalism, utilitarianism and others. Acts are good or bad depending on their consequences or their purposes or their "use". Gouging out the eyes of liars may be considered acceptable if it keeps people from lying. The ends can justify the means and so any means is potentially acceptable. If someone thinks that a country has too large a population, they would be justified in blowing up a few cities to thin out the ranks. This is what happens when relativism and the appeal to pluralism migrate from the realm of knowing to the sphere of morality.

Ultimately, in this environment, the rules of God will be replaced by the rules of tyrants. Human societies need "rules" to survive and these rules either have to be created by the rulers or derive from rules established by the Creator of the human family. If society's "thinkers" reject God and the idea of rules established by God, they will propose their own rules and these will be adopted, adapted or rejected by different rulers according to their whims. From there it will all be downhill. Remember the rulers best-known for rejecting God and setting their own rules: Hitler, Stalin, Pol Pot. The fruits of their "rules" were millions of corpses and societies laid to waste. Recent history has shown that the end result of rejecting moral absolutes is the triumph of evil.

LH: Let us do a reality check. Are you saying there was no war or destruction in societies ruled by those who accepted an objective moral law independent of humanity? Have you forgotten about the crusades, the pogroms, the jihads, the onslaughts of colonialists and imperialists?

Lucas: As I have said, there was savagery aplenty in other eras. But there was also a sense of a higher authority that acted as a check and balance on the blood-thirsty impulses of the barbarous brutes who reigned in the name of God. They were recognized as evil and culpable by their subjects because there was a moral order they were consciously breaching.

True, this may not have helped their victims, but society itself was governed by an awareness of a moral order greater than any ruler. Thus, there was a permanent possibility of progress in aligning society's laws with the moral order. The world of Hitler, Stalin and Pol Pot, on the other hand, was a world without any underlying moral foundation: they were recreating societies in their image and they were accountable to no one. Of course, since you reject the moral order, you cannot call them "evil". "Evil" is a word that can be used only if the "good" is transcendent and absolute.

Good and evil make no sense in a world where survival is the priority and the only law is to kill or be killed. You see human persons as simply conglomerations of quantum fields – and physical conglomerations cannot be described as "good" or "bad." You see human actions as the product of subconscious drives and disordered childhoods. There is no room for right and wrong in that framework.

LH: You know well that philosophers have shown that you cannot derive the "is" from the "ought." In other words, the facts we learn about the world are all descriptions of it but descriptions are not prescriptions for how we should behave. So, there is nothing we can know about right and wrong, good and bad. "Evil" is simply an emotive word. There is no content we can attach to it because it's not something tangible. You have said there are benefits for society if we believe in moral absolutes but you have given no reason for believing in such absolutes.

Lucas: There are taboos today that are just as strong as they were in religious societies. It is no different today. Anything that violates contemporary "woke" principles is greeted with the same horror as adultery or blasphemy in a previous era. Similarly, when something inexplicable happened in medieval times, society might have said it was divine retribution or a supernatural mystery. Today, that explanatory function is performed by climate change, evolution and other factors even when speculation and not hard evidence is the only basis for making correlations.

LH: I do not know where you're going with this. I am still waiting to hear your case for a moral universe.

Lucas: I wanted you to recognize the tendency to find explanations for events via sheer superstition. You attempt to explain the moral code with unverifiable events from the evolutionary past or unidentifiable drives in your unconscious. This is an example of such superstition. It is not very different from the view that lightning was caused by the anger of the gods.

The affirmation that the moral code is objective and absolute is based on immediate experience. To wit:

- Human beings cannot create moral obligations for themselves or establish any act as good or bad in an absolute sense. Moral foundations and obligations can only derive from an ultimate transcendent moral authority – what humankind has called God. God is goodness itself. Acts are not good because God "makes" them good but because they participate in the Absolute Good that is God. Bertrand Russell made the mistake of supposing that there is a distinction between God and what is good. On the contrary, goodness itself issues from conformity to the nature of God who is the Absolute Good.

- On another level, what is a good for any kind of being depends on the nature of that being. God creates each being with a purpose and gives it its nature. Its goodness is to be found in its conformity with both its nature and purpose. Different beings – butterflies, daffodils, humans – have different natures and purposes and therefore different goods. Humans should optimize the operations of body and soul and there are goods proper to the physical, emotional, mental and spiritual dimensions of humanity. Above all, they should cultivate the virtues because these are good in themselves, help them grow to their full potential, and prepare them for their destiny of union with God. Remember that the virtues are not simply a list of do's and don'ts but are the path to true happiness because they are conducive to the fulfillment of your nature.

- Being and acting are two different things. You are a human being with all the potentialities of body and soul. These are goods simply because they are the creation of God understood as the Absolute Good. But you are also a being who acts freely and it is in your free actions – from intention to execution – that you do what is morally good or evil.

- All human beings have an inner voice that tells them what they ought and ought not to do. I grant that different people hear different things but they do hear something. More important, human societies have shown that certain moral principles are universal: cowardice is bad, altruism is good, care for the aged is honorable, sacrifice in atonement is necessary, worship is obligatory. The basic truths embodied in the Ten Commandments are found in other cultures – and one would expect this to be the case if these truths originate in a single Source.

- Thus, humanity has given birth to numerous rule-books in the course of its history. The Codex Hammurabi, the Way of the Buddha, the *Tao Te Ching* of Lao Tzu, the *Gathas* of Zoroaster, to name a few. As we have heard, what is common to the codes of morality in different societies is the Golden Rule – do unto others as you would have them do unto you. The moral law ultimately concerns love: the love of neighbor and God. Only in "leaving" our selves can we love and only in loving can we be united with God. Each moral law shapes and refines our capacity for love. Each such law molds our souls into vehicles of love.

- If we remain true to our most basic insights into ourselves, we will recognize the absolute and universal nature of principles that we know to be fundamental – thou shalt not murder for instance. We will come to see too that these are manifestations of the divine in everyday experience.

- The moral principles governing human societies did not arise from any evolutionary legacy because the animal kingdom is ruled by the law of kill or be killed. There is no compassion or altruism there. Yes, some have spoken of empathy shown by animals for their distressed fellows, say of one chimpanzee licking the wounds of another. This is certainly a reality. And it is equally true that not all animals are carnivorous. And some also use objects as tools. Just as there is autonomy of a kind in certain species so also there is rudimentary consciousness in many. But there is an unbridgeable gap between animals and humans as manifested most obviously in the conceptual reach given by language, the bond of family that is unique to humans, the first person perspective, the freedom of the will and the notions of worship and sacrifice. Also, there are clear instances of empathy in the animal world but these are a far cry from the imaginative and cognitional processes involved in human pity, sympathy and compassion. You can "feel" the pain of a friend who lost a mother or be distraught by a massacre in a far-away continent in a way that is not possible for non-human animals.

- Studies show that certain areas of the brain light up when a person is about to commit a given act. But this does not show that the act concerned, whether good or bad, is a result of such activity in these areas. On the contrary, it is your thought or your intention that causes the associated brain activity and not the other way round. Yes, dementia may cause the deadly sin of sloth but not all sloth can be traced to dementia.

- Can there be progress in morality? Yes, but not necessarily. Just as you make progress in your knowledge of the natural world as you refine your methodologies (with scientific theories and instruments), so also you make progress in your knowledge of the moral law when you refine your baser instincts and habits (slavery is now recognized as abominable). This does not mean that there is a change in the moral law. It simply means there has been an improvement in your ability to recognize and live by it. Then again, lack of sensitivity to the law inscribed in your heart can lead easily to regress and, on a larger scale, it leads to the contagious coarseness of the prevalent culture.

- Then there is the question of who is the arbiter of the moral law in this world. In principle, all its tenets should be obvious to all peoples. But there is a darkness in the human soul that all cultures and societies recognize to be real. They also recognized that only a transcendent source can help them return to the fullness of their humanity which also means returning to the fullness of the moral law.

LH: Oh please! The so-called moral laws are simply control structures created by the hucksters who call themselves priests and pastors. If there is one clear example of evil, it is the morality invented by religion.

The superstition of divine retribution illustrates the damage to the human psyche caused by the virus called Christianity. You have validated its virulence and the urgency of eliminating it as well as developing a vaccine to protect the general population from this deadly infection.

"THE HELLFIRE BRIEF"

Witness – Jose Mendoza (JM), Exorcist
Witness – Harold Montefiore (HM), NDE Survivor

MA: This is our final stop and appropriately we are addressing life's final destination. A key weapon in the Plaintiff's arsenal was the Christian revelation of the possibility of freely-chosen eternal separation from God. Hell. The Plaintiff's counsel and his witnesses were not interested in the far more significant unveiling of the universal invitation to Heaven, everlasting ecstasy in union with God. That luminous truth didn't help their case. So they steered us all to Hell because their sole focus has been on the negative. Ironically, they are literally guilty of being blind to the Gospel which means "Good news."

Hell is an inextricable element of the Christian message in a negative sense. It is inextricable in the same way that the idea of "good" must include the idea of the "absence of good" which is what we mean by evil. The idea of a freely-chosen Heaven, the true purpose of human life, carries with it the possibility of the free rejection of Heaven, i.e. Hell.

Strictly speaking we do not know if any human person is in Hell or how many will choose Hell. But we do know this: the highest of the angels and a multitude of other angels chose to enter into this state of eternal separation; it is possible for human beings to "choose" Hell while in this world; and several individuals who have had Near Death Experiences report the presence of humans in Hell.

Given this, we have an obligation to warn our fellow beings about the very real possibility of Hell and the urgent need to do all we can to avoid choosing this state. This is not emotional terrorism, as the Plaintiff alleges, but an act of compassion and mercy. If you see someone unwittingly plunging themselves into shark-infested waters, it would be an act of humanity to warn them of the danger in which they are placing themselves (the sharks in this example would not only be evil spirits but vices and weaknesses).

Jesus spoke of eternal life. But he also spoke of the possibility of eternal and total separation from God. There can be no getting around the fact that Jesus graphically warned us of Hell. *Matthew* 25 is the classic text.

What is entailed by Hell? The essential suffering of Hell lies in its separation from God and therefore the separation from everything that is required by human nature. Ultimately, the choice is between God and self. If we choose the self we are left with the self – and the self alone. And since our entire being is made for God, the suffering experienced by the self left to itself is the greatest imaginable – worse than unending hunger or thirst in a desolate wilderness or endless separation from one's loved ones. There is no sleep, no death, in eternity, no end to the state of insufferable suffering in which those who choose Hell place themselves.

Hell is the ultimate lockdown, an endless quarantine.

Where is Hell?

According to Peter Geach, since separated souls and lost angels "are *ex hypothesi* immaterial, no place can be straightforwardly ascribed to them; and their damnation is in any event a state not a place. As Mehistopheles said to Faustus's question 'How comes it then that thou art out of Hell?'; 'Why, this is Hell, nor am I out of it.'"[247]

---

247 Peter Geach, *Providence and Evil* (Cambridge: Cambridge University Press, 1977), 144.

This insight is well captured in a line from the movie *Lord of War*. The conscientious lawman is ultimately out-maneuvered by the ruthless and venal gunrunner. As the latter gloats in triumph, the lawman comments that he would like to say, "Go to Hell" but he does not have to because, as he says, "I think you're already there."

Bad Boys for Life has a similarly memorable insight into Hell. When one of the protagonists says, "I don't believe in hell," his colleague responds, "Well, it believes in you … that's a darkness that swallows you whole."

Even enemies of religion have taken Hell seriously. In a 1994 interview with *Paris Match*, Cuban ruler Fidel Castro said, "You know, I'll go to Hell, and I know the heat will be unbearable, but it will be less painful than having expected so much from Heaven, which never kept its promises. (…) And also, when I arrive, I will meet Marx, Engels, Lenin."[248]

Those who revel in brutality and butchery seem to relish the thought of going to Hell. Yevgeny Prigozhin, founder of the Wagner Group, said in a video shot just before his death, "We will all go to hell. But in hell, we will be the best."[249]

For the damned, writes Geach, "all love and joy and peace are things that were once, and were once going to be, but now will never be, never any more. For them, the Blessed and God's grace have disappeared from the world for ever. With no hope of death, they are left for ever with their own dreadful company."[250]

As I have repeatedly said, God does not wish anyone to go to Hell. God has created us for Heaven and will do everything in the realm of logical possibility to take us there. But happiness can only be enjoyed by free beings and not machines or puppets and Heaven is therefore a result of a free choice to love. But this freedom implies the equal possibility of saying "No" to

248 http://lanic.utexas.edu/project/castro/db/1994/19941027.html
249 *Wall Street Journal*, August 25, 2023.
250 Peter Geach, Op cit., 145.

love – which means that the very possibility of Heaven inescapably leads to the possibility of Hell. Love means Hell is possible. We cannot be rational creatures capable of true happiness if we were not free and we cannot be free without the option of withholding love.

In the end, everything is about love. We must love if we want to live with Love Itself. The great dramas of history inevitably pass away: nothing left, all glory gone. All that matters are souls, persons and what they have become. It is this that lasts FOREVER. No one can claim that we are condemned to eternal separation for an original sin that we did not commit. The Cross has taken away that barrier. We are offered the endless ecstasy of the Trinity. All life's sufferings pale before eternal joy. But here and now we must choose our own eternal destiny. We have to say Yes to Love: a Love that is self-giving, all-holy and everlasting.

There are two extremes in thinking about God. One is to think of God as some kind of super-human: this is the anthropomorphic misconception. The other is to think of him as an abstraction: this is the idea of God as an impersonal force. But the true God is revealed to us as the infinite Lover. This infinite Lover is experienced as Heaven or as Hell. We cannot have it any other way. These are not just the rules of the game. These are the only rules possible given what we mean by love.

Martin D'Arcy reminds us that "God is living and has personality and … for the full story of Heaven and Hell we have to bring out this essential clue. God cannot be inactive, and just because His infinite gratuitous love is so dynamic as to lift the good into a supernatural union with Himself …. it will have a pronounced and positive effect upon what is evil and opposed, shining through it like a fire … Where, however, there is unyielding resistance, that love must mean an excruciating pain to the recipient of it. … Love repelled can be called hate when the effect of that love produces pain because of the resistance to it."[251]

---

251 Martin D'Arcy, *Death and Life* (London: Longmans, Green & Co., 1942), 134-5.

The possibility of Hell is terrifying to those who recognize the seriousness of their moral choices and still choose evil. But the Plaintiff has taken the position that it is a superstition and has, on that basis, charged Christians with deliberately and culpably using it to cause emotional distress. So how do we show that Hell exists? Does anyone have empirical evidence for the existence of Hell?

We do. Our next two witnesses have encountered Hell, albeit each in different settings. The first is the Reverend Jose Mendoza, an exorcist who is called on to expel spirits from Hell, also called demons, that oppress or possess people on earth. The second is Mr. Harold Montefiore, the survivor of a Near Death Experience who was shown Hell. Fortunately for him, it was a round-trip visit! Neither of them is an academic. But they are expert witnesses when it comes to Hell because they have had personal encounters with "the Other Side".

After they have given their testimonies, I will invite the Plaintiff's counsel to cross-examine them. Rev. Mendoza, please take the stand and tell us what you know of Hell from personal experience.

Mendoza: I have agreed to share my testimony with you today because I strongly believe in the importance of sharing the reality of the spiritual war zone in which we live. There is more going on in your everyday life than most of you realize. My topic is the manifestation of Hell here on earth. I can testify to the existence of Hell not because I have been there but because I have met various of its inhabitants.

Many people wonder if there is such a thing as the Devil, reputedly the principal inhabitant of Hell. Psychiatrists say the Devil is only in the mind. Scientists and philosophers find the idea amusing. Theologians warn against a belief in mysticism and the supernatural.

I am here to tell you that the Devil does exist. I have met him.

Human history cannot be understood if we do not understand the role of the occult and the diabolic. Human life and history as a whole is replete with interventions of evil spirits. If we want to understand what is going on in human history, we have to realize that it is essentially a battle between good and evil and, in fact, it is Satan's assault on both God and humanity. Today this battle is waged in the media and social media, the entertainment industry, universities, and all professions.

Returning to the occult, the single greatest source of God's anger in Old Testament times is the worship of idols and strange deities. This is not because he is the "jealous Jehovah" but because this is enslavement to Satan and to demons. That path leads only to destruction and damnation. God's people are constantly seduced by the lure of idolatry. Also forbidden on pain of death is sorcery, magic and all forms of the occult.

If you look at the life and ministry of Christ, again you see the theme of diabolic intervention as when it is reported that Satan enters Judas. Jesus is constantly casting demons out of people. There are exchanges between the demons and Jesus. Jesus warns us frequently of Satan's interventions. Many modern scholars have either downplayed or dismissed these accounts of the demonic in the New Testament but this means ignoring what is obvious in the biblical texts.

A new light is shed on all this from the experience of those of us who are exorcists. If scientists offer us knowledge through empirical observation, philosophers through their application of human reason and theologians through the study of biblical passages and concepts, exorcists offers a new window of knowledge that comes from direct experience of evil and of personages from below.

The Devil is not what most people picture him to be. He is not some creature in red tights with horns. There is nothing funny about the Devil. In fact, he hates laughter, and that is one of my favorite weapons against him. The Devil is a spirit, a most powerful and intelligent spirit. But a vile and malicious spirit bent on destroying us all.

When I said I have met him, I meant this quite literally. We exorcists have an insight here that is not available to the psychiatrists and theologians. We actually encounter the Devil and his minions in their most fearsome form on earth – when they actually "possess" the soul and body of a human being. And we have the authority to make them reveal their secrets and plans. We are the scientists of the spiritual world because we have direct contact with what we are studying. We are not mere speculators like the philosophers.

You may ask, does the Devil really exist, and what is he doing here in our world? The Book of *Revelation* says the Devil and his demons have been sent here on earth. Their final destination is an everlasting abyss in which they are frozen out of contact with anyone else. But, until the Final Judgment, they are allowed to stay here distracting themselves from their miserable state by drawing human persons down with them. *Luke* tells us when Jesus drove the demons out of the possessed man, he sent them into a herd of swine because "they pleaded with him not to order them to depart to the abyss." So, they are here with us until the end of time. This is where they are "kept for judgment." And they are desperate. "Woe to you, earth and sea," says *Revelation* 12:12, "for the Devil has come to you in great fury, for he knows he has but a short time."

In our own exorcisms we find that the demons initially behave arrogantly telling us we cannot touch them. Then, as we start making progress, they get more desperate and violent – afraid of being sent to the final abyss. They start calling us killers and torturers. They only leave their victims because, as they tell us, the exorcism itself becomes more painful than Hell.

To those who think the Devil is an abstraction, I say, 'beware'. The diabolic is all around us. Movies, the Internet, music, your local bookstore, they all purvey the most dangerous vehicles of the occult. Right in their school-grounds, your children are introduced to séances, white magic, witchcraft, ouija boards, you name it. These are not harmless pastimes. They are sug-ar-coated poison pills – spiritual toxins – seducing you step by step into the clutches of an enemy that seeks your soul. I cannot tell you how many of the poor possessed souls I have exorcised were first enticed by these instruments of the Devil. At one time, the occult was reserved for eccentric characters at the fringes of society. I am afraid it's now part of the mainstream.

I know there are skeptics, those who believe that the Devil does not exist, or if he does, has no influence over our actions in this world. But I challenge those unbelievers to account for a little child suddenly having the strength of four men. Or being able to speak in exotic languages without knowing any of them before. Or showing encyclopedic knowledge without a formal education. Not all of this behavior can be explained as psychiatric disorders. Exorcists offer a new window of knowledge that comes from direct experience of evil and personalities from below. The Devil does indeed exist and has made his presence felt here in this world. And he will win the battle to bring down humanity with him, soul-by-soul, unless we recognize this fact and take action to stop him.

You should also know that many of the demons we have exorcised tell us that Hell was created by them, not by God, and that they would rather be in Hell than not exist.

MA: Thank you, Rev. Mendoza. Mr. Montefiore, I would like now to invite you to share your experience of Hell with us.

Montefiore: This is very painful for me but I agreed to share my testimony because I want everyone to know that there is another world of endless agony after death. We can avoid going there and that is why I want to sound this warning.

I am not an intellectual so I am just going to tell you what I was like before my experience, what I went through, what I witnessed and what it did to me.

In my life before death, I lived for three things: sex, drugs and alcohol. I was not consciously an atheist but I just did not like religious people and was turned off by religious rituals. I believed in all the right rights: abortion on demand, every possible sexual experiment, legalization of every narcotic. I made money every which way I could without any thought of whether it was moral or legal.

But there is one thing I remember from those days that makes more sense than I could have imagined. An underworld friend of mine told me that, in the old days, the Mafia had a procedure for knocking off rival gang members. They would wait until they found him (it was always a him) in bed with his mistress then take him out. Their chilling rationale was that this way they did not just kill him but sent him straight to Hell. At the time, I found it funny if only because I thought it strange that these cold-blooded killers believed in an after-life.

Little did I know!

Two years ago, I was driving down the highway when a car came right at us going the wrong way. Head-on collision. I died instantly. I say "died" because I felt myself leaving my body and seeing all the chaos below – the fire trucks, the ambulance, the twisted metal. I heard the medical personnel at the scene talking of me in the past tense although they were still attaching devices to my body to try to bring me back. If that did not work, the ambulance would take my body to the county morgue. Just then, I was suddenly transported from the scene of the accident to my parents' house. They were out of town. I saw them getting the phone call with news of my death, their shock, their uncontrollable grief. I wanted to go down and tell them I am OK but then again I felt a force pulling me away.

Of course, in the months following the accident, I have heard of people going through a tunnel and meeting a being of light who guides them through a life review. In my case, I felt I was tunneling through something but it felt more like being flushed down a toilet.

Suddenly, the temperature started getting hotter and hotter – thousands of degrees I would say – and the stink was unbearable but none of that was as bad as what I saw before me. It was an ocean of fire, like the Pacific Ocean and all the oceans of the world combined, with millions of beings in it shrieking and struggling. What I could literally feel coming from them was hatred and despair and rage and loneliness. These beings had claws and sharp teeth and looked like strange terrifying animals. But I could tell they were human beings. I was dismayed to recognize a few of my friends among them and they actually seemed angry to see me. I could also see that they were being tortured and abused by ferocious beings that were not human and that appeared to be powerful intelligences of some kind that I came to recognize later were demons.

It was then that I realized the force pulling me was a demon – a being that was terrifying but also strangely familiar. It seemed to embody all my worst vices: my promiscuity, my self-indulgence, all that was worst in me. I saw that it had been empowered, every time I used "Jesus" or "God" as a curse word; I was, in fact, placing a curse on myself every time I cursed. I saw right away that all the evil of my life was in some way connected to this being. Now these evils had taken a life of their own and were totally out of control. People talk about having guardian angels. This being seemed to be the demonic counterpart. It looked triumphant.

Then hundreds, perhaps thousands, of these creatures – demons and monster-humans – started tearing me apart, clawing at me, gnawing at my limbs, prodding my organs, squeezing my emotions. My pain seemed to energize them. It was the worst possible abuse I could imagine, psychic, physical, intellectual all at once. Even today I cannot bear to think about all they did let alone talk about it. It was as if I was their meal or a snack, something they would continue to feast on forever. They seemed to have been waiting for me, thirsting for me, lusting for me. It was a feeding frenzy. Like sharks being drawn by blood.

In the midst of this torture, my life flashed before me. It was as if I saw every second of my life and the ripple effect of all my actions. I could see the effects of my actions on other people, on the world. I could feel the pain I had caused and the damage I had done to the human race. There was a direct correlation between all this and my being where I was. This was where I was meant to be, given the life I led. I had chosen this.

At that point, I gave up. I knew I could never get out and this would never end.

It was then that I started crying, bawling my heart out. It had been years since I had any feeling but now I felt bitter remorse and regret. I also had the sense I had offended my Creator and saw how many times I had turned down what were actually his attempts to reach out to me. At that moment, something told me to pray to God. But I did not know any prayer. All I knew was that there was a reference to God in the Pledge of Allegiance so I started to recite it.

The instant they heard the name of God, my captors let go. But only for a moment. Enraged, they yelled at me saying they would hurt me even more if I did not stop uttering that name. I finally realized that I had something I could use to stop them and kept saying "God" until they seemed to melt away.

In the darkness I glimpsed a light that kept getting brighter until I saw that I was in front of someone who looked like all the images I had seen of Jesus. He was Love itself. I could see that he loved me despite my wretchedness, that he wanted me to be with him and that I was the one who had pushed him away. I knew that to be with him would be to be happy beyond all I could ask for. And I wanted to be with him.

He did not speak, but in my heart I heard him say: your time has not yet come. I am sending you back. Be a beacon of my love. Turn away from sin. Cherish life and marriage and family because this is how God becomes present in the world. Do not waste the time and talent God has given you.

Just at that moment, I felt piercing, agonizing pain. I felt myself back in my body. The people around me who saw me open my eyes appeared wonder-struck. Some device they had attached to me had kick-started me back into their midst. Instead of the morgue, they took me to a hospital.

And that's how I am here today.

I have given my story many times, often with groups of people who have had near-death experiences. What I found out is that a large number of those who have had NDEs have had what they call negative NDEs. Like me, they went to Hell. But most of them do not talk about their NDEs simply because it is personally embarrassing. In my case, I feel an obligation to warn the world that there is another kind of world awaiting us after we die and we need to live in a way that unites us with God instead of the other way round.

MA: Thank you, Mr. Montefiore. How moving. It is one thing to talk about the idea of Hell. It is quite another to actually go there and see it for yourself. Let us hope that none of us has to go through what you did.

Your Honor, Mr. Montefiore was the last of the witnesses for the Defense.

Judge: Counsel, you may cross-examine the witnesses.

LH: Thank you. I have heard more weirdness and wackiness in the last two testimonies than I ever expected to hear in a court of law. No court would admit any of what they said as evidence. I am hesitant about cross examining these witnesses because I do not want to lend any credibility to people who have none to begin with.

Your Honor, I move that the testimonies of the last two witnesses be struck from the record because they concern subjects that are not a matter of tangible evidence. And please instruct the jury to ignore all that they heard.

MA: Objection, Your Honor. Keep in mind that the Plaintiff is suing my Client who is not tangible although Plaintiff's Counsel claims at the same time not to believe in my Client's existence. But he is nevertheless suing my Client. What is sauce for the goose is sauce for the gander. I move that my witnesses' testimonies be retained but we have no objection to the Plaintiff's counsel not cross-examining them. In fact, we welcome that.

Judge: Objection sustained. Counsel, you do not have to cross-examine the witnesses, but their testimonies will remain a part of the record.

LH: I am disappointed, Your Honor. Despite the obvious vacuity of their testimonies, I have no choice but to cross-examine the witnesses because the jury has been exposed to this nonsense.

I request Mr. Mendoza to please take the stand.

Mr. Mendoza, your kind of thinking has no place in the 21st century. We do not burn witches anymore. Your obsession with the dark arts is an invitation to return to the dark ages. What you call exorcism is simply a pre-scientific attempt to deal with a medical condition called dissociative identity disorder and other disorders of the nervous system including schizophrenia, and the recently popular Tourette syndrome. Dissociative identity disorder has many of the symptoms you people call possession. One or more identities or personality states that are entirely distinct from each other take control of the patient's behavior and speech patterns. Patients may roll their eyes in strange ways or have apparent seizures. Bodily symptoms can include wounds suddenly appearing on the patient. These patients sometimes show extraordinary abilities such as apparently reading people's thoughts or causing observers to feel cold. The main cause for this condition is usually severe childhood abuse.

Then there is schizophrenia which causes delusions and catatonic behavior. These delusions include the idea that a demon is speaking through the patient and that religious objects will cause harm. Facial and other bodily contortions are common. Schizophrenia and other psychoses are caused by malfunctioning of the dopamine system in the brain. Bipolar disorders are the main cause of the apparent superhuman strength shown by some subjects. Tourette syndrome, caused by another brain malfunction, results in such behavior as shouting obscenities and can also be treated medically.

For all these reasons, scientists call exorcism what it is: quackery, but dangerous quackery. We all know about child abuse among the clergy.

Exorcism is a far more insidious form of abuse. Many patients owe their conditions in adolescence and adulthood to abuse in their earliest years. They can only be helped with pharmacological treatment and counseling. The ritual of exorcism is very destructive for them and exacerbates their suffering. You are dealing with highly traumatized people who've been terribly abused. They are very vulnerable. When you confront them with an exorcist and his high-pressure tactics, you re-awaken memories of childhood horror and create in their minds the idea that they are possessed by some evil external force.

These patients need to be treated by competent doctors, not by self-appointed witch-hunters.

Mendoza: I did not come here for a debate. Our Lord said, "Don't throw pearls to swine." I am a witness to this other world. I have looked into the eyes of the possessed. I have seen the demonic. No, this is not some creation of the victim's psyche. There was another intelligence, another being, sometimes more than one, at work in the victim's soul tearing it apart. What you seem to be unaware of is that modern medicine does not claim to explain or even understand major symptoms associated with possession.

Undoubtedly, there are personality disorders that can be treated with drugs and counseling. But we must be reminded that there is no consensus among the specialists about the actual causes of dissociative identity disorder. Anyway, these or other brain disorders are not the issue.

The subjects of exorcism exhibit such behavior as levitation, knowledge of languages to which they had no previous access, penetration into the thoughts of observers. No respectable scientific theory can explain how a person can be suspended in thin air because this defies known scientific law. No number of changes to the brain can cause a person to levitate in the air. Neither is there any scientific explanation for children suddenly speaking in languages they have never heard before or reading the thoughts of the people around them. For that matter, there is no explanation for the measurable reduction in temperature observed during exorcisms.

These are all hard data. To say that the data are associated with one physical malady or another is simply a higher form of superstition. You are simply slapping a label on these data and calling it X without any evidence for your assumption and no idea how the X got there.

You are obviously not aware of the video of an actual exorcism made by William Friedkin, the director of the movie, *The Exorcist*. He showed the video to some of the leading neurosurgeons and psychiatrists in the US, expecting them to explain it with their scientific tools. The neurosurgeons had no explanation for the possessed party's behavior and said it was not a condition they could treat with surgery. Unexpectedly, the psychiatrists did not diagnose it as a known psychosomatic disorder. One of them said the person being exorcised in the video is suffering from a pathology that psychiatrists call possession, the cause of which is unknown.

LH: This is what I was afraid of. You are trying to gain credibility by preying on peoples' ignorance with your mumbo jumbo straight out of medieval sorcery. It is obvious we need to update our current laws to stop this nonsense. That and a few lawsuits will put you exorcists out of business. I will be reporting you to the authorities once this affair is over.

Mendoza: It is obvious that you are motivated by nothing but malice. You want to remove the only remedy that can alleviate the suffering of those who are in the clutches of Satan and his minions. The only weapon I have to stop you is prayer and this is my prayer of deliverance over you:

> "Almighty Lord, Word of God the Father, Jesus Christ, God and Lord of all creation; who gave to your holy apostles the power to tramp underfoot serpents and scorpions; who along with the other mandates to work miracles was pleased to grant them the authority to say: "Depart, you devils!" and by whose might Satan was made to fall from heaven like lightning; I humbly call on your holy name in fear

and trembling, asking that you grant me, your unworthy servant, pardon for all my sins, steadfast faith, and the power – supported by your mighty arm – to confront with confidence and resolution this cruel demon. I ask this through you, Jesus Christ, our Lord and God, who are coming to judge both the living and the dead and the world by fire."

LH: Your Honor, this is an outrage. I ask that this last statement from the witness be struck from the record.

Judge: Sustained. Reverend Mendoza please step down. The next witness please take the stand.

LH: Mr. Montefiore, are you aware that your whole illusion of going to Hell was caused by a lack of oxygen to the brain? All this NDE business is stuff happening in the brain. When you are dying, your brain plays tricks on you. It is calling the Dying Brain syndrome.

Montefiore: NDE is a new world to me. But I have been learning a lot about it from meeting other NDE survivors and going to these meetings of the International Association for Near Death Experience Studies. Did you know that that there are over 10 million documented cases of NDEs? Or that numerous doctors have published studies on their work with thousands of patients who have had NDEs? The doctors themselves have said that these experiences are real.

Normally, if you come out of oxygen deprivation or cardiac arrest, you are disoriented and confused and very little of what you say makes sense. But those who have had NDEs are lucid no matter how bad their physical condition. And their subsequent lives are transformed as a result of their experience.

Congenitally blind people and children have had NDEs and have reported the same kinds of experiences as others. In one case, two soldiers who clinically died at the same time of a bomb blast left their bodies together. Both were resuscitated and reported the same experiences including seeing each other leaving their bodies. This is why the doctors say NDEs are real.

LH: All of what you said fits in with the Dying Brain syndrome. Like it or not, everything reported would appear the way you describe it even if it is just stuff happening in the brain. Which is all it is.

Montefiore: You might be interested to know that *The Annals of the New York Academy of Sciences* reported in February 2022 that "Scientific advances in the 20th and 21st centuries have led to a major evolution in the understanding of death. (…) A multidisciplinary team of national and international leaders (…) examined the accumulated scientific evidence to date." Their report "represents the first-ever, peer-reviewed consensus statement for the scientific study of recalled experiences surrounding death. Among their conclusions:

- Due to advances in resuscitation and critical care medicine, many people have survived encounters with death or being near-death. These people — who are estimated to comprise hundreds of millions of people around the world based on previous population studies — have consistently described recalled experiences surrounding death, which involve a unique set of mental recollections with universal themes.

- *The recalled experiences surrounding death are not consistent with hallucinations, illusions or psychedelic drug induced experiences*, according to several previously published studies. Instead, they follow a specific narrative arc involving a perception of: (a) separation from the body with a heightened, vast sense of consciousness and recognition of death; (b) travel to a destination; (c) a meaningful and purposeful review of life, involving a critical analysis of all actions, intentions and thoughts towards others."[252]

---

252 https://nyaspubs.onlinelibrary.wiley.com/doi/10.1111/nyas.14740

The authors included scientists from New York University, Harvard and the University of California.

On a personal note, I should tell you that my experience could not have been dying-brain-induced. I was transported hundreds of miles away to my parents' home, where I saw all they were doing while my body was being prepared for transport to the morgue. They later confirmed what I told them. How could the dying brain enable you to travel far away?

LH: That is just anecdotal. Why should I believe you?

Montefiore: You do not have to believe me. But many other NDErs have reported similar experiences of seeing things that were happening far away while they were out of their bodies.

LH: Belief in an after-life is simply wish-fulfillment.

Montefiore: That can cut both ways. Denial of the after-life can be seen as a fear-fulfillment. Or maybe you deny the after-life because you are terrified of Hell.

I am just curious. Why are you so resistant to at least considering that my experience might be real? Is it because you are afraid of going to Hell and so do not want to even entertain it as a possibility? Let me tell you, if you entrust yourself to Jesus, you have nothing to worry about.

LH: What imbecility! Remember, you have no academic background, no scientific training. You are just a blue collar lowlife who had a brain injury and got your fifteen seconds of fame because of a story you created.

Montefiore: I know what I saw. If you do not want to accept it, that is your business. I love you no matter how angry you might be. This is what I learned on the other side. Love everybody and everything will be alright.

LH: Talking of love, you obviously ended up being brainwashed by the Christian Fundamentalists. Did it ever occur to you that it is impossible to believe in their claim of a god of love if this same god is condemning millions of people to eternal suffering? If what you say were indeed true, you of all people should know that there cannot be a loving god of any kind.

Montefiore: This is a difficult question. I know what I saw. I saw many many people suffering in this terrible state of being and I knew that there was no way out for them. How could that be possible? But it is a reality that we must deal with. I wish it were not the case, but it is an existential fact. We better live in its light if we want to do what is best for us. Yet, I also know that the God I experienced is infinitely loving and desperately wants us all to love him and be with him. Desperately. But our fate is in our hands. God has no obligation to take us to Heaven but he still wants to do this. Yet, he cannot force us. This I saw in my own case. I wanted to just do my own thing no matter what the consequences and no one could stop me. This is the problem. God does not want us to choose Hell but ultimately the decision is in our hands. And the time is short.

LH: Please step down. This discussion is pointless. There is no "other side." There is no hell other than the hell on earth created by those who believe in a hell hereafter.

CLOSING STATEMENT –
PLAINTIFF'S ATTORNEY

Your Honor, Ladies and Gentlemen of the Jury!

Here we are now.

As you have seen, every one of our original charges have not only been vindicated but verified beyond any reasonable doubt. The Defendant's counsel himself is our strongest witness.

In a display of the very arrogance that led to this lawsuit, the Defendant's counsel proudly proclaimed that the god he supposedly defends is not good or moral. What more do we need to prove? Of course, he dressed up this absurdity in more gobbledygook saying that his deity somehow lies beyond good and evil. In the most charitable reading, that means the deity is an irrelevant abstraction. In the normal reading, it means the deity is unconcerned about human pain and suffering because it has more important things to do. Animal violence and pain are of no consequence to this imperious potentate. The spectacle of humans killing each other does not move him to take any preventive action. Instead, the Old Testament shows him directing the killing. The New Testament does one better and promises eternal suffering for his creatures. Remember too that since he is the creator of everything, he is also the creator of evil. The Christian deity is an evil deity responsible for all evil.

Tragically, sociopathic beliefs such as this affect the behavior of those who cling to them – even if the object of belief is imaginary as is the case with the Christian deity. Just as the antisemitism of Christianity led directly to the Holocaust, Christians' belief in an evil deity is directly responsible for their savagery throughout the history of their religion.

As you have seen, the Defendant did not deny the charges we brought against the institutional practices and deeds of the Christian religion: the Inquisition and the crusades; the killing of so-called witches; the persecution and often murder of the pioneers of modern science with Galileo being just one example; slavery; racism; patriarchal oppression; repression of reproductive rights; and so much more. Neither did the Defendant deny their allegiance to the genocide-ordering god of the Old Testament and admitted in fact that this deity is the same as the deity of the Christians.

Even worse, the Defendant not only did not deny their savage doctrine of Hell but desperately tried to defend it. This horrendous creation of sadistic minds has traumatized millions and is directly responsible for multiple psychiatric conditions, suicides and homicides.

When you think of anyone promoting such a debilitating idea as this, it is hard to keep your composure. No civilized society can tolerate the propagation of ideas that call for destroying its citizens. Remember how antisemitism went from being a popular idea to the ovens of Dachau and Auschwitz. The Defendant not only tried to push their repulsive doctrine down our throats but had the gall to inflict on the jury the testimony of two mentally disturbed Hell-promoters. If nothing else, this final display was a powerful illustration of the mortal threat they pose to society.

In sum, the Defendant not only did not deny our charges but brandished them as virtues that they proudly stood behind. What more is there to be said?

As you will remember, in our opening statement we asked the Court to ban propagation and practice of the Christian religion and for Christian churches to pay reparations to their victims for their past and current actions. To this end, we request the Court institute this ban effective immediately and instruct all Christian churches to turn over all their assets as reparations for their victims. These reparations would serve as compensatory and punitive damages for Christianity's crimes against humanity. The reparations cannot reverse the tragedies of the past but they will bring to an end the cycle of death and destruction, pain and suffering that entered this world with the birth of Christianity.

Ladies and Gentlemen of the jury, you have a chance now to change the course of human history, to end the greatest barrier to the well-being of humanity, and to inaugurate a new era of unparalleled peace and prosperity, health and happiness. Generations to come will thank you for your courage and vision.

CLOSING STATEMENT – DEFENDANT'S ATTORNEY

MA: Your Honor, Ladies and Gentlemen of the jury.

I am bewildered but not surprised by my opponent's closing statement. I am not surprised because his approach throughout has been one of hurling invective without offering serious or sufficient evidence and without deigning to address the fatal flaws I exposed in his position. In contrast, we have offered comprehensive bodies of evidence for our rebuttals and assertions, whereas he has chosen to ignore these and simply repeated his initial charges pretending that nothing more had transpired. He has repeated this same procedure in his closing statement. But abuse certainly cannot serve as an argument and in a proceeding of this magnitude this cavalier approach is a travesty of the legal process. His attitude and actions demand that he be held in contempt of court.

Fortunately, our objective was not to play games with the Plaintiff but to present to you, the jury, the truth, the whole truth and nothing but the truth.

In a case of this kind, the burden of proof is on the Plaintiff to provide a preponderance of the evidence in support of their claim. We submit that the Plaintiff's counsel has, in fact, provided no evidence whatsoever to support their claim and has simply ignored the overwhelming evidence supporting the veracity of our counter-claim.

My Client is innocent of all his slanderous charges and demonstrably so.

We have responded to every one of the Plaintiff's charges head-on and have not tried to evade even the most egregious and nebulous of their claims. Nothing stuck.

We have shown that, in cynical pursuit of their goals, the Plaintiff's counsel and his witnesses have invented their own version of a deity and projected it as the Christian God. In fact, their deity has no resemblance to the infinitely loving God revealed in and through Jesus.

Order, Autonomy and Infinite Love

Theirs is a clockwork deity who controls everything that happens in the universe, a master puppeteer. Of course, such a deity would be responsible for everything that exists including evil.

In contrast, the God revealed in the Old Testament – and definitively in Jesus of Nazareth and the New Testament – created us out of love in order to invite us to everlasting union with him. But the invitation had to be accepted and both testaments tell us of a Lover in pursuit of the faithless beloved.

Love is possible only if it is free. And the entire universe is testimony to the fact that the Creator is not a puppeteer. As we have shown, there is a fine balance between order and autonomy in nature which comes to a climax in rational, free creatures, both in the angelic and the human realms. Love is possible if it is freely chosen. We must choose to love God if we wish to be with him forever and the platform where this choice takes place exists here and now, in this world, in history.

In the case of humans, although the choice made by our first parents was negative, so great was the love of God that he took on a human nature to rescue us. The rescue meant that God incarnate had to suffer and die for our redemption as a consequence of our own sinfulness.

In *Genesis*, we see a God who hates violence and killing and seeks to draw us away from our own self-destructive evil. In *Exodus* and other books that talk about wiping out the enemy in their entirety, it is clear from the text itself that these passages were not intended by their authors to be taken literally but were formulaic rhetorical exaggerations for effect that were standard in those times. This is indisputable because, later in the text, the enemies who were supposedly entirely wiped out, re-appear and continue to live in their lands. The laws of *Deuteronomy* were temporary provisions instituted by Moses that conformed to the hardness of heart of the Israelites.

Of course, the Old Testament condemns the demonic as exemplified by occultism, idolatry and polytheism and warns of their fatal consequences. In the New Testament, Jesus' warnings of Satan and Hell were what we would expect from a loving God seeking to save us from self-destruction. He showed his love for us supremely by his own death on the cross, which he offered up willingly for our redemption.

The death and resurrection of Jesus is the greatest manifestation of God's love for each and every human person. And in Jesus, we came to see that the Godhead is a Relationship – a tri-personal Relationship of love. Love was not something incidental or peripheral but fundamental, the Alpha and the Omega.

Once we recognize the nature of the Triune God, we realize why there is pain and evil and suffering in the world. The non-human natural world in all its splendor involves a dynamism of interacting autonomous agents of all kinds that are precursors to a New Heaven and a New Earth where all of creation will thrive in harmony. But all moral evil in the world comes from us: it is an exercise of our negative power to say "No" to God. God does all in his power to get us to Yes but ultimately only we can give our selves to him. There is no love without self-giving and self-giving is by its very nature a giving of the self by the self. Eternal separation from God and the resultant suffering is self-chosen as the demons themselves have testified.

Even those who become Christians remain free to say "Yes" or "No" to God in their lives. As a result, there are Christians who have committed great evils in history. We do not deny this. That is quite obviously not the fault of the Christian faith which prohibits such acts but of the individual Christians who choose to go against their faith.

Since God is the infinite plenitude of perfections it is obvious that all that is good is a reflection of the Absolute Good that is the Godhead. To attempt to judge God by determining if he conforms to a moral standard is as silly as trying to determine if the moral law conforms to moral standards. God is the moral law. God is the ultimate moral standard.

Contrary to the Plaintiff's argument, we are not saying that God is beyond goodness and morality. *God IS goodness and morality.*

Infinite-eternal Mind

We should note also that, barring snide remarks, the Plaintiff had no satisfactory response to the overwhelming evidence we have adduced both for the existence of the infinite Mind who created the universe and for his ultimate self-revelation in Jesus of Nazareth.

The Plaintiff's counsel and his witnesses have repeatedly said they want to stay with what is ordinary, normal, and natural eschewing anything that is "extra"-ordinary. They saw no reason to go beyond what is available through the senses and quantifiable by science.

This way of thinking illustrates one of their fundamental errors. Nothing is normal. Nothing is natural. The fact that anything at all exists, the fact there are sensory channels, laws of Nature and structures and processes of various kinds – these are all utterly extraordinary and entirely inexplicable on their own terms. Possibility and probability have no applicability here. Nothing is possible if something is not actual. We then ask what is the Source of what is actual.

How is it that anything exists, how is it that it follows specific laws, how is agency possible? No scientist or philosopher has the faintest idea. To point to a multiverse or gravity creating a physical universe or an endless cycle of big bangs or the Landscape solves NOTHING. We want to know how it is that ANYTHING exists. The answer is that things exist only because there exists One who cannot not-exist, who exists without beginning or end or any conceivable limitation.

Furthermore, the most obvious reality in our experience is the fact that we are conscious, thinking, unitary beings (selfs). The inescapable explanation for this reality is its derivation from an infinite-eternal Mind. The Plaintiff's counsel could not dispute this explanation without contradicting himself and so chose to evade.

Next, the extraordinary transformation of eleven peasants and fishermen in first century Galilee in the face of the most powerful empire of the time and the unprecedented personal encounters of millions of people over the last 2000 years and today with the Jesus of the New Testament can only be explained in terms of his resurrection from the dead and his presence with us here-and-now.

The universal testimony of the human race to a Triune God, to the redemptive death of God incarnate and to the existence of a hereafter coincides with and culminates in the revelation of Jesus, the human locus of the divine.

Consciousness, thought and the self are real. The Jesus Cloud is real. The Trinity is the Ultimate Reality.

Christianity and the Creation of the Modern World

We have tried to show too that it is the Christian revelation that stands behind the "success" of the modern world in many realms.

- First, there is higher-order abstraction which is a direct product of monotheism. Even Sigmund Freud acknowledged that the higher-order abstraction required in modern thought (think of physics, mathematics, et al) was possible because the Jews had to believe in a God who could not be seen and who it was prohibited to represent physically. As a result of the Ten Commandments' "compulsion to worship a God whom one cannot see," Freud points out that in Judaism "a sensory perception was given second place to what may be called an abstract idea — a triumph of intellectuality over sensuality." (*Moses and*

Monotheism). Monotheism thus resulted in an "advance in intellectuality" which bore fruit in later mathematics and science that relied heavily on abstraction.

- Secondly, the truths of divine revelation elevated the mental capabilities of those who formulated the associated doctrines and resulted in intellectual breakthroughs for humanity as a whole. Peter Geach writes, "If what is claimed for the Christian mysteries is true, then knowledge of them ought to advance our understanding of other things, just as the sun, too bright to gaze upon, illumines all other things we see. And just this, it may be argued, is what we do find. ... Our concept of a person was forged by the theological controversies about the Trinity; and this term, for which there is no equivalent in Plato or Aristotle, was defined in the context of those very controversies by Boethius, as 'an individual substance of rational nature.' Again, the natural science of the Greeks was fatally held up by their way of regarding intensive magnitudes, like temperature, as due to some sort of mixture of opposites, say heat and cold. Our concept of intensive magnitude was worked out first not for the exigencies of physics but for those of theology; greater grace, or greater charity, had to be explained in terms of more of the same quality, which could vary continuously upwards or downwards without any admixture of an opposite. (...) We may not realise how paradoxical this idea of intension and remission of forms must once have seemed; change simply in respect of a quality, not from one species of a quality to another; and this quality remains the same and yet changes! The Church needed this concept to defeat the Manichees; but once achieved, the concept could be used to think e.g. about intension and remission of velocity; and from medieval speculations about that we can trace a continuous chain to the thought of Galileo and on to the giant growth of modern science. How impossible electrical and thermodynamic and gravitational theories would be if we were still fossicking around with ideas of warring opposites! I could give many other illustrations. (…) I think therefore that a very good case could be made out for the thesis that the mind of Western man has been illumined and strengthened by the intellectual work of elucidating the mysteries of faith."[253]

- Third, there is modern science as a whole. Stanley Jaki lists four reasons (as pointed out earlier) for holding that it was the Christian intellectual matrix that gave birth to modern science: (a) the Creator was truly transcendental and therefore nature was independent and had its autonomous laws (b) the doctrine of *creatio ex nihilo* made it clear that the physical universe and all material objects belonged to the level of creatures and were not semi-divine and the laws of Nature applied to heavenly and earthly bodies (c) the human person was made in the image of God and could therefore understand the rationality inherent in nature (d) the experimental method came out of the Christian matrix because as a mere creation nature had to be taken on its own terms.

Finally, we want you to consider the implications of all that you heard: Only Jesus can heal the wounds suffered by the human family. Only Jesus can draw us to the eternal destiny of union with the Creator for which we were created.

On the terrestrial plane, Christianity has given humankind its new understanding of the uniqueness and dignity of the human person. It is the Christian intellectual and cultural matrix that bore fruit in modern science, the modern university, the hospital and love for the poor and the suffering.

Slurs and Facts

---

253 Peter Geach, *The Virtues* (Cambridge, UK: Cambridge University Press, 1977), 41-3.

The Plaintiff's charge that Christian antisemitism led to the Holocaust has been rejected by Jewish scholars among others. In an article titled, "No Hitler, No Holocaust," Jewish sociographer Milton Himmelfarb concluded:

- "Hitler made the Holocaust because he wanted to make it. Anti-Semitism did not make him make it.

- Hitler was ex-Christian and anti-Christian.

- There was much and there remains some Christian anti-Semitism. Hitler's anti-Semitism was anti-Christian.

- Marxist anti-Semitism also is anti-Christian.

- Anti-Christian anti-Semitism is descended ideologically from pagan disdain for Judaism and the Jews, and emotionally from Christian hatred of Judaism and the Jews.

- In Hitler's time the world capital of anti-Semitism was Berlin. Since then it has been Moscow.

- Jews now have more to fear from anti-Christians than from Christians, and from the Christian Left than from the Christian Right."[254]

Today, antisemitism is especially prevalent in anti-Christian progressive circles.

Christians, as I said, are not always faithful to the teaching of Jesus but when the restraints of the Christian matrix are removed, we end up with the monstrous killing machines produced by the Enlightenment. Without an infrastructure of moral absolutes, we will be creatures of the Void driven only by the Will to Power.

The World to Come

---

254 https://www.commentary.org/articles/milton-himmelfarb-2/no-hitler-no-holocaust/

So, is this the best possible world? I said in my opening statement that it is the only possible world if autonomous agents and free rational creatures are part of the equation. And, as James Ross pointed out, "With respect to created things, all possibility with content is the product of divine creative election, not something antecedent or independent. ... 'Being,' actuality without qualification, is explanatorily prior to 'possibility,' not the reverse."[255]

But it is truly the best possible world since it became a platform for the incarnation of God in creation and, thereafter, its redemption and glorification.

By his death, Jesus overcame the destructive power of sin. By his own resurrection, he redeemed all creation and set all of history on the path of the indwelling of the divine Spirit that will culminate in the glorification of the universe in its entirety. There is no going back, no return to the age before the incarnation of God in Christ. Battles there will be and some will leave the Kingdom of the Most High and enter the outer darkness but, in the end, there will be a new heaven and a new earth.

> "Then I saw a new heaven and a new earth. The former heaven and the former earth had passed away." (*Revelation* 21:1)

> "Creation itself would be set free from slavery to corruption and share in the glorious freedom of the children of God. We know that all creation is groaning in labor pains even until now." (*Romans* 8:21-22)

> "In all wisdom and insight, he has made known to us the mystery of his will in accord with his favor that he set forth in him as a plan for the fullness of times, to sum up all things in Christ, in heaven and on earth." (*Ephesians* 1:8-10)

---

255 James Ross, *Thought and World* (Notre Dame, Indiana: University of Notre Dame Press, 2008), 34.

"I heard a loud voice from the throne saying, "Behold, God's dwelling is with the human race. He will dwell with them and they will be his people and God himself will always be with them [as their God]. He will wipe every tear from their eyes, and there shall be no more death or mourning, wailing or pain, [for] the old order has passed away." The one who sat on the throne said, "Behold, I make all things new."" (*Revelation 21:3-5*)

God is Creator; the universe is his creation and is therefore good in itself; the end of the reign of sin over creation began with the death of Jesus; sin itself will cease to have any place in God's creation on "the last day" when all creatures face the final judgment; we will once again be body and soul but this time with a glorified body and a purified soul; the world as we know it will be transformed, liberated from the effects of sin and powered by the life of God.

How will the world be physically different in this new state?

This we can say: the attributes of the Risen Body of Jesus are a reliable model for the attributes enjoyed both by our own resurrected bodies and in some sense of the "risen" universe; the transformation of matter that began with the incarnation of God in creation reaches its culmination in the New World and we can expect a union of the physical and the spiritual to form a universe filled with the divine Life; the everlasting joy that we will find in the Vision of the infinite-eternal Lover is tailored to our own humanness and, since to be human is to be physical and spiritual, our eternal union with God will involve the physical and spiritual dimensions of our being.

A wake-up call

One final word. Let me point out a hard fact that shows the utmost urgency of our deliberations here. Our academic pundits, entertainment icons, government structures, social media networks, media platforms and the Plaintiff have blinded us to an essential truth that is as obvious as it is ignored. *Each of us lives on the brink of oblivion.*

Close your eyes for an instant. Imagine that you have died. In the darkness of that moment, you realize how transient and temporary is the world in which you grew up – its historical events and current politics, its social structures and cultural achievements, its celebrities and fads, your awards and accomplishments, your dearest friends and loving families. As far as you are concerned, they are all gone, instantly and totally, when you die. And you will most certainly die as will all those who made and make up the world. And that one moment with your eyes closed may help you see what you cannot see when they are open: our life on earth lasts for a ephemeral nanosecond and everything about it disappears without a trace before you know it.

Now let me ask you this. Have any of you ever heard anything about this fundamental fact from any of your reliable mainstream data sources, the talking heads, the prophets of "cool" or the Plaintiff? They ignore and evade this most important and obvious truth. Why? Because it exposes the darkest despair lurking in the atheism they profess and purvey.

From the atheist standpoint, human history is a momentary, forever forgotten flicker in the all-enveloping, never-ending darkness of "death's dateless night." Countries, cultures, empires are just accidents of geography and history which, for all their pomposity, strut into a void without end.

And yet the intellectual and cultural elites say not a word about the imminence of oblivion.

It gets worse. The elites hide not just the bad news but also the good news. Jesus did not come to issue do's and don'ts but to proclaim a call to constant joy. For this is what is offered us by God if we choose to live in communion with him: We are to have FOREVER. In the most fantastic, and yet the most realistic, of fairy tales, we are to "live happily ever after." Mere reflection on this tremendous truth will change our perspectives, attitudes, views, totally. If we know that, with the passing of the nanosecond (namely, our life on earth), we will enjoy eternal ecstasy, we cannot but be joyful during that nanosecond.

But the decision to live in communion with God must be made here-and-now. It is too late after death.

Jesus, along with the major pre-Christian religions, tells us that we have the option to refuse communion with God. And this is a choice we make with the kind of lives we lead. To reject the laws of God is to reject God and to reject God is to choose eternal misery. Hell. This we know from the universal testimony of the human race as recorded in the world religions. In the modern era, many Near Death Experience survivors testify to their own encounter with the terror and despair of the darkness that is Hell. Endless suffering. Horrendous and unthinkable – but an option that any one of us can choose for ourselves. On the other hand, by turning to God incarnate, Jesus, we are granted everlasting joy.

In the light of all this, we see that the Plaintiff's message of moral nihilism, the rejection of the moral order and the embrace of intrinsic evils, is a path to eternal death and destruction.

It is not simply that mainstream information sources ignore the reality of our imminent death. They also cause unutterably more damage by blinding us to the possibility of Hell, of our choosing everlasting suffering. It is suffering we bring on ourselves by living the kind of life promoted and celebrated by the Plaintiff. If we try to live as gods we will lose God. And if we lose God, we lose all that our nature needs – forever!

By Hell we mean as total a separation from God as Heaven is the most total possible union with him. "These will pay the penalty of eternal ruin, separated from the presence of the Lord and from the glory of his power," (2 *Thessalonians* 1:9) God is the greatest need of human nature and total separation from him – a separation unmitigated by sleep or death – causes us the greatest possible suffering. Forever!

It is a numbing thought that we need to keep in mind in every waking moment. Our choices in our one nanosecond between womb and tomb determine our destiny for all eternity. Ruthless rulers and amoral tycoons, drug-addled celebrities and worldly clerics, cannot save us. They come and go: some live for riches, some are power-seekers, some are lost in sin. None of them can save us. Only Christ can. May we let him lead us to make choices that lead to union with God. So, I implore you all to turn to the Truth taught by Jesus, to follow his Way and to live with his Life. Let us answer "Yes" to his call to constant joy!

OUR Father

To follow Jesus is to embrace the revolution he proclaimed: "The hour is coming, and is now here, when true worshipers will worship the Father in Spirit and truth." (*John* 4:23)

Jesus revealed to us that there is a Creator of all things, that this Creator, God, is "our" Father, that the purpose of life is to become children of the Father, our hearts one with the divine Heart, and that we are called to live from this moment forward in the Kingdom of the Father, GodSpace.

Jesus' whole identity and mission centered on the Father. He addressed God only as Father. The Father is "father" because Jesus as Word is his infinite-eternal Son. And the Love between Father and Son is such that it bears fruit as Another, the Holy Spirit.

As I said in the beginning, the Father revealed by Jesus was:

- prodigal in his limitless love, all Heart,
- more intimate than any earthly parent and therefore called *Abba* (the affectionate Aramaic expression for one's own father) and, above all,
- "our" Father meeting all our needs, all the time, and drawing us into GodSpace, the protection and provision of his Providence.

Henceforth, we cannot see God except as the Father who makes us his children through his Son and in his Holy Spirit. God 2.0. God *as* Heart. The Father is infinite perfection, majestic beyond comprehension, and yet he is infinitely intimate, inconceivably more intimate than even the most affectionate of our expressions – be it "daddy" or "father" – can convey.

I am sorry to say that, even among Christians, two millennia later, this infinitely loving Father and the treasure-house he bequeaths us remain a secret! Among Christians we hear about Jesus and the Holy Spirit but very little about the Father who "so loved" us as to send his Son and his Spirit for our salvation and sanctification.

By his death and resurrection, Jesus made the perfect sacrifice and removed the barrier to our union with God. Through the waters of baptism, we are invited to be re-invented as a new race: redeemed by the Son, filled with the Spirit and thereby children of the Father in the fullest sense who will live "happily ever after."

Christianity may be thought of as unbelievable in two different respects.

First, it seems simply unbelievable that what it says can be true – that we are to live forever, that we have the opportunity to enter into endless joy in union with our loved ones and our Creator. Too unbelievably good to be true.

But then you think about the nature of the Christian revelation. It is the revelation of the truth about things received from the One who created all that exists from nothingness, who keeps trillions of galaxies in being, the One who is the here-and-now Source of our consciousness and thought and self-hood and who exists without beginning or end.

Certainly, this infinite-eternal, omnipotent, omniscient Transcendent/ Immanent Ultimate Reality is capable of bringing about what has been revealed. And we know this revelation to be true from our coming to see that the Godhead was incarnate in Jesus of Nazareth, the overpowering phenomenon of unconditional Love that continues to manifest itself across the world and in our own lives.

Which leads us to the second level of unbelievability. Christianity is unbelievably exciting. We have only to say "Yes" and we will inherit the Kingdom prepared for us from the foundation of the world. We will live happily ever after in this Promised Land prepared for us by our infinitely loving Father who stands right here, right now, waiting for us to rush to him so that he can embrace us and lead us into everlasting ecstasy. Let us neither tarry nor turn back. Let us close our eyes and say, "Thy will be done!"

Finale

In conclusion, Ladies and Gentlemen of the Jury, we request you to dismiss this lawsuit with prejudice and levy a penalty fee on the Plaintiff to cover all court costs for this deliberate and utterly wasteful exercise in frivolity.

Thank you for your patience and understanding throughout this proceeding.

STATEMENT BY THE COURT

LADIES AND GENTLEMEN:

As members of the jury, you have been provided with the final instructions for reaching a verdict and you have heard the final arguments of the Plaintiff and the Defendant. At this time, you are excused and you may begin your deliberations.